# ZAGAT SURVEY®

# 2005/06

## CHICAGO RESTAURANTS

Including
Milwaukee

**Chicago Editor: Alice Van Housen**

**Milwaukee Editor: Ann Christenson**

**Coordinator: Jill Van Cleave**

**Editor: Daniel Simmons**

Published and distributed by
ZAGAT SURVEY, LLC
4 Columbus Circle
New York, New York 10019
Tel: 212 977 6000
E-mail: chicago@zagat.com
Web site: www.zagat.com

# Acknowledgments

We thank Lisa Futterman, Bill Rice, Brenda and Earl Shapiro, Laura Levy Shatkin, Steven Shukow and Tom Van Housen. We are also grateful to our associate editor, Anne Cole, as well as the following members of our staff: Reni Chin, Griff Foxley, Schuyler Frazier, Natalie Lebert, Mike Liao, Dave Makulec, Robert Poole, Robert Seixas, Thomas Sheehan, Joshua Siegel and Sharon Yates.

The reviews published in this guide are based on public opinion surveys, with numerical ratings reflecting the average scores given by all survey participants who voted on each establishment and text based on direct quotes from, or fair paraphrasings of, participants' comments. Phone numbers, addresses and other factual information were correct to the best of our knowledge when published in this guide; any subsequent changes may not be reflected.

# Contents

About This Survey . . . . . . . . . . . . . . . . . . . . . . .  5
What's New . . . . . . . . . . . . . . . . . . . . . . . . . . . . . .  6
Ratings & Symbols . . . . . . . . . . . . . . . . . . . . . .  7
Most Popular . . . . . . . . . . . . . . . . . . . . . . . . . . .  9
**TOP RATINGS**
  • **Food:** Cuisines, Features, Locations . . . . . .  10
  • **Decor:** Outdoors, Romance, Rooms, Views .  14
  • **Service** . . . . . . . . . . . . . . . . . . . . . . . . . . . .  15
  • **Best Buys** . . . . . . . . . . . . . . . . . . . . . . . . . . .  16
**RESTAURANT DIRECTORY**
  Names, Addresses, Phone Numbers, Web
  Sites, Ratings and Reviews . . . . . . . . . . . .  17
**INDEXES**
  Cuisines . . . . . . . . . . . . . . . . . . . . . . . . . . . . . . 182
  Locations . . . . . . . . . . . . . . . . . . . . . . . . . . . . . 194
  Special Features
    Additions . . . . . . . . . . . . . . . . . . . . . . . . . . 206
    Breakfast . . . . . . . . . . . . . . . . . . . . . . . . . . 207
    Brunch . . . . . . . . . . . . . . . . . . . . . . . . . . . . 208
    Buffet Served . . . . . . . . . . . . . . . . . . . . . . 209
    Business Dining . . . . . . . . . . . . . . . . . . . . 209
    BYO . . . . . . . . . . . . . . . . . . . . . . . . . . . . . . . 210
    Celebrity Chefs . . . . . . . . . . . . . . . . . . . . . 211
    Child-Friendly . . . . . . . . . . . . . . . . . . . . . . 212
    Cigars Welcome . . . . . . . . . . . . . . . . . . . . 213
    Critic-Proof . . . . . . . . . . . . . . . . . . . . . . . . 214
    Dancing . . . . . . . . . . . . . . . . . . . . . . . . . . . 214
    Delivery/Takeout . . . . . . . . . . . . . . . . . . . 214
    Dining Alone . . . . . . . . . . . . . . . . . . . . . . . 215
    Entertainment . . . . . . . . . . . . . . . . . . . . . . 216
    Fireplaces . . . . . . . . . . . . . . . . . . . . . . . . . 216
    Game in Season . . . . . . . . . . . . . . . . . . . . 217
    Historic Places . . . . . . . . . . . . . . . . . . . . . 218
    Hotel Dining . . . . . . . . . . . . . . . . . . . . . . . 219
    Jacket Required . . . . . . . . . . . . . . . . . . . . 220
    Late Dining . . . . . . . . . . . . . . . . . . . . . . . . 220
    Meet for a Drink . . . . . . . . . . . . . . . . . . . . 221
    Microbreweries . . . . . . . . . . . . . . . . . . . . . 222
    Old City Feel . . . . . . . . . . . . . . . . . . . . . . . 222
    Outdoor Dining . . . . . . . . . . . . . . . . . . . . . 222
    People-Watching . . . . . . . . . . . . . . . . . . . 223
    Power Scenes . . . . . . . . . . . . . . . . . . . . . . 224
    Private Rooms . . . . . . . . . . . . . . . . . . . . . . 224
    Prix Fixe Menus . . . . . . . . . . . . . . . . . . . . 225
    Quick Bites . . . . . . . . . . . . . . . . . . . . . . . . 225
    Quiet Conversation . . . . . . . . . . . . . . . . . 226
    Raw Bars . . . . . . . . . . . . . . . . . . . . . . . . . . 227
    Romantic Places . . . . . . . . . . . . . . . . . . . . 227

Senior Appeal . . . . . . . . . . . . . . . . . . . . . . 228
Singles Scenes . . . . . . . . . . . . . . . . . . . . 229
Sleepers. . . . . . . . . . . . . . . . . . . . . . . . . . 229
Teen Appeal . . . . . . . . . . . . . . . . . . . . . . 230
Theme Restaurants. . . . . . . . . . . . . . . . . 230
Trendy . . . . . . . . . . . . . . . . . . . . . . . . . . . 230
Views. . . . . . . . . . . . . . . . . . . . . . . . . . . . 231
Visitors on Expense Account . . . . . . . . . . 231
Wine Bars . . . . . . . . . . . . . . . . . . . . . . . . 232
Winning Wine Lists. . . . . . . . . . . . . . . . . . 232
Worth a Trip . . . . . . . . . . . . . . . . . . . . . . . 233
**MILWAUKEE**
  **Top Ratings**. . . . . . . . . . . . . . . . . . . . . . 235
  **Restaurant Directory** . . . . . . . . . . . . . . . 239
  **Indexes** . . . . . . . . . . . . . . . . . . . . . . . . . 255
**Wine Chart** . . . . . . . . . . . . . . . . . . . . . . . 268

# About This Survey

This *2005/06 Chicago Restaurant Survey* is an update reflecting significant developments as reported by our editors since our last *Survey* was published. For example, we have added 140 important new restaurants, as well as indicated new addresses, chef changes and other major developments. All told, this guide now covers 1,156 of the Chicago area's best restaurants.

This marks the 26th year that Zagat Survey has reported on the shared experiences of diners like you. What started in 1979 as a hobby involving 200 of our friends rating local NYC restaurants has come a long way. Today we have over 250,000 active surveyors and now cover entertaining, golf, hotels, resorts, spas, movies, music, nightlife, shopping, sites and attractions as well as theater. All of these guides are based on consumer surveys. Our *Surveys* are also available on PDAs, cell phones and by subscription at zagat.com, where you can vote and shop as well.

By regularly surveying large numbers of avid (and hence educated) customers, we hope to have achieved a uniquely current and reliable guide. More than a quarter-century of experience has verified this. For this book, over 4,700 restaurant-goers participated, dining out an average of 3.1 times per week, for a total of roughly 750,000 meals. Our editors have synopsized these surveyors' opinions, with their comments shown in quotation marks. We sincerely thank each of these people; this book is really "theirs."

We are especially grateful to our Chicago editor, Alice Van Housen, a freelance writer and editor; to our Chicago coordinator, Jill Van Cleave, a cookbook author and food consultant; and to our Milwaukee editor, Ann Christenson, the dining critic for *Milwaukee Magazine*.

To help guide our readers to Chicago's best meals and best buys, we have prepared a number of lists. See Most Popular (page 9), Top Ratings (pages 10–15) and Best Buys (page 16). In addition, we have provided 46 handy indexes.

**To vote in any of our upcoming *Surveys*, just register at zagat.com.** Each participant will receive a free copy of the resulting guide (or a comparable reward). Your comments and even criticisms of this guide are also solicited. There is always room for improvement with your help. We look forward to hearing from you – just contact us with your suggestions at chicago@zagat.com

New York, NY
July 18, 2005

Nina and Tim Zagat

# What's New

It's been a busy year for Windy City restaurants, as exemplified by an impromptu game of musical toques that resulted in numerous upper-echelon upheavals.

**We've Got the Moves:** Within moments of our going to press last year, the floodgates opened: first the Ritz-Carlton Dining Room's A-team exited, then Grant Achatz sailed out of Trio (now Trio Atelier) with a big tailwind to begin work on his high-profile Alinea, after which Graham Elliot Bowles took charge of the Avenues kitchen to great fanfare and Roland Liccioni departed Les Nomades (returning to Le Français). On a bittersweet note, Geneva's revered 302 West managed to transcend the untimely passing of chef-owner Joel Findlay.

**Hot Stuff:** Folks are fired up over a host of new city spots ranging from higher-end venues (Acqualina, China Grill) to moderately priced yet chic eateries (JP Chicago, Osteria Via Stato) to hip comfort-food specialists (De Cero, Hot Chocolate, Hot Doug's). Even the 'burbs are getting in on the action, with a spate of sizzling newcomers including the North Shore's Miramar and Prairie Grass Cafe, and the Western Suburbs' Vie. On the ethnic front, hookah huffers have a handful of new hook-up havens, including Babylon, Kan Zaman and Samah. And the Japanese juggernaut steamrolls ahead with the likes of Kaze Sushi, Kizoku, Triad, Tsuki and Usagi Ya.

**Sunset, Sunrise:** Surprise goodbyes issued from Atlantique, Erawan Royal Thai, Ohba, The Outpost, Pili.Pili, Prairie and The Room. Also, Eli's the Place for Steaks lost its building to progress and is looking for a new home, while Michael Kornick sidelined his mk North in favor of A Milano, a simple Italian grill concept. Meanwhile, on the horizon we can make out Custom House, a meatier concept from Shawn McClain (Green Zebra, Spring); a spin-off of Michael Jordan's The Steakhouse NYC; the return of Eric Aubriot at Evanston's Narra; Italian small plates from the Gibsons guys at Quartino; and the Shanghai Club, chic Chinese in the erstwhile Biggs mansion.

**Northern Exposure:** Chicago's nearby neighbor, Milwaukee, maintains its rep for restaurant stability, but this year did see some notable bows, including Bacchus, local legend Joe Bartolotta's big-city high-ender; Barossa, a wine bar–meets–organic eatery; Saffron, an envelope-pushing Indian bistro; and Zarletti, a cozy Italian.

**The Price Is Right:** At $31.64, the average cost of a Chicago meal is still a smidge less than our national average of $31.82.

Chicago, IL
Milwaukee, WI
July 18, 2005

Alice Van Housen
Ann Christenson

# Ratings & Symbols

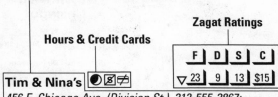

**Name, Address, Phone Number & Web Site**

**Hours & Credit Cards**

**Zagat Ratings**

| F | D | S | C |
|---|---|---|---|
| ▽ 23 | 9 | 13 | $15 |

**Tim & Nina's** ●🖼⊘
*456 E. Chicago Ave. (Division St.), 312-555-3867;
www.zagat.com*

> Hordes of "unkempt" U of C students have discovered
> this "never-closing" "eyesore", which "single-handedly"
> started the "deep-dish sushi pizza craze" that's "sweeping
> the Windy City like a lake-effect storm"; "try the eel-
> pepperoni-wasabi-mozzarella or Osaka-Napolitano pies" –
> "they're to die for" – but bring cash, since "T & N never
> heard of credit cards or checks."

**Review, with surveyors' comments in quotes**

**Top Spots:** Places with the highest overall ratings, popularity
and importance are listed in BLOCK CAPITAL LETTERS.

**Hours:** ● serves after 11 PM
🖼 closed on Sunday

**Credit Cards:** ⊘ no credit cards accepted

**Ratings** are on a scale of **0** to **30. Cost (C)** reflects our
surveyors' estimate of the price of dinner with one
drink and tip.

| F Food | D Decor | S Service | C Cost |
|---|---|---|---|
| 23 | 9 | 13 | $15 |

| | |
|---|---|
| **0–9** poor to fair | **20–25** very good to excellent |
| **10–15** fair to good | **26–30** extraordinary to perfection |
| **16–19** good to very good | ▽ low response/less reliable |

For newcomers or survey write-ins listed without ratings,
the price range is indicated as follows:

| | | | |
|---|---|---|---|
| **I** | $25 and below | **E** | $41 to $65 |
| **M** | $26 to $40 | **VE** | $66 or more |

# Chicago's Most Popular

**Downtown Chicago**

Lake Michigan

Division St.
Elm St.
Gibsons Steakhouse
Morton's*
Bellevue Pl.
Oak St.
Spiaggia
Walton St.
Delaware St.
Cheescake Factory*
Chestnut St.
mk
Ritz-Carlton Dining Room
Locust St.
Chicago Ave.
NoMi
Pearson St.
Café Iberico
Superior St.
Tru
Huron St.
Fogo de Chão
Chicago Chop House
Erie St.
Wildfire*
Les Nomades
Maggiano's*
Ontario St.
Heaven on Seven
Frontera Grill
Ohio St.
Joe's Seafood
Topolobampo
P.F. Chang's
Grand Ave.
Coco Pazzo
Hubbard St.
Shaw's Crab House
Illinois St.
Lou Malnati's
Kinzie St.
Kevin
Carroll Ave.
N. Water St.
Bin 36
Chicago R.
Ruth's Chris
Catch 35*
Wacker Dr.
S. Water St.
Lake St.
Heaven on Seven
Randolph St.
Giordano's
Daley Bicentennial Plaza
Washington Blvd.
Trattoria No. 10
Wabash Ave.
Madison St.
The Berghoff
Adams St.
Jackson Blvd.
Van Buren St.
Everest
Congress Pkwy.
Harrison St.

*Check for other locations

**Inset detail (center)**

Arun's
Irving Park Rd.
Lincoln Ave.
Ashland Ave.
Clark St.
Halsted St.
Lake Michigan
Kedzie Ave.
North Branch Chicago River
Mia Francesca
Belmont Ave.
Diversey Pkwy.
North Pond
Lou Malnati's
Ambria
Fullerton Ave.
Armitage Ave.
Charlie Trotter's
North Ave.
Spring
Western Ave.
Milwaukee Ave.
Division St.
Damen Ave.
W. Chicago Ave.
Ogden Ave.
Blackbird
Washington Blvd.
Randolph St.

Francesca's*
Lake Forest
Carlos'
Bin 36
Highland Park
Lincolnshire
P.F. Chang's
Northbrook
Bob Chinn's
Wheeling
Ruth's Chris
Francesca*
Arlington Heights
Shaw's Crab House
Schaumburg
Evanston
Lake Michigan
Chicago-O'Hare Int'l Airport
The Berghoff
Gibsons Steakhouse
Rosemont
Inset detail (center)
P.F. Chang's
Lombard
Westchester
Downtown Chicago (top detail)
Francesca's*
Chicago
ILLINOIS

Miles
0    5

# Most Popular

| | |
|---|---|
| 1. Tru | 21. NoMI |
| 2. Charlie Trotter's | 22. North Pond |
| 3. Frontera Grill | 23. Blackbird |
| 4. Everest | 24. Francesca's |
| 5. Gibsons Steak | 25. P.F. Chang's |
| 6. mk | 26. Ritz Carlton Din. Rm. |
| 7. Ambria | 27. Heaven on Seven |
| 8. Topolobampo | 28. Catch 35 |
| 9. Joe's Sea/Steak | 29. Café Iberico |
| 10. Wildfire | 30. Chicago Chop Hse. |
| 11. Maggiano's | 31. Bin 36 |
| 12. Morton's Steak | 32. Bob Chinn Crab Hse. |
| 13. Shaw's Crab Hse. | 33. Cheesecake Factory* |
| 14. Spiaggia | 34. Coco Pazzo* |
| 15. Berghoff | 35. Trattoria No. 10 |
| 16. Les Nomades | 36. Lou Malnati Pizza |
| 17. Giordano's | 37. Mia Francesca |
| 18. Fogo de Chão | 38. Arun's |
| 19. Kevin | 39. Carlos'* |
| 20. Spring | 40. Ruth's Chris Steak |

It's obvious that many of the restaurants on the above list are among Chicago's most expensive, but if popularity were calibrated to price, we suspect that a number of other restaurants would join the above ranks. Given the fact that both our surveyors and readers love to discover dining bargains, we have added a list of 80 Best Buys on page 16. These are restaurants that give real quality at extremely reasonable prices.

* Indicates a tie with restaurant above

# Top Ratings

Excludes places with low voting.

## Top 40 Food

28 Tallgrass
Carlos'
Tru
Ambria
Mirai Sushi
Seasons
27 Charlie Trotter's
Le Titi de Paris
302 West
Everest
mk
Arun's
Topolobampo
Le Vichyssois
Bistro Banlieue
Oceanique*
Kevin
26 Avec
Eclectic
Spiaggia

Gabriel's
Morton's Steak
NoMI
Frontera Grill
Blackbird
Café 36
Spring
Shanghai Terrace
Naha
25 Crofton on Wells
Bongo Room
Courtright's
Joe's Sea/Steak
Gibsons Steak
Ixcapuzalco
D & J Bistro
Merlo
Sushi Wabi
Capital Grille
one sixtyblue

## By Cuisine

### American (New)
28 Seasons
27 Charlie Trotter's
302 West
mk
Oceanique

### American (Traditional)
25 Bongo Room
Cornelia's
23 Lawry's Prime Rib
Seasons Café
Walker Bros. Pancake

### Asian
26 Shanghai Terrace
23 Catch 35
Red Light
22 Opera
21 Karma

### Barbecue
23 Twin Anchors
21 Carson's Ribs
20 Merle's
Smoke Daddy
19 Weber Grill

### Cajun/Creole
21 Pappadeaux Seafood
20 Heaven on Seven
19 Dixie Kitchen
Davis St. Fishmkt.
16 Redfish

### Chinese
23 Phoenix
22 Opera
21 Emperor's Choice
Lao Sze Chuan
Dee's

### Eclectic
26 Eclectic
24 Orange
23 Lula
22 Aria
Park Grill

### French (Bistro)
27 Bistro Banlieue
26 Café 36
25 D & J Bistro
Barrington Country
Cafe Pyrenees

# Top Food

## French (New)
*28* Tallgrass
Carlos'
Tru
Ambria
*27* Le Titi de Paris

## Greek
*22* Costa's
*21* Santorini
Parthenon
*20* Artopolis Bakery
Pegasus

## Hamburgers
*23* Superdawg
*22* Pete Miller's
*21* Wiener's Circle
*19* Twisted Spoke
Weber Grill

## Hot Dogs
*23* Superdawg
*21* Wiener's Circle
*19* Gold Coast Dogs
*18* Fluky's

## Indian
*23* Tiffin
*22* Indian Garden
Klay Oven
Mt. Everest
*21* Gaylord Indian

## Italian
*26* Spiaggia
Gabriel's
*25* Merlo
Café Spiaggia
Va Pensiero

## Japanese
*28* Mirai Sushi
*25* Sushi Wabi
Heat
Matsuya*
*24* Japonais

## Mediterranean
*26* Avec
Naha
*22* Costa's
Tizi Melloul
Café des Architectes

## Mexican
*27* Topolobampo
*26* Frontera Grill
*25* Ixcapuzalco
Salpicón
*24* Cafe 28

## Pizza
*23* Art of Pizza
Lou Malnati Pizza
*22* Chicago Pizza
Aurelio's
Nancy's Original

## Seafood
*27* Oceanique
*26* Spring
*25* Joe's Sea/Steak
Hugo's Frog/Fish
Avenues

## Spanish/Tapas
*24* La Tasca
*23* Mesón Sabika
*22* Twist
*21* Café Iberico
Cafe Ba-Ba-Reeba

## Steakhouses
*26* Morton's Steak
*25* Gibsons Steak
Capital Grille
Ruth's Chris Steak
Chicago Chop Hse.

## Thai
*27* Arun's
*24* Amarind's
*23* Thai Classic
*22* P.S. Bangkok
Ruby of Siam

## Vegetarian
*23* Addis Abeba
Lula
Maza
*20* Reza's
Wishbone

## Wild Cards
*24* Fogo de Chão/*Brazil.*
Geja's/*Fondue*
Le Colonial/*French-Viet.*
*23* Addis Abeba/*Ethiop.*
Tre Kronor/*Scand.*

# Top Food

## By Special Feature

**Breakfast**
*28* Seasons
*26* NoMI
*25* Bongo Room
*24* Lobby, The
    Orange

**Brunch**
*28* Seasons
*26* Frontera Grill
*25* Bongo Room
    Salpicón
    Avenues

**Business Dining**
*28* Seasons
*27* Charlie Trotter's
    Le Titi de Paris
    Everest
    mk

**Hotel Dining**
*28* Ambria
    Belden-Stratford
    Seasons
    Four Seasons
*26* NoMI
    Park Hyatt
    Shanghai Terrace
    Peninsula
*25* Gibsons Steak
    Doubletree

**Late Dining**
*26* Avec
*25* Gibsons Steak
    Hugo's Frog/Fish
    Matsuya
*24* Sabatino's

**Meet for a Drink**
*27* mk
*26* NoMI
    Frontera Grill
*25* Joe's Sea/Steak
    Gibsons Steak

**Newcomers/Unrated**
    Alinea
    Hot Chocolate
    Miramar
    Osteria Via Stato
    Prairie Grass Cafe

**People-Watching**
*28* Mirai Sushi
*27* mk
*26* Avec
    NoMI
    Blackbird

**Worth a Trip**
*28* Tallgrass
    Lockport
    Carlos'
    Highland Park
*27* Le Titi de Paris
    Arlington Heights
    302 West
    Geneva
    Le Vichyssois
    Lakemoor

**Winning Wine Lists**
*28* Tallgrass
    Carlos'
    Tru
    Ambria
    Seasons

## By Location

**Andersonville/Edgewater**
*23* M. Henry
    Francesca's
*22* Jin Ju
    Tomboy
*21* Speakeasy Supperclub

**Bucktown**
*25* Café Absinthe
*24* Meritage Cafe/Wine
*23* Le Bouchon
    Cafe Matou
*22* Coast Sushi

**Chinatown**
*22* Phoenix
*21* Emperor's Choice
    Lao Sze Chuan
    Evergreen
*20* Joy Yee's

**Gold Coast**
*28* Seasons
*26* Spiaggia
    Morton's Steak
    NoMI
*25* Gibsons Steak

12                        subscribe to zagat.com

## Lakeview/Wrigleyville
**25** Yoshi's Café
Matsuya
**24** Mia Francesca
Cornelia's
Cafe 28

## Lincoln Park
**28** Ambria
**27** Charlie Trotter's
**25** Merlo
North Pond
**24** Geja's Cafe

## Little Italy
**23** Francesca's
**22** Chez Joel
**21** Tuscany
Lao Sze Chuan
**20** Rosebud

## Loop
**27** Everest
**24** Nick's Fishmarket
Trattoria No. 10
**23** Catch 35
Palm, The

## Market District
**25** Sushi Wabi
one sixtyblue
**23** Red Light
Rushmore
**22** Vivo

## River North
**27** mk
Topolobampo
Kevin
**26** Frontera Grill
Shanghai Terrace

## Streeterville
**28** Tru
**25** Capital Grille
**23** Saloon Steak
**22** Original Pancake Hse.
Caliterra

## Suburban North
**28** Carlos'
**27** Oceanique
**26** Gabriel's
**25** Ruth's Chris
Va Pensiero

## Uptown/Lincoln Square
**24** Magnolia Cafe
**22** Tournesol
Thai Pastry
**21** Pizza D.O.C.
La Bocca/Verità

## West Loop
**26** Avec
Blackbird
**23** Lou Mitchell's
**22** Nine
**20** Wishbone

## Wicker Park
**28** Mirai Sushi
**26** Spring
**25** Bongo Room
**23** Bob San
Mas

# Top 40 Decor

| | | | |
|---|---|---|---|
| 28 | Ritz-Carlton Din. Rm. | | Nine |
| | Karma | | Charlie Trotter's |
| 27 | Japonais | | Signature Room |
| | NoMI | | Le Colonial |
| | Tizi Melloul | 24 | one sixtyblue |
| | Cité | | Ritz-Carlton Café |
| | Tru | | Carlos' |
| | Courtright's | | Atwood Cafe |
| | North Pond | | Lovell's/Lake Forest |
| | Seasons | | Avenues |
| 26 | Ambria | | 120 Ocean Place |
| | 302 West | | Seasons Café |
| | Spiaggia | | Red Light |
| | RL | | mk |
| | Everest | | Zealous |
| | Les Nomades | | Le Titi de Paris |
| | Shanghai Terrace | | Spring |
| 25 | Lobby, The | | Naha |
| | Pump Room | | Nacional 27 |
| | Sushisamba rio | | Capital Grille |

## Outdoors

| | |
|---|---|
| Athena | Pegasus |
| Japonais | Puck's at the MCA |
| Meritage/Wine | Shanghai Terrace |
| Mesón Sabika | Smith & Wollensky |
| NoMI | Thyme |
| Park Grill | Topo Gigio |

## Romance

| | |
|---|---|
| Ambria | L8 |
| Café Absinthe | Nacional 27 |
| Everest | Narcisse |
| Geja's Cafe | Tallgrass |
| Japonais | 302 West |
| Le Colonial | Tizi Melloul |

## Rooms

| | |
|---|---|
| Alinea | North Pond |
| Café des Architectes | Ritz-Carlton Din. Rm. |
| Japonais | RL |
| Marché | Shanghai Terrace |
| Nine | Sushisamba rio |
| NoMI | Tizi Melloul |

## Views

| | |
|---|---|
| Cité | Park Grill |
| Courtright's | Riva |
| Everest | Seasons |
| NoMI | Signature Room |
| North Pond | Spiaggia |

**subscribe to zagat.com**

# Top 40 Service

**28** Ritz-Carlton Din. Rm.
Les Nomades
**27** Tru
Charlie Trotter's
Everest
Seasons
Carlos'
Ambria
**26** Le Français
Shanghai Terrace
Arun's
Seasons Café
302 West
**25** Café 36
Tallgrass
Gabriel's
Spiaggia
Le Titi de Paris
Lobby, The
Barrington Bistro

Fogo de Chão
Topolobampo
**24** Bistro Banlieue
mk
Va Pensiero
Sal & Carvao
Ritz-Carlton Café
Courtright's
NoMI
Morton's Steak
Naha
Spring
West Town Tavern
Kevin
Capital Grille
Maza
D & J Bistro
Nick's Fishmarket
Lawry's Prime Rib
Ruth's Chris Steak

# Best Buys

## Top 40 Bangs for the Buck

1. Superdawg
2. Potbelly Sandwich
3. Wiener's Circle
4. Margie's Candies
5. Gold Coast Dogs
6. Fluky's
7. Walker Bros. Pancake
8. Aladdin's Eatery
9. M. Henry
10. Original Pancake Hse.
11. Penny's Noodle
12. Lou Mitchell's
13. Bongo Room
14. Kitsch'n on Roscoe
15. Art of Pizza
16. Orange
17. Milk & Honey
18. Corner Bakery
19. Pompei Bakery
20. Breakfast Club
21. Artopolis Bakery
22. Aurelio's Pizza
23. Manny's
24. Toast
25. Billy Goat Tavern
26. Nookies
27. Flo
28. Uncommon Ground
29. Chicago Flat Sammies
30. Thai Classic
31. Leo's Lunchroom
32. Tre Kronor
33. Tempo
34. Nancy's Original
35. White Fence Farm
36. Hilary's Urban
37. Ann Sather
38. Lutz Continental
39. Pizzeria Uno/Due
40. Chicago Diner

## Other Good Values

Addis Abeba
Amitabul
Andies
BD's Mongolian
Best Hunan
Big Bowl
Bite
Dave's
De Cero
Dell Rhea's Chicken
Flat Top Grill
Half Shell
Hashalom
Indie Cafe
Irazu
Joy Yee's Noodles
Kabul House
La Cazuela Mariscos
La Crêperie
Lem's BBQ

Lincoln Noodle
LuLu's Dim Sum
Noon-O-Kabab
Nuevo Leon
Old Jerusalem
Pasta Palazzo
Ping Pong
Reza's
Ringo
Ruby of Siam
Russell's BBQ
Shiroi Hana
Silver Seafood
Star of Siam
Tango Sur
Thai Pastry
Tokyo Marina
Tufano's Vernon
Victory's Banner
Wishbone

# Chicago
# Restaurant Directory

### Abbey Pub & Restaurant   14  14  17  $19
*3420 W. Grace St. (Elston Ave.), 773-463-5808;*
*www.abbeypub.com*
Approvers assess this Northwest Side Irish installation as
a "great place to kick back with friends and listen to live
music" ("surprisingly good bands play here") or watch
sports ("more soccer than football"); the fare is "not bad
for pub grub" and the "friendly" atmosphere is suitably
"dark"; P.S. the entertainment "venue is separate from the
restaurant" but you'll "get preferred seating for the shows
if you go for dinner."

### Acqualina   –  –  –  M
*4363 N. Lincoln Ave. (Montrose Ave.), 773-770-4363*
Booming Lincoln Square is home to this Cal-Med hot spot
(from Tizi Melloul's owners) that turns out contemporary
dishes with earthy undertones, accompanied by a seasonal
martini list; the modern space is done up in orange and
chocolate with curved walls, a color-changing LED bar
and accents of exposed yellow brick and dried bamboo.

### Adelle's   –  –  –  M
*1060 College Ave. (bet. N. President St. & Stoddard Ave.),*
*Wheaton, 630-784-8015; www.adelles.com*
Bistro Banlieue veterans Debbie and Todd Williams aspire
to a spot on the West Suburban culinary map with this New
American in the former Cochon Sauvage space, serving up
a seasonal menu featuring upscale versions of classic
comfort food (e.g. pot roast with carmelized sweet potatoes)
in a warm, stylish room with copper accents and mosaic
chandeliers; N.B. monthly wine dinners with prominent
vintners are a highlight.

### Adobo Grill   22  20  19  $31
*1610 N. Wells St. (North Ave.), 312-266-7999*
*2005 W. Division St. (Damen Ave.), 773-252-9990*
*www.adobogrill.com*
Captivated commenters can't get enough of this "Old Town
favorite's" "inspired presentations" of "authentic gourmet
Mexican food" (including "orgasmic" guac "made fresh at
your table") served with an "encyclopedic tequila list" amid
a "hip", "interesting multiroom setup" with an "upscale but
unpretentious" feel; "it can get crowded" and "loud", "and
service can be affected, but after a few of those perfect
margaritas who cares?"; N.B. the Wicker Park branch,
which features a larger patio, opened post-*Survey.*

### Akai Hana   20  13  17  $24
*3223 W. Lake Ave. (Skokie Blvd.), Wilmette, 847-251-0384*
Raters recommend this "no-frills" North Suburban Japanese
spot for "reliable" "fresh fish" and "a good assortment of
other entrees" at a "tremendous value", touting it as a "kid-
friendly" "place to just grab a bite" – in short, "everything

a neighborhood sushi bar needs" to be; still, the "spotty service", "crowds", "noise" and "basic", "dressed-down environment" detract for some; N.B. the Gold Coast branch closed post-*Survey*.

### Aladdin's Eatery    20   16   18   $13

*614 W. Diversey Pkwy. (N. Clark St.), 773-327-6300*
*622 Davis St. (Chicago Ave.), Evanston, 847-475-1498*
*www.aladdinseatery.com*

"Thank goodness for" these Lincoln Park/North Suburban outlets of a regional chain where the "seemingly limitless" "vegetarian-friendly" menu of "healthy", "fresh" Lebanese-Med eats offers a "great quick bite" and good "bang for your buck"; the "attentive" staffers are "polite" and the "lack of ambiance" is beside the point; P.S. "the fresh fruit smoothies are good", plus beer and wine are now served.

### A La Turka    18   19   19   $24

*3134 N. Lincoln Ave. (Belmont Ave.), 773-935-6447;*
*www.turkishkitchen.us*

"Excellent lamb" is part of the "exciting experience" at this "authentic", "dimly lit" "world of Turkish intrigue" in Lakeview; even some converts concede the "atmosphere overshadows the service and food", while infidels insist it's all a bit "hokey" and say the "friendly" staff "moves at a Middle Eastern pace", but "nothing makes you forgive like a belly dance" (Thursday–Sunday nights); P.S. "try the opulent hookahs" in the new second-floor lounge.

### Albert's Café & Patisserie    19   15   18   $20

*52 W. Elm St. (bet. Clark & Dearborn Sts.), 312-751-0666*

"France meets Chicago" at this Gold Coast "favorite", a "sleepy" "hideaway in a busy neighborhood" with decor that "evokes an authentic" "European bistro", "lace sheers and all"; it "attracts a hip, athletic crowd for breakfast and afternoon tea" (starring "creative sandwiches and great pastries") plus "light" dinners, and though "service can be a little gruff", it's "efficient"; N.B. ratings may not reflect a post-*Survey* change of ownership.

### Al Dente Café & Lounge    –   –   –   M

*1615 N. Clybourn Ave. (W. North Ave.), 312-587-0055;*
*www.aldentecafe.com*

Hearty Italian cuisine and a low-lit, polished-wood space are drawing Lincoln Park locals to this handsome, bi-level newcomer; its downstairs dining room is dominated by high-top tables, while its upstairs lounge is dotted with sultry, oversized booths built for quiet conversation over late-night nibbles and specialty martinis.

### Alice & Friends Vegetarian Cafe    ⊠   –   –   –   I

*5812 N. Broadway (W. Ardmore Ave.), 773-275-8797*

Uptown's popular, quirky Asian-vegetarian haven has a devoted following for its 'unmeats' and vegan vittles prepared with a light hand and paired with smoothies (plus there's a nice selection of cookies and other sweet finishes) in a homespun, funky storefront setting with words of wisdom on the colorful walls; N.B. BYO is not allowed.

**Alinea** – – – VE
*1723 N. Halsted St. (bet. North Ave. & Willow St.), 312-867-0110; www.alinearestaurant.com*
Chef whiz Grant Achatz (ex Trio) plays to full houses of the foodie faithful at his much-vaunted 'molecular gastronomy' gambit in Lincoln Park; acolytes ascend a glass-and-metal staircase floating over a reflecting pool to a sleek, neutral dining room, where they indulge in dramatically presented, cutting-edge New American cuisine to the tune of six courses ($75); 10 courses ($110) or 30 courses ($175), paired with selections from celeb sommelier Joe Catterson's wide-ranging wine list.

**Allen's - New American Café** ⊠ 23 18 22 $45
*217 W. Huron St. (bet. Franklin & Wells Sts.), 312-587-9600; www.allenscafe.com*
"Urban dining" awaits at this River Norther (once Harvest on Huron) where chef-owner Allen Sternweiler's "innovative, well-executed" New American cooking, including "creative game specials", is brokered by a "knowledgeable staff and wine steward"; it's "in the Gallery District and the art crowd hangs there", which may account for the "austere decor" that some find "a bit stark" (and "loud"), but optimists opine that the digs' "simplicity makes you focus more on the food."

**Aloha Grill** – – – ⊥
*2534 N. Clark St. (Deming Pl.), 773-935-6828; www.alohagrillbbq.com*
Lurking under a giant surfboard on Clark Street, this Hawaiian 'homestyle fast-food' specialist in Lincoln Park could be the next wave; it serves up authentic island fare like BBQ, curries, loco moco (burgers with rice, gravy and eggs) and Spam (a luau-state favorite) several ways; bench seating and island photography echo the casual vibe; N.B. there's no alcohol or BYO.

**Al's #1 Italian Beef** – – – ⊥
*7132 183rd St. (Harlem Ave.), Tinley Park, 708-444-2333*
*1079 W. Taylor St. (Damen St.), 312-226-4017* ●◔
*169 W. Ontario St. (Wells St.), 312-943-3222* ●
*1600 W. Lake St. (bet. Lombard & Rohlwing Rds.), Addison, 630-773-4599*
*551 W. 14th St. (Division St.), Chicago Heights, 708-748-2333*
*Lincolnwood Town Center, 3333 W. Touhy Ave. (N. McCormick Blvd.), Lincolnwood, 847-673-2333*
*10276 S. Harlem Ave. (W. 103rd St.), Oak Lawn, 708-636-2333*

(continued)
**Al's #1 Italian Beef**
*33 S. Northwest Hwy. (bet. Euclid & Prospect Aves.),*
*Park Ridge, 847-318-7700*
*www.alsbeef.com*
An "institution" in Little Italy since 1938 (with a "convenient"
River North outpost since '86), this quick-eats hot dog and
sandwich specialist may or may not serve "the best Italian
beef in Chicago" (though fans say "the menu trumpets 'It's
why you're here!', and they're right") as well as "superbly
seasoned sausage bursting at its casing" and now cold
wraps; N.B. the Taylor Street original spun off a slew of
new franchises post-*Survey,* with more in the works.

**Amarind's**  24  13  17  $22
*6822 W. North Ave. (Oak Park Ave.), 773-889-9999*
Located "near the Frank Lloyd Wright neighborhood" in the
Western Suburbs, this "excellent Thai" offers "beautiful
presentations" of "fresh, imaginative" fare that's "not as
costly as the quality would warrant" and "the best" of its
kind "you'll find in this neck of the woods"; the fact that the
"staff is friendly" also makes it "worth the drive"; P.S. the
Decor rating may not reflect a post-*Survey* renovation of
the "simple", "clean" interior.

**Amber Cafe**  –  –  –  M
*13 N. Cass Ave. (Burlington Ave.), Westmont, 630-515-8080*
Westmont's latest dining option is this New American bar
and grill with a seasonally changing menu, set in an amber-
hued rehabbed storefront with high ceilings, exposed-brick
walls, chandeliers and candlelit tables; the separate lounge
area with a handmade cherry bar is a fine spot to explore
the moderately priced global wine list.

**AMBRIA**  ⊠  28  26  27  $72
*Belden-Stratford Hotel, 2300 N. Lincoln Park W. (Belden Ave.),*
*773-472-5959; www.leye.com*
"A gem for years", this "culinary delight" "in a top-end
Lincoln Park residential hotel" has created "many wonderful
memories" with its "unbelievably delicious" Spanish-
influenced New French cuisine served by a "battalion of
waiters" who "make you feel like royalty" within a "quiet,
wood-paneled room that speaks of old money"; a few
find the "jackets-required" policy "stuffy", but most say
this is "what a restaurant should be"; P.S. sommelier Bob
Bansberg is a "guru – trust him."

**American Girl Place Cafe**  14  22  18  $26
*American Girl Pl., 111 E. Chicago Ave. (N. Michigan Ave.),*
*312-943-9400; www.americangirlplace.com*
"Wonderful" for "daughters and granddaughters" "of all
ages", this Gold Coast girl-magnet is a "combo theme store,
teahouse" and "*Eloise*-inspired" "fantasy world" outfitted

with "chairs and china for" the little darlings' "favorite dolls"; its Traditional American menu may be "clever for kids" but most adults assert that "the only reason to eat here is" "the excitement in the eyes" "beaming up at you"; P.S. "reservations are highly recommended."

### A Milano Italian Grill                    – | – | – | M |
*305 S. Happ Rd. (bet. Mt. Pleasant St. & Willow Rd.), Northfield, 847-716-6500; www.amilanogrill.com*
Michael Kornick has transformed his former mk North into this casual-chic North Suburban Italian where the dining room is adorned with bright fabric and Venetian glass tiles and the kitchen boasts both a wood-burning oven and charcoal grill; his simple, moderately priced menu, which goes easy on the red sauce while focusing on fresh ingredients, is matched by a list of affordable wines and grappa martinis.

### Amitabul                    – | – | – | I |
*6207 N. Milwaukee Ave. (Huntington St.), 773-774-0276*
"Worth the trip to the intersection of Milwaukee and nowhere", this Northwest Side Korean BYO caters to vegans and "adventurous" diners seeking "exotic but delicious" "healthy" fare made with all-organic homemade sauces and no oil in the cooking process; regulars swear it's "some of the most inventive vegetarian food in the city", and it's "reasonably priced", to boot.

### Amore 🗷                    – | – | – | M |
*1330 W. Madison St. (bet. Ashland & Racine Aves.), 312-829-3333; www.amorechicago.com*
Formerly of Bloomingdale, this relocated Northern Italian brings to the West Loop an extensive menu of made-to-order fare that covers all the classics and offers a generous selection of salads, sandwiches and pizzas for lighter appetites; the cozy exposed-brick-and-wood interior boasts a long bar and colorful fabric lanterns, and there's sidewalk dining in warm weather (plus a free shuttle to United Center events).

### Amy Thai and Sushi Bar                    – | – | – | M |
*1624 W. Belmont Ave. (Ashland Ave.), 773-929-6999*
Thai and Japanese food come together at this low-key Lakeview BYO with an extensive menu of Siamese staples, raw-fish options and teriyaki items; the simple storefront space has a small sushi bar, wood floors and unadorned walls, giving it a refreshingly spare feel; N.B. sip something from the fruity bubble tea selection.

### Andalucia                    – | – | – | M |
*1820 W. Montrose Ave. (N. Honore St.), 773-334-6900*
The owner plays the role of convivial host at this intimate Uptown entry done in sunny yellow and blue with Spanish artwork; the kitchen specializes in authentic Andalusian

tapas, with more than 40 small hot and cold plates, plus a few entrees (including half a dozen paellas).

### Andies  20  17  17  $21
*5253 N. Clark St. (Berwyn Ave.), 773-784-8616* ◗
*1467 W. Montrose Ave. (Greenview Ave.), 773-348-0654*
*www.andiesres.com*
"Comfortable" and "casual", these Middle Eastern–Med sibs are "popular" for the "terrific selections" on their "moderately priced", "enormous menus" (they're "great for vegetarians", too); some suggest the "friendly service" can be "hit-or-miss", while insiders insist the Uptown location retains more of the duo's original "humble" "charm" than the "expanded" Andersonville outpost with a fireplace.

### Angelina Ristorante  21  18  19  $26
*3561 N. Broadway (Addison St.), 773-935-5993*
A "dependable" "neighborhood haunt" with a "gay-friendly atmosphere" befitting its Boys Town address, this "casual", "quintessential first-date spot" cooks up a "nice menu" of "simple but hearty" Southern Italian "comfort food" and a "creative" Sunday "champagne brunch", plus the "window seats make for good people-watching"; N.B. ratings may not reflect a post-*Survey* change in ownership.

### Anna Maria Pasteria  20  14  19  $23
*4400 N. Clark St. (W. Montrose Ave.), 773-506-2662*
Satisfied scribes sanction this "friendly" place – named after its owners, sisters Anna Picciolini and Maria Spinelli – for "generous portions" of "reasonably priced" "traditional Italian fare" ("nothing fancy, just good") including, of course, lots of "old-fashioned pastas"; P.S. the former Wrigleyville "favorite" moved post-*Survey* from its "small" "storefront" to new Uptown digs.

### Ann Sather  18  13  18  $16
*5207 N. Clark St. (Foster Ave.), 773-271-6677*
*929 W. Belmont Ave. (Sheffield Ave.), 773-348-2378*
### Ann Sather Café
*3411 N. Broadway (W. Roscoe St.), 773-305-0024*
*1448 N. Milwaukee Ave. (North Ave.), 773-394-1812*
*3416 N. Southport Ave. (W. Roscoe St.), 773-404-4475*
*www.annsather.com*
A "Chicago institution", these "family-friendly" Traditional American–Swedish restaurants and cafes "remain a guilty pleasure" for those looking for "an unrestrained calorie" and "comfort-food" "splurge", "especially at breakfast" given their "legendary cinnamon rolls"; while locations vary from "homey" to "cramped", there's always "plenty of character and characters" – including more than a few "screaming kids and harried moms"; N.B. the Wrigleyville and Lakeview locations are BYO.

Chicago

F D S C

## Antico Posto
20 | 19 | 18 | $30

*Oakbrook Center Mall, 118 Oakbrook Ctr. (Rte. 83), Oak Brook,
630-586-9200; www.leye.com*
Mallrats maintain that this "sophisticated Italian place"
is "worth a trip to Oakbrook Center, even if you're not
shopping", thanks to its "fresh, tasty" and "reasonably
priced" fare, a wine list designed to allow you to "make your
own tasting" and "upscale", "minimalist decor"; what's
"high energy" to some, however, is "noisy" to others, and
there are those who feel it's "a bit formulaic."

## Arco de Cuchilleros
20 | 15 | 18 | $25

*3445 N. Halsted St. (Cornelia Ave.), 773-296-6046*
Small-plate seekers salute this "reliable" Boys Town "tapas
joint" as a touch "of Spain in Lakeview" that's "worth the
wait" on "crowded weekends" for its "authentic", "not-
Americanized" offerings; the interior may be "cramped" but
service is "efficient", and "sitting out back in the summer
and sipping sangria" is a "beautiful" "urban escape."

## Aria
22 | 22 | 21 | $48

*Fairmont Chicago Hotel, 200 N. Columbus Dr. (South Water St.),
312-444-9494; www.ariachicago.com*
Surveyors sing that this "pleasantly surprising" Loop
youngster offers "a feast for the eyes as well as the palate";
an "innovative use of ingredients" and a "blending of
influences" from "many cultures" mix in its "delectable",
"adventurous" New American–Eclectic cuisine, and its
"dramatic", "upscale" space is a "sexy place for a date"
or "perfect business lunch spot"; still, some sigh "if only
the service would catch up with the food."

## Army & Lou's
▽ 22 | 11 | 21 | $19

*422 E. 75th St. (Martin Luther King Dr.), 773-483-3100*
It's "some of the best soul food in town, and reasonably
priced" swoon stalwarts seeking "the real thing" at this
Far South Side Southern specialist, a "Chicago institution"
since 1945; "good people and parking" don't hurt, either,
even if "the place is getting shopworn."

## Aroma
– | – | – | M

*941 W. Randolph St. (Morgan St.), 312-492-7889*
It was inevitable that the Market District strip would get a
Thai restaurant, and this casually hip entry fills the bill with
Siamese classics and a funky feel – exposed-brick walls, a
red concrete floor, wood tables, an open kitchen, intriguing
color photography – plus outdoor dining in season.

## Art of Pizza, The
23 | 7 | 16 | $13

*3033 N. Ashland Ave. (W. Nelson St.), 773-327-5600*
The "yummy, buttery crust and deelish sauce" delight
devotees of this Lakeview pie place who call it "a slice
above the rest" for its "phenomenal pan pizza" (the top-

**24**                    **subscribe to zagat.com**

rated in our *Survey*) and "great pasta"; the diminutive size and "no-frills" "dive" atmosphere cause some contributors to caution "takeout is the best way to experience Art."

### Artopolis Bakery, Cafe & Agora
20 19 16 $16

*306 S. Halsted St. (W. Jackson Blvd.), 312-559-9000; www.artopolischicago.com*
"Filled to the gills with real Greeks", this "informal" Hellenic-Med "in Greektown" that "feels like a European cafe" is a "wonderful" place for an "affordable lunch" that's "not as heavy as most neighborhood fare"; it's also "good for late-evening noshing", to "meet friends for coffee and dessert" or to "sit near the window and watch passersby" – even if service "has taken a back seat" of late.

### ARUN'S
27 23 26 $86

*4156 N. Kedzie Ave. (bet. Belle Plaine & Berteau Aves.), 773-539-1909; www.arunsthai.com*
Chef-owner Arun Sampanthavivat "brings you to a unique, enchanting world" with his "ultimate Thai food" at this top-rated, "refined" Northwest Side Siamese; "plan to spend a few hours" "blowing the budget" on the tasting menu (no à la carte), each "exquisitely prepared course" "customized to your tastes"; the "smooth" service is "accommodating", the "vast wine list has unexpected choices" and the "quiet" space with "gorgeous artwork" has "nice niches for conversation" – in short, "these folks got it" right.

### a tavola ⊠
23 20 23 $37

*2148 W. Chicago Ave. (bet. Hoyne Ave. & Leavitt St.), 773-276-7567; www.atavolachicago.com*
Grateful gourmets are "always surprised" that this "out-of-the-way" Ukrainian Village "jewel" "is not more crowded", considering the "helpful" staff and "wonderful" Northern Italian food (including what may be the "best gnocchi in town"); its "quaint", "intimate atmosphere" makes it "perfect for a romantic, leisurely meal", and the "nice outdoor seating" adds to the appeal.

### Athena ◑
19 21 20 $28

*212 S. Halsted St. (Adams St.), 312-655-0000; www.athenarestaurant.com*
Fresh-air fanatics favor the "unmatched" patio at this Greektown "favorite", which offers a "beautiful setting" in which to "get away from urban noise" while still enjoying "a magnificent city view"; the "solid Greek cuisine" is "consistently good" and "authentic", and "service is friendly" amid the "charming, ethnic atmosphere."

### Atwater's
∇ 20 23 22 $45

*Herrington Inn, 15 S. River Ln. (State St.), Geneva, 630-208-7433; www.herringtoninn.com*
"Located in the absolutely charming Herrington Inn with beautiful views of the Fox River", this West Suburban

seasonal New American–New French offers "very good" food and "great martinis" within an atmosphere that feels like "your private dining room", making it "an outstanding choice for a quiet, romantic dinner"; P.S. patio access in warm weather maximizes the "nice setting."

### Atwood Cafe    | 21 | 24 | 20 | $35 |
*Hotel Burnham, 1 W. Washington St. (State St.), 312-368-1900*
"One feels so cosmopolitan" during an "intimate lunch", "business meeting" or "pre/post-theater dinner" in this "posh", "cozy dining room" of a "landmark" Loop hotel, "even when tucking into its homey" "Americana cuisine" such as "wonderful pot pies" and "out-of-this-world bread pudding"; it's like "stepping into an art deco painting", with "whimsical", "eclectic furniture and tableware", "a great view of revitalized State Street" and a mix of "characters" from "young arty types to old widows dressed to the nines" being tended to by an "accommodating staff."

### Aurelio's Pizza    | 22 | 14 | 17 | $15 |
*Centennial Plaza, 1455 W. Lake St. (Lombard Rd.), Addison, 630-889-9560*
*1509 W. Sibley Blvd. (bet. Bensley & Calhoun Aves.), Calumet City, 708-730-1400*
*1545 S. Western Ave. (1 block south of Rte. 30), Chicago Heights, 708-481-5040*
*1002 Warren Ave. (Highland Ave.), Downers Grove, 630-810-0078*
*13001 W. 143rd St. (Bell Rd.), Homer Glen, 708-645-4400*
*18162 Harwood Ave. (183rd St.), Homewood, 708-798-8050*
*17 W. 711 Roosevelt Rd. (Summit Rd.), Oak Brook, 630-629-3200*
*6543 W. 127th St. (Ridgeland Ave.), Palos Heights, 708-389-5170*
*601 E. 170th St. (South Park Ave.), South Holland, 708-333-0310*
*15901 Oak Park Ave. (Rte. 6), Tinley Park, 708-429-4600*
*www.aureliospizza.com*
*Additional locations throughout the Chicago area*
There's "no other like it anywhere" – so say die-hard fans delighted by the "distinctive thin-crust pizza" with a "sassy, slightly sweet sauce" at this "family-friendly" franchise of pie purveyors; avid aficionados aver that "the original" "Homewood flagship" location, open since 1959, "is the best", deeming its decor "dark and cozy" whereas the chain-wide ambiance is berated as "bare-bones."

### AVEC ●    | 26 | 19 | 23 | $37 |
*615 W. Randolph St. (Jefferson St.), 312-377-2002;*
*www.avecrestaurant.com*
"Foodies" feel that Koren Grieveson's "profound" "merry-go-round of Med" small plates "blows the competition away" at this West Loop wunderkind (spin-off of Blackbird), where oenophiles enjoy "lovely big pours" of "unusual" wines and service is "energetic" and "attentive"; "you have to like minimalism to get" the "stark", "sauna" decor, and the "elbow-to-elbow" "communal" "table setup" isn't for

introverts, but it does "enable" social-ists "to meet sexy, interesting and sophisticated people."

### Avenue Ale House ◑

| 15 | 15 | 15 | $19 |

*825 S. Oak Park Ave. (Harrison St.), Oak Park, 708-848-2801; www.alehouseop.com*

"Fun, noisy and good for an ale house", this kid-friendly "Oak Park hangout" is "a great place to watch a game and have some burgers" and other "pub/bar food" (including "some updated items") with your choice of over 70 beers; while naysayers natter that it's "nothing special", all appreciate the "wonderful roof garden in the summer"; N.B. there's live entertainment on weekends.

### AVENUES

| 25 | 24 | 23 | $71 |

*Peninsula Hotel, 108 E. Superior St. (bet. Michigan Ave. & Rush St.), 312-573-6754; www.peninsula.com*

A "civilized, quiet" space studded with "comfortable chairs" and agreeably "far-apart tables" (some of which boast "wonderful views of Water Tower") sets the stage at this River North "gourmet" Eclectic; enthusiasts eat up the "exquisite service", even if dissenters decry the "expense-account" prices and "attitude" (jacket suggested); N.B. the Food rating may not reflect the post-*Survey* arrival of noted chef Graham Elliot Bowles.

### Babylon Middle Eastern Kitchen

| ─ | ─ | ─ | I |

*2023 N. Damen Ave. (McLean Ave.), 773-342-7482*

This inexpensive BYO offers Bucktowners traditional Middle Eastern fare — couscous, dolmades, kebabs — made from the owner's family recipes, along with fruit-honey smoothies and juices; the vibrantly colored room has an array of hookahs on display, available for smoking (including at outdoor tables) on Fridays and Saturdays after 10 PM, when a small menu of sampler platters is also available (until 2 AM).

### Bacchanalia ⊘

| ▽ 25 | 15 | 22 | $29 |

*2413 S. Oakley Ave. (bet. 24th & 25th Sts.), 773-254-6555*

Heart of Italy habitués hanker for this "great old Italian eatery" where the "flavorful, hearty" Northern fare is "a garlic lover's dream"; it's "a joint" "right out of *Moonstruck*", with the "ultimate old-school" decor of "gold veined mirrors, Xmas lights and false vines", and the "tables are on top of each other"; P.S. you no longer have to "make sure you bring along cash" as they've recently installed an ATM.

### Bacino's

| 20 | 12 | 15 | $19 |

*2204 N. Lincoln Ave. (Webster Ave.), 773-472-7400*
*118 S. Clinton St. (Adams St.), 312-876-1188* ⊠

Loyalists of this "reliable" Lincoln Park and West Loop pizza-and-pasta pair stand by its "tasty" "deep dish" with "thicker crust and lots of cheese" (especially the "stuffed spinach" variety) as well as its "good-quality" "traditional

Italian fare", saying either outpost is "always a yummy" (if "not fabulous") choice.

### Bagel, The                    17 | 11 | 15 | $15
*3107 N. Broadway (Belmont Ave.), 773-477-0300*
*Westfield Shoppingtown, 50 Old Orchard Ctr. (Old Orchard Rd.),*
*Skokie, 847-677-0100*
*www.bagelrestaurant.com*
"All the standard fixings" of "Jewish soul food" can be found at this "old-time", "authentic" deli duo in Lakeview and the Northern Suburbs – including "matzo balls as big as your head" and other such "comfort food with a pickle" that "pleases both grandparents and kids"; so what if the "service is inconsistent" and the facilities "could use a face-lift"?

### Balagio                    ▽ 19 | 22 | 21 | $29
*19917 S. LaGrange Rd. (W. La Porte Rd.), Frankfort, 815-469-2204*
*18042 Martin Ave. (Ridge Rd.), Homewood, 708-957-1650* ⊠
*Westbrook Corporate Center, Tower II (22nd St.), Westchester,*
*708-409-1111*
*www.balagio-restaurant.com*
"Some of the best Italian food in the South" and Southwest Suburbs can be found at these "jumping places" that each boast "comfortable surroundings", a "fun piano bar" and a "great Sinatra singer" (who alternates between the various locations); still, the lukewarm lament that "the overall-good experience could be better"; N.B. the Westchester branch opened post-*Survey*.

### Ballo                    – | – | – | M
*445 N. Dearborn St. (bet. Hubbard & Illinois Sts.),*
*312-832-7700*
Alex Dana (of the Rosebud Restaurant Group) assumes the River North space that formerly housed the Dearborn and Fog City Diners (among others), bringing a red-on-red remodel and a tried-and-true Italian comfort food concept; the small, oft-changing menu includes wood-oven pizzas, meatball salad and osso buco, and servers engage in a steakhouse-style menu presentation with the antipasti and fresh pasta choices.

### Bandera                    19 | 18 | 18 | $29
*535 N. Michigan Ave., 2nd fl. (bet. Grand Ave. & Ohio St.),*
*312-644-3524; www.houstons.com*
"A good staple" for a "quick dinner when shopping" "or a drink and a bite after work with jazz", this Mag Mile member of a "casual" chain serves "generous portions" of "good American food" (band-itos "love" the "rotisserie chicken" and "down-home cornbread"); the staffers have "great personality", and the "cozy" room with "window views" "above Michigan Avenue" is "perfect" for "people-watching."

## Bank Lane Bistro 🎲  22  19  20  $37
*670 Bank Ln. (Deerpath Rd.), Lake Forest, 847-234-8802*
Believers boost this "intimate", "not overly pretentious"
bistro in "the sleepy [North] Suburb of Lake Forest", saying
"you can always" bank on the "varied" and "innovative"
French–New American menu; the "charming", "surprisingly
sophisticated" decor helps make this "one of the better"
local spots "for a quiet dinner" – and it's a "great stop
for lunch, too."

## BaPi  –  –  –  M
*1510 E. Hintz Rd. (Buffalo Grove Rd.), Arlington Heights,*
*847-253-2333*
Chef Cristiano Bassani (ex Carlucci, Cristiano's) takes his
Northern Italian itinerary to this cozy (read: small) but
modern Northwest Suburban ristorante with a simple,
moderately priced menu that carries diners from calamari
through tiramisu; daily risotto, fish and housemade pasta
specials are offered, with panini selections added to
the lunch menu.

## Bar Louie ⚫  14  13  15  $19
*3545 N. Clark St. (Addison St.), 773-296-2500*
*1704 N. Damen Ave. (Wabansia Ave.), 773-645-7500*
*123 N. Halsted St. (bet. Randolph St. & Washington Blvd.),*
*312-207-0500*
*5500 S. Shore Dr. (E. 55th St.), 773-363-5300*
*226 W. Chicago Ave. (Franklin St.), 312-337-3313*
*47 W. Polk St. (Dearborn St.), 312-347-0848*
*1321 W. Taylor St. (S. Ashland Ave.), 312-633-9393*
*1520 N. Sherman Ave. (Grove St.), Evanston, 847-733-8300*
*22 E. Chicago Ave. (Washington St.), Naperville,*
*630-983-1600*

## Louie on the Park ⚫
*1816 N. Lincoln Ave. (Clark St.), 312-337-9800*
*www.barlouieamerica.com*
Pals of this "popular" pack of "funky" "places to hang out"
postulate it amounts to "a solid back-up plan" for "meeting
up with friends" or getting "late-night munchies" and "killer
martinis", even if "service is hit-or-miss" and the "wide
selection" of American eats is "a slight step above typical
bar fare"; cooler heads, though, say it's getting "formulaic"
now that there's "one on every corner."

## Barn of Barrington  18  20  18  $33
*1415 S. Barrington Rd. (¼ mi. north of Dundee Rd.), Barrington,*
*847-381-8585; www.barnofbarrington.com*
Stalwarts are satisfied with this "old-fashioned" North
Suburban Traditional American they call a "special place"
that's "reliable and cozy" "for a romantic dinner, family
get-together" or "very good Sunday brunch"; still, barn-
burners berate it as "stuffy" and "tacky", mooing that it's
"Medieval Times with a maitre d'."

### Barrington Country Bistro
25 | 20 | 25 | $39

*Foundry Shopping Ctr., 700 W. Northwest Hwy. (Hart Rd.),*
*Barrington, 847-842-1300; www.barringtoncountrybistro.com*
Francophiles "feel at home" in the "relaxing" atmosphere of
this "first-rate" "gem" of a bistro; the "efficient" staff helps
it "shine in comparison to the competition", even if its
"upscale" "strip-mall" setting is "not exactly in the country",
but rather in the Northwest Suburbs' "culinary vacuum";
N.B. ratings may not reflect a post-*Survey* renovation,
chef change and introduction of a Provence-style menu
with Asian accents.

### Basil Leaf Cafe
– | – | – | M

*2460 N. Clark St. (Fullerton St.), 773-935-3388; www.basilleaf.com*
A "consistently reliable" "Lincoln Park secret" serving
"amazing" Northern Italian "chef's special pasta dishes",
"interesting salads and appetizers" and "homemade
dessert", this "cozy" "storefront" cafe is a "nice date spot"
that's also noteworthy for its "air of sophistication" and
"impressive" if limited wine list.

### BD's Mongolian Barbeque
17 | 13 | 16 | $19

*221 S. Washington St. (Jefferson Ave.), Naperville, 630-428-0300*
*445 E. Townline Rd. (Milwaukee Ave.), Vernon Hills, 847-247-9600*
*www.bdsmongolianbarbeque.com*
Make-your-own mavens mob this North and West Suburban
"eat-until-you-explode" barbecue duo for the "multiple
customer-driven choices" of "buffet-style meats and
veggies" prepared for you by stir-fry "cooks who add to the
fun"; disenchanted diners, though, flame the food as "filler",
give the service so-so marks and naysay the "noisy"
atmosphere (one reason "it's a good spot to bring the kids");
N.B. the Wrigleyville branch closed post-*Survey*.

### bella! Bacino's
19 | 16 | 15 | $24

*75 E. Wacker Dr. (Michigan Ave.), 312-263-2350*
*36 S. La Grange Rd. (Harris Ave.), La Grange, 708-352-8882*
Though the bistro-style menu of this City and Suburban West
pair goes beyond that of their pie-palace sibs, longtime
devotees of the extended family still swear by the "good
deep-dish" and "super-thin pizza" ("try the spinach even if
you don't like" Popeye's favorite green); some say the La
Grange location "is a step up" for the area, but detractors
describe the "something-to-be-desired" Downtown decor
as having "lost its charm and coziness."

### Bella Notte
21 | 11 | 16 | $31

*1374 W. Grand Ave. (Noble St.), 312-733-5136;*
*www.bellanottechicago.com*
It's unanimous: this Near West "hole-in-the-wall" is a
"reliable" "mainstay" for "red-sauce Italian" "comfort
food" – the kind that "grandma would have cooked had she
been" born on The Boot – served in "mammoth" portions

and at "reasonable prices"; P.S. the Decor score may not reflect the post-*Survey* move from its former "no-frills", "tavern"-like digs next door.

### Benihana
| 18 | 16 | 19 | $31 |

*Fitzpatrick Hotel, 166 E. Superior St. (Michigan Ave.), 312-664-9643*
*747 E. Butterfield Rd. (Meyers Rd.), Lombard, 630-571-4440*
*1200 E. Higgins Rd. (Meacham Rd.), Schaumburg, 847-995-8201*
*150 N. Milwaukee Ave. (Dundee Rd.), Wheeling, 847-465-6021*
*www.benihana.com*

A divided demographic yo-yos about this teppanyaki chain where the "entertaining" "hibachi chefs" "like to play with the food" — boosters tout the "always tasty and fun" "flying" fare, but bashers blast the "tired", "gimmicky" "concept" as "overpriced" "Japanese flash" (except for the "cheap sushi") and also cite some housekeeping concerns; P.S. "some may not like the communal tables."

### Ben Pao
| 20 | 23 | 19 | $29 |

*52 W. Illinois St. (Dearborn St.), 312-222-1888; www.benpao.com*

"Dates and business diners" head to River North's "hip", "chichi Chinese" for "a sassy dining experience" amid "stunning decor" that's "exotic and romantic"; partialists are pleased that the "creative" menu offers "something for everyone", though purists pan it as "pricey" "pseudo-Asian cuisine" when compared to "the real deal in Chinatown"; P.S. honorable mention for the "homemade ginger ale" "and sake flights."

### BERGHOFF, THE ⌧
| 19 | 19 | 18 | $25 |

*17 W. Adams St. (bet. Dearborn & State Sts.), 312-427-3170*
### BERGHOFF CAFE O'HARE
*O'Hare Int'l Airport, Concourse C, 773-601-9180*
*www.berghoff.com*

"*Ach du lieber!*" exclaim addicts of this German-American "relic" in the Loop, a "classic, big-shoulders" schnitzel-haus "rich with Chicago history" and "lots of wood and beer" that proves "old is still good"; expect "long lines at lunch", despite the downstairs cafe added in a 2003 remodeling, and remember: "if you haven't been abused by the waiter, you haven't had the complete experience"; N.B. on-the-go noshers give a nod to the shortened menu at the airport outpost.

### Best Hunan
| 20 | 15 | 19 | $21 |

*Hawthorn Fashion Sq., 700 N. Milwaukee Ave. (Rte. 60),*
*Vernon Hills, 847-680-8855*

Hungry Hunan-hounds hail this "consistently good" North Suburbanite as "a must-visit for people in the area", saying its "large variety" of "authentic Chinese" fare fashioned from "fresh ingredients" truly is "some of the best available" (regulars report that "the crispy chicken and crab Rangoon are not to be missed"); also, the service is "fast and friendly."

### Bêtise, A Bistro on the Lake     19 | 20 | 19 | $37

*Plaza del Lago, 1515 Sheridan Rd. (Lake Ave.), Wilmette,
847-853-1711; www.betisebistro.com*

A dramatic dichotomy divides the *ouis* and the *nons* when
it comes to this North Suburban bistro that's near, though
"not exactly on, the lake" – for every claim that it "almost
always pleases" with "creative and satisfying" French fare,
there's a counterclaim that it's "inconsistent" or "getting a
bit stale"; similarly, service is either "excellent" or "erratic",
so it's no wonder some "regulars" report it's been something
of "a roller coaster ride" over the years.

### Bice Grill ⊠     19 | 17 | 16 | $40

*158 E. Ontario St. (bet. Michigan Ave. & St. Clair St.),
312-664-1474; www.biceristorante.com*

"Comfort-food" cousin to the adjacent ristorante, this
"upbeat" Streeterviller serves "cafeteria-style" Northern
Italian ("pizza, soft drinks, salads") for weekday lunch only;
it's "a bargain for the area" and a "great alternative to the
[loud] expense-account spots", even if service is "not
always attentive"; N.B. they do serve alcohol from next door.

### Bice Ristorante     22 | 19 | 21 | $42

*158 E. Ontario St. (bet. Michigan Ave. & St. Clair St.),
312-664-1474; www.biceristorante.com*

"Terrific choices" such as "fresh handmade pastas" make
this "fine-dining experience" from a "classic [Northern]
Italian chain" a microcosm of "Milano in Chicago"; it's a
"good place for a power dinner" or a "shopping break", with
a "wonderful" "see-and-be-seen" Streeterville "streetside
cafe" for "people-watching on a summer evening"; still,
penne-pinchers peg it as "pricey."

### Big Bowl Asian Kitchen     17 | 17 | 17 | $21

*6 E. Cedar St. (State St.), 312-640-8888
60 E. Ohio St. (Rush St.), 312-951-1888
215 Parkway Dr. (Milwaukee Ave.), Lincolnshire, 847-808-8880
1950 E. Higgins Rd. (Rte. 53), Schaumburg, 847-517-8881
www.bigbowl.com*

Stir-frying fans of these "cheap, cheerful" and "casual"
city and suburban "staples" "enjoy the creativity" of
"customizing" their own "good", "dependable Asian fusion"
fare, which may "not [be] authentic" but still makes for a
"fun, quick meal"; that said, the "unimpressed" underscore
that "quantity doesn't make up for" "ok quality", and say
"what started out as a unique concept" is now "pretty
plebian"; N.B. ratings may not reflect the post-*Survey*
return of original owners Lettuce Entertain You.

### Bijan's Bistro ◖     17 | 15 | 18 | $29

*663 N. State St. (Erie St.), 312-202-1904; www.bijansbistro.com*
A reincarnation of River North's former "great late-night
option" of the same name, this "comfortable neighborhood

spot" has a "better-than-adequate" and "varied" New American menu that's "always there for an easy dinner", so even if "it's not as quirky" as the original, most are "glad to see it's back"; N.B. the kitchen closes at 4 AM nightly.

### Billy Goat Tavern                14  10  13  $11

*Navy Pier, 700 E. Grand Ave. (Lake Shore Dr.), 312-670-8789*
*430 N. Lower Michigan Ave. (Illinois St.), 312-222-1525* ◐ ⊘
*330 S. Wells St. (Van Buren St.), 312-554-0297* ⊠ ⊘
*1535 W. Madison St. (Ogden Ave.), 312-733-9132* ⊘
*309 W. Washington St. (Franklin St.), 312-899-1873* ⊠ ⊘
*O'Hare Field Terminal 1, Concourse C, Gate 18 (I-90),*
*773-462-9368*

Featured in "that famous *SNL*" "cheezborger" sketch, this "cheap, greasy" "Chicago legend" and its spin-offs may be "rude and crude" with "crummy service" (regulars "love to watch them deal with first-timers"), but stubborn surveyors swear "that makes them all the more perfect"; also, the Lower Michigan "original under Wacker Drive is the real McCoy", with its "walls lined with autographed celebrity pictures", "Cubs kitsch, clippings" and "nicotine stains"; P.S. "they now serve Coke, no Pepsi."

### BIN 36                          20  20  20  $39

*339 N. Dearborn St. (Kinzie St.), 312-755-9463*
*275 Parkway Dr. (Aptakisic Rd.), Lincolnshire, 847-808-9463*
*www.bin36.com*

"Everything for the wine lover" awaits at this "trendy", "metrosexual" River North and North Suburban "date-place" duo where oenophiles "enjoy" "building flights" from an "exceptional list" crafted to complement the "inventive", "full-of-flavor" New American fare; still, bin-busters bemoan the "numbing noise" of the "exuberant crowd", claiming it "distracts" the "unpretentious, courteous" staff; N.B. a branch of Kamehachi, offering a limited sushi menu, opened post-*Survey* at the Lincolnshire location.

### Bistro Banlieue                 27  21  24  $40

*44 Yorktown Convenience Ctr. (bet. Butterfield Rd. &*
*Highland Ave.), Lombard, 630-629-6560; www.bistrobanlieue.com*

Advocates aver this "lovely" West Suburban bistro offering "outstanding", "innovative French cuisine" is just "getting better with age"; expect "an impeccable dining experience" with "attentive, friendly service" and "reasonable prices" (especially since they "offer half portions – a great idea"), but be sure to allow yourself plenty of time to find its "hidden strip-mall location."

### Bistro Campagne                 23  21  21  $37

*4518 N. Lincoln Ave. (bet. Sunnyside & Wilson Aves.),*
*773-271-6100*

A relative of Evanston's Campagnola, this "cozy", "charming bistro" in Lincoln Square has earned its "favorite" status by offering "terrific", "authentic" French fare at "reasonable prices"; "the mostly organic items are vibrant", the "wine list is impressive but not overwhelming" and the "staff knows its stuff"; P.S. the "outdoor garden is enchanting."

### Bistro Kirkou ⊠

▽ 25 | 19 | 22 | $45

*500 Ela Rd. (Maple Ave.), Lake Zurich, 847-438-0200*
A "tiny French bistro tucked away from almost everything" in the Suburban Northwest, this "great place" combines a seasonally changing menu of "excellent fare" "with an affordable wine list" in a "casual atmosphere"; "nice owner Kirk", who named the venue after the childhood sobriquet given him by his Gallic father, "is always there making sure everything is up to his standards"; N.B. open for lunch on Thursday and Friday only.

### Bistro Marbuzet

20 | 19 | 18 | $33

*7600 W. Madison St. (Des Plaines Ave.), Forest Park, 708-366-9090; www.bistromarbuzet.com*
"Fresh", "imaginative bistro fare" and a "great" wine list are assets of this "comfortable" New American–French that's "an easy pick in the Western Suburbs" according to eager enthusiasts who find it to be a "nice surprise" "in an unexpected locale"; the hesitant hedge a bit, though, claiming that the kitchen creates "no fireworks" and saying that "spotty service" "sometimes mars the experience."

### Bistro 110

20 | 19 | 19 | $37

*110 E. Pearson St. (bet. Michigan Ave. & Rush St.), 312-266-3110; www.bistro110restaurant.com*
Supporters suggest it's "easy to drop in" to this "charming and rustic" Gold Coast Gallic "right off Michigan" for some "French comfort food", whether you're looking for some "romance", a "good client" meal or just to "wind down a long day of shopping"; bothered bistro-goers backhand it as "noisy and crowded", though, and say the staff "doesn't handle peak" periods well.

### Bistrot Margot

21 | 20 | 19 | $36

*1437 N. Wells St. (bet. North Ave. & Schiller St.), 312-587-3660; www.bistrotmargot.com*
"Enjoy French comfort foods" such as "consistently prepared steaks" accompanied by "enough frites for a small country" at this "classic" Old Town neighborhood bistro, "a charming slice of France on Wells Street"; in keeping with its "nice Parisian feel", the "closely spaced tables" make for a "vibrant atmosphere" (it "can be a little noisy"), and the "wonderful upstairs" space is "warmed" by a working fireplace; N.B. a Naperville branch is in the works.

### Bistrot Zinc

20 | 19 | 18 | $34

*1131 N. State St. (bet. Cedar & Elm Sts.), 312-337-1131*
"Loyal regulars" "love to drop in" and "linger over coffee and conversation" at this "great Gold Coast" "favorite",

where the "hearty, varied and tasty" bistro menu is served amid "romantic, seductive French ambiance" that's both "authentic" ("like a meal in the Latin Quarter" of Paris) and "classy for everyday"; P.S. it's also a "good value."

**Bite** ⬤　　　　　　　　　　▽ 20 12 17 $17
*1039 N. Western Ave. (Cortez St.), 773-395-2483*
"Off the beaten path", this "hip", "funky" Ukrainian Village BYO "diner" does "cheap" Eclectic "comfort food" in a "less-than-posh" – ok, "pitiful" – environment "friendly" enough to make you "feel like you're eating dinner at someone's house"; known as a "breakfast and brunch spot" that's "guaranteed to cure any hangover", it's also handy for "seeing a show at the Empty Bottle afterwards."

**BJ's Market & Bakery**　　　　▽ 17 9 12 $12
*1156 W. 79th St. (Racine Ave.), 773-723-7000*
*8734 S. Stony Island Ave. (87th St.), 773-374-4700*
*9645 S. Western Ave. (bet. 96th & 97th Sts.), 773-445-3400*
"Northsiders don't know what they're missing" at this Far South Side "Southern cooking" specialist with "varied menu choices" of "affordable and filling" "self-serve soul food"; the space "is utilitarian" but "clean", and don't be surprised if service is "slow, especially since some items are made to order"; N.B. the Western Avenue and 79th Street branches opened post-*Survey.*

**BLACKBIRD** 🖾　　　　　　26 20 22 $53
*619 W. Randolph St. (bet. Desplaines & Jefferson Sts.), 312-715-0708; www.blackbirdrestaurant.com*
Faithful fans "flock" to this "absolute pinnacle of hip" in the West Loop where Paul Kahan's "outstanding" "seasonal" New American fare "will knock your socks off", "service is unexpectedly friendly" and the "modern, austere" digs are part of the "high concept"; contrarily, critics crow that the "cold", "sterile decor", "noise" and "too-close tables" "detract from the food."

**Black Duck Tavern & Grille**　　16 16 15 $28
*1800 N. Halsted St. (Willow St.), 312-664-1801; www.blackducktavern.com*
Lincoln Park locals land at this "neighborhood standby" for "huge portions" of "decent" Traditional and New American cooking in a "comfortable atmosphere"; birds of a feather feel it's "good" for a "date night" or "if you're going to the theater nearby", but quibblers quack it's "a loud sports bar" and "meat market" "trying to be something else", saying "go for drinks and move on."

**Blandino's Sorriso** 🖾　　　　　　– – – E
*321 N. Clark St. (bet. Kinzie & Wacker Sts.), 312-644-0283; www.sorrisoristorante.com*
The "home-cooked-style food" at this Northern Italian (from restaurateur John Blandino) on the edge of River North

doesn't draw the same raves as the "rare and beautiful riverside setting", but smiles abound for its "outdoor seating in summer" – and there are even boat-docking facilities for peckish pilots.

**Blind Faith Café**                    17  12  16  $18
*525 Dempster St. (Chicago Ave.), Evanston, 847-328-6875; www.blindfaithcafe.com*
"Not your father's hippie joint", this "mellow", "seitan-sational" North Suburban Eclectic has veteran vegetarians vowing that it's not only a "great place for vegans" thanks to a host of "healthy choices" but even has enough "flavorful", "interesting alternatives" "to convert beast eaters"; still, downers denounce the food and decor as "bland" and wonder "why are they charging so much?"; P.S. "there's a cheaper, faster" "self-serve section in front."

**Blue Bayou**                    15  17  18  $23
*3734 N. Southport Ave. (bet. Grace St. & Waveland Ave.), 773-871-3300*
N'Awlins' nostalgics like this "fun" Lakeview Regional American for giving "good Creole-Cajun" cooking, calling it a "comfy" "gathering place" for "friends" over "a casual dinner" and "great hurricanes" or for "people-watching while listening to a live band"; nevertheless, needlers who are "not impressed" jibe it's "just ok"; N.B. the Food rating may not reflect a post-*Survey* chef change.

**Blue Cactus**                    – – – I
*1938 W. Chicago Ave. (Damen Ave.), 773-227-5777*
Low-key and bargain-priced, this Ukrainian Villager is an intimate place for a casual date or Sunday brunch over authentic Mexican fare and BYO beer or wine (tote along some tequila and they'll whip up margaritas for you); a dimly lit dining area with ochre and terra-cotta walls, wood floors and cafe tables is separated by funky white drapery, and the storefront window gives a view onto the cooks' line.

**Bluefin**                    21  18  19  $30
*1952 W. North Ave. (Milwaukee Ave.), 773-394-7373; www.bluefinsushibar.com*
"Don't be fooled by the exterior" of this "small", "under-discovered" "neighborhood sushi place" in Bucktown that fin fans find "better than your average" Japanese joint; inside it's "hip and chic" (with half-priced drinks and a DJ on Thursday nights), and the "fresh" fish "melts in your mouth"; still, foes throw it back for being "overpriced."

**Bluegrass**                    – – – M
*1636 Old Deerfield Rd. (Richfield Ave.), Highland Park, 847-831-0595; www.bluegrasshp.com*
North Suburban Highland Park is home to this family-friendly, Southern-accented Traditional American, serving everything from a classic burger and ribeye to jambalaya

and chicken-sausage gumbo (along with an all-American beer and wine list that focuses on smaller producers); the simple interior has a warm, modern cafe feel, with lots of woods and neutral colors, and there's a cozy bar and a seasonal outdoor patio.

**Blue Line Club Car** ◑ ⊠    ▽ 17 | 20 | 14 | $18

*1548 N. Damen Ave. (bet. North & Pierce Aves.), 773-395-3700*
"Imagine yourself transported into an old-time train car" at this "comfortable" "great meeting place" in Wicker Park; it's a "nice addition" for "snacks and drinks after work" or a dinner of "solid, slightly creative" New American eats at "reasonable prices" — though peeved passengers pan the proferrings as "typical."

**Bluepoint Oyster Bar**    19 | 16 | 19 | $38

*741 W. Randolph St. (Halsted St.), 312-207-1222;*
*www.rdgchicago.com*
Satiated slurpers swear by the "wonderful selection of oysters" and other "fresh, well-prepared fish dishes" at this "pleasant" Market District "seafood place on Randolph Street"; with a "good happy-hour bar food" menu, it's a "nice place to meet for after-dinner drinks and cocktails", but some get the blues over "expensive" eats they feel are "good but not great."

**Blue Water Grill**    – | – | – | E

*520 N. Dearborn St. (bet. W. Grand Ave. & W. Illinois St.),*
*312-777-1400; www.brguestrestaurants.com*
In the River North space that formerly housed Spago, the NYC-based B.R. Guest group has opened this chic spin-off of its popular Manhattan spot; courtesy of chef Dirk Flanigan (ex Meritage), the creative New American slate is sexed up by a sushi bar, raw bar (including caviar), specialty cocktails and small-production wines by the glass, and the second-floor lounge presents live music nightly.

**Blu 47**    – | – | – | E

*4655 S. Martin Luther King Dr. (E. 46th St.), 773-536-6000*
Bronzeville, Chicago's erstwhile South Side blues district, is home to this New American serving Cajun/Creole-influenced cuisine in a contemporary, white-tablecloth setting done up in chocolate brown and sky blue; brunch is served on Sundays, and live jazz is featured in the lounge on Thursday nights.

**BOB CHINN'S CRAB HOUSE**    20 | 13 | 17 | $35

*393 S. Milwaukee Ave. (Dundee Rd.), Wheeling, 847-520-3633;*
*www.bobchinns.com*
"If you love seafood and garlic, this is the place" prate pros of this "reliable", "rollicking" Wheeling "warehouse" famous for a "huge variety of" "fresh fish", "long waits" and "delicious mai tais"; contrarily, cons can't abide being "herded like cattle" in "Disney-like lines" for what they

call "overpriced", "ordinary food" served in "charmless" "ballpark decor"; N.B. the distantly related River North branch closed post-*Survey*.

**Bob San** ◗  23  19  19  $37

*1805 W. Division St. (Wood St.), 773-235-8888; www.bob-san.com*
"Bob's the man" state stalwarts of this "trendy" Wicker Park Japanese "favorite", where the "consistently fresh fish" is "first rate" and "the cooked food's good too"; "hipper than its River North brother, Sushi Naniwa", it offers "trendy atmosphere" that's "much better than that of your typical" raw-fish restaurant, while remaining "laid-back" and "not at all pretentious"; N.B. there's summer sidewalk seating.

**Bogart's Charhouse**  19  17  18  $34

*18225 Dixie Hwy. (183rd St.), Homewood, 708-798-2000*
*17344 Oak Park Ave. (171st St.), Tinley Park, 708-532-5592*
"Beef, beef and more beef is what brings 'em back" to these Suburban South and Southwest steakhouses that are popular with partialists of "a lot of food" ("bring the big car"); to some, it's "good steak" "with all the fixings" "at a reasonable price" in a "step-back-in-time" setting, but others say the offerings are "bland", adding that Bogie "needs a face-lift"; N.B. the ratings may not reflect a change of ownership at the Homewood location.

**BOKA**  23  21  22  $43

*1729 N. Halsted St. (W. North Ave.), 312-337-6070;*
*www.bokachicago.com*
"Cutting-edge" and "sophisticated for Lincoln Park", this "excellent" venue enlivens "the tired pre-theater scene" with "well-prepared" New American cuisine made from "high-quality ingredients" then served in small and large plates within a "sleek", "modern" setting ("check out the cell phone booth!"); still, negs needle that it "needs to iron out a few kinks"; P.S. there's an "active bar scene at night."

**BONGO ROOM**  25  18  17  $17

*1470 N. Milwaukee Ave. (W. Evergreen Ave.), 773-489-0690*
"Before you die, have the chocolate French toast" at this "funky", "urban" Wicker Park American pancake palace where the "enormous breakfast", "unforgettable brunch" and "killer lunch" ("wish they had dinner") are "decadent and inventive"; "they need a bigger space", so "hipsters" "line out the door", but at least you can indulge in some "great people-watching" during the "long wait."

**Boston Blackie's**  18  12  17  $17

*164 E. Grand Ave. (St. Clair St.), 312-938-8700*
*120 S. Riverside Plaza (bet. Adams & Monroe Sts.),*
*312-382-0700* ☒
*222 E. Algonquin Rd. (Tonne Dr.), Arlington Heights,*
*847-952-4700*
*405 Lake Cook Rd. (Waukegan Rd.), Deerfield, 847-418-3400*

(continued)

**Boston Blackie's**

*Hubbard Woods Plaza, 73 Green Bay Rd. (Scott Ave.), Glencoe,*
*847-242-9400*
*www.bostonblackies.com*

Burger-meisters maintain that the house hunk is a "huge
and tasty" "value" at these "comfortable" Streeterville,
Loop and Suburban sibs (the "garbage salad is great", too),
so they're lenient about the "limited menu" and "not-fancy"
atmosphere; still, crabby carnivores "won't rush back",
calling them "average meat-lovers hangouts" with "dingy,
dark, dated" digs that are "often crowded" and "noisy";
N.B. the Arlington Heights location opened post-*Survey.*

**Brasserie Jo**   22 | 21 | 20 | $38 |

*59 W. Hubbard St. (bet. Clark & Dearborn Sts.), 312-595-0800;*
*www.brasseriejo.com*

"Big, boisterous" and "bustling", this "real brasserie" in
River North is a "staple" to stalwarts, who say it's "still one
of the best" thanks to Jean Joho's "outstanding" New
French and "interesting bistro fare" served in a "convivial
atmosphere"; conversely, complainers conclude the "food
and service sometimes seem a bit tired."

**Breakfast Club, The** ⊅   20 | 11 | 18 | $14 |

*1381 W. Hubbard St. (Noble St.), 312-666-3166;*
*www.chicagobreakfastclub.com*

"Forget all diets" at this "cute and cozy", "cash-only"
clubhouse that's "worth trying to find" in its Near West
niche for its "good food, smilin' service and neighborhood
atmosphere"; look for all-American "breakfast and lunch
in the grand tradition" including "wonderful pancakes,
waffles and omelets" with "great Bloody Marys."

**Brett's Café Americain**   ∇ 20 | 15 | 18 | $29 |

*2011 W. Roscoe St. (Damen Ave.), 773-248-0999;*
*www.brettscafe.com*

*Casablanca* it's not, but it's "pretty fancy for Roscoe Village"
at this "civilized" "find" with a "creative American menu" of
"good" Asian- and Latin-influenced "seasonal creations"
and "unbelievable" "homemade breads" (plus a "fantastic
brunch"); the "relaxed" atmosphere makes it "a great
place to enjoy the company of your dining companions."

**Bricks**   22 | 13 | 17 | $18 |

*1909 N. Lincoln Ave. (Wisconsin St.), 312-255-0851;*
*www.brickspetaluma.com*

Lincoln Park's "underground", "grottolike" "pizza joint"
"has its own thing going on" when it comes to "gourmet"
"thin-crust pizza" with "creative toppings" of the "freshest
ingredients", "a large beer selection" and "great music";
it's a "friendly" place for "casual times with friends", even if
the setting is "just like your college boyfriend's basement."

## Bruna's Ristorante    ▽ 21 | 14 | 19 | $29

*2424 S. Oakley Ave. (24th Pl.), 773-254-5550*

"Another great Heart of Italy joint", this "old-line classic Chicago Italian" is "worth going" "down memory lane" for, with "solid cuisine" and an "unpretentious", "welcoming" vibe ("the owner will pull you in off the street – and that's a good thing"); eaters insist it's "eras and miles from its modern Downtown" competitors.

## Bubba Gump Shrimp Co.    13 | 15 | 15 | $25

*Navy Pier, 700 E. Grand Ave. (Lake Shore Dr.), 312-252-4867;*
*www.bubbagump.com*

For some "fried-food" fanatics, this *Gump* film-inspired seafood spot and "tourist magnet" on Streeterville's Navy Pier is "fun" (and especially "good for families with kids"); critics, though, pan it as a "predictable", "overpriced" "concept restaurant" that "was better left on a producer's floor", quipping "run, Forrest, run!"

## Buca di Beppo    16 | 18 | 17 | $25

*2941 N. Clark St. (bet. Oakdale & Wellington Aves.), 773-348-7673*
*521 Rush St. (Grand Ave.), 312-396-0001*
*90 Yorktown Shopping Ctr. (bet. Butterfield Rd. & Highland Ave.),*
*Lombard, 630-932-7673*
*15360 S. 94th Ave. (151st St.), Orland Park, 708-349-6262*
*604 N. Milwaukee Ave. (Lake Cook Rd.), Wheeling, 847-808-9898*
*www.bucadibeppo.com*

Consensus eludes this "national chain serving ersatz Italian home-cooked fare", a "zany family restaurant" that's "fun, festive, feisty" and "best with a crowd" considering the "pile-it-high" "family-style" "portions on steroids"; friends favor its "hearty" eats and "purposely kitschy" "wall-to-wall" "gaudiness", but foes fume "fuggedabout" this "concept run amok", saying the "quantity" of the "bland" "institutional food" "outweighs the quality."

## Buona Terra Ristorante    ▽ 22 | 21 | 22 | $24

*2535 N. California Ave. (Logan Blvd.), 773-289-3800*

"Some inventive dishes" from a "solid and tasty" Northern Italian menu sway surveyors to seek out this "comfy" Logan Square spot, "especially those living in" the "burgeoning retail and restaurant corridor"; with its "nice staff" and "mellow scene", it's a "lovely place to meet friends" among "an interesting mix of clientele."

## Burgundy Inn    – | – | – | M

*2706 N. Ashland Ave. (Deversey Pkwy.), 773-327-0303;*
*www.burgundy-inn.com*

A "small but varied menu" of "good", "reasonably priced" Traditional American cooking that's "a cut above homestyle" makes for a "great casual dinner" at this "classic Chicago" "charmer" in Lakeview, where the "filling" fare and "old-style service" "welcome you back again and again."

### Butera Ristorante
– | – | – | M |

*2200 N. Lincoln Ave. (W. Webster Ave.), 773-525-8400*
Occupying a prime corner in Lincoln Park, this upscale-casual neighborhood Italian steakhouse has a simple interior of brick and neutral walls, tile floors and an open kitchen; it's an understated backdrop for the traditional appetizers, salads and handmade pastas, as well as steak and seafood selections.

### Butter
– | – | – | E |

*130 S. Green St. (bet. Adams & Monroe Sts.), 312-666-9813;*
*www.butterchicago.com*
This posh, pricey New American – located in the Greektown space that once housed the Green Room – shows off the creative cooking of chef Ryan Poli (a vet of The French Laundry and Le Français); a luxury raw bar, late-night service (1 AM weeknights, 2 AM Saturdays) and a funky second-floor lounge that's festooned with polka dots add to the seduction.

### Cab's Wine Bar Bistro
23 | 18 | 22 | $36 |

*430 N. Main St. (Duane St.), Glen Ellyn, 630-942-9463;*
*www.cabswinebarbistro.com*
"Do I have to give up my secret?" ask admirers of this "wonderful little" West Suburban bistro where the "creative chef" ensures "there's always something interesting on" the New American menu, and the "well-versed staff" "helps you navigate" the "extensive wine list"; its "cute", "quaint" surroundings in "a small storefront next to a wine store" complete the "charming" package.

### Café Absinthe
25 | 21 | 21 | $42 |

*1954 W. North Ave. (Damen Ave.), 773-278-4488*
New American lovers laud the "amazing", "sophisticated menu" at Bucktown's "consistent upscale star" for the "serious foodie palate", assuring it's "still going strong"; among its numerous other assets are a "low-key glam" feel that's "romantic" (even when "noisy") and "hip without the attitude", as well as a "knowledgeable", "affable" staff; N.B. the Food score may not reflect a post-*Survey* chef change.

### Cafe Ba-Ba-Reeba!
21 | 19 | 18 | $28 |

*2024 N. Halsted St. (Armitage Ave.), 773-935-5000;*
*www.cafebabareeba.com*
"Good ol' Ba-Ba-Reeba!" gush gregarious gourmands who gather in "groups" at this "steady" Lincoln Park Spaniard, a "perennial favorite" for a "tapas food orgy", with an "excellent sherry list" and "great outdoor dining"; worriers wonder, though, if the small plates justify the "noisy" "crowds" and "spotty service" – and "wallet-watchers" warn "the price adds up rapidly"; N.B. the Food rating may not reflect a post-*Survey* chef change.

### Café Bernard                    23 | 18 | 22 | $34
*2100 N. Halsted St. (Dickens Ave.), 773-871-2100;*
*www.cafebernard.com*
An "oldie but goodie", this Lincoln Park "bistro without an
attitude" "continues to get better with time"; the "excellent
French country fare", "attentive staff" and "casual feel"
make this "romantic" "hideaway" a "mainstay", plus its
"sister" spot, the "Red Rooster [wine bar] in back", is "a
bargain alternative"; N.B. the Decor score may not reflect
a post-*Survey* redecoration.

### Cafe Bolero                    ▽ 21 | 17 | 17 | $25
*2252 N. Western Ave. (W. Belden Ave.), 773-227-9000;*
*www.cafebolero.net*
"I've died and gone to Cuba" insist impressed individuals
who indulge in the "tasty", "authentic food" at Bucktown's
"casual", "reasonably priced" Cuban cantina with "outdoor
dining" and periodic live entertainment; respondents
report they "must go back for plantains" and the "great
empanadas with a flaky crust and flavorful fillings" on a
regular basis; P.S. "people-watching picks up around 10."

### Cafe Borgia                    ▽ 23 | 15 | 22 | $28
*17923 Torrence Ave. (179th St.), Lansing, 708-474-5515;*
*www.cafeborgia.com*
"Not just a spaghetti and lasagna place", this "gem in
the South Suburbs" "has been around so long" because
the folks there "know how to put together a tremendous
meal" of "diverse and interesting" Italian fare, which is
offered with "simply great service" in an "unpretentious"
environment; P.S. "the outdoor patio is wonderful during
the summer months."

### Cafe Central                    23 | 19 | 23 | $34
*455 Central Ave. (St. Johns Ave.), Highland Park, 847-266-7878;*
*www.cafecentral.net*
North Suburban cafe society sanctions this spin-off "sister
of Carlos'" for "excellent French bistro" cooking that's
"well prepared, fresh and interesting", and ambiance
that's both "cozy" and "friendly" (including in the "terrific
sidewalk cafe"); those who think the "bill is always more
than expected" also tell us the "tables are too close."

### Café des Architectes                    22 | 22 | 19 | $42
*Sofitel Chicago Water Tower, 20 E. Chestnut St. (Wabash Ave.),*
*312-324-4063; www.sofitel.com*
If you build it, they will come to this "sleek, contemporary"
Gold Coast New French–Mediterranean in the "upscale"
Sofitel hotel, which is "well designed, as befits its name",
with a "stylish" ambiance; believers brand the "beautifully
presented" output as "*très* tasty", but deconstructionists
declare it's an "expensive" spot that may just be "better
for breakfast than dinner."

## CAFÉ IBERICO ◑                          21 | 14 | 16 | $24

*739 N. La Salle Blvd. (bet. Chicago Ave. & Superior St.),*
*312-573-1510; www.cafe-iberico.com*

"Go early, hungry, thirsty and bring earplugs" comment
conquistadors craving the "inspiring creations" and
"yummy" "red and white sangrias" at this "jam-packed"
River North Spanish small-plate specialist "where the
action is with the younger crowd" for "an informal dinner" or
"group outing"; inquisitionists are irritated, though, by the
"hit-or-miss" eats, "cramped", "tired decor" and "average
service", complaining "you could grow old waiting."

### Café La Cave                         22 | 21 | 22 | $49

*2777 Mannheim Rd. (bet. Higgins Rd. & Touhy Ave.), Des Plaines,*
*847-827-7818*

Habitués head to the O'Hare area and this "classic" "old
favorite" where "perusing the menu is a step back in time"
thanks to "great" Continental "classics" that make for "a
beautiful experience" for a "date" or a "business deal";
some "enjoy" hibernating in the "unique" atmosphere of
its "dark grotto" space while others prefer the "spacious
main room", though detractors wish the place would
"become more value-conscious"; N.B. the Decor rating may
not reflect a post-*Survey* renovation.

### Café le Coq ⊟                    ▽ 24 | 21 | 22 | $36

*734 Lake St. (Oak Park Ave.), Oak Park, 708-848-2233*

"It's the real thing" crow coq-ettes who are crazy about
this "cozy" "shining star", a "nice addition to Oak Park"
where Steve Chiappetti's "deftly prepared" French "bistro
food" is accompanied by a "wonderful wine menu" and
served by an "intelligent staff"; sure, there may still be "a
few wrinkles", but patient patrons "hope they'll be ironed
out" in short order.

### Café Luciano                         17 | 17 | 18 | $30

*871 N. Rush St. (Chestnut St.), 312-266-1414*
*2676 Green Bay Rd. (Central St.), Evanston, 847-864-6060*

There's a split decision over this "bustling", "casual" Italian
Gold Coaster and its North Suburban spin-off: some say
"both locations provide reliable food", "good service" and a
"nice setting" (plus "sidewalk dining" Downtown); others
are underwhelmed, though, by the "uninspired" menu and
overwhelmed by the "crowded seating."

### Cafe Matou                           23 | 20 | 23 | $41

*1846 N. Milwaukee Ave. (bet. Armitage & North Aves.),*
*773-384-8911*

"You can feel the love of" chef-owner Charlie Socher at
Bucktown's "trendy" tomcat (translation of the name) that
"rarely puts a paw wrong" with its "heartwarming", "honest
French bistro food", augmented by a "smart, approachable
wine list" and "delightful service" – and all for "just a few

euros" amid "homey" "storefront" "surroundings" with "local art on the walls."

### Cafe Pyrenees
25 | 19 | 23 | $36

*River Tree Court Mall, Rte. 60 & Milwaukee Ave. (Rte. 21), Vernon Hills, 847-918-8850; www.cafepyrenees.com*
Surveyors strike it rich at this "gold mine", a "true gourmet restaurant" with "outstanding" "bistro food and wine" "for the budget-minded" served by a "friendly staff" providing "polite service with a French accent"; with its "comfy", "conversation-friendly" digs (set "in an unlikely spot" – a North "Suburban strip mall"), it's "a winner" "oozing charm."

### Cafe Selmarie
19 | 17 | 17 | $19

*4729 N. Lincoln Ave. (Lawrence Ave.), 773-989-5595; www.cafeselmarie.com*
"All types meet to eat, drink and converse" over a "good" "light meal" (especially the "great outdoor brunch in warm weather") from the "small but interesting" New American menu of "delicious breads, pastries, sandwiches, coffee" and "killer desserts" at this "comfy", "reliable" "little spot" "in the heart of [Lincoln] Square"; in fact, it's so "yummy" some night-owls hoot "why can't they stay open later?"

### CAFÉ SPIAGGIA
25 | 23 | 24 | $46

*980 N. Michigan Ave., 2nd fl. (Oak St.), 312-280-2750; www.cafespiaggia.com*
Approvers assert *"andiamo"* to this "casual" spawn of Spiaggia (almost "as good as the parent only cheaper" and "less stuck-up") for "contemporary Italian cuisine" "with flair" – including "pasta to die for" and "great thin-crust pizzas" – and a "fabulous view" of the Gold Coast's "North Michigan Avenue passing parade"; fence-sitters, though, find "issues with the value", "limited menu" and "tight quarters."

### CAFÉ 36
26 | 20 | 25 | $41

*22-24 W. Calendar Ct. (La Grange Rd.), La Grange, 708-354-5722; www.cafe36.com*
"For a memorable night out" (or a "top-notch" lunch), fans frequent this "first-class" "favorite" whose menu of "classic French" bistro fare (with a specialty in wild game) is marked by "excellent preparation and presentation"; factor in "cordial service" and a "classy, not stuffy", setting and you'll see why this "oasis" in a "small" West Suburban town is a "special find."

### Cafe 28
24 | 17 | 19 | $26

*1800-1806 W. Irving Park Rd. (Ravenswood Ave.), 773-528-2883*
"Thank God they expanded" gab grateful goers to this "Lakeview jewel", a "casual, family-run" "Havana nirvana" where "excellent Cuban and Mexican food" (including "terrific" weekend "brunch") and "good prices" make selfish sorts wish "others did not know about" it; helpful

hint: if you must endure a "long wait", "try the mojitos" – they're "freshly mixed" and very "refreshing."

## Caliente 🖾  – – – I

*3910 N. Sheridan Ave. (bet. Dakin St. & Sheridan Rd.),
773-525-0129; www.calientechicago.com*

A Latin-themed mural and Day of the Dead skeletons add sizzle to this warm, vibrantly colored storefront BYO Mexican on the fringe of Wrigleyville; the inexpensive, hearty cooking includes fresh tamales as well as some unusual items like chicken with red chiles and pumpkin-seed mole.

## California Pizza Kitchen  17  13  16  $19

*52 E. Ohio St. (bet. Rush St. & Wabash Ave.), 312-787-6075
Water Tower Pl. Shopping Ctr., 835 N. Michigan Ave., 7th fl.
(bet. Chestnut & Pearson Sts.), 312-787-7300
North Ave. Collections, 939 W. North Ave. (Sheffield Ave.),
312-337-1281
Arlington Town Square, 3 S. Evergreen Ave. (Campbell St.),
Arlington Heights, 847-590-0801
Oakbrook Center Mall, 551 Oakbrook Ctr., 2nd level (Rte. 83),
Oak Brook, 630-571-7800
Woodfield Village Green, 1550 E. Golf Rd. (Meacham Rd.),
Schaumburg, 847-413-9200
Westfield Shoppingtown, 374 Old Orchard Ctr. (Old Orchard Rd.),
Skokie, 847-673-1144
www.cpk.com*

Friends of "always-dependable CPK" find it a "fail-safe" for a "novelty" pie that's "good, interesting and consistent", and say it remains the "best compromise place for pleasing both parents and kids"; foes fault the "early '80s shopping-mall decor" and "standard chain fare", though, harping "how dare you bring California pizza to Chicago?"

## Caliterra Bar & Grille ☽  22  22  22  $45

*Wyndham Chicago, 633 N. St. Clair St. (Erie St.), 312-274-4444;
www.wyndhamchicago.com*

A rash of raters reward this "relatively undiscovered gem" for its "unique menu" of "contemporary Californian-Italian cuisine" "featuring whatever fresh ingredients the season is offering"; the "attentive service" and "beautiful, open location" "tucked away" on the "second floor" of the Wyndham Chicago hotel also win praise, even if a quorum of quibblers quote it's "nothing special."

## Calypso Cafe  17  15  16  $20

*Harper Ct., 5211 S. Harper Ave. (bet. 52nd & 53rd Sts.),
773-955-0229*

Chicagoans who "have a hankering for the Caribbean" take a "quick trip to the islands" at this "informal", "friendly and cheerful" Hyde Park pit stop for "family dining" featuring "tasty" if "not-fancy" fare; the "must-have jerk" specialties and "plantains are not to be missed", as are the "numerous

tropical mixed drinks", but weary travelers still warn that
"connoisseurs would be disappointed."

### Campagnola                              – – – M
*815 Chicago Ave. (Washington St.), Evanston, 847-475-6100*
The evolution of this rustic Evanston trattoria has included
a recent stint as an outpost of Bistro Campagne, but it's
returned to its thinking-man's Italian roots, retaining a
commitment to fresh local and organic ingredients but not
the dual-menu concept (the upstairs, serving the same bill
of fare, is now only open on Saturdays).

### Cannella's on Grand              ▽  20   12   21   $33
*1132 W. Grand Ave. (May St.), 312-433-9400*
"Go for the crispy and garlicky chicken Vesuvio" erupt
enthusiasts of this "casual" Near West "hangout" in a
"simple storefront", where the "friendly atmosphere" is
home to "enormous" servings of "reasonably priced"
"traditional Italian food"; "every entree comes with soup or
salad and pizza bread, too", making for "great value."

### Canoe Club                             – – – M
*15200 S. 94th Ave. (W. 151st St.), Orland Park, 708-460-9611;*
*www.thecanoeclubrestaurant.com*
Island attitude comes to the Southwest Suburbs by way of
this sprawling New American getaway, where the decor
encompasses a full-grown palm tree, a 25-ft. waterfall and
a floor-to-ceiling shark tank that's the centerpiece of the
spacious bar; the menu is rife with tropical touches –
particularly exotic seafood – but landlubbers can also find
plenty of steaks and chops; N.B. there's a large patio, too.

### Cape Cod Room                       21   21   22   $49
*Drake Hotel, 140 E. Walton Pl. (Michigan Ave.), 312-787-2200;*
*www.thedrakehotel.com*
One school of surveyors savors being "shot back 50 years"
at this "venerable" "Chicago seafood" "tradition" in the
"basement of the Drake Hotel", where "classy" "dressed-
up" customers dine on "fresh fish", an "excellent raw
bar" and "executive martinis" served by "mature" staffers
in an "old-fashioned men's club" setting; "to some it's
reassuring, to others tired" (the latter fillet it as "flat",
"overpriced" and "stuffy").

### CAPITAL GRILLE, THE                  25   24   24   $53
*633 N. St. Clair St. (Ontario St.), 312-337-9400;*
*www.thecapitalgrille.com*
"Monstrous", "melt-in-your-mouth" "dry-aged steaks",
"wonderful fish" and "martinis to die for" have happy
honchos handing high marks to this "good representative
of the national chain" of steakhouses; "consistency",
"extraordinary service" and a "comfortable", "clubby"
setting where "you can actually hold a conversation"
combine in this admittedly "pricey" "meat-eaters' paradise."

## CARLOS'    28  24  27  $80
*429 Temple Ave. (Waukegan Ave.), Highland Park, 847-432-0770;*
*www.carlos-restaurant.com*
"Bring a Polaroid camera" (and gentlemen, wear a jacket) to
Carlos and Debbie Nieto's "beautiful" North Shore "temple"
of "exciting, inspired" "New French cuisine" to capture the
"meticulous presentation" of its "fabulous food"; also
expect "personalized service" from a "courteous staff"
that's "knowledgeable about" the "outstanding list" of
"amazing wines", but be warned that "high prices" make
this "a special-occasion favorite" for penny-wise pen pals.

## Carlucci    20  20  19  $39
*1801 Butterfield Rd. (I-355), Downers Grove, 630-512-0990*
*250 Marriott Dr. (Milwaukee Ave.), Lincolnshire, 847-478-0990*
*Riverway Complex, 6111 N. River Rd. (Higgins Rd.), Rosemont,*
*847-518-0990*
*www.carluccirestaurant.com*
Contradictory correspondents can't be conclusive about
this suburban Northern Italian trio that "varies by location" –
they're either "inventive" and "upscale", offering "great-
tasting food" "served with a smile" in a "classy" setting, or
"dependable" and "decent" but "not dazzling", with
"amateurish" service and "loud" ambiance.

## Carmichael's Chicago Steak House    20  18  19  $42
*1052 W. Monroe St. (bet. Morgan St. & Racine Ave.), 312-433-0025*
Meat is the message at this "West Loop mainstay", a
steakhouse whose fans praise its "great steaks and sides",
"lovely courtyard" and proximity to the "United Center for
before or after" a "game or concert"; the opposing team,
though, takes issue with what it calls "ok" offerings that are
"overpriced", especially "for an out-of-the-way restaurant."

## Carmine's    20  18  18  $36
*1043 N. Rush St. (bet. Bellevue Pl. & Cedar St.), 312-988-7676;*
*www.rosebudrestaurants.com*
Friends of this Gold Coast petal of the Rosebud *famiglia*
gather for "heaping portions of" "great Italian food" in a
"cute", "fun" setting that's "right in the heart of everything",
with an "inviting outdoor patio" to "watch the Rush Street
crowd"; foes, though, find that its fare is "typical" and say
it's teeming with "tourists."

## Carson's Ribs    21  13  17  $29
*5970 N. Ridge Ave. (Clark St.), 773-271-4000*
*612 N. Wells St. (Ontario St.), 312-280-9200*
*200 N. Waukegan Rd. (bet. Deerfield & Lake Cook Rds.),*
*Deerfield, 847-374-8500*
*5050 N. Harlem Ave. (Foster Ave.), Harwood Heights, 708-867-4200*
*www.ribs.com*
"Sometimes you just have to go back to the source", and
"it's the ribs, baby", that have sauce-smeared regulars of

this "solid" city and suburban barbecue "classic" raving "who cares about" the "dark, unexciting decor"?; still, a rack of remaining raters report being less than tickled about the "stale atmosphere", not to mention the "spotty service."

**CATCH 35**  23 21 21 $43
*Leo Burnett Bldg., 35 W. Wacker Dr. (bet. Dearborn & State Sts.), 312-346-3500*
*35 S. Washington St. (bet. Benton & Van Buren Aves.), Naperville, 630-717-3500*
*www.catch35.com*
A surfeit of fish feasters supports this Loop location for its "unique menu selection of extremely fresh seafood" dishes with "lots of Asian touches" prepared "any way you like" and served within an "elegant" context ("eat farther away from" "the lively bar" if it's "quiet" you seek); yes, it's "a little pricey" – some say "overly" so – but most maintain it's "worth it"; N.B. the Naperville branch opened post-*Survey*.

**Cerise**  ▽ 19 16 20 $44
*Le Méridien Hotel, 521 N. Rush St., 5th fl. (Grand Ave.), 312-645-1500; www.lemeridienchicago.com*
Pleased patrons pick this "romantic", "hidden" French bistro "tucked away" in a "classy" River North hotel for its "original offerings" and "pleasant", "quiet ambiance" (it's also a "great place for a meeting" or "business breakfast"); still, supporters are pitted against "bored" sorts who label it "uninspired"; N.B. the Food rating may not reflect the post-*Survey* arrival of chef David Burns (ex Le Bouchon).

**Charlie's Ale House**  16 15 15 $20
*Navy Pier, 700 E. Grand Ave. (Lake Shore Dr.), 312-595-1440*
*5308 N. Clark St. (Berwyn Ave.), 773-751-0140*
*1224 W. Webster Ave. (Magnolia Ave.), 773-871-1440*
*www.charliesalehouse.com*
"Definitive pub grub" such as "wonderful pot pie and meatloaf" makes habitués happy at this trio of Traditional American "hangouts"; the Clark Street branch is a "good" "choice in Andersonville", the Streeterville spot on Grand is "a great escape from the commotion of Navy Pier", while the "quaint" original "Lincoln Park institution" on Webster separated from the pack post-*Survey* and will be renamed; N.B. a Wheaton outpost is in the works.

**Charlie's on Leavitt**  _ _ _ M
*4352 N. Leavitt St. (Montrose Ave.), 773-279-1600*
A spin-off of Charlie Socher's Cafe Matou, this long-awaited Lincoln Square New American has a clean, modern feel with lots of neutral colors, polished wood, glass and abstract artwork; the medium-priced menu combines the warming, rustic elements of bistro fare with a stateside sensibility, complemented by a small, global boutique wine list whose by-the-glass options change daily.

## CHARLIE TROTTER'S ⊠          27   25   27   $119
*816 W. Armitage Ave. (Halsted St.), 773-248-6228;*
*www.charlietrotters.com*
"If food can be poetic, orgasmic or intoxicating", you'll find it
at this "benchmark" New American in Lincoln Park, where
"master" chef and owner Charlie Trotter "still reigns",
creating cuisine that "can change your life"; believers
"bow down before" the "perfect harmony" of "sublime"
"food-as-art", a "wonderful wine list" "as thick as a phone
book" and "unbelievably attentive", "top-tier service" —
even if a few infidels insinuate it's "a bit full of itself" and
are "not sure it's worth the price."

## CHEESECAKE FACTORY          20   19   17   $24
*John Hancock Ctr., 875 N. Michigan Ave. (bet. Chestnut &*
*Delaware Sts.), 312-337-1101* ◖
*Oakbrook Center, 2020 Spring Rd. (bet. Harger Rd. & W. 22nd St.),*
*Oak Brook, 630-573-1800*
*Woodfield Mall, 53 Woodfield Rd. (Gulf Rd.), Schaumburg,*
*847-619-1090*
*Westfield Shoppingtown, 374 Old Orchard Ctr. (Skokie Blvd.),*
*Skokie, 847-329-8077*
*www.thecheesecakefactory.com*
A sizable slice of submitters is sweet on these city-and-
suburban stops for their "skyscraper-high cheesecakes"
and "something-for-everyone" Traditional American
menu delivered by "perky" servers amid "over-the-top"
"funhouse decor"; conversely, a chunk of cheesed-off
challengers chastises their "chain"-ness and complains
about "the constant crush of customers" that "creates
a cattle-car atmosphere"; N.B. the Oak Brook branch
opened post-*Survey.*

### Chef's Station          24   20   21   $41
*Davis Street Metra Station, 915 Davis St. (Church St),*
*Evanston, 847-570-9821*
Pleased passengers profess things "are on the right track"
at this "well-guarded" New American "secret" in "the
train station" in North Suburban Evanston, a "relaxed,
quiet" venue that's home to "haute cuisine at bargain
prices" (including an "outstanding fixed-price" menu); a few
miss the connection, though, finding the service "friendly
but somewhat erratic."

### Chen's          _   _   _   M
*3506 N. Clark St. (Addison St.), 773-549-9100;*
*www.chenschicago.com*
Even eaters who are "usually skeptical of split-cuisine
restaurants" praise the "well-prepared" Chinese-Japanese
provender with "lots of options" (including "the freshest
sushi") at this "upscale" Wrigleyville spot with "refined
ambiance"; N.B. its large windows open up to the street
in warm weather.

## Chestnut Grill & Wine Bar                    – | – | – | E
*200 E. Chestnut St. (Mies van der Rohe Way),*
*312-266-4500*
The former Cantare has resurfaced as this Streeterville
New American supper club focused on updated classics,
many served in both full and half portions; its posh decor
(overstuffed leather chairs, ceiling fans, vintage Hollywood
photographs) sets an indulgent tone, as does its global wine
list, which features numerous boutique and by-the-glass
selections; N.B. separate bar and late-night menus are
available, and live music is performed nightly in the lounge.

## Chez François ⊠                              – | – | – | E
*14 S. Third St. (State St.), Geneva, 630-262-1000;*
*www.chezfrancoisrest.com*
Beguiled boosters bellow "bravo!" to chef-partner Francois
Sanchez for his weekly changing menu of "superb" seasonal
Southern French cooking at this "delightful" bistro in the
Western Suburbs, which is decorated with large murals of
the Gallic countryside; N.B. the three-course prix fixe lunch
is a bargain.

## Chez Joel                                    22 | 17 | 21 | $39
*1119 W. Taylor St. (Racine Ave.), 312-226-6479*
"You're made to feel welcome from the first moment to the
last" at this "romantic, unique" French "hideout" "smack
in the middle of Little Italy", with a "terrific selection" of
"hearty", "heartfelt" and "well-priced bistro" fare; the
"quaint", "sunny" space can "get cramped" "but the food
is worth it" – and there's also "delightful outside [dining]
in fair weather."

## CHICAGO CHOP HOUSE                           25 | 19 | 22 | $49
*60 W. Ontario St. (bet. Clark & Dearborn Sts.), 312-787-7100;*
*www.chicagochophouse.com*
"Mainline" and "testosterone-laced" (though you may see
"women smoking cigars"), this "old-school" River North
steakhouse with "piano bar" rouses raves from red-meat
eaters for its "superb beef" selections – such as roasted or
"char-grilled prime rib" – that are "not à la carte" (potato
and salad included) and for servers with "lotsa hustle"
"who remember what being a waiter is all about"; still,
unkind cattlemen call it "touristy" and "cramped."

## Chicago Diner                                19 | 12 | 16 | $16
*3411 N. Halsted St. (Roscoe St.), 773-935-6696;*
*www.veggiediner.com*
Loyalists "love" this "crunchy oasis" in Lakeview, a
"vegetarian's dream come true" with "great healthy food"
"full of flavor" "to satisfy even the most devout" carnivore
(and "not saving room for" one of their "wonderful",
"hard-to-get vegan desserts" "is a crime"); still, doubters
guess it's "good enough but think they could try harder."

### Chicago Firehouse Restaurant     18    22    19   $38

*1401 S. Michigan Ave. (14th St.), 312-786-1401;*
*www.chicagofirehouse.com*
Fired-up fans find this "cozy" "old firehouse with original
fittings" and a "romantic outdoor patio area" a "hospitable"
South Loop home for "good-quality" Traditional American
cooking; foes dampen the flames, though, wondering why
the "food doesn't keep up" with the "great setting."

### Chicago Flat Sammies     14    9    9   $10

*163 E. Pearson St. (Michigan Ave.), 312-664-2733*
An "oasis for Michigan Avenue shoppers", this "casual"
Gold Coast "sandwich joint" "in the old Pumping Station" is
"good for a fast", "reasonable and tasty lunch" according to
flatterers who feel it's "a great Chicago secret"; flat-liners
flame it for being "crammed", though, and claim it's "nothing
to write home about"; N.B. kitchen closes at 5 PM.

### Chicago Kalbi ●     –    –    –    M

*3752 W. Lawrence Ave. (Hamlin Ave.), 773-604-8183*
"A favorite of native" *kalbi* coveters, this unassuming
Northwest Side spot is "so good" "if you're looking for
Korean BBQ" grilled at your table; solicitous service is
another reason that no one seems to mind the simple digs.

### Chicago Pizza & Oven Grinder Co. ⊘     22    15    17   $19

*2121 N. Clark St. (bet. Dickens & Webster Aves.),*
*773-248-2570; www.chicagopizzaandovengrinder.com*
The "delish" "upside-down" "pizza pot pie" is "heaven with
a crust" to cronies of this Lincoln Park "staple", "a true
Chicago experience" where "the host has the uncanny
ability to remember" "and to find you" "when a table is
ready"; those with an axe to grind grump that its unusual
offerings are "not the real" thing, the "wait is often quite
long" and the cash-only policy "is a pain."

### Chicago Prime Steakhouse     25    22    23   $49

*1370 Bank Dr. (Meacham Dr.), Schaumburg, 847-969-9900;*
*www.chicagoprimesteakhouse.com*
"Exceptional steaks" of prime beef, "generous portions" and
"an extensive wine list" combine with "attentive service", an
"elegant" interior and live jazz (Tuesday–Saturday nights)
to make this "one of the area's finer steakhouses" and "a
perfect place for business dinners in the [Northwest]
Suburbs" – even if it is "expensive"; N.B. the Decor rating
may not reflect a post-*Survey* renovation of the lounge area.

### CHIC Cafe     ▽    19    10    15   $24

*Cooking and Hospitality Institute of Chicago, 361 W. Chestnut St.*
*(Orleans St.), 312-873-2032*
Good sports say this "sincere" "cooking-school" proving
ground "that supports a good cause" "makes the grade"

as a "great" "BYO" spot for "real cheap" New French–
Eclectic edibles ("Sunday brunch is a favorite", with the
added bonus of a "year-round farmer's market"); tougher
tutors take points off for "uneven cooking", though, and
tease that "it's clear they aren't training waiters."

### Chief O'Neill's Pub    ▽ 18 | 16 | 18 | $22 |
*3471 N. Elston Ave. (Addison St.), 773-583-3066;*
*www.chiefoneillspub.com*
A wee bit o' "surprisingly good" "bar food" (including
"wonderful fish 'n' chips") plus "great live music" and a
"fun beer garden" add up to a "truly authentic Irish" pub
experience at this Northwest Side spot; N.B. there's a dozen
imported brews on tap.

### Chilpancingo    22 | 21 | 19 | $38 |
*358 W. Ontario St. (Orleans St.), 312-266-9525;*
*www.chilpancingorestaurant.com*
Amigos approve of this River North "mole heaven" where
the "highly flavored", "creative Mexican cuisine" (including
an "incredible chef's tasting menu") goes down smoothly
with "killer" "tableside[-prepped] margaritas", "a superb
wine list" and "tequila flights" amid "interesting", "colorful"
"decor"; grumpy gringos groan about "inflated prices" and
"service with a frown."

### China Grill    – | – | – | VE |
*Hard Rock Hotel, 230 N. Michigan Ave. (Lake St.), 312-334-6700;*
*www.hardrockhotelchicago.com*
A new Loop hot spot in the Hard Rock Hotel, this upscale
chain link offers creative, globally influenced Asian cuisine
in large, pricey sharing portions (go with a group if you want
to sample lots of dishes); the contemporary red-lacquer
interior is accented by gold mesh draping, an open kitchen
and a wall of windows overlooking Michigan Avenue.

### Chinn's 34th St. Fishery    22 | 13 | 18 | $29 |
*3011 W. Ogden Ave. (bet. Fender Ave. & Naper Blvd.), Lisle,*
*630-637-1777*
The "wonderful" fish is so "fresh" it "jumps onto your plate"
(it's flown in "daily", with "air-freight waybills tacked to the
wall that prove it") at this "casual" West Suburban seafood
server, a distant relation to Bob Chinn's Crab House; it's
generally "jammed" with devotees who aren't deterred by
"uneven service" and "pedestrian" "diner decor" that may
"need a makeover."

### Chinoiserie ⌿    20 | 10 | 13 | $24 |
*509 Fourth St. (Linden Ave.), Wilmette, 847-256-0306*
Eclectic Asian offerings ("mashed potatoes with Chinese
food – who'd have thought?") and an "eccentric" vibe make
this "one of the quirkiest restaurants on the North Shore";
pals praise "some gems on the menu" of "interesting
concoctions", while reserved reviewers report kitchen

"inconstancy", but most agree that the "flowery decor" is "strange" ("don't look, just eat"); P.S. though a liquor license is pending, the "great BYO" policy will continue.

### Cielo                    ▽  16  21  18  $37

*Omni Chicago Hotel, 676 N. Michigan Ave., 4th fl. (Huron St.), 312-944-7676*

"A great" Gold Coast "respite above Michigan Avenue", this "tony" "hotel dining room" with an "open feeling" and "beautiful domed ceiling" captures compliments as a "light and lively" "place for drinks and people-watching" or "a nicely presented, all-around decent meal"; less lofty lauders love the "Mag Mile views" but would "like to see a little more variety" in the "nothing-spectacular" Northern Italian–accented New American fare.

### CITÉ                    22  27  23  $64

*Lake Point Tower, 505 N. Lake Shore Dr., 70th fl. (Navy Pier), 312-644-4050; www.citechicago.com*

"Breathtaking views" from atop a Streeterville skyscraper qualify this "quiet", "romantic" New American–New French as a "great special-occasion spot"; high-fliers find the food "excellent", though crestfallen cité-dwellers deem it "good but not great" and "secondary to" the "awesome" scenery – which, by the way, "you're paying for"; N.B. gents, jackets are suggested.

### Clubhouse, The                    20  22  19  $33

*Oakbrook Center Mall, 298 Oakbrook Ctr. (Rte. 83), Oak Brook, 630-472-0600; www.theclubhouse.com*

Swingers score this West Suburban mall "surprise" as "sophisticated", praising the "huge portions" of "very enjoyable" American edibles (special mention for the "wonderful Sunday brunch") and "private-clubhouse feel"; others take shots at the "loud", "smoky" "meet-market" atmosphere, "not-very-impressive food" and "erratic service"; P.S. "eat upstairs if you don't like noise."

### Club Lago 🗷                    −  −  −  M

*331 W. Superior St. (Orleans St.), 312-951-2849*

"A great [Northern] Italian hole-in-the-wall", this River North "neighborhood joint" "run by two brothers", Giancarlo and Guido Nardini, has been serving "awesome home-cooked" Tuscan fare (including steakhouse specialties) at "super-cheap" prices since 1952; sensitive sorts "watch out", though – the "minimalist atmosphere" complete with tin ceiling and a "quite fun bar" sometimes gets "smoky."

### Club Lucky                    19  18  19  $28

*1824 W. Wabansia St. (1 block north of North Ave.), 773-227-2300; www.clubluckychicago.com*

Lucky ladies and gents love the "consistently great" "basic Italian cuisine", "killer martinis" and "cool", "kitschy" "Rat Pack" "scene" with "soul" and "staff spirit" at this "bustling" Bucktown "neighborhood mainstay"; it's "upbeat and fun if you're looking for a casual bite", and the budget-minded brag "it won't break the bank."

**Coast Sushi Bar** ◑          22  17  15  $28
*2045 N. Damen Ave. (bet. Dickens & McLean Aves.), 773-235-5775; www.coastsushibar.com*
"Superb fish quality" and "imaginative rolls" sliced up in a "young and minimalist" "club atmosphere" make this Japanese spot "a great sushi option" for the Bucktown neighborhood, even if "service is ok, not outstanding" – besides, "BYO keeps prices down"; N.B. the Decor rating may not reflect a post-*Survey* renovation.

**Coco**          – – – E
*2723 W. Division St. (California Ave.), 773-384-4811; www.cocochicago.com*
A handsome jewel amid an urban stretch of Humboldt Park storefronts, this pioneering 'modern Puerto Rican' is a sophisticated surprise, serving refined versions of island favorites in a beautiful, open room with richly painted walls, wood and tile floors, bright artwork and an imposing 1930s-era mahogany bar; N.B. they claim to be amassing one of the nation's largest collections of native rums from the Shining Star of the Caribbean.

**COCO PAZZO**          24  21  22  $45
*300 W. Hubbard St. (Franklin St.), 312-836-0900*
"A slice of Northern Italy in River North", this "upscale" but "not pretentious" spot pairs "outstanding", "authentic" cuisine with "fine wine" in a "comfortable, sophisticated" "converted loft space" "with golden lighting"; it all amounts to an "absolutely delightful", "truly grown-up experience" for "business or pleasure" that's "expensive, but worth it" – even if it "can be noisy" and "service is more variable than it should be."

**Coco Pazzo Cafe**          22  19  20  $36
*Red Roof Inn, 636 N. St. Clair St. (Ontario St.), 312-664-2777*
For "calm dining just off Michigan Avenue", it's "easy to like" this "charming, small" Streeterville "Italian cafe" ("the more casual" counterpart of its "upscale sibling", Coco Pazzo) thanks to its "always-well-prepared" Northern Italian cooking ("fantastic fresh pasta" and "panini" plus an "authentic antipasti bar"), "personal service" and a "great outdoor patio" – just "don't let the fact that it's on the ground floor of the Red Roof Inn influence you."

**Cold Comfort Cafe & Deli**     ▽ 22  15  15  $14
*2211 W. North Ave. (Leavitt St.), 773-772-4552*
Deli denizens are devoted to this "great little" breakfast and lunch BYO in Bucktown for "authentic selections" such as "perfectly prepared, gut-busting sandwiches" made with "high-quality" provender and Carnegie Deli cheesecake at

"decent prices"; the "tiny" space with "local art on the walls" "gets crowded", "so be prepared to wait."

### Convito Italiano    18 | 12 | 16 | $27

*Plaza del Lago, 1515 Sheridan Rd. (3 blocks north of Lake Ave.), Wilmette, 847-251-3654; www.convitoitaliano.com*

A "reliable" "place to hang in the 'hood" for "good honest Italian food" "and great wine", this North Shore restaurant/deli/grocery hybrid is "especially nice in the summer when you can sit outside"; nevertheless, nagging neighbors say it's "nothing special" and there's "no decor to speak of" – one reason it's "better for picnics and catering than sit-down."

### Coobah ◐    19 | 20 | 16 | $31

*3423 N. Southport Ave. (bet. Newport Ave. & Roscoe St.), 773-528-2220; www.coobah.com*

"Scene"-sters swarm this "trendy" Lakeview spot for "tempting", "creative" Latin-Filipino fusion cuisine "with lots of spice" paired with "funky drinks" in a "lively", "pumping urban" atmosphere; still, cavalier commenters complain of "barely attentive service" and call it "loud", "dark" and "too cool for thou", whispering "wake me when the mojito craze is over"; P.S. it's a "late-night gourmet treat."

### Cornelia's    24 | 22 | 21 | $34

*750 W. Cornelia Ave. (bet. Broadway & Halsted St.), 773-248-8333; www.ilovecornelias.com*

"Gourmet" Traditional American and Italian fare "without the fine-dining attitude" is on the "inspired menu" at this "cute" "locals' gem" where the "unique", "inventive" "comfort food" gets approval for both "quality and quantity"; plus, the "charming", "homey feel" of its "small, cozy" space and its "nice location" in Boys Town make it "a perfect gay-date restaurant"; N.B. the Decor rating may not reflect a post-*Survey* renovation.

### Corner Bakery Cafe    18 | 13 | 13 | $12

*516 N. Clark St. (Grand Ave.), 312-644-8100*
*900 N. Michigan Ave. (Outer Dr.), 312-573-9900*
*360 N. Michigan Ave. (bet. Wacker Dr. & Water St.), 312-236-2400*
*676 N. St. Clair St. (Erie St.), 312-266-2570*
*1121 N. State St. (Cedar St.), 312-787-1969*
*123 N. Wacker Dr. (Randolph St.), 312-372-3624* ✉
*Market Bldg., 140 S. Dearborn St. (Marble Pl.), 312-920-9100* ✉
*Field Museum, 1400 S. Lake Shore Dr. (opp. Soldier Field Stadium), 312-588-1040*
*Santa Fe Bldg., 224 S. Michigan Ave. (Adams St.), 312-431-7600*
*Goodman Theatre, 56 W. Randolph St. (Dearborn St.), 312-346-9492*
*www.cornerbakery.com*
*Additional locations throughout the Chicago area*

Converts claim the "twists on traditional sandwiches", "great soups and salads" and "decadent baked goods" at this "popular chain" of "speedy in-out spots" amount to a "nice alternative to burgers" that "will eventually take over the world" (don't forget to "take some bread home"); conversely, cons call the comestibles "overpriced" and "uninspiring" ("more variety would be nice"), cold-shoulder the "uninvolved" staffers and carp it "could stand a more efficient process."

## Corner Grille ∅                  _ | _ | _ | I

*5200 N. Clark St. (W. Foster Ave.), 773-271-3663*
Casual American comfort food comes to Andersonville courtesy of the Jack's on Halsted/Atlantique folks, who cater to cravers of homey breakfast fare and hearty PM foodstuffs like club sandwiches, chopped salad, meatloaf and milkshakes, all dished up in a modern chrome-black-and-white interior that's a cut above the classic diner's.

## Costa's                     22 | 20 | 21 | $30

*340 S. Halsted St. (Van Buren St.), 312-263-9700*
*1 S. 130 Summit Ave. (Roosevelt Rd.), Oakbrook Terrace,*
*630-620-1100*
*www.costasdining.com*
"Real Greeks eat" at this "upscale", "authentic Greektown gem" and its West Suburban sequel, where "excellent", "honest" "versions of the standards" are presented amid a "warm, inviting" environment that's "quieter and more sophisticated than the typical" competitor – though a "roaring fireplace" at both locations and a weekend "piano player" at the Oakbrook Terrace branch make "nice" noise.

## Costumbres Argentinas           _ | _ | _ | I

*1309 N. Ashland Ave. (bet. Blackhawk St. & Milwaukee Ave.),*
*773-489-6214; www.costumbresargentinas.net*
Enlivening a bleak stretch of Bucktown's Ashland Avenue is this subterranean taste of Buenos Aires; expect a come-as-you-are casual ambiance and a menu featuring traditional Argentinean fare – particularly empanadas and beef cooked on tabletop grills – along with a handful of Mexican dishes such as fajitas and enchiladas, all complemented by a selection of native wines, sangria or *yerba mate,* the homeland's tealike herbal stimulant.

## COURTRIGHT'S                 25 | 27 | 24 | $53

*8989 S. Archer Ave. (Willow Springs Rd.), Willow Springs,*
*708-839-8000; www.courtrights.com*
Take an "easy drive out" to the Southwest Suburbs for a "tranquil dining experience" amid "gorgeous", "understated decor" at this "warm, friendly place" where "picture windows" allow you to "watch the forest wildlife while you dine"; not only is "innovative" chef Jonathan Harootunian's New American cooking "terrific", but a "knowledgeable staff" and an "extensive list" of "excellent" vintages make it a "wine lover's paradise"; N.B. lunch is no longer served.

### Cousin's                              18   17   16   $21

*2833 N. Broadway (Diversey Pkwy.), 773-880-0063*
"Those who really want to feel they're in Turkey" "can sit on cushions at low tables in a raised", "shoes-free area" at this "nice hideaway for Middle Eastern fare" in Lakeview that's "great for vegetarians", though "there's also plenty of meat for carnivores"; still, pouty pashas pan the profferings as purely "passable"; N.B. it's no longer affiliated with Cousin's Turkish Dining on Irving Park Road.

### CROFTON ON WELLS ⌧          25   19   23   $49

*535 N. Wells St. (bet. Grand Ave. & Ohio St.), 312-755-1790;*
*www.croftononwells.com*
Supporters of this "intimate", "first-class" River North New American's chef-owner and namesake Crofton say "Suzy satisfies" with her "comfortable, haute" seasonal cuisine served in an "understated" setting that assures "the only art is the food" on your dinner plate; the subject of service splits surveyors, though, and some wish the "tables weren't so close together", while detractors of "minimalist decor" declare that it "could use a decorator."

### Cru Cafe & Wine Bar ◑          16   19   15   $28

*888 N. Wabash Ave. (Delaware Pl.), 312-337-4001*
The vibe is "laid-back" and "loungey" with "low lighting", "chic furniture" and a "snuggly fireplace" at this "romantic" Gold Coast grape bar with Eclectic light fare to pair with the "terrific wine list"; even so, some surveyors are sour on the "hit-or-miss service" and suggest they "don't come here for the food"; P.S. there's "a lot of outdoor seating" when weather warrants.

### Cucina Bella Osteria & Wine Bar    19   16   18   $28

*1612 N. Sedgwick Ave. (North Ave.), 312-274-1119;*
*www.cucinabella.com*
"Old-school" "Italian comfort food" finds a home at this "comfy" Old Town outpost "with a lot of personality" and "down-to-earth" service; contrarians may call the cuisine "nothing special", but more find the fare "enjoyable" – plus they "welcome dogs outside in the summer"; N.B. the Lincoln Park branch closed post-*Survey*.

### Cullen's Bar & Grill              18   18   18   $19

*3741 N. Southport Ave. (bet. Addison St. & Irving Park Rd.),*
*773-975-0600*
Grill-goers get to this "Wrigleyville favorite" for "good, old-fashioned" American and Irish "comfort food" including "huge burgers" and "onion rings that can make a hung-over man cry"; there can be "a long wait" "on weekends" (it's a "brunch standby") to enter the "dark, wood interior", whether there's a performance at the next-door Mercury "Theater or not", and it may get "loud", but "it is a pub after all"; P.S. their "excellent sidewalk seating" is "dog friendly."

**Cyrano's Bistrot & Wine Bar** ⌧   19 | 18 | 19 | $33
*546 N. Wells St. (Ohio St.), 312-467-0546; www.cyranosbistrot.com*
Aficionados "feel transported to France" at this "charming",
"fun" River Norther, where the "delicious", "bargain" "bistro
food" is "the real thing" and the "low-key" "European" vibe
is refreshingly "untrendy"; chef-owner Didier Durand, "a
treasure" who sometimes "comes out to chat", "and his wife
[Jamie Pellar] are wonderful hosts", and they've recently
added the Café Simone Parisian Cabaret on the lower level,
offering live music and a lighter, seafood-focused menu.

**D & J BISTRO**   25 | 20 | 24 | $37
*First Bank Plaza Ctr., 466 S. Rand Rd./Rte. 12 (Rte. 22),*
*Lake Zurich, 847-438-8001; www.dj-bistro.com*
Northwest Suburban seekers of "excellent" "seasonal"
French bistro fare find "truly wonderful dining" at this "solid
culinary performer", a "terrific" "surprise" "in a strip-mall
locale"; add in the "excellent wine choices" plus "charming
service" from an "experienced staff" and you have some
selfish surveyors suggesting they'd like to "keep it a secret";
P.S. "the prix fixe option is a steal."

**Dave's Italian Kitchen**   16 | 11 | 15 | $18
*1635 Chicago Ave., downstairs (bet. Church & Davis Sts.),*
*Evanston, 847-864-6000; www.davesik.com*
Dave's devotees delight in "carbo-loading" on the "large
portions" of "basic Italian grub" at this "inexpensive", "kid-
friendly" Evanston "staple" that's "not trying to be anything
more than it is"; "thriving for over 30 years" ("there's a good
reason this place is always full"), it "keeps chugging along"
despite discontents who decry what they call "mediocre"
eats and "so-so service."

**David's Bistro**   21 | 17 | 19 | $36
*Norwood Plaza, 623 N. Wolf Rd. (Central Ave.), Des Plaines,*
*847-803-3233; www.davidsbistro.com*
Supporters say you "can't beat this choice", "a wonderful
find in the Northwest Suburbs" for "surprisingly good"
seasonal New American food accompanied by a "solid
wine list" and served in a "small but nice" "strip-mall
storefront"; still, though friends feel eponymous chef-owner
"David [Maish] really has it together", dissenters describe
his staff as "slow as escargots."

**Davis Street Fishmarket**   19 | 14 | 16 | $29
*501 Davis St. (Hinman Ave.), Evanston, 847-869-3474;*
*www.cleanplate.net*
Reel-ists report an "outstanding school of fish dishes" and a
raw bar with a "variety of fresh oysters" at this "reliable",
"few-frills" Cajun-influenced "seafooder" in the North
Suburbs that makes you feel "like you're eating dinner on
a dock"; cons continue to carp about "fishy service",
though, and room rankings range from "rather rustic" to

"authentic-looking dive"; N.B. ratings may not reflect post-*Survey* changes to the menu and interior.

### De Cero ⊠     – ⎪ – ⎪ – ⎪ M
*814 W. Randolph St. (bet. Green & Halsted Sts.), 312-455-8114;*
*www.decerotaqueria.com*
A self-described 'modern-day taqueria', this much-needed Market District hot spot fills a niche for casual Mexican fare, with everything made to order – including hot-off-the-griddle tortillas comprising unusual ingredients and accompanied by the likes of pear-cilantro or hibiscus margaritas; equally refreshing are the blue floors and walls that evoke a south-of-the-border beach escape.

### Dee's     21 ⎪ 17 ⎪ 18 ⎪ $24
*1114 Armitage Ave. (Seminary Ave.), 773-477-1500;*
*www.deesrestaurant.com*
Gourmands gush about this "reliable" Lincoln Park Asian hybrid's "inventive and elegant" Mandarin and Szechuan menu augmented with a "good selection" of "fine sushi" and "fresh sashimi"; others experience it as "expensive", and choose to pass on the Japanese profferings, noting "it is a Chinese restaurant after all!"

### Deleece     21 ⎪ 16 ⎪ 20 ⎪ $28
*4004 N. Southport Ave. (Irving Park Rd.), 773-325-1710;*
*www.deleece.com*
"Reasonably priced, innovative dining" (including a "terrific brunch"), a "hip setting with exposed brick and copper pipes" and a "personable staff" are a recipe for success at this Eclectic Wrigleyville "treasure"; plus, "the owners make you feel at home", adding to the "warm, relaxed" vibe.

### Dell Rhea's Chicken Basket     ▽ 18 ⎪ 10 ⎪ 15 ⎪ $16
*645 Joliet Rd. (I-55/Rte. 83), Willowbrook, 630-325-0780*
Take "a trip down memory lane" at this "rooster-themed [American] roadhouse" a "little off the beaten path" in the Southwest Suburbs, where you "step back in time" – 1946 to be precise – "for a great chicken dinner"; the setting may be a tad "kitschy", but "the food is just plain good."

### Del Rio ⊠     20 ⎪ 16 ⎪ 22 ⎪ $34
*228 Green Bay Rd. (Rte. 22), Highwood, 847-432-4608*
Allies of this "old-fashioned" North Shore "red-sauce favorite" "can count on" the "no froufrou" Northern Italian fare, "homey" setting and "great wine list"; opened in 1930, it's among a "vanishing breed" and reminds many of their "grandma's food in [their] grandpa's favorite hangout."

### Dick's Last Resort ◑     13 ⎪ 13 ⎪ 14 ⎪ $22
*River East Plaza, 435 E. Illinois St. (bet. Lake Shore Dr. & McClurg Ct.), 312-836-7870; www.dickslastresort.com*
"If one enjoys abuse", this "down-and-dirty" BBQ and seafood spot "is the place" "to have a ton of fun" according

to fans of the "aggressive" servers, who "trade insults with you" ("masochists welcome"); it's "not for refined" foes of "crude commentary" and "rowdy" revelry, especially given the "mediocre" fare, though some say "your impression of the food" depends on "how drunk you are."

### Dining Room at                     − | − | − | M |
### Kendall College, The
*Kendall College, 900 N. North Branch St. (Halsted St.), 312-752-2328; www.kendall.edu*
Homework never tasted better than at this Near West culinary classroom, a sophisticated, white-tablecloth setting with third-floor views of the Chicago skyline and a menu featuring New French cuisine cooked and served by Kendall College students; below-market pricing and a BYO policy with a $5 corkage fee seal the deal.

### Dinotto Ristorante                22 | 17 | 21 | $32 |
*215 W. North Ave. (Wells St.), 312-202-0302; www.dinotto.com*
Old Town optimists opine positively on the "reasonably priced" "fresh pastas, great sauces and some less-than-traditional [Northern] Italian dishes" at this "intimate" "find" with an "attentive" staff and "excellent location near Piper's Alley"; still, those who dub the dining "undistinguished" miss the "old" incarnation (fka Trattoria Dinotto).

### Dixie Kitchen & Bait Shop         19 | 17 | 18 | $19 |
*5225 S. Harper Ave. (53rd St.), 773-363-4943*
*825 Church St. (Benson Ave.), Evanston, 847-733-9030*
*2352 E. 172 St. (Torrence Ave.), Lansing, 708-474-1378*
Soul-satisfied surveyors savor the "Southern comfort" food and Cajun dishes, "from fried green tomatoes to blackened catfish", at these "lively", "crowded" "bits of the bayou" in Hyde Park, Evanston and Lansing, with "kitschy" "rusted-metal-sign decor" and "down-home" "hospitality"; still, some Yankees yammer about the "hit-or-miss flavors" of it's "faux" fare and fault the "hokey decor."

### Dolce ⊠                            − | − | − | M |
*1600 W. 16th St. (Rte. 83), Oak Brook, 630-571-9500*
Despite the name, this is not a dessert bar – rather, it's a sleek 'Italian tapas' specialist and martini lounge luring stylish Oak Brook mallrats for savory and sweet small plates (and, yes, unusual confections, such as a fried Snickers bar in puff pastry); glass and metal meet drapes and leather in the chic space, with photos and flat-screen TVs providing visual stimulation.

### Don Juan                           20 | 13 | 17 | $25 |
*6730 N. Northwest Hwy. (bet. Devon & Ozark Aves.), 773-775-6438*
This long-standing Edison Park eatery still pleases partialists with its combo of "traditional" and "creative" "*nuevo Mexicano*" dishes (both "high brow and no-brow"), "delicious, potent margaritas" and "civilized" surroundings;

still, a portion of participants perceive the service as "iffy" and the overall experience "not what it used to be."

## Don Roth's Blackhawk　　　21 ⏐ 18 ⏐ 20 ⏐ $37 ⏐

*61 N. Milwaukee Ave. (Dundee Rd.), Wheeling, 847-537-5800; www.donroths.com*

Nostalgics befriend this Northwest Suburban "flashback", the late Don Roth's "shrine to pre-war Chicago" where management "keeps it simple" with "old favorites from the original Blackhawk Downtown" – namely "excellent spinning salad", "quality steaks", "juicy prime rib and delicious Boston scrod" that are "always as expected"; still, futurists fault the "dated decor and menu."

## Don's Fishmarket & Tavern　　16 ⏐ 14 ⏐ 16 ⏐ $29 ⏐

*9335 Skokie Blvd. (Gross Point Rd.), Skokie, 847-677-3424*

Fans favor this "friendly", "solid" North Suburban "fish place" for its "great variety" and "staffers who take pride in their work", though foes feel it's "nothing special"; P.S. regulars recommend you "get there for their early-bird special", while "proximity to the Northlight Theater" means it's a "good" "pre-show stop."

## Dorado　　　　　　　　– ⏐ – ⏐ – ⏐ M ⏐

*2301 W. Foster Ave. (bet. Claremont & Oakley Aves.), 773-561-3780*

More ambitious than most Mexican spots, this Lincoln Square BYO is owned by Luis Perez (ex Bistro Marbuzet, Jack's on Halsted), who employs classic French techniques and ingredients in some preparations; an open kitchen accents the colorful, casually upscale storefront setting.

## Dover Straits　　　　19 ⏐ 16 ⏐ 19 ⏐ $33 ⏐

*1149 W. Golf Rd. (Gannon Dr.), Hoffman Estates, 847-884-3900*
*890 E. US Hwy. 45 (Butterfield Rd.), Mundelein, 847-949-1550*
*www.doverstraits.net*

Denizens of this duo of "suburban seafooders" "feel comfortable" dining on its "fine selection" of fish including "real Dover sole" (the "best deal is the early-bird dinner") served by a "polite, pleasant" staff amid "nautical decor" that's "simple but not tacky"; still, detractors swim away from what they consider "standard" fin-food and "so-so service"; P.S. both offer "live entertainment and dancing" on certain nights.

## Dragon Court　　　　　– ⏐ – ⏐ – ⏐ I ⏐

*2414 S. Wentworth Ave. (W. 24th St.), 312-791-1882*

Worth a trip to the southern tip of Chinatown's Wentworth Avenue, this family-run Cantonese BYO affords seafood lovers the opportunity to select their swimming dinner straight from the tank; other specialties include hot pots and sizzling plates, all served family-style; N.B. this is one of those dual-menu establishments, with the Chinese version harboring the more interesting dishes.

### Dragonfly Mandarin | – | – | – | M |
*832 W. Randolph St. (Green St.), 312-787-7600;*
*www.dragonflymandarin.com*
Set in the former Azuré space in the Randolph Street
Market District, this swanky venue features a regional
Chinese menu (Mandarin, Szechuan, Hunan and a touch of
Cantonese); the decor is evolving, but will continue to
showcase the space's impressive bi-level exhibition wine
display and sweeping staircase to the second floor, along
with eye-popping artwork and huge gold foo dog statues
flanking the entrance.

### Drake Bros.' Steaks Chicago | – | – | – | E |
*The Drake Hotel, 140 E. Walton St. (Michigan Ave.),*
*312-932-4626; www.drakebros.com*
Replacing the old Oak Terrace, this upscale Streeterville
meatery capitalizes on the classic Chicago steakhouse
concept with prime steaks dominating its American menu,
complemented by a few contemporary dishes (Asian salad,
peppered ahi tuna) and nods to nostalgia (Bookbinder's
soup, steak tartare); the tony, tasteful interior is more
modern than old-style clubby, and offers killer views of
Lake Michigan and Michigan Avenue.

### Duke of Perth | 17 | 16 | 18 | $18 |
*2913 N. Clark St. (W. Oakdale Ave.), 773-477-1741*
Lads and lasses "love" this "great little pub" in Lakeview for
its "authentic Scottish" feel, "hearty saloon grub" (including
on Wednesdays and Fridays what many call the "best all-
you-can-eat fish 'n' chips deal in town") and "terrific
selection of single-malt scotches" and European beers;
its "quaint and cozy" atmosphere makes it a "warm" place
to "snuggle up", so "who needs glitzy decor" anyway?

### Dunlays on Clark | 18 | 14 | 18 | $25 |
*2600 N. Clark St. (Wrightwood Ave.), 773-883-6000;*
*www.dunlaysonclark.com*
### Dunlays on the Square
*3137 W. Logan Blvd. (Milwaukee Blvd.), 773-227-2400;*
*www.dunlaysonthesquare.com*
"It's like a top chef crashed a bar" and started cooking up
"a wide range of foodstuffs" at this Lincoln Park New
American "neighborhood joint" (with an adjacent wine bar)
that boasts "a lot of class" and "friendly, accommodating"
staffers; check it out "for a simple dinner", "great Sunday
brunch" or "after work" "for some of the best martinis in
town"; N.B. the Logan Square branch opened post-*Survey*.

### ECLECTIC ⊠ | 26 | 18 | 23 | $42 |
*117 E. North Ave. (Lake Cook Rd.), Barrington, 847-277-7300*
"They take their name so seriously that each dish seems to
draw upon four or five continents for its inspiration" at
"fantastically creative" chef-owner Patrick Cassata's

Northwest Suburban Eclectic, an "intimate" "find" set in a "charming historic old schoolhouse" whose atmosphere gives the impression of "dining in someone's private home"; add in "excellent service" by a "hip, knowledgeable staff" and it's one "terrific package for a night out."

### Ed Debevic's                           14 | 18 | 16 | $17

*640 N. Wells St. (Ontario St.), 312-664-1707*
*157 Yorktown Shopping Center (bet. Butterfield Rd. & W. 22nd St.), Lombard, 630-495-1700*
*www.eddebevics.com*

An "irreverent feeding frenzy" of "fair food" at "fair prices" awaits at this River North "'50s diner with attitude", a "noisy" "riot of a good time" "for tourists" where burgers and malts come with "wise-guy" service that may include "tabletop dancing"; those who don't "like shtick" warn "only eat here if you're eight years old"; N.B. the branch in Lombard's Yorktown Center opened post-*Survey*.

### Edelweiss                          ▽ 21 | 20 | 21 | $33

*7650 W. Irving Park Rd. (bet. Cumberland & Harlem Aves.), Norridge, 708-452-6040*

Bavaria-boosters believe it's "better than a trip to Germany" at this "always-Oktoberfest" outpost, "one of the few places left in Chicago to get authentic" Deutsch cuisine (with some American items); the "surprisingly tasty but heavy meals" go "beyond knockwurst" and pair well with "a wide selection" of native beers, plus "lederhosen-clad musicians" "make for a festive experience" Thursday–Sunday nights.

### Edwardo's Natural Pizza              18 | 10 | 14 | $17

*1321 E. 57th St. (Kimbark Ave.), 773-241-7960*
*1212 N. Dearborn St. (Division St.), 312-337-4490*
*2662 N. Halsted St. (1 block south of Diversey Pkwy.), 773-871-3400*
*521 S. Dearborn St. (bet. Congress Pkwy. & Harrison St.), 312-939-3366*
*6831 North Ave. (Grove Ave.), Oak Park, 708-524-2400*
*9300 Skokie Blvd. (Gross Point Rd.), Skokie, 847-674-0008*
*401 E. Dundee Rd. (Milwaukee Ave.), Wheeling, 847-520-0666*
*www.edwardos.com*

Facing off in an ongoing contest, fans of this city and suburban franchise's "signature stuffed spinach pizza" ("psst . . . the wheat crust is fantabulous") feel "you can't beat the flavor", and they're happy to overlook decor that's "not the best" (just keep your "expectations low" – after all, "they deliver"); still, foes find the deep-dish "disappointing", the service "slow" and the atmosphere "uninviting."

### 18 Esperienza ⊠                        – | – | – | E
(fka Old Church Inn)
*18 N. Fourth St. (Main St.), St. Charles, 630-443-8400*

For those experiencing innovative-cooking ennui, this West Suburban site comforts with a menu of American and Italian

classics, from Dover sole and veal scallopine to banana
cream pie; the handsome interior in a restored church
harbors a piano-martini-cigar lounge with live music on
Friday and Saturday nights.

### EJ's Place                      20  17  18  $42

*10027 Skokie Blvd. (Old Orchard Rd.), Skokie, 847-933-9800*
Diners divide over the merits of this North Suburban
"neighborhood" Italian "steak-and-martini-joint-meets-
hunting-lodge" cousin to Gene & Georgetti: regulars respect
the "large portions" of "very tasty", "well-executed" fare
and "great old-time waiters", while the resistance reports
"overpriced", "ordinary" offerings and "rude" service.

### El Jardin                      12  11  14  $19

*3335 N. Clark St. (bet. Addison St. & Belmont Ave.), 773-528-6775*
Commenters concur on the "tasty", "potent margaritas",
"small-town" decor, "great garden" and "slack service" at
this Mexican mainstay in Wrigleyville, but the revolution is
on when it comes to the "cheap" eats, which are either
"basic" but "delicious" or merely "mediocre" (depending on
whether you've had "one or two" of those "killer" cocktails);
N.B. they brought back Sunday brunch post-*Survey.*

### El Nandu                    ▽ 18  15  17  $22

*2731 W. Fullerton Ave. (California Ave.), 773-278-0900*
They "make you feel like you're in Argentina" at this South
American steakhouse in Logan Square, "a diamond-in-the-
rough" "place to go with friends" where the "reasonably"
priced "food has a special taste and authenticity" (folks
really "like the empanadas") and the "sangria is strong
and tasty"; P.S. "come for the live [entertainment] on
Thursday" through Saturday nights.

### El Presidente ◑                14  9  16  $14

*2558 N. Ashland Ave. (Wrightwood Ave.), 773-525-7938*
"Every city should have a 24-hour Mexican place", and "it's
comforting to know" this "low-profile" "dive" "is there" and
"always open" on the fringes of Lincoln Park; "just get the
food and put it in your mouth" pen pragmatists who praise
the "tasty, cheap" eats, though purists purport that the "dull"
fodder is only good "if you're three sheets to the wind."

### Ember Grille                    –  –  –  E

*Westin Chicago River North Hotel, 320 N. Dearborn St.
(Kinzie St.), 312-836-5499; www.westin.com/rivernorth*
This Eclectic in the Westin Chicago River North Hotel
offers patrons various ordering options, including buffet
(breakfast), prix fixe (lunch and dinner) and à la carte (all
meals); done in warm woods and earth-tone fabrics, with a
granite bar and view of the Japanese garden and lake, it also
features warmers for side dishes on each table as well as
an eclectic wine list divided between domestic wines and
those 'from the other side of the planet.'

**Emilio's Tapas**                                   21 | 18 | 18 | $29
*444 W. Fullerton Pkwy. (Clark St.), 773-327-5100*
*4100 W. Roosevelt Rd. (Mannheim Rd.), Hillside, 708-547-7177*
**Emilio's Tapas La Rioja**
*230 W. Front St. (Wheaton Ave.), Wheaton, 630-653-7177*
**Emilio's Tapas Sol y Nieve**
*215 E. Ohio St. (N. St. Clair St.), 312-467-7177*
*www.emiliostapas.com*
You "could be in Spain" "munching on an array of" "hot-
and-cold" "small plates" at this "trustworthy" group that
was serving "high-quality" Spanish "tapas before they
became trendy"; moods are mixed about the merits of
various locations, but the "fun"-"to-share" concept amounts
to "multitasking at its best", and "great sangria" adds to a
"wonderful after-work attitude adjustment."

**Emperor's Choice** ◑                               21 | 11 | 18 | $25
*2238 S. Wentworth Ave. (Cermak Rd.), 312-225-8800*
Chopstick-wielding chowhounds champion this "oasis
amid the hubbub of Chinatown", a Chinese "favorite" for
"great" Cantonese-Mandarin dishes made from "seafood
[so] fresh" it comes "directly from the fish tank"; most
maintain that "they generally do it right", especially "if you
can overlook" the "dim decor."

**Enoteca Piattini**                            ▽ 19 | 19 | 20 | $30
*934 W. Webster Ave. (bet. Bissell St. & Sheffield Ave.),
773-281-3898; www.enotecapiattini.com*
The "knowledgeable" staff at this "delightful" Lincoln Park
two-year-old serves "flavorful" Southern Italian fare in
"portions sized to enable tapas-style sampling", paired
with "lots of wines by the glass" (some 30) and followed by
"well-executed desserts"; with its "cozy atmosphere"
(including a fireplace), it's not only a "great spot" "for a date
or a small" gathering but is also a "family-friendly" "find."

**Erie Cafe**                                        19 | 15 | 20 | $43
*536 W. Erie St. (Kingsbury St.), 312-266-2300; www.eriecafe.com*
*Amici* of this "classic Chicago" Italian steakhouse (a Gene
& Georgetti relation) in River North are in it for the "huge
quantities" of "traditional" fare and "urban" "men's club
atmosphere" that make this "a regular hangout for pols, the
business crowd, locals and conventioneers"; conversely,
contrarians cry you'll need the "corporate credit card" to
cover the "good-but-not-great" food.

**erwin, an american cafe & bar**                    23 | 19 | 21 | $35
*2925 N. Halsted St. (Oakdale Ave.), 773-528-7200;
www.erwincafe.com*
"They go out of their way to make you feel at home" at this
"laid-back" Lakeview "gem" where chef-owner Erwin
Drechsler's "flavorful", "fresh seasonal" New American
cooking, which "only seems basic", is partnered with a

"good, unusual and fair-priced wine list" (be sure to "save room for dessert"); "knowledgeable, unassuming" service and a "charming", "mellow" atmosphere make it "an inspired choice for dates"; P.S. folks "love their brunch."

### Essence of India                          _ | _ | _ | M
*4601 N. Lincoln Ave. (Wilson Ave.), 773-506-0002*
Serving an extensive menu of authentic Indian fare – including tandoori dishes, biriyanis, vindaloos and numerous vegetarian selections, plus yogurt shakes – this serene storefront BYO in Lincoln Square boasts a dining room done in rose and soft browns with embroidered tablecloths and traditional artwork; N.B. a lunch buffet is available seven days a week.

### Ethiopian Diamond                   ▽ 20 | 11 | 18 | $18
*6120 N. Broadway (Glenlake Ave.), 773-338-6100*
Enthusiasts exclaim that "all the Ethiopian folk go" to this "authentic" Edgewater outpost, where the "rich and subtly flavored" fare is accompanied by "honey wine or house tea" and "brought to your table with a big smile"; it's "an incredible value", which is one reason the "cheap decor" doesn't detract – although some say the one-man band on Friday nights "leaves a bit to be desired."

### EVEREST 🛇                            27 | 26 | 27 | $86
*One Financial Pl., 440 S. La Salle Blvd., 40th fl. (Congress Pkwy.), 312-663-8920; www.leye.com*
High-minded Francophiles seeking "the summit of Chicago dining" say "chef [Jean] Joho continues to weave magic" with his "world-class", Alsatian-accented New French cuisine at this "special place" with a "million-dollar view" above the Loop; "noble service", a "posh setting" and sommelier Alpana Singh, a "wonderful guide" to the "extraordinary wine list", also help justify the "steep prices", though a segment says the "polished staff" can be "stiff" and the "room needs updating"; N.B. jacket suggested.

### Evergreen ◑                           21 | 10 | 16 | $20
*2411 S. Wentworth Ave. (24th St.), 312-225-8898*
A portion of panelists pines for the "outstanding Peking duck" and "inexpensive", "authentic [Cantonese-Mandarin] cooking" at this "fun Chinatown spot" where "big groups" and "families go" to indulge in "excellent entrees that are large enough to share"; nevertheless, pot-sticklers swear there are "better choices" considering what they call "dreary decor" and "ok" output.

### Fadó Irish Pub                        15 | 20 | 16 | $21
*100 W. Grand Ave. (Clark St.), 312-836-0066; www.fadoirishpub.com*
Pub-goers populate this "lively", "cozy" River North pint-peddler because it's a "lot o' fun", the staff "pulls an excellent" "room-temperature Guinness" and the "basic"

American and Irish eats – including "a mean breakfast" all day long – are offered up "in a casual atmosphere"; cooler heads chide this "chain" outpost for its "contrived" concept, though, and claim it's a better "hangout [than] restaurant."

## Famous Dave's    18 | 15 | 16 | $19 |

*1631 W. Lake St. (½ mi. east of Hwy. 53), Addison, 630-261-0100*
*113 S. Western Ave. (Main St.), Carpentersville, 847-428-9190*
*Yorktown Ctr., 206B Yorktown Ctr. (Highland Ave.), Lombard, 630-620-6363*
*1126 E. Ogden Ave. (Burlington Ave.), Naperville, 630-428-3500*
*North Riverside Park Mall, 7201 W. 25th St. (Harlem Ave.), North Riverside, 708-447-8848*
*15657 S. Harlem Ave. (157th St.), Orland Park, 708-532-7850*
*1101 E. Dundee Rd. (N. Rand Rd.), Palatine, 847-202-2213*
*948 S. Barrington Rd. (Ramblewood Dr.), Streamwood, 630-483-2480*
*99 Townline Rd. (Deerpath Dr.), Vernon Hills, 847-549-9933*
*www.famousdaves.com*
For a "down-home" "good time", confederates call on these "family-friendly" suburban sauce-slatherers serving up "consistently good ribs" and "BBQ with a choice of five different sauces" – just "don't expect nothin' fancy" from the "informal" digs; miffed meat eaters malign the makin's as "mediocre", though, and slam the service as "weak."

## Fattoush    – | – | – | I |

*2652 N. Halsted St. (bet. Deversey Pkwy. & Wrightwood Ave.), 773-327-2652; www.fattoushrestaurant.com*
Bargain-hunters back this Lincoln Parker serving Lebanese classics in casual, cafe-style confines; the quaint, second-level dining room is light and airy, simply decorated in white with swirling ceiling fans; N.B. it's BYO indefinitely, but it does offer spiced Lebanese coffee, mint tea and fresh-squeezed juices.

## Fat Willy's    – | – | – | I |

*2416 W. Schubert Ave. (Western Ave.), 773-782-1800; www.fatwillysribshack.com*
Cue cravers who quip "may Willy get even fatter" "hate to let people know about this great" "no-frills" BBQ and Southern "joint" in Logan Square, where the "substantial" "comfort-food" fare like "good brisket" and ribs along with "great cornbread and mac 'n' cheese" "makes you start planning your trip back the minute you leave."

## Feast    19 | 18 | 17 | $26 |

*1616 N. Damen Ave. (North Ave.), 773-772-7100; www.feastrestaurant.com*
Chums of Debra Sharpe's New American "standby" in Bucktown champion its "Eclectic menu full of inventive, delicious dishes" (especially at the "bustling brunch"), offered in an "open and relaxed" space with a "cozy

fireplace" in winter and "a little garden paradise" in summer; the less loyal label the cooking "a little hit-or-miss", though, and say the service is "not so awesome."

### Figo Ristorante
| – | – | – | M |

*433 Main St. (Duane St.), Glen Ellyn, 630-469-4232; www.figoristorante.com*

Chef and co-owner Luca Corazzina (ex Vivo) has rebuilt the former Glen Ellyn Brewery into this stylish Northern Italian featuring cooking that's both modern and authentic – he's even got his mom helping out in the high-ceilinged restaurant's open kitchen – and matched with a moderately priced wine list that's 90 percent Italian.

### Filippo's
| 23 | 15 | 20 | $27 |

*2211 N. Clybourn Ave. (Webster Ave.), 773-528-2211*
*833 Unit B Deerfield Rd. (Robert York Ave.), Deerfield, 847-948-8333*

There's "hidden talent" at this "comfortable" "gem" in a "relatively" obscure location in Lincoln Park's Clybourn corridor; its "creative" kitchen turns out "unexpectedly great" Southern Italian offerings at an "excellent value", making it a sometimes "crowded" spot for "a casual but solid dinner"; N.B. the Deerfield location is unrated.

### Fio
| ▽ 21 | 23 | 21 | $38 |

*566 Chestnut St. (Spruce St.), Winnetka, 847-441-4600*

Not only are the "food, decor and service very good" at this "quiet", "enjoyable" North Suburban New American two-year-old, which is "the locale of [former] Karizma chef" Martin Rogak, but fans report they're "improving all the time"; N.B. additional seafood dishes were added to the menu post-*Survey*.

### Firefly ●
| ▽ 16 | 19 | 19 | $28 |

*3335 N. Halsted St. (Buckingham Pl.), 773-525-2505*

Most who alight at this "intimate bistro" "in the heart of Chicago's gay neighborhood", aka Boys Town, do so more for the "good people-watching", the "casual" and "intimate" atmosphere of its "dark" digs, the "outdoor dining when weather permits" and the list of 30-plus martinis than for the French fare whose "quality doesn't match" ("some real kitchen talent could make this place a winner").

### Fireplace Inn, The ●
| 17 | 13 | 16 | $26 |

*1448 N. Wells St. (bet. North Ave. & Schiller St.), 312-664-5264; www.fireplaceinn.com*

"As the name suggests, you can expect a roaring fire" during winter "within the log-cabinlike surroundings" of this "old-timer" in Old Town, a "Traditional" American bastion of BBQ since 1969; fans also "enjoy" "watching a game" "on the huge projection TV" or sitting in the "nice outdoor area" in summer, but foes would rather skip what they call the "standard" fare and "so-so service."

## Flatlander's Restaurant & Brewery ─ ─ ─ I
(aka Flatlander's)
*200 Village Green (Rtes. 21 & 45), Lincolnshire, 847-821-1234;*
*www.flatlanders.com*
Fresh beers, Traditional American eats that go beyond bar
food and vast confines done in rustic wood-on-wood
distinguish this popular, casual Lincolnshire brewpub;
there's also a green scene in the garden when weather
permits, as well as brunch and live music on weekends.

## Flat Top Grill 18 14 16 $19
*3200 N. Southport Ave. (Belmont Ave.), 773-665-8100*
*319 W. North Ave. (Orleans St.), 312-787-7676*
*1000 W. Washington Blvd. (Carpenter St.), 312-829-4800*
*707 Church St. (bet. Orrington & Sherman Aves.), Evanston,*
*847-570-0100*
*726 Lake St. (Oak Park Ave.), Oak Park, 708-358-8200*
*www.flattopgrill.com*
When it comes to this "family-friendly" faction of "fun",
"festive" Asian stir-fry stations, stalwarts "love that you can
experiment" by "picking your own ingredients" (or take the
house's "suggestions for combinations") then watch as
"they cook it right there for you" – and "if your creation
doesn't suit you, go back up to the line"; still, tepid tasters
talk of "typical" food that's "only as good as you can make
it" and served in a "crowded" context.

## Flight ◑ ─ ─ ─ M
*1820 Tower Dr. (Patriot Blvd.), Glenview, 847-729-9463;*
*www.flightwinebar.com*
Situated in the Glen Town Center, site of the old Glenview
Naval air station, this North Suburban spot lifts off with
chef Quoc Luong's Eclectic array of Asian-influenced
Continental small plates paired with flights of wine and 80
by-the-glass choices; the casual, modern atmosphere
is grazer-friendly, with an open kitchen, live music on
weekends and outdoor dining in warm weather.

## Flo 23 17 19 $18
*1434 W. Chicago Ave. (bet. Bishop & Noble Sts.), 312-243-0477*
Flo-rid fans of this "fun", "casual" "little nook" in West Town
claim it's cooking up a "surprisingly interesting menu"
(including a frequently mentioned "great breakfast") of
American fare with some "Southwest flair" and coddling
customers with "caring" service; N.B. the addition of a full
bar has obviated the old BYO policy.

## Flourchild's ─ ─ ─ M
*185 Milwaukee Ave. (Old Half Day Rd.), Lincolnshire, 847-478-9600;*
*www.flourchilds.com*
Amid time-warped, tie-dyed, shag-carpeted environs, this
new North Suburban noshery serves up hearty Italian
comfort food including heros and hand-tossed, brick-oven

pizzas (steak and potato, curried chicken and Caribbean jerk are among the groovy toppings); N.B. leave room for one of the nostalgic desserts.

### Fluky's     18 | 9 | 13 | $8

*The Shops at Northridge, 520 N. Michigan Ave. (bet. Grand & Ohio Sts.), 312-245-0702*
*6821 N. Western Ave. (W. Pratt Blvd.), 773-274-3652* ⊟
*Lincolnwood Town Ctr., 3333 W. Touhy Ave. (McCormick Blvd.), Lincolnwood, 847-677-7726* ⊟
*www.flukys.com*

It's "the quintessential Chicago hot dog" and "best-of-breed Polish sausage" ("greasy, but in a really good way") that whistle to well-wishers of this "dirt-cheap" family of "conveniently located franchises" started in 1929; still, some strays snarl it's "not what it used to be", wondering "who's in charge?"

### FOGO DE CHÃO     24 | 20 | 25 | $53

*661 N. LaSalle St. (Erie St.), 312-932-9330; www.fogodechao.com*

"Gorging" gauchos glory in the "carnivorous orgy" and "noisy" "*carnivale* atmosphere" at this international chain outpost in River North, a "stylized take on Brazilian meat-houses" where the "incessant parade of" "melt-in-your-mouth" flesh (most every kind "except brontosaurus") is "hot off the spit and carved at your table"; moderates, though, maintain it's "too much of a good thing" – and "expensive", to boot.

### Follia     22 | 20 | 20 | $43

*953 W. Fulton St. (Morgan St.), 312-243-2888*

Fashionable foodies find the "authentic Northern Italian" fare "served with panache" at this "modern", "out-of-the-way" Randolph Market ristorante "amazing", including its "outstanding pastas" and "fresh" "thin-crust pizzas" "just like in Italy"; plus, it's "a fun place to take out-of-towners who thought that trendy meatpacking-district hot spots existed only on *Sex and the City*"; P.S. they now "have a liquor license", so no more BYO.

### Fondue Stube     ▽ 19 | 11 | 18 | $29

*2717 W. Peterson Ave. (Fairfield Ave.), 773-784-2200*

"Throw back some fondue while enjoying the '70s decor" at this "romantic" West Rogers Park Swiss dipping station that fans feel is just "like it oughta be" (even if the "self-serve" setup means you may "smell of the oil" "when you leave"); with this "old trend becoming 'in' again", it's "a fun place to go with a group of people."

### foodlife     17 | 14 | 12 | $16

*Water Tower Pl., 835 N. Michigan Ave. (bet. Chestnut & Pearson Sts.), 312-335-3663; www.leye.com*

Combining a "cornucopia of the world's cuisines" under one roof, this Eclectic "mother of all food courts" in the "upscale" Water Tower Place mall makes for a "quick, tasty" trip "that will satisfy any mix of people"; just the same, jesters jibe that the "concept is interesting" but the "overpriced" "food less so", while others malign the "mandatory tip" and "chaotic" confines.

### Fornetto Mei    – | – | – | M

*107 E. Delaware Pl. (bet. Michigan Ave. & Rush St.), 312-573-6300*
Marco Polo would be proud of this Chinese-Italian hybrid next to the Gold Coast's Whitehall Hotel: though the decor hasn't changed much since Molive resided here, the menu has, ranging from dumplings, noodle soups and a three-course 'Oriental fixed-price dinner' to pastas and thin-crust pizzas wood-fired in the restaurant's namesake 'small oven.'

### Four Farthings    17 | 14 | 17 | $25

*2060 N. Cleveland Ave. (Lincoln Ave.), 773-935-2060;*
*www.fourfarthings.com*
Happy hangers-out hail this Lincoln Parker as their "home away from home" when they "don't feel like cooking"; it's "exactly what a neighborhood place should be", with an American "comfort-food" menu emphasizing steak and seafood, "friendly service" and "reasonable prices" in a "cozy" "upscale bar setting" that's "good for dates, singles and families"; P.S. it's also "great for eating outside."

### 1492 Tapas Bar    17 | 17 | 17 | $29

*42 E. Superior St. (Wabash Ave.), 312-867-1492;*
*www.1492tapasbar.com*
A sangria-swilling segment of "the Michigan Avenue crowd" supports this River North Spanish spread over "three floors" in a "cozy" "old brownstone", saying "come with a group and share" its "exotic array" of "upscale tapas" served by a "personable" staff; skeptics snipe, though, that it's "still sailing the ocean blue without discovering" "food that matches the price."

### FRANCESCA'S AMICI    23 | 19 | 20 | $30

*174 N. York Rd. (2nd St.), Elmhurst, 630-279-7970*
### FRANCESCA'S BRYN MAWR
*1039 W. Bryn Mawr Ave. (Kenmore Ave.), 773-506-9261*
### FRANCESCA'S BY THE RIVER
*200 S. Second St. (Illinois St.), St. Charles, 630-587-8221*
### FRANCESCA'S CAMPAGNA
*127 W. Main St. (2nd St.), West Dundee, 847-844-7099*
### FRANCESCA'S FORTUNATO
*40 Kansas St. (Rte. 19), Frankfort, 815-464-1890*
### FRANCESCA'S INTIMO
*293 E. Illinois Rd. (Western Ave.), Lake Forest, 847-735-9235*
### FRANCESCA'S NORTH
*Northbrook Shopping Ctr., 1145 Church St. (Shermer Rd.),*
*Northbrook, 847-559-0260*

(continued)

(continued)

**FRANCESCA'S ON TAYLOR**
*1400 W. Taylor St. (Loomis St.), 312-829-2828*
**FRANCESCA'S TAVOLA**
*208 S. Arlington Heights Rd. (Northwest Hwy.), Arlington Heights, 847-394-3950*
**LA SORELLA DI FRANCESCA**
*18 W. Jefferson Ave. (bet. Main & Washington Sts.), Naperville, 630-961-2706*
*www.miafrancesca.com*
*Additional locations throughout the Chicago area*
Advocates adhere to the "excellent" and "affordable" "contemporary Italian meals" offered at this "reliable", "crowd-pleasing" city and suburban sisterhood born of the original Mia Francesca; the "comfortable", "attractive" environs and reservations policy "vary by location", and some feel that all of this family's features are "inconsistent"; N.B. Wicker Park and Barrington outposts are in the works.

**Francesco's Hole in the Wall** ⊅   24 | 15 | 21 | $31
*254 Skokie Blvd. (bet. Dundee & Lake Cook Rds.), Northbrook, 847-272-0155*
"Regulars" at this "reliable", "homey" North Suburban Southern Italian order the "excellent", "well-prepared specialties" posted on its "blackboard menu", which are delivered "in large quantities" by an "accommodating staff"; others, though, gang up on the "painful" prime-time "waits", "jammed" setting and "cash-only" policy.

**Frankie J's on Broadway**   – | – | – | M
*4437 N. Broadway (Montrose Ave.), 773-769-2959*
It's "quirky", yes, "but the food and service are surprisingly good" at this Uptown New American BYO owned by local comic and chef Frankie Janisch, whose "big idea" was to create a single venue in which to express his "love for" "cooking" and couple it with a "comedy club upstairs" (Friday–Saturday nights); a "great staff" and "excellent-value" pricing also make it "a nice addition to the 'hood."

**Froggy's French Cafe** ⊠   24 | 18 | 23 | $40
*306 Green Bay Rd. (Highwood Ave.), Highwood, 847-433-7080; www.froggyscatering.com*
Habitués hop to this "ultrafriendly" "old favorite" in the Northern Suburbs, "still going strong" with classic and bistro-style French cuisine that's "the best bargain there is" and served by a "charming and personable staff"; still, a few critics croak that the "drab" decor "needs an update."

**FRONTERA GRILL** ⊠   26 | 21 | 22 | $37
*445 N. Clark St. (bet. Hubbard & Illinois Sts.), 312-661-1434; www.fronterakitchens.com*
"Genius" Rick Bayless' "more casual alternative to its swankier [sibling] Topolobampo" "remains spirited, fresh

and fun" for "amazing" "non-gringo" "regional Mexican" cooking "that lives up to the hype" and "changes with the seasons" (and oh, "those incomparable margaritas" and that "wide variety of tequila"), all in a "boisterous" setting filled with "festive art"; a soupçon of spoilsports submits that "service can vary greatly" when it's "crowded", while "long waits" sadden even some supporters.

### Furama                    15  9  12  $17
*4936 N. Broadway (Argyle St.), 773-271-1161*
"Inexpensive dim sum daily" draws diners to this Chinese outpost Uptown, which also serves "traditional [Mandarin and] Cantonese food" with a "good selection of seafood"; still, some dis the "no-scenery" decor and say the sum of all its parts is "hit-or-miss"; N.B. the Chinatown branch closed post-*Survey*.

### GABRIEL'S ⊠               26  22  25  $60
*310 Green Bay Rd. (Highwood Ave.), Highwood, 847-433-0031;*
*www.egabriels.com*
Chef-owner and "consummate host" Gabriel Viti's "personal touch", not to mention his New French and Italian cuisine, which is "creatively prepared" with "fresh ingredients", mingle with "exceptional service" in "lively", "pretty surroundings" to create a "top-notch experience" at this North Suburban spot; still, some would prefer that the provender weren't so "pricey."

### Gale Street Inn            19  14  18  $27
*4914 N. Milwaukee Ave. (Lawrence Ave.), 773-725-1300;*
*www.galestreet.com*
*935 Diamond Lake Rd. (Rte. 45), Mundelein, 847-566-1090;*
*www.galest.com*
Alumni of the "old school" of "basic Americana" approve of these identically named but separately owned "local neighborhood restaurants" (one in Jefferson Park, the other with a view of Diamond Lake in Mundelein), where the "fall-off-the-bone" signature ribs have "some zing"; fans feel the Traditional fodder, "friendly"-if-"basic" "service" and "comforting ambiance" make them "great for a date or family" meal, but foes fault the output as "average."

### Gaylord Fine Indian Cuisine    21  16  18  $24
*678 N. Clark St. (Huron St.), 312-664-1700*
*555 Mall Dr. (Higgins Rd.), Schaumburg, 847-619-3300*
"Excellent" Indian cuisine including "mouthwatering curries" and "wonderful samosas" are among the assets of this "plain but tasteful" River North "original" and its Northwest Suburban sibling; diners diverge over whether they "beat Devon Avenue" and its delights, with some pun-jabbing that they're "pedestrian" and "pricey" (though virtually all agree their "economical buffet lunches" are a "great value").

### Geja's Cafe                          24 | 23 | 23 | $43 |
*340 W. Armitage Ave. (bet. Clark St. & Lincoln Ave.), 773-281-9101;*
*www.gejascafe.com*
The "fun is in the interaction" at this "reliable" "retro"
Lincoln Park fondue "classic", perennially rated as one of
the "most romantic restaurants" around ("flamenco guitar
music", "dark corners and hot oil – what else could you ask
for?"); still, the "delicious", diverse dipping and "helpful
staff" don't appease antis who are weary of the "long waits"
and wish management would "offer disposable clothes"
(you may "smell like sterno" "when you leave").

### Gene & Georgetti ⌧               22 | 14 | 19 | $50 |
*500 N. Franklin St. (Illinois St.), 312-527-3718;*
*www.geneandgeorgetti.com*
"Loyal followers" of River North's "hallmark" meat mainstay
revere it as a "very Chicago" "steakhouse at its finest",
the "kind of place Al Capone would have loved" for its
"delicious" "prime beef" ("love that char"), "must-have
garbage salad", "saloon" vibe with "lots of old-timers" and
"seasoned" staff; grumps get it as "a guy thing" and a
"pricey" "private club for the regulars" where the "waiters
have attitudes" and the whole vibe "needs some Viagra."

### Genesee Depot                    ▽ 16 | 10 | 18 | $24 |
*3736 N. Broadway (bet. Grace St. & Waveland Ave.), 773-528-6990*
"Time has stood still" at this Boys Town BYO in a "small
storefront", where a "friendly" staff serves "large portions"
of "good" Traditional American "comfort food like your
grandmother prepared when she entertained guests"; sure,
the "decor is a bit blah" and the fare "is nothing to write
home about", but it's also "not expensive."

### GIBSONS STEAKHOUSE ◑            25 | 19 | 23 | $54 |
*1028 N. Rush St. (Bellevue Pl.), 312-266-8999*
*Doubletree Hotel, 5464 N. River Rd. (bet. Balmoral &*
*Bryn Mawr Aves.), Rosemont, 847-928-9900*
*www.gibsonssteakhouse.com*
This "A-list" Gold Coast steakhouse "is da place" for "pretty
people" (including "locals, tourists, conventioneers",
"politicos" and those "looking for a mistress" or a "sugar
daddy") who hanker for "a hunka hunka burnin'" "prime-
aged beef" in a "high-energy" "boys'-club" atmosphere (the
"bar scene is jumping"); those who eschew this "expense-
account" "meatery" say "service suffers" from "crowding"
and "reservations are rarely on schedule" ("it helps to be
the mayor"); P.S. the O'Hare area spin-off is "a nice sibling."

### Gilardi's                          21 | 20 | 21 | $35 |
*23397 N. Rte. 45 (Rte. 21), Vernon Hills, 847-634-1811*
It "smells and tastes great" at this "family-run" "favorite"
in the Northwest Suburbs, where "they take an interest in
everyone", the "real Italian cooking" is "prepared by

capable hands" and the "luxurious old-house" setting
features "rooms filled with charm" and a screened-in
veranda that's "like being on a Southern plantation"; even
so, a few faultfinders feel the fare is a tad "typical."

### Gio                                 19 | 19 | 19 | $31 |
*1631 Chicago Ave. (bet. Church & Davis Sts.), Evanston,*
*847-869-3900; www.giorestaurant.com*
Bringing "some sophistication to the [North] Suburbs",
this Northern Italian "find" is "a fine value for fresh and
honest food", including "excellent" brick-oven pizzas and
"delicious pastas", served amid "attractive" if "sparse"
"surroundings"; there's also a "selection of reasonably
priced wines", so "don't be afraid to ask for help from
the friendly sommelier."

### Gioco                               21 | 21 | 19 | $38 |
*1312 S. Wabash Ave. (13th St.), 312-939-3870;*
*www.gioco-chicago.com*
Twists on traditional" Northern Italian fare can be found at
this "trendy" "trailblazer" in the South Loop, where the
"flavors are fresh" and "interesting", the staff "is attentive
but not intrusive" and the "upscale" yet "rustic" atmosphere
is "lively and noisy"; critics call the "prices a bit higher than
necessary", though, and say "service varies"; N.B. the Food
rating may not reflect a post-*Survey* chef change.

### GIORDANO'S                          21 | 12 | 15 | $18 |
*135 E. Lake St. (Upper Michigan Ave.), 312-616-1200*
*2855 N. Milwaukee Ave. (Wolfram St.), 773-862-4200*
*730 N. Rush St. (W. Superior St.), 312-951-0747*
*5159 S. Pulaski Rd. (Archer Ave.), 773-582-7676* ●
*236 S. Wabash Ave. (Jackson Blvd.), 312-939-4646*
*1040 W. Belmont Ave. (Kenmore Ave.), 773-327-1200*
*5927 W. Irving Park Rd. (Austin Ave.), 773-736-5553*
*223 W. Jackson Blvd. (Franklin St.), 312-583-9400*
*310 W. Randolph St. (Franklin St.), 312-201-1441*
*815 W. Van Buren St. (Halsted St.), 312-421-1221*
*www.giordanos.com*
*Additional locations throughout the Chicago area*
Pie partisanship continues, with diehards of this "longtime
favorite" deeming it "worthy of time-capsule status" for its
"ooey-gooey" "inimitable stuffed pizzas" possessing "a
perfect mixture of cheese, toppings and incredible" "rich,
buttery crust"; conversely, crusty critics claim the "service
is slow", the proprietary product is "not the best" of its kind
and quality "varies by location."

### Glunz Bavarian Haus                  – | – | – | M |
*4128 N. Lincoln Ave. (bet. W. Belle Plaine & W. Warner Aves.),*
*773-472-4287; www.glunzbavarianhaus.com*
A branch of the House of Glunz wine family tree has sprouted
this Lincoln Square outpost for German dining, situated in

a tastefully Alpine update of the former Great Beer Palace (whose patrons will appreciate the extensive Bavarian beer selections); the Austrian chef's menu covers the expected classics, with a few surprise twists and specials that transcend the concept's geographic boundaries.

### Gold Coast Dogs    19   7   13   $8
*2415 N. Clark St. (Fullerton St.), 773-770-3555*
*159 N. Wabash Ave. (bet. Lake & Randolph Sts.), 312-917-1677*
*U of C Center for Advanced Medicine, 5758 S. Maryland Ave.*
*(E 58th St.), 773-834-7261* ☒
*17 S. Wabash Ave. (Monroe St.), 312-578-1133* ☒
*1429 W. Montrose Ave. (Clark St.), 773-472-3600*
*Westfield Shoppingtown, 275 Old Orchard Arcade (bet. Golf Rd. & Skokie Blvd.), Skokie, 847-674-4171*
*16707 Oak Park Ave. (167th St.), Tinley Park, 708-429-9052*
*Midway Airport, food court, 773-735-6789*
*O'Hare Int'l Airport, Terminal 3, 773-462-9942*
*Union Station, 225 S. Canal St. (Jackson Blvd.), 312-258-8585*
*www.goldcoastdogs.net*
*Additional locations throughout the Chicago area*
If you're panting for some "excellent fast food" – namely, "classic Chicago dogs" and "the best cheese fries bar none" – along "with hideous decor and loud service", "this reliable chain delivers the goods"; faithful fans feel it's "still among the top wiener" purveyors "despite having lost some of the [shuttered] original location's hard-won grease build-up", though a litter of off-leash observers object, opining they're "not as good as they think."

### Golden Budha Chinese Steakhouse    –   –   –   M
*312 W. Randolph St. (bet. Franklin St. & Wacker Dr.), 312-609-0000*
Though classic, midpriced Szechuan fare dominates the menu, some premium Asian-sauced steaks and seafood dishes up the ante at this subterranean Loop locale (with an intentionally misspelled name) whose traditionally red-and-gold decor achieves a sleek, modern look – and features a waterfall, fresh bamboo on the tables and a view into the building's towering atrium; N.B. weekday lunch bargains suit the local business crowd.

### Goose Island Brewing Co.    16   14   15   $20
*3535 N. Clark St. (Addison St.), 773-832-9040*
*1800 N. Clybourn Ave. (Sheffield Ave.), 312-915-0071*
*www.gooseisland.com*
"Some of the best beer anywhere" in "many varieties" "matches perfectly with" the "tasty bar food" at this "pubbish" pair of "tavern-type" "brewhouses" in Lincoln Park and Wrigleyville, a "favorite choice" for "meeting friends" or "a casual get-together"; voters who evaluate the vittles as "variable", though, feel the signature suds are "the reason to go"; P.S. you can "take home a growler" (a refillable 64-ounce to-go container).

## Grace O'Malley's                 _  _  _  M

*1416 S. Michigan Ave. (14th St.), 312-588-1800;*
*www.graceomalleychicago.com*
Set in an 1891 building, and featuring a two-story vaulted bar
with library ladder, replicas of vintage streetlights and wood
dining booths sporting coat hooks and checked tablecloths,
this upscale restaurant/pub serves Irish-accented American
fare as well as specialty cocktails, 10 handles of draft beer
and a nice selection of Irish whiskeys.

## Gracie's on Webster 🗷            _  _  _  M

(fka Gracie's)
*1119 W. Webster Ave. (Clifton Ave.), 773-528-1788;*
*www.graciesonwebster.net*
New owners have massaged the menu and decor a bit
at this mid-casual Lincoln Park New American with a
warm yet spiffy setting (tin ceiling, lots of wood, big front
windows); a light bar menu, lunch and weekend brunch
offer plenty of options, and DJs rock the house on Friday
and Saturday nights; N.B. loungey late hours run to 2 AM
nightly, 3 AM on Saturdays.

## Grand Lux Cafe                   18  22  18  $26

*600 N. Michigan Ave. (Ontario St.), 312-276-2500*
Proponents of this River North New American, a "classier
sibling of the Cheesecake Factory", praise its "fabulous
variety" of "delicious options", saying it offers "something
for everyone" in a "great location" that feels "like a crazy
carnival of color and activity" (with "a fantastic view of
Michigan Avenue"); foes, though, fault what they find to be
an "overwhelming menu" of "factory food", "long waits",
"glitzy" "faux decor" and "spotty service."

## Graziano's Brick Oven Pizza      18  17  17  $21

*5960 W. Touhy Ave. (Lehigh Ave.), Niles, 847-647-4096;*
*www.grazianos.net*
Believers "can't get enough of" the "generous" amounts
of "hearty Italian cuisine" at this "family-style" Northwest
Suburbanite whose "create-your-own" concept "pleases
different tastes" with a wide variety of "really good brick-
oven pizzas"; nevertheless, naysayers nix the "noise level"
and say the sustenance is "so-so."

## Greek Islands                    19  18  19  $26

*200 S. Halsted St. (Adams St.), 312-782-9855 ◑*
*300 E. 22nd St. (Highland Ave.), Lombard, 630-932-4545*
*www.greekislands.net*
Socratic surveyors support the Grecian formula of this
Greektown "institution" and its West Suburban sequel for
their "extensive menus" of "great" "traditional food",
"served with flair"; "atmosphere that reminds you of the
Isles" encourages a "spirited", "party" vibe; N.B. both
locations offer outdoor dining.

**Green Dolphin Street** ⊠　　　20 | 20 | 19 | $42

*2200 N. Ashland Ave. (Webster Ave.), 773-395-0066;*
*www.jazzitup.com*

Would-be members of this "contemporary urban-chic
version" of an "old-fashioned supper club" on the "out-of-
the-way" outskirts of Lincoln Park go for "an outstanding
evening" of New American cuisine followed by a visit to
the separate "jazz bar" that's "free after dinner"; some say
it's swimming upstream, though, with "great music" that
"overshadows the good" but "inconsistent" food (which is
"a bit pricey", to boot).

**Green Door Tavern**　　　　14 | 16 | 16 | $18

*678 N. Orleans St. (Huron St.), 312-664-5496;*
*www.greendoorchicago.com*

River North's "super-casual" Traditional American tavern
"treasure" has "been around forever" (since 1921 to be
precise) "with the memorabilia on the walls to prove it",
making it a "vintage Chi-town" "burger and beer joint"
with "great history"; skeptics, though, "skip the food" and
"go for the bar."

**Green Ginger**　　　　∇ 16 | 14 | 17 | $24

*2050 W. Division St. (Hoyne Ave.), 773-486-6700;*
*www.greengingercafe.com*

Some say this "upscale" Wicker Parker offers "innovative
Asian" fare made from "high-quality ingredients" (including
"admirable dim sum on weekends") and a "real sense of
style", qualifying it as a "favorite" that's "great for small
gatherings with friends"; others are holding back, "hoping
that they find their groove."

**Green Zebra**　　　　　　－ | － | － | E

*1460 W. Chicago Ave. (Greenview Ave.), 312-243-7100;*
*www.greenzebrachicago.com*

Spring chef-partner Shawn McClain gives his upscale New
American cuisine a vegetarian slant at this Wicker Park
encore named for an heirloom tomato variety; the menu
showcases organic and locally raised produce (with a few
fish and poultry items), the wine list emphasizes artisanal
producers and the soothing, harvest-hued space (a former
hat shop) is accented with stainless steel and live greenery.

**Grille on Laurel, The**　　　　－ | － | － | E

*181 E. Laurel Ave. (Western Ave.), Lake Forest, 847-234-9660;*
*www.thegrilleonlaurel.com*

A nostalgic nod to the golden age of the supper club, this
natty North Suburbanite complements Continental classics
with retro cocktails and a global wine list; its setting (a
former Mercedes dealership) has a swanky feel, with warm
woods and a double-sided fireplace that divides the dining
room and lounge, the latter home to piano music Thursday–
Saturday nights; N.B. there's a Sunday buffet brunch.

### Grill on the Alley, The    18  20  18  $40

*Westin Hotel, 909 N. Michigan Ave. (Delaware Pl.), 312-255-9009;*
*www.thegrill.com*

Approving alley cats come for the "clubby atmosphere"
and "quite good" American fare that's "not just hotel food" at
this Beverly Hills–born Streeterville steakhouse; proponents
praise it as a "pleasant" "place for weary shoppers to rest"
or for "a romantic tête-à-tête", but others roast the offerings
as "ordinary" and wonder when service will "improve."

### Grillroom, The    18  17  19  $35

*33 W. Monroe St. (bet. Dearborn & State Sts.), 312-960-0000;*
*www.rdgchicago.com*

"Juicy steaks, big martinis and 40 wines by the glass"
(plus "filling salads at lunch") draw Loop denizens to this
"conversation-friendly" steakhouse and seafood specialist,
a "lovely respite in the middle of Downtown" – and one
that's "great for a pre-show meal" before the Shubert
Theatre "or an after-work cocktail"; doubters define it as
merely "decent", though, deciding it "won't knock any of
the top contenders out."

### Grotto    ∇  15  16  16  $43

*1030 N. State St. (Rush St.), 312-280-1005; www.grottoonstate.com*

Some suggest this Italian meating place is "a hot spot" with
"food that's better than it has to be considering the popularity
of" its "huge bar area" (open until 2 AM), "where Gold Coast
locals go" for "lots of action"; still, others surmise it "delivers
average", "standard fare" in "Chicago steakhouse terms"
and "fails to measure up to its [local] brethren."

### Gulliver's Pizzeria & Restaurant ●    ⎯  ⎯  ⎯  M

*2727 W. Howard St. (California St.), 773-338-2166;*
*www.gulliverspizza.com*

Travelers to this West Rogers Park "mainstay pizzeria and
food experience established in 1965" say it really "knows
deep-dish, Chicago-style pizza" and also has a "massive
menu" of American eats, not to mention "over-the-top
decor" teeming with "tons of turn-of-the-century antiques";
throw in outdoor seating, "late-night hours" (1 AM on
weekdays, 2 AM on weekends) "and delivery, as well", and
"what more could you want?"

### Hacienda Tecalitlan    ⎯  ⎯  ⎯  M

*820 N. Ashland Ave. (W. Chicago Ave.), 312-243-6667*

Somewhere between bargain-bin burritos and high-end
Mexican, this charming East Villager's cuisine comprises
standards as well as delicacies such as broiled quail and
smoked marlin (plus margs made with fresh fruit and a top-
drawer tequila selection); the setting, a tiered courtyard
replica, comes complete with burbling fountain, roving
mariachi band and an intimate bar with Casablanca
chairs and fireplace.

**Hackney's**     17 | 13 | 17 | $19
*733 S. Dearborn St. (Polk St.), 312-461-1116*
*1514 E. Lake Ave. (bet. Sunset Ridge & Waukegan Rds.),*
*Glenview, 847-724-7171*
*1241 Harms Rd. (Lake Ave.), Glenview, 847-724-5577*
*880 N. Old Rand Rd. (Rand Rd.), Lake Zurich, 847-438-2103*
*9550 W. 123rd St. (La Grange Rd.), Palos Park, 708-448-8300*
*241 S. Milwaukee Ave. (Dundee Rd.), Wheeling, 847-537-2100*
*www.hackneys.net*
Allegiants of these "institutions" known for "great old-
fashioned American food" say they're city-and-suburban
"standbys" that still serve an "outstanding hamburger" and
"scrumptious onion ring loaf" "worth every drop of fat and
cholesterol"; turncoats tell us they're "tired", though, with
"passable but undistinguished" profferings and "terribly
dated decor" at some locations; P.S. "the original Harms
Road" branch's "wonderful patio" is "relaxing."

**Hai Yen**     ▽ 21 | 11 | 14 | $17
*1055 W. Argyle St. (bet. Kenmore & Winthrop Aves.), 773-561-4077;*
*www.haiyenrestaurant.com*
"You can't go wrong" with the "excellent" "traditional
Vietnamese" and Mandarin Chinese food fashioned from
"fresh ingredients" and washed down with "great bubble
teas" at this Uptown "fave" in a "clean storefront" setting;
the "helpful" service and "prices you can't easily match"
all help make up for "awful decor."

**Half Shell** ◑⇸     23 | 7 | 14 | $26
*676 W. Diversey Pkwy. (Orchard St.), 773-549-1773*
"One of the best for" "seafood in the city" ("especially the
raw bar" and "fantastic crab legs"), this Lakeview "local
hangout" in a "stealth location" is equally known for its
"rough service" and "the world's worst decor" ("a dank
basement" setting); "prices are dirt cheap" but "bring
cash", because they don't take credit cards.

**Hama Matsu**     – | – | – | M
*5143 N. Clark St. (W. Winona St.), 773-506-2978;*
*www.hamamatsu-restaurant.com*
Serving both raw fish and cooked fare from the land of the
rising sun and its neighbor to the west, this Andersonville
Japanese-Korean decorated in a spare style (with pressed
bamboo floors and hanging box lanterns over a long wood
sushi bar) is a peaceful stop; N.B. the BYO policy will remain
in effect even after the liquor license comes through.

**Handlebar** ◑     ▽ 18 | 16 | 18 | $19
*2311 W. North Ave. (2 blocks east of Western Ave.), 773-384-9546;*
*www.handlebarchicago.com*
"You just have to get past the hippie anti-car thing to
realize" this bicycle-themed "neighborhood bar", "off
the beaten path" in Wicker Park, "is a great local place";

"a diverse menu" of "good", "mostly vegetarian fare"
(the only flesh is from fish) rides in tandem with "friendly
service" and "creative decor" to make it a "pleasant" spot.

**Happy Chef Dim Sum House** ◖  19 | 8 | 14 | $16
*2164 S. Archer Ave. (Cermak Rd.), 312-808-3689*
The chef's not the only one "happy" at this "crowded and
noisy" Chinatown chowhouse where "mouthfuls of heaven"
come in the form of "great", "piping hot dim sum" ("few
dishes are brought around to the tables" – "instead you
order from a menu"); it's "an incredible value", but don't
expect great service, and the "decor is nil", unless you
count the "nice" "plastic trash-bag tablecloths that are
summarily scooped up after each party finishes its meal."

**Hard Rock Cafe**  12 | 20 | 13 | $24
*63 W. Ontario St. (bet. Clark & Dearborn Sts.), 312-943-2252;*
*www.hardrock.com*
Rockers reckon the "casual American fare" and "fun
atmosphere" with "lots of cool" "music memorabilia" make
this River North "chain" member and "kid pleaser" "one of
the few theme restaurants worth going to"; but buzzkills
believe it's a "tourist trap" that's "getting a bit old hat", with
"overpriced" "pedestrian" food.

**Harry Caray's**  19 | 19 | 19 | $36
*33 W. Kinzie St. (Dearborn St.), 312-828-0966*
*Holiday Inn, 10233 W. Higgins Rd. (Mannheim Rd.), Rosemont,*
*847-699-1200*
**Harry Caray's Seventh Inning Stretch**
*Midway Airport, 5757 S. Cicero Ave. (55th St.), 773-948-6300*
*www.harrycarays.com*
Passionate proponents pick this three-peat of Italian
steakhouses for pitching "better food than you'd ever
expect" (the "Vesuvio dishes are fantastic") amid "fun"
"baseball memorabilia" "galore"; still, spoilsports assess
their hitting as "average"; P.S. "the River North location is
the mecca" "for die-hard Cubs fans to cry in their beer",
and the airport-area satellites are "conveniently located
for a meal on the way or during a delay."

**Hashalom** ⊠⇗  – | – | – | I
*2905 W. Devon Ave. (Francisco Ave.), 773-465-5675*
Some of the city's "best Middle Eastern food" is to be
found at this "great, cheap and authentic" Northwest Side
spot, the "real thing" for Moroccan and Israeli specialties,
where patrons "sit at the front table and argue politics";
N.B. it's BYO and cash only.

**Heartland Cafe**  17 | 14 | 15 | $17
*7000 N. Glenwood Ave. (Lunt Ave.), 773-465-8005;*
*www.heartlandcafe.com*
"Take a trip in the way-back machine" to the "'60s and '70s"
for "a socially responsible meal that really satisfies" at this

"bohemian" Rogers Park "institution with a conscience"
that "keeps on truckin'"; its Traditional American and
vegetarian vittles are "delicious, surprising and uniquely
nurturing", though wags warn you'll have to "endure
the music and artistic types" and "a heaping helping of
activism" "to get to the food."

### Heat ⌧                          25  20  20  $69
*1507 N. Sedgwick St. (North Ave.), 312-397-9818;*
*www.heatsushi.com*
Writers who warm up to this "sleek", "ultramodern" and
"hard-to-find" Old Town Japanese say the "authentic",
"sublime sushi" "can't get any fresher" "unless you swallow
a goldfish alive" "since the fish come from tanks under the
bar"; the parsimonious perceive it as "overpriced" (it's
"definitely one for the corporate card"), though, and the
conscientious call the "scary live-kill" concept "macabre."

### HEAVEN ON SEVEN                  20  16  17  $23
*3478 N. Clark St. (Cornelia Ave.), 773-477-7818*
*600 N. Michigan Ave., 2nd fl. (bet. Ohio & Ontario Sts.),*
*312-280-7774*
*Garland Building, 111 N. Wabash Ave., 7th fl. (Washington Blvd.),*
*312-263-6443 ⌧⊟*
*224 S. Main St. (bet. Jackson & Jefferson Sts.), Naperville,*
*630-717-0777*
*www.heavenonseven.com*
"Great chow" that's "spicy, not pricey", and as "Looz-ee-
ann" "as you'll find this far north" garners groupies for these
Cajun-Creole specialists, where the "noisy" "party" vibe is
augmented by a "wall-of-fire" hot-sauce display; still, the
earthbound expound that "expansion has taken its toll"
and service is "hit-or-miss"; P.S. the cash-only "original on
Wabash" ("on the 7th floor – get it?") is dearest to many.

### Hecky's Barbecue                  ─ ─ ─ I
(aka Hecky's)
*1902 Green Bay Rd. (Emerson St.), Evanston, 847-492-1182*
### Hecky's of Chicago
*1234 N. Halsted St. (Division St.), 312-377-7427*
*www.heckys.com*
Slathering sauce at the original Evanston location since
1983, Hecky Powell is a North Suburban barbecue legend
with a devoted following addicted to his babyback ribs,
pulled pork and sweet potato pie; the city outpost, in a
rapidly gentrifying strip of the Near West side, also slings
his 'slow-cooked fast food', plus salads and wraps.

### Hema's Kitchen                    ─ ─ ─ I
*2411 N. Clark St. (Fullerton Pkwy.), 773-529-1705*
*6406 N. Oakley Ave. (2300 W. Devon St.), 773-338-1627*
"One of the best" and most "original" restaurants "on
Devon" is this Northwest Side Indian-Pakistani "hole-in-

the-wall" and BYO where every "spicy", "out-of-this-world"
item "is made fresh to order"; you may have to "wait" for
such "fine food", plus the "service is usually awful" and
the decor is "tacky – but who cares?"; N.B. the Lincoln Park
branch opened post-*Survey.*

### Hemmingway's Bistro     ▽ 20 | 18 | 17 | $35 |
*211 N. Oak Park Ave. (Ontario St.), Oak Park, 708-524-0806;*
*www.hemmingwaysbistro.com*
Adventurers seeking "great" Traditional American and
French bistro fare "keep coming back" to this Oak Parker, a
"cozy neighborhood spot" in the Western Suburbs; fence-
sitters submit it's "improving", and say "service is very good
unless the establishment is busy."

### Hilary's Urban Eatery     19 | 17 | 18 | $17 |
*1500 W. Division St. (Greenview St.), 773-235-4327;*
*www.hilarysurbaneatery.com*
"Scrumptious" "down-home cooking", including "freakin'
fantastic" breakfasts and brunches "that almost make it
worthwhile to get out of bed", draws drooling devotees to
this "cute and quirky" Wicker Park Eclectic, "the epitome of
a great neighborhood eatery" with "laid-back" service and a
"patio [that's] especially nice in summer"; N.B. though it's
BYO, they offer a 'wine on wheels' option (i.e. they'll run to
the liquor store for you).

### Hot Chocolate     – | – | – | M |
*1747 N. Damen Ave. (Wabansia Ave.), 773-489-1747;*
*www.hotchocolatechicago.com*
Acclaimed pastry chef Mindy Segal (ex mk) goes it alone at
this Bucktown cafe, widening her scope to incorporate a
full menu of creative American comfort food and desserts
(including some of her cult-status signatures), as well as
artisanal cheeses and global wines; decorated in shades
of light and dark chocolate, the room also features an open
kitchen and pastry case; N.B. lunch and brunch expand
the dining options.

### Hot Doug's ⌧⌿     – | – | – | I |
*3324 N. California Ave. (Roscoe Blvd.), 773-279-9550;*
*www.hotdougs.com*
Gourmet sausage addicts rejoice: Doug Sohn's encased-
meats mecca has reopened a half-mile west of its original
Northwest Side location, which closed due to a fire; the new
incarnation offers plenty of street parking, more seating
(plus outdoor tables), the chef's trademark duck-fat french
fries on Fridays and Saturdays, and a full lineup of unusual,
high-quality dogs – but, alas, it still closes at 4 PM.

### Hot Tamales     22 | 14 | 19 | $21 |
*493 Central Ave. (St. John Ave.), Highland Park, 847-433-4070*
"Bring a shoehorn, because getting in is worth it" at this
"popular local" Highland Park "hangout" where "flavorful

food" that's "not your average Mexican" fare – including "great tamales" (try the "interesting pumpkin" ones) and "*muy bueno* duck tacos" – ensures that the "funky", "family-friendly" "storefront" setting is "packed every night of the week"; P.S. the "outdoor tables are a summer treat."

## House of Blues Back Porch      15  20  16  $32

*329 N. Dearborn St. (Kinzie St.), 312-923-2007; www.hob.com*
Porch-sitters who patronize this River North place perceive its "Southern selections" with Cajun-Creole accents as "consistently good" and served "in a fun atmosphere" with "cool decor" and "great music" nightly ("check out the gospel brunch on Sundays"); yard-birds yawp that the "overpriced" meals are "mediocre", but add that if you "don't expect perfection you'll have a great time."

## HUGO'S FROG BAR & FISH HOUSE  25  20  22  $46

*55 S. Main St. (bet. Benton & Van Buren Aves.), Naperville, 630-548-3764*
*1024 N. Rush St. (bet. Bellevue Pl. & Oak St.), 312-640-0999* ●
*www.hugosfrogbar.com*
In addition to "fantastic" aquatic fare and "humongous desserts", this "loud, fun and friendly" Gold Coast "fish version of Gibson's" also offers the latter's meat-centric menu from their mutual kitchen; it's "brash", "packed to the gills" and "pricey but still manages to feel like" a "fairly reasonable" "alternative to the hustle bustle next door", plus folks "love the [nightly] piano" music; N.B. the Naperville location opened post-*Survey*.

## Iggy's ●       17  18  16  $27

*1840 W. North Ave. (bet. Wolcott Ave. & Wood St.), 312-829-4449*
"It's late, you're hungry", so head for this Eclectic Near West "joint" with a "fun lounge" vibe, where "scenesters and a lot of restaurant/hospitality industry people hang out" over "good" wee-hour "snacks or bowls of pasta" and a "vast selection of martinis"; still, some say that its "just-ok" food makes it a "better bar scene than" dining destination.

## Improv Kitchen ⊠       –  –  –  M

*3419 N. Clark St. (bet. Newport Ave. & Roscoe St.), 773-868-6423; www.improvkitchen.com*
Interactive dining comes to Wrigleyville thanks to this food-and-comedy hybrid where patrons suggest improv topics to comedians viewed on flat-screen TVs at each table (the performers are secreted away in a high-tech studio next door); the seasonal New American menu is complemented by microbrews, whimsical martinis and a limited wine list.

## Ina's       18  15  19  $21

*1235 W. Randolph St. (Elizabeth St.), 312-226-8227; www.breakfastqueen.com*
Ina-philes insist that the "homey" American "comfort food" at this Market District mainstay is "better than grandma's",

especially the "fabulous breakfasts" – the "'Heavenly Hots' [pancakes] are what makes Ina's a legend" – and "less-crowded lunches", all in a "comfortable" setting where the namesake owner's "energy is evident" (as is her "salt- and pepper-shaker collection"); P.S. the "free parking" "is a great perk."

### India House     – | – | – | M
*59 W. Grand Ave. (bet. Clark & Dearborn Sts.), 312-645-9500*
*228-230 McHenry Rd. (E. Lake Cook Rd.), Buffalo Grove, 847-520-5569*
*1521 W. Schaumburg Rd. (N. Springinsguth Rd.), Schaumburg, 847-895-5501; www.indiahouseschaumburg.com*
This civilized River North offshoot of a Northwest Suburban Indian duo offers an exhaustive menu (145 items), as well as a generous lunch buffet that's a steal; the refined service and decor of warm wood and deep yellow walls, carved Indian artworks and white tablecloths promise a sedate dining experience.

### Indian Garden, The     22 | 13 | 16 | $22
*247 E. Ontario St., 2nd fl. (Fairbanks Ct.), 312-280-4910*
*2546 W. Devon Ave. (Rockwell St.), 773-338-2929*
*855 E. Schaumburg Rd. (Plum Grove Rd.), Schaumburg, 847-524-3007*
*6020 S. Cass Ave. (60th St.), Westmont, 630-769-9662*
Survey says this city-and-suburban foursome delivers an "amazing quality and quantity" of "traditional Indian cuisine", including "fluffy, fresh naan", "always-moist tandoori" and "fabulous tikka masala chicken"; the fact that the "food is always good" helps compensate for the "bland decor" and "erratic service"; P.S. check out the "superb lunch buffet."

### Indie Cafe     – | – | – | M
*5951 N. Broadway (bet. Elmdale & Thorndale Aves.), 773-561-5577*
You wouldn't know it from the spartan digs, a tiny room minimally decorated with paper lanterns, but this Edgewater BYO is a hot destination for well-priced Thai and Japanese fare that's a cut above the neighborhood norm, including beautifully presented sushi, noodles and curries; N.B. check out the bargain lunch special.

### Irazu ⌧⇟     ▽ 24 | 8 | 18 | $11
*1865 N. Milwaukee Ave. (Western Ave.), 773-252-5687*
Just a "random little shack" in Bucktown, this "absolute treasure" is "on target" with its "sensational", "authentic" Mexican and Costa Rican eats "done with care" (plus "tropical-fruit"-"oatmeal shakes" that "defy imagination"); it's also "inexpensive and BYO to boot", which helps regulars ignore the "lack of decor"; in fact, locals who "want to keep it to" themselves plead "please don't eat here."

## Irish Oak Restaurant & Pub ▽ 16 | 17 | 18 | $16

*3511 N. Clark St. (Addison St.), 773-935-6669; www.irishoak.com*

There's no argument about the assets of this "authentic" Emerald Isle pub in Wrigleyville, where the "traditional dishes done the traditional way" include a "good Irish breakfast" and some American faves for good measure; "they make you feel welcome, and as if you are in Ireland" "without the jet lag" – plus the trip is "a good value."

## Isabella's Estiatorio – | – | – | E

*330 W. State St. (4th St.), Geneva, 630-845-8624*

Set in "charming Geneva", in the Western Suburbs, this "excellent" venue (whose name pays tribute to one of the owner's grandmothers) "wows" with an "interesting" seasonal menu of "thoughtful and well-prepared" Med cuisine offered up within a "warm, caring atmosphere"; N.B. there's patio dining.

## Itto Sushi ●🅍 19 | 10 | 17 | $25

*2616 N. Halsted St. (Wrightwood Ave.), 773-871-1800*

Most raw-fish raters rank this "comfortable, kid-friendly, well-established" Lincoln Park "hole-in-the-wall" as a "good standard" Japanese where they can "get out of the trendy" "sushi fad" and into some "quality seafood" sliced by "knowledgeable chefs" – "just don't expect luxury."

## IXCAPUZALCO 25 | – | 21 | $35

*2165 N. Western Ave. (bet. Armitage & Fullerton Aves.), 773-486-7340*

Lauders "love" this "upscale but unpretentious" Bucktown Mexican (which relocated post-*Survey* from its former Logan Square digs), where the "unquestionably authentic" yet "innovative" menu of "outstanding" "high-end" cuisine changes monthly but always includes an "incredible" "mole of the day"; a "helpful" and "attentive staff" as well as "incredible margaritas" made from a "huge tequila list" help seal the deal.

## Izumi Sushi Bar & Restaurant ● ▽ 23 | 17 | 20 | $32

*731 W. Randolph St. (Halsted St.), 312-207-5299; www.izumisushi.com*

Located in the Market District, this loungey sushi spot offers "quality, down home–style Japanese food" including some intriguing *maki* and fusion items complemented by sake flights; the focal point of its ultramodern black-and-blond-wood decor is a dramatic paper-lantern chandelier; N.B. hip music and a late-night menu (until 2 AM on weekends) lure a wee-hours crowd.

## Jack's on Halsted 23 | 18 | 21 | $35

*3201 N. Halsted St. (Belmont Ave.), 773-244-9191*

Nice guys say this New American "treasure" and "good, steady drop-in" spot is "one of the few respectable Boys

Town" spots, where chef-owner Jack Jones' "flavorful"
"quality meals" are offered in a "cozy", "lively atmosphere"
with "wonderful service"; P.S. a location "convenient to
the North Side theater area" means "dining before 8 PM
may result in being seated around suburbanites and teens
headed to Blue Man Group" at the Briar Street.

**Jacky's Bistro**                    24  19  20  $41
*2545 Prairie Ave. (Central St.), Evanston, 847-733-0899;*
*www.jackysbistro.com*
Delighted diners dig this "adorable but classy" venue in
the North Suburbs for its "inventive", "palate-pleasing"
New American and French bistro "fare in a lively setting"
with "charming decor"; antagonists argue about "variable
quality" and "Gold Coast prices"; N.B. eponymous owner
Jacky Pluton sold the restaurant post-*Survey,* though he
will continue to consult.

**Jake Melnick's Corner Tap** ●    15  12  15  $22
*41 E. Superior St. (Wabash Ave.), 312-266-0400;*
*www.jakemelnicks.com*
A "huge pub" serving "reliable" American "bar food",
including "great burgers", this Gold Coast "hangout" with
a "typical tavern" vibe is to some "a great place to watch
sports" or "grab a beer" (there are "tons to choose from");
tapped-out tipsters take issue with "mediocre" fare, though,
saying "bring back" the Blackhawk Lodge.

**J. Alexander's**                    –  –  –  E
*1832 N. Clybourn Ave. (bet. W. Willow & W. Wisconsin Sts.),*
*773-435-1018*
*4077 Lake Cook Rd. (bet. I-294 & Sanders Rd.), Northbrook,*
*847-564-3093*
*1410 16th St. (bet. Castle Dr. & Spring Rd.), Oak Brook,*
*630-573-8180*
*www.jalexanders.com*
The "great", "casual American food" (kudos for the "fresh"
seafood and "prime rib and BBQ ribs prepared in an open
kitchen") manages to be "basic but innovative" at these
city-and-suburban chain links, where "beautiful decor"
and "good service" help make dining "a real value."

**Jane's**                    22  19  20  $30
*1655 W. Cortland St. (Paulina St.), 773-862-5263;*
*www.janesrestaurant.com*
Surveyors are sweet on this "darling", "quaint" New
American–Eclectic eatery in a "romantic" Bucktown
"storefront" setting that "feels like eating at home with
good friends"; the seasonal menu holds "a wide variety
of foods including old favorites and inventive culinary
delicacies" (plus there's an "excellent brunch"), and the
"attentive" staff takes good care of customers within the
"dark, candlelit" "brick" interior.

**JAPONAIS** 24 27 19 $56

*600 W. Chicago Ave. (Larrabee St.), 312-822-9600;*
*www.japonaischicago.com*
Superlatives surrounding this "ultrachic" Near West
Japanese, "one of the brightest lights on the local dining
scene", cover the "drop-dead gorgeous" decor that
"transports" "the 'it'-crowd" patrons "out of Chicago", the
"amazing sushi and innovative menu items" and the
"Indochine-sexy" "bar"-cum-"patio that opens up to the
river"; still, unswayed raters report that all that "style
comes at a high price" and the "service is not the best."

**Jewel of India** – – – I

*2401 W. Devon Ave. (Western Ave.), 773-465-3269*
Another intriguing Asian fusion concept takes shape on
the Northwest Side in the form of this upscale Indian-
Chinese hybrid, which traverses familiar territory with
straightforward selections from both culinary categories
but also explores uncharted terrain via 'Indian-style
Chinese dishes' (vegetarian, chicken and seafood), fusing
spices and sauces from the former cuisine with traditional
preparations from the latter; the serene room combines
formal, white-tablecloth dining and a traditional low-
seating area for 20.

**Jilly's Cafe** 22 16 23 $38

*2614 Green Bay Rd. (Central St.), Evanston, 847-869-7636;*
*www.jillyscafe.com*
Enthusiasts of the "excellent" New French and New
American cuisine created by chef-owner Brian Newkirk
find this "storefront" bistro to be "one of the North Shore's
most charming", adding that "lovely service" contributes
to the feeling that "you're dining in someone's home";
fainter flatterers fault the "cramped" confines, though,
saying "the size of the room does not allow" this blossom
to fully flower.

**Jin Ju** 22 19 21 $28

*5203 N. Clark St. (Foster Ave.), 773-334-6377*
"Exquisite dishes" that are "inventive" yet "surprisingly
faithful to the native cuisine" along with "fabulous specialty
cocktails" such as "excellent sojutinis" (made with *soju*, a
sweet-potato liquor) and "attentive service" "make for a
night to remember" at this "modern, hip" and "Western-
friendly Korean" in Andersonville; the fact that it's usually full
of "beautiful people" helps cement its "favorite" status.

**Joe's Be-Bop Cafe** 15 16 15 $23

*Navy Pier, 600 E. Grand Ave. (Lake Shore Dr.),*
*312-595-5299; www.joesbebop.com*
Boppers buy into this "noisy" "BBQ-type" Streeterville
"joint" with "lively jazz bands" nightly, calling it "a lot of
fun" thanks to its "terrific" Navy Pier "location" complete

with a "great outdoor patio"; though some say it's "a good place to sit and have a few cocktails" along with some "decent" Southern food, others feel the "mediocre" fare hits a sour note.

**JOE'S SEAFOOD, PRIME STEAK &**  25 | 21 | 23 | $51 |
**STONE CRAB**

*60 E. Grand Ave. (Rush St.), 312-379-5637; www.leye.com*
"Power diners and tourists" pour into this "good imitation" of its Miami "namesake" in River North for its "deliciously simple" surf 'n' turf menu ("terrific" "for those times you can't decide between fish and meat"), "consistently" "excellent service" from "well-trained professionals" and "sophisticated masculine atmosphere", including a "nice-looking bar" with lots of "action"; still, vice cops vent that it's "a madhouse at peak hours", which leads to "long waits despite reservations", and claim "prices leave you crabby."

**Joey's Brickhouse**                 – | – | – | M |

*1258 W. Belmont Ave. (Racine Ave.), 773-296-1300;*
*www.joeysbrickhouse.com*
Named for its chef-owner, Joey Morelli, and freestanding brick building, this casual Lakeview American pairs a largely straightforward menu with craft-brewed beers and 18 varieties of Long Island iced tea; the open space has a painted concrete floor, wood tables, a mosaic tile bar and large doors, which in nice weather open onto a small sidewalk dining area shaded by trees; N.B. jazz brunch is available on Sundays.

**John Barleycorn** ●                 13 | 14 | 14 | $18 |

*3524 N. Clark St. (bet. Addison St. & Sheffield Ave.), 773-549-6000*
*658 W. Belden Ave. (Lincoln Ave.), 773-348-8899*
*www.johnbarleycorn.com*
"Fun bars" "for family or friends", these fraternal twins serve "huge burgers" and other Traditional American fodder with an "extensive beer selection" in disparate settings – the Lincoln Park "institution" (dating from the 1890s) has more "interesting decor" and "great outdoor seating", whereas "sports-bar ambiance dominates" at the Wrigleyville branch (opened in 2000); nevertheless, bummed barflies berate the "so-so" "neighborhood pub fare" and "slow service."

**John's Place**                      16 | 13 | 15 | $20 |

*1200 W. Webster Ave. (Racine Ave.), 773-525-6670*
Stroll on into the "warm environs" of this "reliable", "friendly" Lincoln Park "neighborhood spot" that fans call "a great family place" thanks to "somewhat creative" Eclectic fare (including a "great brunch") made from lots of "natural ingredients"; still, some former regulars rue the rug rats "running rampant" in this "kiddy central" (there must be a "zillion babies") and report "standard fare", "long waits" and "slow service."

### Joy Yee's Noodle Shop　20 12 14 $16
*2159 Chinatown Sq. (Archer Ave.), 312-328-0001*
*521 Davis St. (Chicago Ave.), Evanston, 847-733-1900*
*1163 E. Ogden Ave. (Iroquois Ave.), Naperville, 630-579-6800*
*www.joyyee.com*
The "abundant" menu of "delightful", "freshly prepared"
Asian fare at these "cheap", "noisy", "upbeat" "noodleries"
makes each "a great place to try something new", and the
"fabulous bubble teas and fruit smoothies" are a bonus (or
you can BYO); nonetheless, indifferent ingesters imply that
"inconsistent food", "long waits" and "crammed tables"
diminish the joy; N.B. the Naperville branch opened post-
*Survey,* and a fourth location is planned for South Halsted.

### JP Chicago　　– – – M
*901 W. Weed St. (Freemont St.), 312-337-2001;*
*www.jpchicago.com*
An out-of-the-way Lincoln Park locale has not deterred
hipsters from flocking to Jason Paskewitz's casual, upscale
New American set in a former motocross repair shop; the
bistro-like setting with antique mirrors and red leather
banquettes creates a chic backdrop for cool comfort food,
and there's an imposing mahogany bar serving house
cocktails and wines listed on blackboards.

### Julio's Cocina Latina ⊠　▽ 22 20 20 $29
*Lakeview Plaza, 95 S. Rand Rd. (Rte. 22), Lake Zurich,*
*847-438-3484; www.julioslatincafe.com*
"Excellent" and "always-tasty" South American and
Caribbean cooking awaits adventurers at this Northwest
Suburban outpost, where the "unusual", "upscale" offerings
and "great margaritas" are served by "lovely people";
furthermore, live jazz and "Latin music on weekends adds to
the already great" "comfortable" and "casual atmosphere."

### Kabul House　19 11 19 $17
*1629 N. Halsted St. (North Ave.), 312-751-1029*
*3320 Dempster St. (McCormick Blvd.), Skokie, 847-763-9930*
*www.kabulhouse.com*
They've got "the real thing", even "for a world traveler", at
this "traditional" Afghani BYO twosome in the North Suburbs
and Lincoln Park; each is "a real treat" that affords "an
opportunity to sample" "wonderful flavors", including
"surprisingly good vegetarian options", and the "solicitude
of the staff" offsets the "plain" decor; P.S. the city locale is
a "great pre-Steppenwolf" Theater stop.

### Kamehachi　22 19 19 $33
*240 E. Ontario St. (bet. Fairbanks & St. Claire St.), 312-587-0600*
*Westin River North, 320 N. Dearborn St. (Kinzie St.), 312-744-1900*
*1400 N. Wells St. (Schiller St.), 312-664-3663* ☽
*City Park Complex @ BIN 36, 275 Parkway Dr. (Aptakisic Rd.),*
*Lincolnshire, 847-541-8807*

(continued)
## Kamehachi
*Village Green Shopping Ctr., 1320 Shermer Rd. (Waukegan Rd.), Northbrook, 847-562-0064*
*www.kamehachi.com*
"Fresh and consistent", these raw-fish "favorites" strike supporters as some of "the best" options, especially for "larger groups" in which "some like sushi but others want cooked" selections from a "full Japanese menu"; still, wafflers "wish" the "uneven" "service would match the food" and find the "portions small"; N.B. the Lincolnshire location (which opened post-*Survey* within Bin 36) and the River North branch offer a limited bill of fare.

## Kaminari          – – – E
*2124 Algonquin Rd. (Randall Rd.), Lake in the Hills, 847-854-4909*
Improbably located in an unassuming Lake in the Hills mall, this ambitious new Japanese outpost offers a lengthy, hip-for-the-'burbs menu complemented by an urban interior of wood, exposed ductwork, track lighting, matte black walls and clubby music.

## Kan Zaman          – – – I
*617 N. Wells St. (Ontario St.), 312-751-9600;*
*www.kanzamanwells.com*
The owners of the original Andersonville branch (closed in 2003) begat this identically named River North spot offering the same inexpensive, vegetarian-focused Lebanese food and hookah hook-ups; the interior includes both traditional Middle Eastern cushioned seating and a more formal white-tablecloth dining room, both of which host a belly dancer who shakes it on Fridays and Saturdays.

## KARMA          21 28 20 $39
*Crowne Plaza Hotel, 510 E. Rte. 83 (Rte. 45), Mundelein, 847-970-6900*
"An oasis of calm and gourmet food" in "an out-of-the-way" North Suburban hotel, this "inviting", "citified" Asian incarnation wows with its "sophisticated", "soothing" "modern" decor that's "a feast for the eyes"; the "exciting menu" draws divergent declarations, though, ranging from "creative" and "excellent" to "good, not great."

## Karyn's Cooked 🚫          – – – I
*738 N. Wells St. (W. Superior St.), 312-587-1050;*
*www.karynraw.com*
Karyn Calabrese, founder of Chicago's only raw-food restaurant, Karyn's Fresh Corner, now feeds fans of cooked cuisine at this small, storefront 'gourmet vegan' haven in River North, offering a generous array of hot and cold sandwiches, wraps and entrees like tofu ribs and eggplant stuffed with soy-based ricotta; N.B. thirst quenchers include herbal teas, fruity elixirs and organic beer and wine.

## Karyn's Fresh Corner                          – – – | I

*1901 N. Halsted St. (Armitage St.), 312-255-1590;*
*www.karynraw.com*
Raw foodists revere Karyn Calabrese's original outpost,
this Lincoln Park purveyor of uncooked vegan fare (which
proponents purport retains more nutrients and enzymes)
featuring salads, meatless entrees, sandwiches, desserts
and a Sunday brunch buffet served in a serene wood and
off-white space; N.B. there's also an attached day spa and
health shop with takeout, a juice bar and non-food products.

## Katsu Japanese                                – – – M

*2651 W. Peterson Ave. (California Ave.), 773-784-3383*
"Consistently excellent" Japanese fare – including "fresh,
well-prepared sushi" "selections of the highest quality",
"creative maki" and a "good range" of cooked dishes –
shines at this "hidden", "not-too-glitzy" Northwest Sider,
where the "welcoming" modern atmosphere is also home
to "great service" that's "not rushed."

## Kaze Sushi                                    – – – M

*2032 W. Roscoe St. (Seeley Ave.), 773-327-4860;*
*www.kazesushi.com*
Though it serves classic maki, nigiri and sashimi, this
Roscoe Village new wave Japanese outpost specializes in
creative, seasonal dishes – both hot and cold – including
sushi jazzed up with toppings; the sleek, modern setting
features a gleaming gold raw-fish bar and Louis XIV-
style upholstered chairs.

## Keefer's ☒                                    23  21  21  $49

*20 W. Kinzie St. (Dearborn St.), 312-467-9525;*
*www.keefersrestaurant.com*
Ayes aver that this "swanky" "standout" in River North is
a keeper thanks to chef John Hogan's "high-quality",
"classic" steakhouse fare (as well as "great seafood"), its
"see-and-be-seen" "energy" (including a "strong bar
crowd with media types") and its "modern", "clubby"
"Arts and Crafts decor"; nays note that it's "noisy", though,
and some eaters "expected more" considering that it's
"kind of pricey."

## KEVIN ☒                                       27  23  24  $55

*9 W. Hubbard St. (State St.), 312-595-0055;*
*www.kevinrestaurant.com*
Kindred spirits contribute copious kudos for Kevin Shikami's
"beautifully prepared", "inventive" New American–New
French "fusion cuisine with definite Asian overtones", the
foundation of a "superb dining experience" at his "high-
power" River North namesake where the "spare and
elegant" surroundings glow in "flattering low lighting";
still, skeptical scribes suggest it's "pricey" and pick up a
whiff of "attitude."

### KiKi's Bistro ☒
23 | 20 | 23 | $40

*900 N. Franklin St. (Locust St.), 312-335-5454; www.kikisbistro.com*
Like a "favorite pair of jeans", this "comfortable" River North
bistro has "stood the test of time" according to its "steady
clientele", who submit that it's "always a pleasure" for a
"*très bon*" "romantic meal or to meet an old friend" over
"solid renditions" of "great-tasting French fare" (and at
"reasonable" prices); a few killjoys, though, suspect this
"reliable standby" still has the potential "to be better."

### Kinzie Chophouse
18 | 17 | 20 | $40

*400 N. Wells St. (Kinzie St.), 312-822-0191;*
*www.kinziechophouse.com*
Pals of this "pleasant" River North "steak joint" praise
the "large portions of well-aged, well-cooked beef" and
"chophouse/tavern" ambiance in the "Midwest tradition",
adding that the "attentive staff" "takes care of customers";
paradoxically, other pens pall at what they call "standard"
fare that's "a step below the high-end" competition, though
they like that it comes "without the lines" or "attitude."

### Kit Kat Lounge & Supper Club ◑
14 | 20 | 15 | $33

*3700 N. Halsted St. (Waveland Ave.), 773-525-1111;*
*www.kitkatchicago.com*
The "great bartenders" at this "*très* gay" "supper club" in
Boys Town shake up "classic lounge cocktails", including "a
million martinis", while a coterie of "outrageous" "camp
entertainers in drag" shake their groove things; still, the
wary warn "don't go for" the "disappointing" Eclectic eats or
"spotty service", though the "tables outside" are "pleasant"
on a "Chicago summer evening"; N.B. the Decor rating may
not reflect a post-*Survey* renovation.

### Kitsch'n on Roscoe
19 | 20 | 17 | $15

*2005 W. Roscoe St. (Damen Ave.), 773-248-7372*
### Kitsch'n River North
*Montgomery Bldg., 600 W. Chicago Ave. (Larrabee St.),
312-644-1500*
*www.kitschn.com*
Reminiscers "can't help but smile" and "feel like a kid
again" at Roscoe Village's "hip, funky and any-other-
synonym-for-cool" eatery that dishes up an Eclectic menu
of "childhood" "treats" such as "PB&Js" and "green eggs
and ham" amid "fun decor" featuring lunchboxes, lava
lamps and televisions playing "clips of old reruns"; grumpy
gourmets groan that the "gimmick" is "overdone", though,
and feel the food "should be better"; N.B. the River North
location opened post-*Survey*.

### Kizoku Sushi & Sake Lounge
‒ | ‒ | ‒ | E

*358 W. Ontario St. (Orleans St.), 312-335-9888*
Two veterans of Heat headed to River North to create this
contemporary Japanese, with a broad menu of raw and

cooked items complemented by numerous sakes, tequilas and signature drinks (which are also available in the clubby lounge, where DJs occasionally man the decks); snazzy design elements include a waterfall, three-tiered red chandelier and a big sushi bar.

**Klay Oven**                          22 │ 17 │ 21 │ $31 │
*414 N. Orleans St. (Hubbard St.), 312-527-3999;*
*www.klayovenrestaurant.com*
"A range" of "well-presented and tasty" "gourmet Indian foods in a beautiful setting" sums up statements surrounding this "upscale", "quiet" River North "gem" where "you can actually have a conversation"; "knowledgeable service" and an "all-you-can-eat lunch buffet" that's a real "deal" also help make this "a great alternative to [other] city spots."

**Koi**                                 – │ – │ – │ M │
*624 Davis St. (bet. Chicago & Orrington Aves.), Evanston,*
*847-866-6969; www.koievanston.com*
The owners of Chen's are behind this sophisticated North Suburban hybrid where sushi and traditional Chinese fare share equal billing, and the beverage list includes 45 wines plus dozens of specialty martinis and some rare teas; the space (formerly Lulu's) has been expanded and refined into a white-walled, slate-floored oasis with a mahogany raw-fish bar and a loungelike conversation pit with fireplace.

**Koryo**                               – │ – │ – │ M │
*2936 N. Broadway (bet. Oakdale & Wellington Aves.),*
*773-477-8510*
"Wonderful" "homestyle Korean dishes" come with "a wide selection of kimchi" and "fast service" from an "attentive staff" at this Lakeview spot, where the "music is always pumping" amid the "modern decor"; N.B. they have their liquor license but you can BYO for a small corkage fee.

**Kuni's**                              21 │ 14 │ 16 │ $29 │
*511 Main St. (bet. Chicago & Hinman Aves.), Evanston,*
*847-328-2004*
"Fresh", "tasty, well-executed sushi and other delights" lure lauders to this North Suburban "storefront" Japanese, the namesake of "great chef" and owner Yuji Kunii, "a master in preparing the best fish"; the "portions are great", too, and the atmosphere is "lively", though malcontents make middling memoranda, noting it's "nothing fancy."

**Kyoto**                         ▽ 20 │ 14 │ 19 │ $25 │
*2534 N. Lincoln Ave. (Altgeld St.), 773-477-2788;*
*www.kyotochicago.com*
*Best Buy Shopping Center, 1408 Butterfield Rd. (bet. Finley Rd. &*
*Highland Ave.), Downers Grove, 630-627-8588* ☒
*1062 Gage St. (Green Bay Rd.), Winnetka, 847-784-9388*
"Solid Japanese" food, including "excellent sushi for the price" (read: "cheap"), have those who "sit at the bar and

ask for the chef's creations" singing the praises of these
"friendly and warm" city-and-suburban spots; still, others
suggest they serve "relatively standard fare in a standard
environment"; N.B. the Decor rating may not reflect the
post-*Survey* remodeling of the Lincoln Park branch.

### La Bocca della Verità　　　　21 ｜ 14 ｜ 19 ｜ $29

*4618 N. Lincoln Ave. (bet. Lawrence & Wilson Aves.),*
*773-784-6222; www.laboccachicago.com*

The truth about this "relaxed" Italian "joint" in Lincoln
Square may lie somewhere between panelists' praise for
its "consistently mouthwatering", "memorable" fare that's
"a far cry from red-sauce" standards (including "duck
ravioli that answers the Marx Brothers' question"), and the
opinions of those who reveal reticence about "steep prices"
considering the "consignment-shop decor"; N.B. lunch is
served in summer only, when the sidewalk seating is open.

### La Cantina Enoteca ☒　　　　▽ 21 ｜ 21 ｜ 22 ｜ $27

*71 W. Monroe St. (bet. Clark & Dearborn Sts.), 312-332-7005;*
*www.italianvillage-chicago.com*

"You go from the Loop to Italy" at this "basement" venue
(opened in 1955), "the downstairs restaurant of the Italian
Village trio"; evocative of a wine cellar, it's a "relaxing"
and "romantic" lair where "simply prepared but delicious"
fare is "served proudly" in a "quiet", "cozy" space with
"high-walled booths" and "large fish tanks."

### La Cazuela Mariscos　　　　– ｜ – ｜ – ｜ I

*6922 N. Clark St. (bet. Farwell & Morse Aves.), 773-338-5425*

"Good", "solid" Mexican seafood and "heartfelt" service
"make you forget" the "ticky-tacky decor" at this casual,
unassuming Rogers Park BYO *restaurante,* whose amenities
include garden seating in warm weather and live Latin
guitar on weekend nights.

### La Crêperie　　　　18 ｜ 14 ｜ 17 ｜ $19

*2845 N. Clark St. (bet. Diversey Pkwy. & Surf St.), 773-528-9050;*
*www.lacreperieusa.com*

To cronies, this "deliciously unique" French bistro and
"date spot" is "the closest Lakeview comes to Paris",
proffering "anything you can imagine wrapped in a crêpe" (a
"good diversion" from the "typical" amid "dark-paneled
walls littered with European travel posters" or on the "idyllic
summer patio"; cranks call the concept "limited" and the
decor "dated", though, and nag that it's "not good if you
want anything lighter."

### La Cucina di Donatella　　　　– ｜ – ｜ – ｜ M

*2221 W. Howard St. (Ridge Blvd.), 773-262-6533*

Ranging from rustic to refined, the authentic Italian fare at
this tiny, family-run storefront trattoria in Rogers Park is
moderately priced and lovingly prepared; cracker-crust
pizza, stuffed panini, handmade pasta dishes and meat

entrees like saltimbocca and roast lamb join specials listed on a blackboard; N.B. it's BYO.

### La Donna
17 ❙ 14 ❙ 18 ❙ $26 ❙

*5146 N. Clark St. (Foster Ave.), 773-561-9400;*
*www.ladonnaitaly.com*

Some Andersonvillagers vouch that this "tiny" "treasure" serves "tried-and-true Italian favorites with a creative touch here and there", making for "delightful" dining amid "bistro ambiance"; other opiners pan the "pasta" as "pretty average", though, and insist the space is more "cramped" than "intimate" (the "tables are so close you can easily participate in your neighbors' conversation").

### La Fette
– ❙ – ❙ – ❙ E ❙

*163 W. North Ave. (bet. La Salle Dr. & Wells St.), 312-397-6300;*
*www.lafette.net*

Old Town is home to this prix fixe, seasonal New American bistro that sports a simple wood-on-wood look, earth-toned table appointments and a daily changing five-course set menu ranging in price from $35–$45 (depending on which entree is selected); if that's too restrictive a formula for you, take heart – almost all the wines are available by the glass; N.B. weekend brunch is also one price.

### La Fonda Latino
▽ 20 ❙ 14 ❙ 16 ❙ $21 ❙

*5350 N. Broadway St. (Balmoral Ave.), 773-271-3935*

For "surprisingly good" "upscale" Colombian "food served with love", it's "worth the trip" to this "quiet, low-lit" Andersonville "storefront" venue, which "relocated" in 2002 to its "comfortable but not fancy" digs after its "old location burned down"; the fact that "it's a steal at these prices" also makes it "a fine addition to the neighborhood."

### La Fontanella
– ❙ – ❙ – ❙ M ❙

*2414 S. Oakley Ave. (24th St.), 773-927-5249*

A no-frills, family-run, kid-friendly favorite in the Heart of Italy 'hood, this vintage ristorante – opened in 1961 – specializes in classic Italian fare and cozy, dimly lit dining environs with the traditional checkered tablecloths and photo-lined walls; a cast of locals gathers at the bar.

### La Gondola
▽ 22 ❙ 7 ❙ 18 ❙ $24 ❙

*Wellington Plaza, 2914 N. Ashland Ave. (Wellington Ave.),*
*773-248-4433*

"Just good" "old-time Italian food" including "fab" pizza "more than makes up for the lack in ambiance" at this "great neighborhood" "mall storefront" in Lincoln Park; even so, the "dining room is so tiny" you may want to "consider carryout or delivery."

### Lalo's
14 ❙ 15 ❙ 15 ❙ $24 ❙

*1960 N. Clybourn Ave. (bet. Clifton Ave. & Cortland St.),*
*773-880-5256*

(continued)
**Lalo's**
*500 N. LaSalle St. (Illinois St.), 312-329-0030*
*3515 W. 26th St. (bet. Drake & St. Louis Aves.), 773-522-0345*
*4126 W. 26th St. (Kedvale Ave.), 773-762-1505*
*3011 S. Harlem Ave. (31st St.), Berwyn, 708-484-9311*
*1432 Waukegan Rd. (Lake Ave.), Glenview, 847-832-1388*
*804 S. Oak Park Ave. (Rte. 290), Oak Park, 708-386-3386*
*425 S. Roselle Rd. (bet. Schaumburg Rd. & Weathersfield Way),*
*Schaumburg, 847-891-0911*
*Midway Airport, 5757 S. Cicero Ave. (bet. 55th & 60th Sts.),*
*773-838-1604*
*www.lalos.com*
Amigos of these "cut-above-most-Mexican-chain-dining"
locations dig the "traditional fare at reasonable prices", the
"fun, festive" feel and the "great margaritas" that "will have
you dancing with the mariachi band" (at some branches);
nevertheless, banditos berate the "old-style food" as "below
average" and claim it's "overpriced", to boot.

**L'anne** ⊠               ▽ 24  19  21  $38
*221 W. Front St. (bet. Hale St. & Wheaton Ave.), Wheaton,*
*630-260-1234; www.lannerestaurant.com*
Sophisticated supporters of this West Suburban spot say
that its "exquisite", "unusual French-Asian" fusion cuisine, a
"nice wine list" and "gracious service" combine to create
a dining experience that's "a pleasure in every way";
P.S. expect an oasis of "quiet during the week" and live
"piano music on weekend" evenings.

**Lao Sze Chuan Express** ❶     21  8  16  $18
*1520 W. Taylor St. (Ashland Ave.), 312-455-0667*
**Lao Sze Chuan House** ❶
*Oak Court Shopping Ctr., 500 E. Ogden Ave. (bet. Cass Ave. &*
*Rte. 83), Westmont, 630-455-4488*
**Lao Sze Chuan Spicy City** ❶
*2172 S. Archer Ave. (Princeton Ave.), 312-326-5040*
**Szechuan House**
*321 E. Northwest Hwy. (Hicks Rd.), Palatine, 847-991-0888*
*www.laoszechuan.com*
Sated spice-savorers swoon for this fortunate family's
"gigantic" selection of "homestyle Chinese cooking" with
"beginner and advanced dishes" including "really good
hot pots" and other "authentic" Szechuan and Mandarin
goodies that make natives "miss their homeland" (the
"typically lousy service and ambiance" are beside the
point); N.B. the Little Italy location is BYO.

**La Peña** ❶                 -  -  -  M
*4212 N. Milwaukee Ave. (Montrose Ave.), 773-545-7022;*
*www.lapenachicago.com*
Brightly colored and festooned with tropical bird figurines,
this "fabulous Ecuadorian restaurant" on the Northwest

Side offers "a fun way to visit [another] culture" while enjoying "rare dishes" from South America like "excellent corn tamales and mango margaritas", plus nightly "dancing" to the music of "great live bands" (Thursdays through Sundays) or a DJ.

**la petite folie**                    23  20  21  $42
*Hyde Park Shopping Ctr., 1504 E. 55th St. (Lake Park Blvd.), 773-493-1394*
A "civilized", "white-tablecloth" dining "oasis" that's a "favorite site of University of Chicago faculty and visitors to Court Theater" in Hyde Park, this "elegant yet relaxed" "storefront" spot does "beautiful presentations of classic French food" that are "worth the fee", even if faultfinders feel that the "sparse" "strip-mall setting" is "off-putting."

**La Piazza** 🅱                    –  –  –  M
*410 Circle Ave. (Madison St.), Forest Park, 708-366-4010; www.piazzacafe.com*
Chef-owner Gaetano Di Benedetto is gaining attention for his inspired, authentic regional Italian cooking at this West Suburban spot, where offerings of hand-cut pasta, fresh seafood and Sicilian-style pizza are supplemented by pricier specials; it's all served in a rustic atmosphere creating the feel of an open-air courtyard, and there's an adjacent wine bar and take-out pizza bakery.

**La Sardine** 🅱                    22  20  21  $39
*111 N. Carpenter St. (bet. Randolph St. & Washington Blvd.), 312-421-2800; www.lasardine.com*
Market District denizens descend upon Jean-Claude Poilevey's "quality French bistro" for "delicious" "classic fare" that's both *"très authentique"* and "consistent"; the "large, open space" (name notwithstanding) manages to be both "romantic" and "vibrant", and "personable service" adds to the "intimate, easygoing environment"; P.S. the "nicely priced wine list is even better on Mondays when it's half price."

**Las Bellas Artes**                    ∇ 27  21  26  $38
*112 W. Park Ave. (York St.), Elmhurst, 630-530-7725; www.cafebellasartes.com*
*Camaradas* "love" this "outstanding high-end Mexican" place in the Western Suburbs "so much" that some are "reluctant to give it a good rating for fear people will discover it"; perhaps it's the "fine" cuisine, "amazing margaritas", "elegant setting and classy service" that make it a "rewarding" experience; P.S. "Sunday brunch is a treat."

**La Scarola**                    23  12  19  $33
*721 W. Grand Ave. (bet. Halsted St. & Milwaukee Ave.), 312-243-1740; www.lascarola.com*
"Hearty" eaters hail the "huge portions" and "expansive menu" of "delicious" "Italian favorites" offered "at a decent

price" at this Near West "neighborhood storefront", where the "fun and energetic" environs are "chatty" and there's "always a buzz"; heavies heckle that it's "quantity [over] quality", though, and claim there's "always a wait."

**Las Tablas**    21  13  17  $22
*2965 N. Lincoln Ave. (Wellington Ave.), 773-871-2414*
*4920 W. Irving Park Rd. (Cicero Ave.), 773-202-0999*
*www.lastablas.com*
Champions of this "sizzlin'" churrascaria-style Colombian steakhouse in Lincoln Park are charged up about the "excellent", "authentic", "wonderfully spiced grilled meat" and "love the chimichurri sauce", as well as the "warm service", "good value" and "fun", "happening" scene (it's "always busy" but "worth the wait"); small wonder that in 2002 it spun off a Northwest Side sequel.

**La Strada Ristorante**  ▣    19  17  21  $36
*155 N. Michigan Ave. (Randolph St.), 312-565-2200;*
*www.lastradaristorante.com*
Pasta partisanship has some streetwise surveyors saying this "longtime" Loop locale serves "traditional and well-prepared" Italian cuisine "a stone's throw from the Art Institute", with a "cozy" "atmosphere" that makes it "nice for a client lunch or dinner"; put-out pedestrians, though, are unmoved by what they consider to be "overpriced", "unimaginative" food and "bland decor."

**La Taberna Tapatia**  ◖    _  _  _  M
*3358 N. Ashland Ave. (Roscoe St.), 773-248-5475*
A south-of-the-border twist on "tasty tapas" known as *botanita* makes this casual Roscoe Village sophomore a "great Mexican option"; it also boasts a clubby yet "comfy tavern setting" with a hipper-than-average attitude, as well as "first-rate margaritas", DJ music Thursday through Sunday nights and a "patio to enjoy in the summer."

**La Tache**    20  19  17  $38
*1475 W. Balmoral Ave. (bet. Clark St. & Glenwood Ave.),*
*773-334-7168*
Andersonville inhabitants are "glad to have such a class act on the block" as this "high-end French" spot, where a "surprisingly adept" kitchen turns out "true bistro food" for the "hip crowd" that hangs out in its "warmly lit" space with "worn-in, modern Parisian decor" (or in the sidewalk-seating section that's "great in summer"); still, critics carp that "for these prices, service should be better"; N.B. the Food rating may not reflect a post-*Survey* chef change.

**La Tasca**    24  21  22  $29
*25 W. Davis St. (Vail Ave.), Arlington Heights, 847-398-2400;*
*www.latascatapas.com*
"Totally top-notch tapas" wow those who wander into this Northwest Suburban spot, where the "original" small

Spanish plates and paellas are "quite good, fresh" and "fantastic" "to share" amid the "great ambiance" of a nearly century-old building; the periodic live music and flamenco shows are also "a nice change of pace", and help this "favorite" live up to its name, which translates as 'a local gathering place.'

### La Vita     – | – | – | M
*1359 W. Taylor St. (S. Loomis St.), 312-491-1414;*
*www.lavitarestaurant.com*
A relative latecomer by Little Italy standards, this casual-chic, chrome-and-curves Northern Italian has a more modern menu and attitude than the *mangia* mainstays, with an open kitchen, rooftop patio and sociable bar scene adding to the ambiance.

### Lawry's The Prime Rib     23 | 21 | 24 | $45
*100 E. Ontario St. (Rush St.), 312-787-5000; www.lawrysonline.com*
This River North Traditional American "meat-eater's mecca", an offshoot of the Beverly Hills original, may have a "limited menu", but it "knows its strengths": "simply succulent" "old-school" "prime rib carved tableside" "with all the fixin's" (plus "hand-carved sandwiches for lunch") and served by "professionals" in a "classy", "boys' club" "time-warp" atmosphere; still, feuding futurists feel it's "a bit pricey" and about "time to update" the "tired decor."

### Le Bouchon ☒     23 | 18 | 19 | $36
*1958 N. Damen Ave. (Armitage Ave.), 773-862-6600;*
*www.lebouchonofchicago.com*
Some *bouches* are amused by the "great traditional bistro fare" at this Bucktown boîte that's "much like a true French cafe", where the "expertly cooked" cuisine finds a home "about as small as a champagne cork"; phobes fear the "tight quarters" with "tables on top of each other", though, and suggest that service is occasionally "snooty."

### Le Colonial     24 | 25 | 21 | $45
*937 N. Rush St. (bet. Oak & Walton Sts.), 312-255-0088;*
*www.lecolonialchicago.com*
"It may be a chain but it's wonderful" wax wordsmiths won over by the "great food" with New "French–Vietnamese flair" that "transports you" to "colonial Vietnam" at this Gold Coast "favorite" whose "stunningly beautiful space" with "bamboo and swaying fans" absolutely "smolders"; still, world-weary wags wonder why it's so "snooty" and find the offerings "overpriced"; P.S. there's a "hopping upstairs bar/lounge" and an "upper-level veranda."

### LE FRANÇAIS ☒     – | 23 | 26 | $89
*269 S. Milwaukee Ave. (Dundee Rd.), Wheeling, 847-541-7470;*
*www.lefrancaisrestaurant.com*
Hope springs anew at this North Suburban "classic" that keeps cycling through chefs, as Roland Liccioni, one of

the venerable restaurant's reputation-building originals –
appointed the first time around by founding chef Jean
Banchet – returns, bringing some contemporary twists to
his new Classic French menu (à la carte or dégustation)
and bargain-priced prix fixe lunch; the "beautiful room"
with plush booths and tastefully placed mirrors is also
home to "impeccable" service and a "fantastic wine list."

### L8 🗷　　　　　　　　　　　　　－ － － M
*222 W. Ontario St. (Wells St.), 312-266-0616; www.l8chicago.com*
Pronounce the name and you'll get the concept of this
hipster redo of the former Lino's, where the Italian–New
American menu of small plates, pastas and pizzas from a
wood-burning oven feeds a River North crowd of pre- and
post-clubbers; the chic, open space has a generous bar
area, draped columns, high-tech sound and lighting, and
massive doors that open onto the Ontario Street action.

### Le Lan 🗷　　　　　　　　　　　－ － － E
*749 N. Clark St. (Chicago Ave.), 312-280-9100;*
*www.lelanrestaurant.com*
River North's new 'orchid' joins the talents of executive
chef Roland Liccioni (Le Francais) and collaborating chef
Arun Sampanthavivat (Arun's), who creatively fuse New
French and Vietnamese cuisine; the tastefully minimalist
setting boasts walnut floors, a bar with jade-green onyx tile
accents and a traditional Vietnamese dragon mural.

### Lem's BBQ ●≠　　　　　　　　　－ － － I
*311 E. 75th St. (bet. Calumet & Prairie Aves.), 773-994-2428*
Though the original State Street location closed after nearly
half a century, this surviving Far South Side BBQ bastion
where the "sauce is the boss" is still serving up "great
spareribs" that are "the best in the city, bar none" and
"the real deal" to aficionados, including some who declare
themselves "born-and-bred Southerners"; N.B. late hours
mean you can get your fix in the middle of the night.

### Leonardo's Ristorante　　　　　－ － － M
*5657 N. Clark St. (Hollywood Ave.), 773-561-5028*
Rosebud alumni have migrated north to Edgewater, opening
this moderately priced Tuscan bistro named for Leonardo
da Vinci; the food is thoughtfully conceived and artfully
presented, while the sleek space is filled with custom
lighting, steelwork, original paintings and sculptures.

### Leo's Lunchroom ≠　　　　　19 11 16 $14
*1809 W. Division St. (bet. Ashland & Damen Aves.), 773-276-6509*
A "piece of history" "reminiscent of pre-gentrification
Wicker Park", this "bohemian" BYO boasts a "cool" if
"limited menu" of "imaginative, comforting" New American
food that includes "unexpected combinations that work"
for "a price that cannot be beat"; N.B. ratings may not
reflect post-*Survey* ownership, chef and interior changes.

### Le P'tit Paris　　　　　　　　–   –   –   E
(fka Zaven's)
*260 E. Chestnut St. (Dewitt Pl.), 312-787-8260*
This Streeterville spot maintains a focus on Continental–
Classic French food ("the chef excels in wild game") and
"the same attentive staff", while ditching its predecessor's
Middle Eastern influence; the intimate space remains
unchanged as well, with the 'Wall of Fame' at the entrance
featuring photos and testimonials of satisfied guests, and
live jazz that energizes the cozy bar on weekends.

### Les Deux Autres　　　　　　　–   –   –   E
*462 Park Blvd. (bet. Crescent Blvd. & Duane St.), Glen Ellyn,
630-469-4002; www.ldafrenchcuisine.com*
Now occupying the West Suburban space that once
housed the unaffiliated 'Two Fat Guys' of Les Deux Gros,
this 'Two Others' successor features toque Greg Lutes'
New French cuisine, pastry chef/owner Louisa Lima's
desserts, a broadly priced and predominantly American
wine list and two comfy, warm-wood dining rooms with
well-spaced, candlelit tables.

### LES NOMADES ⊠　　　　–   26   28   $89
*222 E. Ontario St. (bet. Fairbanks Ct. & St. Clair St.), 312-649-9010;
www.lesnomades.net*
Nomads come and go, and chefs have been doing the same
at this "sophisticated", sedate former "private dining club"
in a "civilized" Streeterville townhouse: the post-*Survey*
departure of Roland Liccioni occasioned a flurry of kitchen
changes culminating in the arrival of Chris Nugent (ex
Bêtise, A Bistro on the Lake), whose pricey New French
prix fixe fare partners well with a "top-notch wine list",
all presented by a "personable", "solicitous" staff that
"unobtrusively" provides "impeccable service."

### LE TITI DE PARIS　　　　27   24   25   $64
*1015 W. Dundee Rd. (Kennicott Ave.), Arlington Heights,
847-506-0222; www.letitideparis.com*
A "rare find in the Northwest Suburbs", this "fine-dining"
"treasure" "maintains its excellence year after year" –
even after the 2004 retirement of former chef-owner Pierre
Pollin – due to longtime collaborator Michael Maddox,
whose "outstanding" New American–influenced New
French fare is offered "at a fair" price by an "exceptional"
staff within a "quiet", "intimate" setting; P.S. the wine list
is as "fantastic" as it is "extensive."

### LE VICHYSSOIS　　　　　27   21   21   $48
*220 W. Rte. 120 (2 mi. west of Rte. 12), Lakemoor, 815-385-8221;
www.levichyssois.com*
"If you want to understand the way French food was
intended to be", head for the Northwest Suburbs to this
"true family-run" "favorite" that's "still excellent after all

these years" thanks to new and "classic cuisine prepared by a real pro", chef-owner Bernard Cretier; throw in "good service", a "quaint" ambiance and "great prices" that make it "a nice value", and you'll see why most contributors proclaim it's "worth the drive."

**Lincoln Noodle House** ⊠        – – – I

*5862 N. Lincoln Ave. (Sacramento Ave.), 773-275-8847*
A longtime Lincoln Square option for "inexpensive, fresh" Asian fare, especially "authentic homestyle" noodles and "very good dumplings", this casual BYO offers "an exotic tour" for the "taste buds" and is "great for the budget" too.

**Lindo Mexico** ◗        16 | 17 | 17 | $22

*2642 N. Lincoln Ave. (bet. Diversey Pkwy. & Wrightwood Ave.), 773-871-4832*
*Muchachos* mingle at this Lincoln Park "find" for "yummy" "Mexican and Cuban all in one place", including "Tex-Mex classics and authentic moles", "good frozen drinks" and "homemade salsa" dished out in a "festive", "colorful room"; still, some find the "standard fare" somewhat "ordinary", pointing out that it's not the best "that Chicago has to offer."

**LOBBY, THE**        24 | 25 | 25 | $52

*Peninsula Hotel, 108 E. Superior St., 5th fl. (bet. Michigan Ave. & Rush St.), 312-573-6760; www.peninsula.com*
More "relaxing" and "grand" than the name might imply, this "hushed" space in River North's Peninsula Hotel offers "divine" Continental "food and drink" with an Asian emphasis, as well as "oh-so-elegant afternoon tea" and a "great view of the Hancock Building"; assets aside, some lobbyists label it "overpriced"; N.B. a chocolate-and-coffee buffet is offered on Friday and Saturday nights.

**LOU MALNATI'S PIZZERIA**        23 | 12 | 16 | $18

*439 N. Wells St. (Hubbard St.), 312-828-9800*
*3859 W. Ogden Ave. (Cermak Rd.), 773-762-0800*
*958 W. Wrightwood Ave. (Lincoln Ave.), 773-832-4030*
*85 S. Buffalo Grove Rd. (Lake Cook Rd.), Buffalo Grove, 847-215-7100*
*1050 E. Higgins Rd. (bet. Arlington Heights & Busse Rds.), Elk Grove Village, 847-439-2000*
*1850 Sherman Ave. (University Pl.), Evanston, 847-328-5400*
*6649 N. Lincoln Ave. (bet. Devon & Pratt Aves.), Lincolnwood, 847-673-0800*
*131 W. Jefferson Ave. (Washington St.), Naperville, 630-717-0700*
*1 S. Roselle Rd. (Schaumburg Rd.), Schaumburg, 847-985-1525*
*www.loumalnatis.com*
Chi-town pizza fanaticism is alive and well, with delirious devotees dubbing this "enduring" "A-list" "institution's" "dangerously addictive deep-dish" pies the "only Chicago-style 'za worth eating" ("you won't be disappointed" by the

"fantastic thin crust", either); whether it's the "just-right mix of ingredients" or the optional "butter crust to die for", fans are "sure that if there's a heaven, they serve Lou's there"; P.S. it "ships well, too."

### Lou Mitchell's  ⌐                    23  10  18  $14
*565 W. Jackson Blvd. (Jefferson St.), 312-939-3111*
*O'Hare Int'l Airport, Terminal 5, 773-601-8989*
An "icon" that's "stood the test of time", this Loop "diner" dating from 1923 "defines the best American breakfast", "even at lunch" time, with "great omelets and eggs" ("double-yolkers are their trademark") and "good bakery items"; other selling points are "sassy" service, "nice prices" and "fresh doughnut holes while you wait" – though weekday visitors can "avoid the weekend lines" entirely; N.B. the O'Hare soup-salad-sandwich spot is takeout only.

### Lovell's of Lake Forest            21  24  22  $53
*915 S. Waukegan Rd. (Everett Rd.), Lake Forest, 847-234-8013;*
*www.lovellsoflakeforest.com*
The lofty lionize this North Shore "space museum's" namesake "astronaut owner", who "often greets guests" in the "traditional" "sage-and-beige, clublike" dining room while his son is in the kitchen cooking "out-of-this-world" New American fare; grounded grumps have a problem, however, grousing they "would prefer more down-to-earth cuisine and prices."

### Lucca's                            21  20  19  $33
*2834 N. Southport Ave. (Wolfram St.), 773-477-2565;*
*www.iloveluccas.com*
Lakeviewers "hope the rest of Chicago never discovers" this "gem", an "excellent" "date place" prized for its "imaginative" Italian and Med cuisine, including selections "for both carnivores and vegetarians"; *amanti* also approve of the "friendly service" and "European feel", not to mention the "wonderful outside seating."

### Lucia Ristorante                   –  –  –  M
*1825 W. North Ave. (Honore St.), 773-292-9700*
There are those who think this Wicker Park Italian BYO merits praise for its "sincere hospitality", "friendly" vibe and "good" "family cooking" (like "delicious sandwiches" made with "paper-thin sliced meats" at their deli, which is open for lunch); nevertheless, other opiners peg the food as "non-memorable" and feel confined by the "tiny room", though there is also patio seating in summer.

### Lula                               23  18  18  $24
*2537-41 N. Kedzie Blvd. (bet. Fullerton Ave. & Logan Blvd.),*
*773-489-9554; www.lulacafe.com*
"Committed to healthy, organic food and extreme culinary creativity", the owners of this Eclectic Logan Square "gem"

generate results that both "middle-aged foodies and young hipsters can agree on" (including "delicious vegetarian" options and "awesome breakfasts"); their "small but comfortable dining room" featuring "art by local artists" and the "best music" is also peopled with what some patient patrons perceive as "spotty (and sometimes dotty) servers."

### LuLu's Dim Sum & Then Sum  19⏐ 14⏐ 17⏐ $19⏐
*804 Davis St. (Sherman Ave.), Evanston, 847-869-4343;*
*www.lulusdimsum.com*
Some sum up the "small eats" as "fun and flavorful" at this North Suburban "family-friendly hangout" where the "interesting Asian dishes" are "innovative, satisfying" and "priced right" (especially the "incredible" "all-you-can-eat deals" that are sum-times available); still, some take a dim view of what they call "disappointing food" and "iffy service", saying "go directly to Chinatown."

### Lupita's  22⏐ 13⏐ 20⏐ $23⏐
*700 Main St. (Custer Ave.), Evanston, 847-328-2255;*
*www.lupitasmexicanrestaurant.com*
"Every dish satisfies" those Evanstonians eager to eat the "innovative" Mexican cuisine, including "creative specials", at this "casual", "consistently good" "favorite" (which is "especially great when they feature the *Like Water for Chocolate*" menu); more dubious diners declaim that it "tries to cross over from ordinary to high-end" but only "sometimes works"; P.S. a guitarist provides live "music on the weekends."

### Lutnia  −⏐ −⏐ −⏐ E⏐
*5532 W. Belmont Ave. (Central Ave.), 773-282-5335*
Cravers of "authentic" "Continental cuisine" come to this "romantic", "candlelit" Northwest Side spot for the feeling that they "have left the country", with "flaming tableside entrees and desserts", as well as "attentive service" from a staff that "tries hard to please"; live music on the "white grand piano" (Friday–Sunday nights) helps enthusiasts ignore that the decor "needs updating."

### Lutz Continental Café & Pastry Shop  20⏐ 16⏐ 19⏐ $18⏐
*2458 W. Montrose Ave. (bet. Campbell St. & Western Ave.),*
*773-478-7785; www.lutzcafe.com*
"You can gain weight just walking through the door" of this Northwest Side German-Continental outpost that's long been beloved as a "sweet-tooth satisfier" serving "great comfort food", "mouthwatering cakes", "exquisite tortes" and "Viennese-style coffee"; Lutz-nutz laud it as "old-world perfection" with "tearoom elegance" and a "charming" "summer courtyard", though weary wags write off the "ladies' lunch fare", saying "skip the restaurant and focus on the pastry" shop.

### L. Woods Tap & Pine Lodge   19  17  18  $28
*7110 N. Lincoln Ave. (Kostner Ave.), Lincolnwood, 847-677-3350;*
*www.leye.com*

"Cheeseheads never had it so good" chime champions of
this "amusing" re-creation of a "pine lodge" that brings "a
little Wisconsin to Chicago", saying its "comfortable and
kid-friendly" environs are just the place for "tender ribs"
and other "simple" Traditional American table treats;
holdouts, however, hanker for something better than what
they call its "ordinary, fattening food."

### Mac's ●   –  –  –  M
*1801 W. Division St. (Wood St.), 773-782-4400*

"Some of the best pub grub in the city" "sweeps [surveyors]
off their feet" at this "cool" "local" American tavern (named
after both its chef-owner, Michael Henry Moorman, and
his father, Henry) in an "up-and-coming" Ukrainian Village
location; "prices are reasonable", "service is decent" and
there's also sidewalk seating in season.

### MAGGIANO'S LITTLE ITALY   20  18  19  $28
*516 N. Clark St. (Grand Ave.), 312-644-7700*
*Oakbrook Center Mall, 240 Oakbrook Ctr. (Rte. 83), Oak Brook,*
*630-368-0300*
*1901 E. Woodfield Rd. (Rte. 53), Schaumburg, 847-240-5600*
*Westfield Shoppingtown, 175 Old Orchard Ctr. (bet. Golf &*
*Old Orchard Rds.), Skokie, 847-933-9555*
*www.maggianos.com*

Big appetites are appeased at this chain of "great family-
style places" "still going strong" with their "abundant"
"red-sauce" Southern "Italian comfort-food" concept and
"vibrant atmosphere" that's "a touch old Italy, a touch Rat
Pack"; still, the jaded jot that "it's not worth the wait" to
tolerate what they find to be "forgettable food", merely
"competent service" and "overcrowded" conditions.

### Magnolia Cafe   24  19  21  $36
*1224 W. Wilson Ave. (Magnolia Ave.), 773-728-8785*

Enthusiasts extol the "excellent", "surprising, delightful"
cooking and "relaxed setting" that's "like stepping into a
cozy living room" at this New American in an "up-and-
coming", "underserved" Uptown location; expansive eaters
would prefer that the tables in this "diamond in the rough"
were "a little less crowded" and "cramped."

### Magnum's Prime Steakhouse   22  19  19  $44
*777 E. Butterfield Rd. (bet. Highland Ave. & Meyers Rd.),*
*Lombard, 630-573-1010*
*1701 W. Golf Rd. (New Wilke Rd.), Rolling Meadows,*
*847-952-8555* ☒
*www.aceplaces.com*

Appreciators of this "upscale" suburban steakhouse duo
find "no-frills good beef" "prepared the right way" (and

"they show you the [meat] before you eat") plus "lunch deals" in a "nice setting" that makes for a "great business venue"; still, critics carp that the "typical" fare "doesn't measure up to" its competition; N.B. both locations offer live piano music.

### Maison

— | — | — | E

*30 S. La Grange Rd. (Harris Ave.), La Grange, 708-588-9890; www.maisondining.com*

Guests of this "charming, intimate" venue in the Western Suburbs dine happily within its "cozy", "lovely" environs, which are manned by a "great" staff; the oft-changing menu of "delicious", "fancy" (some say "fussy") New French–influenced New American cuisine is courtesy of husband-and-wife team Mary and Christopher Spagnola.

### Mama Desta's Red Sea

▽ 17 | 7 | 19 | $17

*3216 N. Clark St. (Belmont Ave.), 773-935-7561*

Mama's boys and girls feel "you won't find a more unique meal" than the "awesome finger food" and "honey wine" at this "delicious cultural experience" in Lakeview ("who would think eating dinner with a pancake instead of silverware would be a good experience?"); still, prodigal pen pals propose that you "get your Ethiopian fix elsewhere"; N.B. vegetarian dishes are a specialty.

### Mama Thai

▽ 22 | 14 | 19 | $17

*1112 W. Madison St. (Harlem Ave.), Oak Park, 708-386-0100*

Thai fanatics in the Western Suburbs beg their fellow surveyors to "please stop telling people about this place" where the "great" "food is fresh", the "menu has a wide variety of selections with lots of spicy or mild options" and the "in-house service is just as good" as the "quick and hot delivery"; in short, so what if the "location is not so great"?

### Mambo Grill ⊠

17 | 15 | 16 | $27

*412 N. Clark St. (bet. Hubbard & Kinzie Sts.), 312-467-9797*

Savorers of the "interesting", "tasty" Nuevo Latino food at this "overlooked value" in River North find it a "friendly", "fun" "destination" with a "varied menu"; others opine that it has two left feet – namely, "disinterested service" and "disappointing" food – making it better for "catching some drinks", like "fantastic mojitos" and "great caipirinhas."

### Manny's

23 | 8 | 15 | $13

*1141 S. Jefferson St. (Roosevelt Rd.), 312-939-2855 ⊠⇲
Midway Int'l Airport, 5700 S. Cicero Ave., Concourse A (55th St.), 773-948-6300
www.mannysdeli.com*

"Chicago's answer to a New York deli", this "legend"-ary South Loop spot boasts "the best corned beef, pastrami and hand-carved roast beef sandwiches" served "with a side of" "sass" from the "seasoned" "countermen" in a "nostalgic" atmosphere that's like "a cafeteria in the afterlife" thanks to "the mix of people eating under one roof" ("you can see anyone here"); N.B. the airport cafe also serves dinner.

### Maple Tree Inn ⌧                  ▽  24  18  18  $27
*13301 S. Old Western Ave. (Canal St.), Blue Island, 708-388-3461*
"Super" Contemporary Louisiana vittles including "Cajun and Creole specialties that don't disappoint" draw drawlers to this "Northern outpost of good Southern food", "a little hidden away" in the South Suburbs with an "ornate bar and tin ceiling" that really "make the place"; N.B. Dixie expats will appreciate that a heated portion of the veranda is now open year-round.

### Marché                            21  23  18  $43
*833 W. Randolph St. (Green St.), 312-226-8399;*
*www.marche-chicago.com*
"Swank"-sters who make the "scene" at this "funky" Market District venue declare it "dishes up the flavor" with its Traditional American and New French fare "done simply but with interesting touches" "along with fanciful attitude", as in the "*Alice-in-Wonderland*-in-a-bordello" decor and "kooky", "vibrant staff"; more staid surveyors find it "over the top", "noisy" and "not a great value", though, adding that "service doesn't match" the food or mood.

### Margie's Candies ●                22  16  15  $10
*1960 N. Western Ave. (Armitage Ave.), 773-384-1035;*
*www.margiescandies.com*
"Smile"-ing 'screamers melt for this "quintessential 1920s" "ice-cream dream", a Bucktown source for "serious" "old-fashioned parlor" creations, "homemade hot fudge" and "delicious candies" that are "worth every minute you wait on a hot summer night"; still, the chilly chide the American food as "forget"-able, fear the "freaky" "dolls staring at" their frozen treats and cite housekeeping issues; N.B. a Ravenswood branch is planned.

### Marina Cafe                       _   _   _   M
*6401 S. Coast Guard Dr. (Hayes Dr.), 773-947-0400*
Set in a former Coast Guard house overlooking Jackson Harbor, this carefree Creole-Caribbean hangout feels farther south than the Far South Side (access is from the parking lot at 63rd St. and Lake Shore Dr.); the main dining room has massive doors that open onto the water and a stage that sometimes hosts jazz musicians; N.B. open weekends only during the off-season, so be sure to call in advance.

### Mario's Gold Coast Ristorante ⌧  ▽  17  13  21  $28
*21 W. Goethe St. (Dearborn St.), 312-944-0199;*
*www.mariosristorante.com*
Seems only the Gold Coast "regulars" get this "non-pretentious" Italian "meeting place" where the portions of "basic Italian fare" are "generous", the atmosphere is

"cozy" and chef-owner "Mario [Stefanini] is always there" "to stop by and say hi"; apparently, outsiders "can't figure out why it's popular", saying it's "nothing special."

### Mas                                    23  19  20  $36
*1670 W. Division St. (Paulina St.), 773-276-8700;*
*www.masrestaurant.com*
"More Mas!" quip raters who rank Wicker Park's "*muy* cool", "happening" "place for Latin lovers" as "one of the best" South American spots thanks to chef John Manion's "creative, inventive and lively" Nuevo Latino dishes "nicely paired with delicious drinks" (including "great" mojitos, caipirinhas and margaritas); too bad the "noise" level means it's "not very conversation-friendly", though sidewalk dining helps alleviate the sometimes "crowded" conditions.

### Masck                                    –  –  –  M
*35 W. Ontario St. (Dearborn St.), 312-440-8880;*
*www.masckrestaurant.com*
Recently unmasked in its new River North Millennium Center location, this spirited North Shore import serves creative New American meat and seafood dishes, wood-fired pizzas, and the signature floppy cheeseburgers and fresh mini-doughnuts in a bright, whimsical setting with a piano bar and open kitchen; N.B. the original Deerfield branch is planning to reopen in a new location.

### Matsuya ●                                    25  13  16  $22
*3469 N. Clark St. (Sheffield Ave.), 773-248-2677*
Those who like it raw are radiant on the subject of this "favorite" Wrigleyville "neighborhood" "hole-in-the-wall" where the "not-cutting-edge-but-dependable" fare includes "excellent", "inexpensive sushi" and "something for non-seafood eaters", as well; P.S. the "low-key" locale draws a "young and vibrant crowd."

### Matsu Yama                                    –  –  –  M
*1059 W. Belmont Ave. (bet. Kenmore & Seminary Aves.),*
*773-327-8838; www.matsuyamasushi.com*
A stylish storefront spot serving an extensive selection of grilled and tempura dishes, standard raw offerings and specialty maki, this Lakeview BYO boasts dove-gray walls and cherry-stained tables and chairs, an ornate stone tile floor and an open kitchen flanked by a corner sushi bar.

### Maza                                    23  16  24  $27
*2748 N. Lincoln Ave. (Diversey Pkwy.), 773-929-9600*
The titular Lebanese-style tapas, including "great vegetarian dishes", are "flawlessly prepared", "authentic" and "a good value" at this "upscale" Lincoln Park Middle Easterner where "the owners go out of their way to make you feel comfortable"; not only is the "delicious" cuisine "more gourmet than most others" in its category, but the "elegant" "setting is nicer than the norm."

## McCormick & Schmick's    21 | 19 | 20 | $40
*41 E. Chestnut St. (Rush St.), 312-397-9500;*
*www.mccormickandschmicks.com*
Satiated seafood lovers laud the "tremendous menu
selection" of "fresh seafood items" that are "always tasty"
(if "not always creatively prepared") at this "great Gold
Coaster watering hole" whose "tasteful", "comfortable"
setting is a "real nice place for a business meeting or
intimate dinner for two"; ranked raters rue that "there's
nothing to get excited about", though, saying it's an
"upscale chain with all the good and bad that come with"
that particular territory.

## Medici on 57th ◑    – | – | – | I
*1327 E. 57th St. (bet. Kenwood & Kimbark Aves.),*
*773-667-7394*
"Every alum returns" to this "longtime University of Chicago
hangout" and "Hyde Park staple" for "excellent thin-crust
pizza", "fresh-squeezed OJ on a Sunday morning" or
something else from the "huge [American] menu selection";
"the service could be better", but the setting is "too
comfortable for words", and some surveyors say it's "still
the best coffeehouse/burger joint in town."

## Meiji    – | – | – | E
*623 W. Randolph St. (bet. Desplaines & Jefferson Sts.),*
*312-887-9999*
A chef from Sapporo adds authenticity to this West Loop
Restaurant Row Japanese (pronounced *may-gee*) with an
ever-changing menu that employs quality ingredients such
as genuine Kobe beef; the swanky space is accented by
rich earth tones and raw architectural details (including
exposed brick and granite) and features a central sushi
bar and lounge area.

## Melting Pot, The    – | – | – | M
*1205 W. Dundee Rd. (Arlington Hts. Rd.), Buffalo Grove,*
*847-342-6022*
*17 W. 633 Roosevelt Rd. (Summit Rd.), Oakbrook Terrace,*
*630-495-5778*
*255 W. Golf Rd. (bet. Higgins & Roselle Rds.), Schaumburg,*
*847-843-8970*
*Millennium Center Towers, 609 N. Dearborn St. (bet. Ohio &*
*Ontario Sts.), 312-573-0011* ◑
*www.meltingpot.com*
Raising the profile of its older suburban siblings, this
new River North subterranean dipping den (a branch of a
national chain) spreads from an unassuming storefront
entrance into cozy, cavernous rooms with built-in tabletop
cookers for do-it-yourself fondue; a glass-enclosed lounge,
kitchen that stays open till 1 AM and nightly entertainment
are other draws for its melting-pot crowd of couples,
families, businesspeople and tourists.

### Menagerie
21 | 18 | 18 | $37

*1232 W. Belmont Ave. (bet. Racine & Southport Aves.),*
*773-404-8333; www.menagerierestaurant.com*
With "one of the most fun and creative menus around", this
New American is "recommended by Lakeview foodies" who
inhale its "imaginative" fare, which features "excellent
combinations of flavors"; the "friendly", "relaxed ambiance"
is enhanced by "nice outdoor dining", and "everyone can
find something on the wine list" (or BYO for no charge);
N.B. a tapas menu was added post-*Survey*.

### Meritage Cafe & Wine Bar
24 | 21 | 22 | $42

*2118 N. Damen Ave. (bet. Armitage & Webster Aves.),*
*773-235-6434; www.meritagecafe.com*
"Consistently" "original", this "sophisticated, urban" corner
of "heaven" in Bucktown offers a "creatively prepared and
presented" New American menu that "changes with the
seasons"; habitués also haunt it for its "enchanting, almost-
hidden courtyard" and "friendly", "professional" staffers
who're "knowledgeable" about the "nice wine list featuring
small West Coast producers"; N.B. the Food rating may not
reflect the post-*Survey* departure of chef Dirk Flanigan.

### Merle's Smokehouse
20 | 15 | 18 | $24

*1727 Benson Ave. (Church St.), Evanston, 847-475-7766;*
*www.merlesbbq.com*
"The best BBQ for miles", this "legit" North Suburban rib
house is "a carnivore's holy grail"; surveyors "mix and match
various types" of "good and hearty" "down-home" 'cue
(Texas-, Tennessee- and North Carolina-style) with "great
chili" in a "blue-jeans casual" setting where the "kitsch is
part of the fun"; P.S. "get a booth if you want to talk."

### MERLO
25 | 20 | 23 | $39

*2638 N. Lincoln Ave. (Wrightwood Ave.), 773-529-0747*
*16 W. Maple St. (bet. Dearborn & State Sts.), 312-335-8200*
Expect a "warm welcome" at this "super" Lincoln Park
"secret" where the "hands-on" "owners are focused on the
right stuff" – "marvelous, home-cooked yet sophisticated"
Northern Italian cuisine ("don't miss anything with truffles
here") and a "superb wine list"; a "wonderful" staff swans
around in the "lovely storefront with several cozy rooms",
which remind rapt raters of "a warm, beautiful Bolognese
home"; N.B. the Gold Coast branch is opened post-*Survey*.

### Mesón Sabika
23 | 21 | 21 | $32

*1025 Aurora Ave. (Washington Ave.), Naperville, 630-983-3000*
*Northfield Village Ctr., 310 Happ Rd. (bet. Willow Rd. &*
*Winnetka Ave.), Northfield, 847-784-9300*
*www.mesonsabika.com*
North or West, Suburban surveyors say these Spanish
sisters represent a "cost-effective" "trip to Spain"; the
itinerary includes a "wide selection" of "delicious tapas"

(both "staple and adventurous"), "tasty port", "great sherry" and "the ever-popular" "white or red sangria", plus the "small rooms" in the Naperville location's "old mansion" "give a lovely dinner-party feel to things" – or spend a "summer night" "on the patio" under "the stars."

### M. Henry    23 | 19 | 20 | $16
*5707 N. Clark St. (W. Hollywood Ave.), 773-561-1600*
Boosters are blissed by one of the "best breakfast", "brunch and lunch" "joints around", namely this "hip" haven in Andersonville, where the "wonderful, creative, delicious" New American daytime dining (no dinner) draws a "cute and fashionable" crowd to the "handsomely decorated", "intimate space"; "service can be slow", though, so you may have to "wait for a table"; N.B. it's BYO.

### Mia Cucina    20 | 18 | 17 | $29
*56 W. Wilson St. (Brockway St.), Palatine, 847-358-4900;*
*www.miacucina.com*
*Mangia*-mavens mete out varying opinions on this Italian entry in the Northwest Suburbs: where some see "high-quality", "interesting" brick-oven cooking in a "quaint", "upscale setting", others discern a "high noise level" and find that the "food isn't good enough to overcome the environmental and service shortcomings."

### MIA FRANCESCA    24 | 18 | 20 | $30
*3311 N. Clark St. (W. School St.), 773-281-3310;*
*www.miafrancesca.com*
"The original, most perfect" of the Francesca "empire", this "cozy, cafe-style" spot in Lakeview has flatterers fawning over its "top-notch" Northern Italian fare and the "delicious hustle-bustle" of its "passionate" patrons; diners divide over the "quiet island" "upstairs" and the "raucous first floor", and those who "hate the noise", "waits" and "close tables" whine that "the whole city is showing up" – so "thank God they finally decided to take reservations."

### Mike Ditka's    20 | 18 | 19 | $38
*Tremont Hotel, 100 E. Chestnut St. (N. Rush St.), 312-587-8989*
A football fellowship fills this Gold Coast "homage to da coach" to down American steakhouse eats, including "awesome pork chops" and "great pot roast", offered in a "museum for sports fanatics" with a "friendly atmosphere" and "nice upstairs cigar bar"; the opposition concedes that "you can have a good steak and watch a ballgame" here but says that the "predictable" "food can't carry it on its own."

### Milk & Honey    21 | 17 | 12 | $14
*1920 W. Division St. (bet. Damen & Wolcott Aves.), 773-395-9434;*
*www.milkandhoneycafe.com*
This "fun, funky and friendly" Wicker Park New American daytime (no-dinner) destination does "great breakfasts" and "scrumptious" "gourmet sandwiches and soups" for the

"hipster and the stroller crowds"; it's "self-service to varying degrees", and "you may have to jockey for a table" in the "tight quarters" of its "bright, cheery" interior, but you can "bring your dog" to its "nice outdoor area" in summer.

### Miller's Pub ◗    15   13   18   $23

*134 S. Wabash Ave. (bet. Adams & Monroe Sts.), 312-263-4988; www.millerspub.com*

Veterans venerate this "comfortable and affordable" "old Chicago warhorse" and Loop "staple", with "dependable", "straightforward" American "meat-and-potatoes" fare, "old-pro service" and a "hearty" history with "memorabilia on the walls"; still, sour surveyors suggest the "so-so food" doesn't justify dealing with the "seedy", "dated" digs; P.S. it's "handy for theater and symphony dining."

### Mill Race Inn    17   21   18   $29

*4 E. State St. (Rte. 25), Geneva, 630-232-2030; www.themillraceinn.com*

"Charm exudes from every corner" of this West Suburban American "oasis in the Fox Valley" that "has been around forever" (or at least since 1933); contributors conclude the food is just "ok" but the "lovely country setting" offers the opportunity to "watch" or "feed the ducks", and "the lower-level Grill is a better deal for good sandwiches" – you can even "grab a bite [during] a bike ride along the river."

### Millrose Restaurant and    19   20   18   $32
### Brewing Co.

*45 S. Barrington Rd. (Central Rd.), Barrington, 847-382-7673; www.millroserestaurant.com*

"Despite its hugeness", this Northwest Suburban spot "created out of" "old barns" is hailed by happy hangers-out for the "warm, cozy" and "rustic" "North Woods–lodge" atmosphere in which it delivers "dependable" Traditional American (including "great ribs"); still, disheartened diners dis the "inconsistent" fare, describing it as "adequate but not very interesting" – but "the beer is still good."

### Mimosa    24   19   22   $37

*1849 Second St. (bet. Central Ave. & Elm Pl.), Highland Park, 847-432-9770; www.mimosacafe.com*

Constituents who call this "lovely" New French and Italian installation a "Downtown Highland Park favorite" appreciate its "creativity and consistency", "reasonable prices", "diverse, well-chosen wine list" and "comfortable, relaxed atmosphere"; as a bonus, "excellent", "efficient service" from the "friendly servers" gives it that "personal touch."

### Mirabell ⊠    ▽ 19   17   19   $30

*3454 W. Addison St. (bet. Kimball & St. Louis Aves.), 773-463-1962; www.mirabellrestaurant.com*

For "a taste of Bavaria", Teutonic traditionalists tout this "charming" Northwest Side "joint" that's "practically the last of the German eateries" in the area; most maintain that it boasts the genuine "feel of Munich", though some surveyors score its schnitzel as strictly "standard."

**MIRAI SUSHI**   | 28 | 21 | 20 | $45 |

*2020 W. Division St. (Damen Ave.), 773-862-8500;*
*www.miraisushi.com*

"The fish swim down Division to get" to this "always-amazing" "trendy Japanese", officially the "best in Chicago" thanks to its "fresh", "creative" and "adventurous sushi" ("love the rare varieties they have") and "cool" "scene" (especially the "great bar upstairs"); nonconformists nag that they "need to work on the service" and pout about the "premium price" you'll pony up for the "edible art", though ayes aver "you get what you pay for."

**Miramar**   | – | – | – | M |

*301 Waukegan Ave. (Highwood Ave.), Highwood, 847-433-1078;*
*www.miramarbistro.com*

Owner Gabe Viti (Gabriel's) is packing in the locals at this sizzling North Shore scene where classic, hearty French bistro fare is complemented by a smart global wine list and 'Havana cocktails'; decorative touches include subway-tile walls, marble-topped sideboards, shelves of fresh bread loaves and an unabashed display of cigarettes over the bar; N.B. the authenticity extends to the sidewalk cafe.

**Misto** ⊠   ▽ | 21 | 15 | 22 | $34 |

*1118 W. Grand Ave. (bet. Halsted St. & Racine Ave.), 312-226-5989;*
*www.mistochicago.com*

"A friend to all" and "a star in his own right", chef-owner "Donny [Greco] makes the place" at this "comfortable" Near West Italian "neighborhood restaurant" with Traditional American mixed into a menu that's "simple, but caters to different tastes"; even foes have faint praise, suggesting perhaps the likable spot is an "underachiever."

**Mity Nice Grill**   | 19 | 15 | 19 | $26 |

*Water Tower Pl., 835 N. Michigan Ave., mezzanine level*
*(bet. Chestnut & Pearson Sts.), 312-335-4745; www.leye.com*

"Lots of locals partake" of the "reliable", "simple" American fare that cronies compare to "home cooking" – they "love the mac 'n' cheese" and "recommend the garlic-crusted whitefish" – at this "relaxed" Streeterville respite in "crazy" Water Tower Place; it's "convenient" for "harried", "weary Michigan Avenue shoppers" and "good for families" because there's "something for everyone."

**Mj2 Bistro**   | – | – | – | M |

*800 W. Devon Ave. (Brophy Ave.), Park Ridge, 847-698-7020;*
*www.mj2bistro.com*

It's a small world after all at this Eclectic bistro in suburban Park Ridge, where the mostly Asian and South American dishes sometimes take on other international accents (Med,

Italian, Creole) and are allied with a globe-spanning list of 30 wines by the bottle or glass; soft lighting, a coppery tin ceiling and black-and-white tile floors lend this casual, family-friendly spot a classic Parisian feel.

## MK

27 | 24 | 24 | $56

*868 N. Franklin St. (bet. Chestnut & Locust Sts.), 312-482-9179; www.mkchicago.com*

"Long adored" and "still among the best", this River North New American proffers chef-owner Michael Kornick's "creative menu", which "delivers on the promise" of "subtle", "sophisticated" cuisine "with minimal pretension" (it "looks simple, but a lot of work went into these dishes") accompanied by "stupendous desserts" and "wonderful wines"; "service is stellar", and the "sleek", "swanky" space is "elegant in that urban warehouse loft kind of way", even if "a bit noisy."

## Mon Ami Gabi

21 | 20 | 20 | $38

*Belden-Stratford Hotel, 2300 N. Lincoln Park W. (Belden Ave.), 773-348-8886*
*Oakbrook Center Mall, 260 Oakbrook Ctr. (Rte. 83), Oak Brook, 630-472-1900*
*www.monamigabi.com*

These Chicago area members of a national group have boosters who bask in their "friendly", "fun and cozy faux-Parisian atmosphere" while downing "first-class" Gallic bistro "comfort food" including "various offerings of steak frites" and a "good variety of seafood"; advocates of their "authenticity", however, are challenged by the gang who say their "chain" status makes them "unoriginal" and "uninspired" (though they concede "service is authentically French, which isn't necessarily a compliment").

## Monsoon

19 | 23 | 18 | $41

*2813 N. Broadway St. (bet. Clark St. & Diversey Pkwy.), 773-665-9463; www.monsoonchicago.com*

Raters blow hot and cold over this "sleek", "high-end" Indian-Asian "fusion restaurant" in Lakeview: some say you'll be swept away by its "beautiful", "interesting decor" ("visit the erotic bathroom") and the "amazing flavors" and "sophistication" of its "different-from-the-usual" dishes, but others warn you'll be ruffled by the ill winds of "inconsistent food", "too-expensive" tabs and "uneven service" that "can't compete" with the "great atmosphere."

## Moody's Pub ●⌀

17 | 12 | 13 | $14

*5910 N. Broadway St. (Thorndale Ave.), 773-275-2696; www.moodyspub.com*

Opened in 1959, this American tavern – a "longtime, well-kept secret" in Edgewater – is best "loved [for its] blue-cheese burger", its "televisions and fireplaces (great when it's cold)" and what some consider "the best beer garden in Chicago", complete with "fountains, overhanging trees, stars and even crickets"; some pub-crawlers grow moody, however, about a "too-dark" interior that can get "smoky."

**Moon Palace**　　　　　- | - | - | I
*216 W. Cermak Rd. (S. Wentworth Ave.), 312-225-4081*
An example of the newer Chinatown breed courting a hipper crowd, this little brick storefront has a more upscale feel than the nearby chow-palaces, with a pop music soundtrack accompanying its big portions of Mandarin and Shanghai-style specialties (some authentic, some Americanized); N.B. check out the noteworthy lunch deals.

**MORTON'S, THE STEAKHOUSE**　26 | 21 | 24 | $56
*65 E. Wacker Pl. (bet. Michigan & Wabash Aves.), 312-201-0410*
*Newberry Plaza, 1050 N. State St. (Maple St.), 312-266-4820*
*9525 W. Bryn Mawr Ave. (River Rd.), Rosemont,*
*847-678-5155*
*1470 McConnor Pkwy. (Meacham Rd.), Schaumburg,*
*847-413-8771*
*1 Westbrook Corporate Ctr. (22nd St.), Westchester,*
*708-562-7000*
*www.mortons.com*
Still edging out stiff competition in its carnivorous category, "Chicago's original" "genteel" "king of the steakhouse chains" "continues to reign supreme" "in a town famous for steak", with the "best" "prime beef", "clubby" digs and "service as crisp as the hash browns" ("save room for" the "must-have" "hot Godiva cake"); a note to wallet-watchers, though: everything's "huge", including the "big prices"; N.B. the Loop location opened post-*Survey*.

**Motel** ◗　　　　　- | - | - | M
*600 W. Chicago Ave. (Larrabee St.), 312-822-2900;*
*www.themotelbar.com*
The decor may be retro, but there's no kitsch in the concept – a neighborhood-friendly take on a motel lobby bar – at this intimate River North hipster hangout in the old Montgomery Ward building (the latest project from the Mas mavens), where the inn crowd orders American room-service eats and classic cocktails amid loungey furniture groupings; N.B. closes at 2 AM nightly (3 AM Saturdays).

**Moto** ☒　　　　　- | - | - | VE
*945 W. Fulton Mkt. (Sangamon St.), 312-491-0058;*
*www.motorestaurant.com*
Inhabiting a warehouse-dotted stretch of the Market District, this minimalist Asian-Eclectic entry features Trotter's alum Homaro Cantu's ambitious and avant-garde tastings-only menu, which ranges from five to 16 courses and can be paired with uncommon wines (mostly from Spain, Italy and Chile); its stark setting, all angles and neutrals, is enlivened by a few bamboo plants.

**Mr. Beef** 🈂️⊘    | – | – | – | I |
*666 N. Orleans St. (bet. Erie & Huron Sts.), 312-337-8500*
You "can't beat a hot-and-juicy Italian beef" – "wet or dry,
with or without peppers" – at this "funky" River North
sandwich "shack" that "Jay Leno raves about"; in fact, the
place is "filled with photos of celebs who come" for a
"savory, sloppy, sliced serving of heaven"; N.B. cash only.

**Mrs. Levy's Delicatessen** 🈂️    | 15 | 12 | 14 | $16 |
*Sears Tower, 233 S. Wacker Dr., 2nd level (bet. Adams St. &
Jackson Blvd.), 312-993-0530; www.levyrestaurants.com*
While some deli-cats purr over the "old-style" "favorites"
("good sandwiches", "big salads", "fresh matzo-ball soup")
and the frequent presence of "Mrs. Levy herself" at this
"efficient" Loop "luncheon [and breakfast] place" with
"dinerlike decor", others growl about "inflated prices" for
"marginal food", and say "service can be lacking" – plus
"dealing with [Sears Tower] security is sometimes a pain."

**Mrs. Park's Tavern**    | 18 | 15 | 17 | $32 |
*Doubletree Guest Suites Hotel, 198 E. Delaware Pl.
(Michigan Ave.), 312-280-8882*
Tavern-goers who appreciate this "pleasant" Streeterville
Traditional American "for after shopping, before movies"
or a "late-night cocktail" also approve of the "large and
tasty entrees and salads" and "great breakfasts", saying
it's "good for a hotel" eatery; tarter tongues wag over food
that's "sometimes too imaginative", though, and suggest
that "service varies"; P.S. "sitting outside in summer offers
a cool view of the city."

**Mt. Everest Restaurant**    | 22 | 17 | 19 | $23 |
*630 Church St. (bet. Chicago & Orrington Aves.), Evanston,
847-491-1069; www.mteverestrestaurant.com*
The "delightful mixture of Nepalese and Indian" fare is
"satisfying, filling" and "finer than average" to those who
are high on this North Suburban "favorite", plus there's
"friendly service" and a "great lunch buffet" every day;
nonetheless, some adventurers announce it's "uneven"
and "on the edge of pricey"; N.B. imbibers should note
that they serve beer and wine only.

**My Pie Pizza**    | 17 | 10 | 13 | $14 |
*2417 N. Clark St. (Fullerton Pkwy.), 773-929-3380
2010 N. Damen Ave. (Armitage Ave.), 773-394-6900*
In the battle for 'za supremacy, the "great pizza (thick or
thin)" and "tasty salad" bars at this Bucktown and Lincoln
Park local "stopping-place" twosome still has its partisans,
who also consider each a "casual", "cheap date place";
those who feel that "other Chicago favorites are better"
pan the pie as "passable", and some wounded warriors
wonder "what happened to what used to be one of the
best in the city?"; P.S. the Damen Avenue outpost is BYO.

### Myron & Phil's Steakhouse    21   16   21   $38
*3900 W. Devon Ave. (bet. Crawford & Lincoln Aves.),*
*Lincolnwood, 847-677-6663; www.myronandphils.com*
"Old-school" chums of this North Suburban steakhouse
"institution" where "little has changed in years" still
champion its status as a "staple" for "generous portions"
of "quite-good" "Chicago-type foods" (plus the "chopped
liver freebie"); the "clubby if somewhat geriatric" scene is
"not exciting but comfortable", and "service" is "reliable";
N.B. there's live piano Thursday through Saturday nights.

### Mysore Woodland    –   –   –   M
*2548 W. Devon Ave. (Rockwell St.), 773-338-8160*
*6020 S. Cass Ave. (60th St.), Westmont, 630-769-9663*
"Delicious" and "authentic Indian cuisine" with a vegetarian
focus makes this pair of subcontinental spots "an easy
choice" when in the Western Suburbs or on the Northwest
Side; some say that service can be "a bit slow, but when
the food arrives, it is well worth it"; N.B. the Devon Avenue
location is BYO.

### Nacional 27 ⊠    22   24   21   $40
*325 W. Huron St. (N. Orleans St.), 312-664-2727; www.leye.com*
Chef Randy Zweiban's "imaginative, explosively flavored"
cuisine isn't the only "saucy and spicy" thing at this Nuevo
Latino specialist in River North, where "the 27 stands
for the number of [Central and South American] nations
represented on the abundant menu"; this "hot date place"
with cool "specialty cocktails" "makes Chicago feel like the
tropics", especially after 11 PM on weekends when "the
tables clear and the dance floor opens."

### NAHA ⊠    26   24   24   $57
*500 N. Clark St. (Illinois St.), 312-321-6242;*
*www.naha-chicago.com*
"Creative" chef-partner Carrie Nahabedian's "amazing"
seasonal New American "dining with daring Mediterranean
touches" tempts travelers to her "flat-out superb" River
North "keeper", where "the *Queer Eye* guys would be
proud of" the "streamlined", "simple" "Zen-like" decor;
sure, her "food is pricey" but most meditate it's "worth the
splurge" – though what's a "great buzz" to some is just plain
"noisy" to others.

### Nancy's Original Stuffed Pizza    22   12   15   $15
*2930 N. Broadway St. (Wellington Ave.), 773-883-1977 ◗*
*3970 N. Elston Ave. (Irving Park Rd.), 773-267-8182 ⊽*
*940 N. York Rd. (Grand Ave.), Elmhurst, 630-834-4374*
*8706 W. Golf Rd. (Milwaukee Ave.), Niles, 847-824-8183*
*www.nancyspizza.com*
Pals of this "reliable" city-and-suburban sisterhood prefer
its "yummy", "cheap" "Chicago-style stuffed pizza" with
"the best sauce" (and "conveniently, they sell" it "by the

slice"); doubters declare that the pie may be "good" but prefer to "pass on the other entrees", adding that "the interiors leave a lot to be desired"; N.B. the Northwest Side spot is BYO.

**Narcisse** ● 18 23 17 $39
*710 N. Clark St. (bet. Huron & Superior Sts.), 312-787-2675; www.narcisse.us*
"The name says it all" about this "decadent", "upscale" River North "champagne-and-caviar" dream — "if you're beautiful and you know it you'll fit right in"; combining "chic dining in elegant" environs with "loud music" "downstairs" in a "disco-bedroom" setting, it's an "excellent" choice for "spending an evening out in one place"; N.B. the Food score may not reflect the post-*Survey* arrival of chef Jason McClain and his full-service Eclectic-Continental menu.

**Negro League Café, The** – – – M
*301 E. 43rd St. (Prairie Ave.), 773-536-7000; www.thenegroleaguecafe.info*
Filled with art and memorabilia honoring the eponymous baseball league that pre-dated the sport's desegregation in the '40s, this Far South Side entry has safely slid into a Bronzeville home, pitching a Southern–soul food buffet (lunch and dinner), plus burgers, sandwiches, a variety of wing dishes and a few entrees (e.g. jerked rib-eye with collards); N.B. live music jazzes up the joint some nights.

**New Japan** ▽ 18 10 20 $25
*1322 Chicago Ave. (Dempster St.), Evanston, 847-475-5980*
North Suburban "neighborhood residents" are grateful for the "great sushi" at this "friendly", "off-the-beaten-path" longtimer that's "more like a taste of old Japan – authentic, right down to the servers"; abstainers assess the fare as "average", though, saying "there's better" in the area; N.B. they serve beer and wine only.

**New Three Happiness** – – – M
*2130 S. Wentworth Ave. (Cermak Rd.), 312-791-1228*
Some Chinatown visitors call this cavernous, crowded old-timer "the place to go for dim sum" seven days a week, saying "food, service, value – what's the fourth happiness?"; still, others swear that "nothing really stands out" on its Cantonese-Mandarin menu, viewing it as "an alternative to [other] local houses only when you can't wait for a table to open up."

**Next Door Bistro** ⌿ 24 16 22 $33
*250 Skokie Blvd. (bet. Dundee & Lake Cook Rds.), Northbrook, 847-272-1491*
A "friendly" and "affordable" North Suburban neighbor to Francesco's Hole in the Wall, this "great restaurant" combines New American and Italian eats (including "the best roasted chicken bar none") in a "relaxed", "easy-

dining" experience; the space is "small" and "often" has "long waits", though, and it "would be nice if the owner took credit cards."

### Nick & Tony's Italian Chophouse  17  17  18  $33
*1 E. Wacker Dr. (bet. State St. & Wabash Ave.), 312-467-9449
Geneva Commons, 1322 Commons Dr. (Bricher Rd.), Geneva,
630-845-0025
www.rdgchicago.com*
The Loop location of this "good (not great)" and "friendly" duo with "corny Sinatra decor" places the accent on Italian, plus they have a "handy quick-service counter", "fun bar", "view of the river" and an "outdoor cafe in summer", while the West Suburban spot is more of a "place to go for steak" or seafood; still, plenty of participants point to the pair's "predictable" provender and "sketchy service."

### Nick's Fishmarket  24  21  24  $51
*Bank One Plaza, 51 S. Clark St. (Monroe St.), 312-621-0200* ⓢ
*O'Hare Int'l Ctr., 10275 W. Higgins Rd. (Mannheim Rd.),
Rosemont, 847-298-8200
www.nicksfishmarketchicago.com*
"Fin fans delight" in the "fancy, fine, fresh fish" such as "wonderful shellfish and excellent grilled items" at this Loop and O'Hare area twin-set, among "the few great seafood joints in a steak town", with assets such as "posh" digs and "smooth-as-silk service" (they "should compete in the Olympics in synchronized swimming"); be advised, though, that "sticker-shock" prices make it best "on somebody else's nickel" or if you "just won the Powerball."

### Nine  ⓢ  22  25  19  $52
*440 W. Randolph St. (Canal St.), 312-575-9900; www.n9ne.com*
Lurking in the West Loop is this "chichi" spot where "sexy people" sup on "excellent steakhouse cuisine" and "even better seafood" in a "sleek", "flashy" space with a ceiling that "changes color" (and if you're "ready for nightlife after dinner", "drop by the Ghostbar upstairs"); contrarians crab, though, that the "expensive" "food is not as amazing as the decor" and "the service gets a little stretched."

### NOMI  ●  26  27  24  $66
*Park Hyatt Chicago, 800 N. Michigan Ave. (Chicago Ave.),
312-239-4030; www.nomirestaurant.com*
Beguiled boulevardiers believe "they built the Park Hyatt hotel around this" "fabulous" "first-class" "favorite", where a "table by the window" offers a "celestial" Gold Coast view and the "stunning modernist decor" sets the stage for "superb", "innovative" New French fare and selections from the "top-notch sommelier"; still, those who aren't "loaded" lament the "inflated prices" and say "the staff needs to loosen up"; N.B. the Food rating may not reflect the post-*Survey* departure of chef Sandro Gamba.

**Nookies** ⊄　　　　　　　18　11　17　$14
*1746 N. Wells St. (bet. Lincoln & North Aves.), 312-337-2454*
**Nookies Too**
*2114 N. Halsted St. (bet. Dickens & Webster Aves.), 773-327-1400*
**Nookies Tree** ◗⊄
*3334 N. Halsted St. (Buckingham Pl.), 773-248-9888*
Ever-"popular" and "extremely fun", this threesome of "laid-back", "friendly" BYOs is home to "good hearty American breakfasts" (aka "hangover cures") and "reliable, affordable diner fare" for lunch or dinner, as well as "interesting sight-seeing"; "watch out for long lines on [weekend] mornings", though, and a "note to prudes: the Belmont location [whose decor was spruced up post-*Survey*] is gay-tastic!"

**Noon-O-Kabab**　　　　▽ 20　7　14　$19
*4661 N. Kedzie Ave. (Leland Ave.), 773-279-8899;*
*www.noonokabab.com*
Persian partialists proudly praise this "cozy" Northwest Side "storefront" for its "yummy", "inexpensive food", including some of "the best kebabs in town" and "fresh bread that could tempt anyone to quit a low-carb diet"; persnickety pen pals pan the "unpredictable service", though, and point out that they're "not much with decor" (as the score indicates); N.B. serving beer and wine only.

**NORTH POND**　　　　25　27　21　$53
*2610 N. Cannon Dr. (bet. Diversey & Fullerton Pkwys.),*
*773-477-5845; www.northpondrestaurant.com*
"Nestled" "lagoon-side" in a "breathtaking" Lincoln Park locale, this "beautiful", "historic" "ice-skating shelter" features a "fantastic" "Prairie School interior", a suitable setting for "gifted chef" Bruce Sherman's "phenomenal seasonal" New American fare employing "local artisan ingredients" and paired with a "unique wine selection"; still, perfectionists point out that the "stiff staff" is "not always as attentive" as you'd expect given the "top-of-the-line prices."

**Northside Bar & Grill** ◗　　15　16　16　$17
*1635 N. Damen Ave. (North Ave.), 773-384-3555;*
*www.northsidechicago.com*
Nice neighbors of this "happening" Bucktown American "staple" happily "hang out" in its "bar atmosphere" for "burgers, salads and simple food" (especially in the "glass atrium in winter and the outdoor seating in summer"); pragmatists posit there's "nothing wrong with this place, but nothing particularly good, either"; N.B. the 1:30 AM kitchen closing (2:30 AM on Saturdays) appeals to insomniacs.

**Noyes Street Café**　　　15　12　17　$22
*828 Noyes St. (Sherman St.), Evanston, 847-475-8683;*
*www.noyescafe.com*
"A mix of everything" draws a similar mix of commentary about this "friendly" North Suburban spot, a "higher-end

version of a Greek diner" that also serves Italian food; pros paint the "solid", "homey" fare, "low prices" and "people-watching" as positives, while cons carp about "mediocre" eats and quip that its name is "Noyes – as in noise."

### Nuevo Leon    20   8   15   $17

*1515 W. 18th St. (bet. Ashland & Blue Island Aves.),*
*312-421-1517* ●🖂
*3657 W. 26th St. (Lawndale Ave.), 773-522-1515*

"Authentic" Mexican mainstays (unrelated but with the same name), these two Near South Siders have a reputation for "huge portions" of "tasty" "homestyle" food that's "greasy and great"; "cheap prices" may help account for occasional "long waits", and don't expect any "pretense or luxuries"; N.B. the 18th Street Pilsen location is BYO.

### Oak Tree    17   16   15   $18

*Bloomingdale's Bldg., 900 N. Michigan Ave., 6th fl.*
*(bet. Delaware Pl. & Walton St.), 312-751-1988*

Offering an "escape from mall food", this Gold Coast American "update of a greasy spoon (with no grease)" serves a "huge breakfast selection" plus "a comfortable lunch" of "fresh salads", "great sandwiches", "enjoyable soups" and "tasty desserts"; "the view out to Michigan Avenue makes for a bright, cheery environment", and lots of "locals" and "shoppers" "wish it were open" later.

### OCEANIQUE 🖂    27   20   23   $51

*505 Main St. (bet. Chicago & Hinman Aves.), Evanston,*
*847-864-3435; www.oceanique.com*

Putting his "creativity on display nightly", "personable" "chef-owner Mark Grosz continues to amaze" at this "unpretentious" but "absolutely fabulous" North Suburban New French–New American "favorite" (the "best seafood" spot in our *Survey*) serving "excellent" fare so "inventive and outstanding" it "should be illegal"; kudos, too, for the "understated storefront" space with "fabric-draped ceiling" and a "knowledgeable staff" "attuned to the needs of the diner"; P.S. the three-course $35 menu is a "great deal."

### O'Famé    19   12   16   $22

*750 W. Webster Ave. (Halsted St.), 773-929-5111; www.ofame.com*

Allies of this "reliable" Lincoln Park spot recommend its "great thin-crust" pies made with "fresh ingredients and sauce", as well as its other "solid" Italian items such as "good salads and calamari"; less enthusiastic eaters "don't understand" the appeal of what they deem "average" fare, but "who doesn't love half-price pizza Tuesdays?"

### Old Jerusalem    18   8   14   $14

*1411 N. Wells St. (bet. North Ave. & Schiller St.), 312-944-0459;*
*www.oldjerusalemrestaurant.com*

Defenders of this "authentic" Middle Eastern BYO "staple" in Old Town take their "non-pretentious friends" for the "best cheap eats" in the 'hood; others, though, "wail" about its "hole-in-the-wall", "fast-food-joint decor."

### Olives                    – – – M
*752 Sheridan Rd. (Old Elm Rd.), Highwood, 847-681-9687; www.oliveswinebar.com*
Bringing urban dining to the suburbs, this upscale bistro offers a value-conscious approach to New French and Italian cuisine; the intimate setting includes a vaulted ceiling and marble bar, as well as white tablecloths set with crystal and china; N.B. 50-plus wines by the glass.

### O'Neil's                  18  15  19  $31
*1003 Green Bay Rd. (Scott Ave.), Winnetka, 847-446-7100; www.oneilsinwinnetka.com*
"Popular with the locals", this "long-established, homey" North Shore spot is known for Traditional American and Italian cooking that's "reliable (if not the most exciting)", as well as an "elegant" but not "stuffy" ambiance and "great" "alfresco dining" in summer; diners who "don't see the attraction" suggest "let's change the menu a little after all these years", and others tire of the "long waits on weekends because of the no-reservations policy."

### One North ☒              18  20  16  $35
*1 N. Wacker Dr. (Madison St.), 312-750-9700; www.rdgchicago.com*
The ayes aver that an "upscale experience" awaits at this "consistent" Loop New American with "swanky" "urban-lodge" decor, "large windows" and "high ceilings" as "a businessperson's staple" (it's a "lunchtime favorite" and has a "happy-hour bar scene"), plus "you can crawl to the Civic Opera House" from here; nays are nonplussed, though, by the "noisy atmosphere", "unimaginative menu" and some "inexperienced" staffers; P.S. the patio "is enjoyable."

### ONE SIXTYBLUE ☒          25  24  23  $58
*1400 W. Randolph St. (Ogden Ave.), 312-850-0303; www.onesixtyblue.com*
"There's a modern freshness to both the food and decor" at "Michael Jordan's" "out-of-the-way" Market District "jewel", where Chef Martial Noguier's "phenomenal" New American cooking "is an object lesson in perfect simplicity", the wine list is "eclectic but appropriate" and the "civilized" setting with a "huge" "open kitchen" is "cosmopolitan" yet "comfortable"; no wonder most say it's "worth every penny", even if a few fans call a financial foul ("I enjoyed my meal until I got the check").

### 120 Ocean Place ☒        22  24  20  $40
*120 N. Hale St. (bet. Front & Wesley Sts.), Wheaton, 630-690-2100; www.one20.com*
Satisfied seafarers swear by this New American seafood specialist whose "classy" environs ("a former funeral

home" replete with a "gorgeous stained-glass window") are the "intriguing setting" for a "great selection" of "excellent seafood with inventive sauces" (plus game dishes) and a "nice little wine list with something for everyone"; still, a few miserly mariners moan about "the cost" and claim that service has "slipped a bit."

**OPA Estiatorio** <u>–</u> <u>–</u> <u>–</u> <u>M</u>
*950 Lakeview Pkwy. (Hawthorn Pkwy.), Vernon Hills,*
*847-968-4300; www.oparestaurant.com*
Expect a large menu of classic, hearty Greek fare such as stewlike dishes baked in clay pots and lots of fresh seafood at this reasonably priced, North Suburban Hellenic; beneath a soaring white ceiling reminiscent of a giant wedding tent lurk multiple dining rooms and a large bar, with picture windows and outdoor dining offering views of Bear Lake.

**Opera** <u>22</u> <u>23</u> <u>21</u> <u>$44</u>
*1301 S. Wabash Ave. (13th St.), 312-461-0161;*
*www.opera-chicago.com*
"As much about scene as cuisine", this "eccentric" eatery in the "up-and-coming" South Loop is "a wild ride" thanks to an "over-the-top" "fantasy" setting "full of urban hipsters" and "fun", "attentive" servers; chef Paul Wildermuth's "original", "upscale" ("expensive") take on Asian and Mandarin Chinese cuisines includes "extensive vegetarian" choices and can be "outrageously spicy", and the night can be "noisy", but it's "romantic" "if you get one of the private vaults" "in this former film warehouse."

**Orange** <u>24</u> <u>17</u> <u>18</u> <u>$16</u>
*3231 N. Clark St. (Belmont Ave.), 773-549-4400*
*75 W. Harrison St. (bet. Clark & Federal Sts.), 312-447-1000*
*www.orangechicago.com*
Squeezing out "a new spin on" breakfast, brunch and lunch, this "bright, cheery" Lakeview Eclectic BYO takes "a unique approach" with "kooky creations" like "chai latte French toast", "special pancake flights", "fruit sushi" and "design-your-own juices", all served by a "fun and energetic staff"; it's so "popular" that "weekend" "waits can be painfully long", and far-flung feasters wonder "orange ya going to open one in the suburbs?"; N.B. the South Loop location opened post-*Survey*.

**Original Gino's East, The** <u>21</u> <u>13</u> <u>14</u> <u>$19</u>
*2801 N. Lincoln Ave. (Diversey Pkwy.), 773-327-3737*
*633 N. Wells St. (Ontario St.), 312-943-1124*
*2516 Green Bay Rd. (Central St.), Evanston, 847-332-2100*
*1807 S. Washington St. (south of 75th St.), Naperville, 630-548-9555*
*15840 S. Harlem Ave. (159th St.), Orland Park, 708-633-1300*
*1321 W. Golf Rd. (Algonquin Rd.), Rolling Meadows, 847-364-6644*
*8725 W. Higgins Rd. (bet. Cumberland & River Rds.), Rosemont,*
*773-444-2244*

(continued)

**Original Gino's East, The**

*Tin Cup Pass Shopping Ctr., 1590 E. Main St. (Tyler Rd.), St. Charles, 630-513-1311*
*315 W. Front St. (West St.), Wheaton, 630-588-1010*
*www.ginoseast.com*

Still a "worthy competitor", this "classic" chain bakes up what some call "the gold standard of deep dish", with "incredible tomato sauce" and "fluffy cornmeal crust"; fans also have "fun" "creating graffiti decor while dining" at the River North site, but many "miss the *real* original", saying "it's lost cred since" "moving to the old Planet Hollywood" space; N.B. the Oak Lawn branch closed post-*Survey*.

**Original Pancake House, The**  22 | 12 | 17 | $14

*22 E. Bellevue Pl. (bet. Michigan Ave. & Rush St.), 312-642-7917* ⊟
*Village Ctr., 1517 E. Hyde Park Blvd. (bet. 51st St. & Lake Park Blvd.), 773-288-2323* ⊟
*2020 N. Lincoln Park W. (Clark St.), 773-929-8130* ⊟
*10437 S. Western Ave. (104th St. & 105th St.), 773-445-6100*
*5148 W. 159th St. (bet. Laramie & Le Claire Aves.), Oak Forest, 708-687-8282* ⊟
*954 Lake St. (Forest St.), Oak Park, 708-524-0955*
*106 S. Northwest Hwy. (Touhy Ave.), Park Ridge, 847-696-1381*
*www.originalpancakehouse.com*

"Always packed, and for a good reason", this gaggle of "great" "old-time breakfast" places ("no goat cheese here") grows on gourmands who go for the "apple pancake and Dutch baby", "fresh-squeezed orange juice" and "darn good coffee", "all the time" (the daytime-only hours vary by location); "there's no scenery", service waffles from "hustling" to "scarce" and there's "sometimes a long wait", but boosters boast "it's worth it."

**Osteria Via Stato**  - | - | - | E

*620 N. State St. (Ontario St.), 312-642-8450; www.leye.com*

To cook up this River North Italian, the Lettuce Entertain You gang folded chefs Rick Tramonto (Tru) and David Di Grigorio (ex Maggiano's) into the erstwhile Papagus space and mixed well; the result is a large venue that feels like a cozy grotto, where three-course, prix fixe meals are enhanced with a vino list overseen by sommelier Belinda Chang (ex Charlie Trotter's); N.B. for lighter eaters, the adjacent wine bar offers a small-plates menu.

**Oysy**  22 | 20 | 22 | $31

*50 E. Grand Ave. (bet. Rush & N. Wabash Sts.), 312-670-6750*
*888 S. Michigan Ave. (9th St.), 312-922-1127*
*315 Skokie Blvd. (Dundee Rd.), Northbrook, 847-714-1188*
*www.oysysushi.com*

South Loopers say this "hip" territory is a "great addition" to the area for serving "fun, fresh, creative sushi" and

"Japanese bistro offerings" at "reasonable prices" in a "sleek", "hi-tech" "setting" with "sincere" "service" and "outdoor seating in summer across from Grant Park" — just be prepared for the "alien green lighting"; N.B. the North Suburban location is unrated, and the River North branch opened post-*Survey*.

### Pacific Blue                    – – – M
*536C Crescent Blvd. (N. Main St.), Glen Ellyn, 630-469-1080*
At his new West Suburban seafooder, Jonji Gaffud (ex 120 Ocean Place, Les Deux Autres) cooks up Asian-influenced dishes from an oft-changing, market-based menu; though some 2,000 miles from its namesake, the casual, blue-painted room feels fittingly fresh, captivating kids with crayon-filled beach buckets while adults do their own California dreaming courtesy of the moderately priced wine list; N.B. weekends feature live music.

### Palm, The                    23 19 21 $51
*Swissôtel, 323 E. Wacker Dr. (bet. Lake Shore Dr. & Michigan Ave.), 312-616-1000*
*Northbrook Court, 2000 Northbrook Ct. (Lake Cook Rd.), Northbrook, 847-239-7256*
*www.thepalm.com*
Offshoots of an "old-school", "upmarket" steakhouse "chain", these "satisfying" Loop and North Suburban spots are magnets for "expense-account" meat eaters who "enjoy" manhandling the "huge portions" of "fantastic steaks and lobsters" "while pondering what it takes to make it onto the walls" of "caricatures" that grace the "classic" decor; truants take issue with some "diffident" servers, though, and mark the pair in the "middle" range of some "very tough competition"; N.B. there's no "power-lunch" service at the Northbrook branch.

### Pane Caldo                    23 19 22 $56
*72 E. Walton St. (bet. Michigan Ave. & Rush St.), 312-649-0055; www.pane-caldo.com*
"Life is better at" this "small", "elegant" Gold Coast "gem" thanks to a frequently changing menu of "memorable" Northern Italian food and "excellent service" from an "attentive" staff; it's "perfect for a decadently long weekday lunch or romantic dinner for two" — especially if you can afford to "spend a ton of money."

### Papagus Greek Taverna                    18 17 19 $30
*Oakbrook Center Mall, 272 Oakbrook Ctr. (Rte. 83), Oak Brook, 630-472-9800; www.leye.com*
"You can rely on" this "friendly", "festive", "good-for-the-whole-family" West Suburban spot for a "solid" selection of "above-average" Greek goodies and "cute decor"; but while supporters assert that it's one of the "best [of its kind] outside of Greektown", those who find it "faux" in feel

chorus that it "lacks the charm of [that] section of the city"; N.B. the River North branch closed post-*Survey*.

### Papa Milano   18 | 11 | 16 | $26
*951 N. State St. (bet. E. Walton Pl. & Oak St.), 312-787-3710*
A Gold Coast "hangout" since "the neighborhood's pre-chic era", this "old-school" Southern Italian "institution" (dating from 1951) continues to cook up "family portions" of "comfort-food" dishes "the way these places used to" in a "warm and casual atmosphere"; those with other opinions find the food "ok" but think "there's better nearby"; N.B. the Food rating may not reflect a post-*Survey* chef change.

### Pappadeaux Seafood Kitchen   21 | 18 | 19 | $32
*798 W. Algonquin Rd. (Golf Rd.), Arlington Heights, 847-228-9551*
*921 Pasquinelli Dr. (Oakmont Ln.), Westmont, 630-455-9846*
*www.pappas.com*
Shellfish fans favor the "outstanding crawfish étouffée" and other Cajun-Creole cookin' from this pair of suburban "chain" representatives specializing in seafood, where the "Mardi Gras fun" goes on all year with various "special" "price breaks" sweetening the pot; still, annoyed anglers point to "sporadic service" and "earsplitting" environs as reasons to go fish elsewhere.

### Parkers' Ocean Grill   24 | 22 | 23 | $44
*1000 31st St. (Highland Ave.), Downers Grove, 630-960-5701;*
*www.selectrestaurants.com*
Expect "lots of interesting choices" of "fresh, carefully prepared" fish dishes "presented with a lot of flair" by a "knowledgeable" staff at this "classy" West Suburban seafooder, where the "upscale clublike environment" is "tastefully decorated" and "the bar is especially festive and fun" on weekends when there's live entertainment; careful, though, as a contingent of frugal fin fans finds it "pricey."

### Park Grill   22 | 21 | 21 | $31
*Millennium Park, 11 N. Michigan Ave. (bet. Madison &*
*Washington Sts.), 312-521-7275; www.parkgrillchicago.com*
"Reasonably priced" and "very good" Eclectic–New American fare gets a "beautiful setting" with "fireplaces, floor-to-ceiling windows" and "great views of the skating rink and Millennium Park" at this Loop location that's also "convenient to the Art Institute"; some say the one-year-old's staffers are still "getting their act together", but most think they have "real possibilities"; N.B. there's outdoor dining in summer.

### Parthenon ◑   21 | 15 | 18 | $25
*314 S. Halsted St. (bet. Jackson Blvd. & Van Buren St.),*
*312-726-2407; www.theparthenon.com*
Groupies of this "Greektown classic" go for "spit-roasted lamb", "flaming cheese" and other "homemade" Hellenic fare from a 100-plus item menu, presented by a "mature

and attentive" staff in a "fun setting" that makes "you feel like dancing (but it's too crowded)"; if that's not enough, it's a "fantastic value" and the "late-hours" kitchen (1 AM on Friday and Saturday) appeals to the night-owl crowd.

## Pasha ●◐図 ▽ | 18 | 21 | 17 | $36 |
*642 N. Clark St. (bet. Erie & Ontario Sts.), 312-397-0100; www.psharestaurant.com*
Exotic name aside, this River North nightspot serves "very good" Italian "eats" with New French and Med influences until 3 AM Monday through Friday (4 AM Saturday) for those who are otherwise "hard pressed to get late-night fare"; service may not always be up to snuff, but the sidewalk seating is "nice in summer", and "women love" to "sneak off to" the "champagne bar hidden" in "the ladies room."

## Pasta Palazzo ⊅ ▽ | 18 | 16 | 17 | $16 |
*1966 N. Halsted St. (Armitage Ave.), 773-248-1400*
"For a casual night out", bargain-hunters hail this "cozy", "dependable" Lincoln Park Italian whose "quick, simple pasta" dishes may be "nothing to write home about" but are "great for the price"; still, some "might not like the communal tables", and "stop by the ATM" first ; N.B. ratings may not reflect a post-*Survey* change in ownership.

## Pasteur | 21 | 21 | 17 | $35 |
*5525 N. Broadway St. (bet. Bryn Mawr & Catalpa Aves.), 773-878-1061; www.pasteurrestaurant.com*
Edgewater excursionists enjoy the "exceptional flavors" and "fresh ingredients" of the "upscale" Vietnamese–New French cuisine at this "dreamy" "Indochina-inspired" spot that's "so realistic you can almost feel the tropical heat", "especially when it's warm enough to open the front windows"; even so, some guerrilla grumps gab about it "resting on its laurels" and being "too pricey"; N.B. it plans to close in late 2005 then reopen with a new concept.

## Pegasus ● | 20 | 19 | 20 | $26 |
*130 S. Halsted St. (bet. Adams & Monroe Sts.), 312-226-4666*
## Pegasus on the Fly ●
*Midway Int'l Airport, 5700 S. Cicero Ave., Concourse A (55th St.), 773-581-1522*
*www.pegasuschicago.com*
Fans fly to this "festive" Greektown "fave" for "reliable", "right-on" Greek fare served by a "professional staff", and fresh-air fanciers feel there's "nothing better on a summer night than drinks and meze" in its "rooftop dining" space with a "wonderful view of the city"; P.S. the Midway location is "surprisingly good for airport food."

## Penang ● | 19 | 15 | 15 | $20 |
*2201 S. Wentworth Ave. (Cermak Rd.), 312-326-6888*
For the faithful, "it's hard to believe" this "popular Chinatown eatery" "is a chain" spot, considering its "interesting"

concept – "a wide range of Malaysian" and other Southeast Asian food that approvers call "authentic" and "cheap, but good", mixed with "Japanese offerings" that many mark as "mediocre"; "tropical drinks and a late [1 AM] closing time are a plus", but no one's raving about the decor or service.

### Penny's Noodle Shop          20  12  17  $13

*1542 N. Damen Ave. (North Ave.), 773-394-0100;*
*www.pennysnoodleshop.com*
*3400 N. Sheffield Ave. (Roscoe St.), 773-281-8222;*
*www.pennysnoodleshop.com*
*950 W. Diversey Pkwy. (Sheffield Ave.), 773-281-8448;*
*www.pennysnoodleshop.com*
*1130 Chicago Ave. (Harlem Ave.), Oak Park, 708-660-1300;*
*www.pennysnoodleshopoakpark.com*

Penny-wise people praise this group of Asian assimilators as a "twentysomething's dream" "for a casual night" of noshing on "delicious noodles of all types"; a few complain that "everything tastes the same", claiming they're "crowded because of price, not quality", but many more maintain that "you can't beat the value"; N.B. the Lakeview locale is BYO, and the Oak Park branch opened post-*Survey.*

### Pepper Lounge ◗          21  21  19  $32

*3441 N. Sheffield Ave. (Clark St.), 773-665-7377;*
*www.pepperlounge.com*

"Surprisingly delightful", this "swank", "cozy" Wrigleyville establishment "right in the heart of Cubs country" gets peppered with praise for its "consistently scrumptious" New American cooking, and for being "upscale" without the commensurate prices; it's also an "excellent date place" thanks to a "romantic garden" and "killer martinis" (including "one of the best chocolate [ones] in town") that are nothing to sneeze at.

### Pete Miller's Seafood &          22  20  20  $42
### Prime Steak

*1557 Sherman Ave. (bet. Davis & Grove Sts.), Evanston,*
*847-328-0399 ◗*
*412 N. Milwaukee Ave. (Dundee Rd.), Wheeling, 847-243-3700*
*www.petemillers.com*

These "well-done" North Suburban steakhouse sibs have some carnivores salivating for their "straightforward steak-and-potato menu" – as well as "incredible burgers" – served in a "dark, masculine atmosphere" that showcases "great live jazz" (Tuesday–Saturday); still, dryer wits won't rush back, calling the "inconsistent" eats "overpriced."

### Petterino's          18  19  19  $38

*Goodman Theatre Bldg., 150 N. Dearborn St. (Randolph St.),*
*312-422-0150; www.leye.com*

A "blast from the past", this Loop "power-lunch" and "pre-theater choice" draws positive reviews from many critics for

its "broad selection" of Traditional American "standards"
and its overall "feel of the '40s"; others, though, pan the
"dated dishes", "fake Sardi's" decor and "service gaffes",
griping that "they should be used to being busy now";
P.S. it gets "crowded" and "loud" "before a show" and
"reservations are a must."

### P.F. CHANG'S CHINA BISTRO          20 | 19 | 18 | $26 |

*530 N. Wabash Ave. (Grand Ave.), 312-828-9977*
*2361 Fountain Square Dr. (bet. Butterfield & Meyers Rds.),*
*Lombard, 630-652-9977*
*1819 Lake Cook Rd. (Northbrook Court Dr.), Northbrook,*
*847-509-8844*
*www.pfchangs.com*
Champions of this "Chinese chain" gang with a national
presence cheer that they're a "consistent", "good choice"
for "great", "upscale" "Americanized food" ("everyone
loves the lettuce wraps") in a "fun", "noisy and crowded"
atmosphere staffed by "upbeat servers"; the quality of the
latter's efforts appears to vary by location, and detractors
who find the chow "derivative" grunt "go to Chinatown."

### Philander's Oak Park          ▽ 19 | 16 | 16 | $40 |

*Carleton Hotel, 1120 Pleasant St. (bet. Maple Ave. & Marion St.),*
*Oak Park, 708-848-4250; www.carletonhotel.com*
New American fare including "good", "fresh seafood" is
dished up in a "dark" setting with "wood walls and vintage
photographs", a "piano bar" and "big, comfy booths spaced
well apart" at this "Oak Park standby"; a few feel it's "not
worth a long trip", but more maintain that it's a "comfortable
place", especially for "the older set"; N.B. the Food rating
may not reflect a post-*Survey* chef change.

### Phil & Lou's          ▽ 21 | – | 17 | $30 |

*1124 W. Madison St. (bet. Halsted St. & Racine Ave.),*
*312-455-0070; www.philandlous.com*
"No ordinary comfort-food" place, this West Loop American
features a "good-variety menu" "with something for
everyone" ("from simple dishes" to "interesting specials"
"with sophisticated flair"); following a post-*Survey* move
from its former Madison location a block away, it remains
a "great" "place to stop before sports or concerts", in part
thanks to "the shuttle to the United Center" offered on some
event days; N.B. lunch is no longer served.

### Phil Stefani's 437 Rush ⊠          22 | 20 | 19 | $43 |

*437 N. Rush St. (E. Hubbard St.), 312-222-0101;*
*www.stefanirestaurants.com*
Raters rush for the "reliable", "good steakhouse" fare
and "Italian specialties" at this "upscale" yet "warm and
inviting" River North restaurant in the "old Riccardo's
space"; perhaps it's "not the greatest place on earth, but it's
reliable" and "pleasant"; P.S. some prospectors purport it

has a "nice sugar-daddy scene", while naturists give a nod to the "outdoor patio for summer lunching (a must)."

### Phoenix     22 | 12 | 15 | $21

*2131 S.Archer Ave., 2nd fl. (Wentworth Ave.), 312-328-0848*
Dim sum-aritans divide over the rolling repasts at this "busy, noisy" Chinatown spot that's "somewhat more sophisticated" "than others in the neighborhood" (and also serves "tasty" Mandarin eats) – most declare those "diverse", "delicious" diminutive dishes (doled out "daily" until 3 PM) are "worth it", even if they're "more expensive", while a few suggest there are "better options"; P.S. some staffers are "only so-so on English."

### Piazza Bella     22 | 18 | 20 | $27

*Roscoe Village, 2116 W. Roscoe St. (bet. Damen & Western Aves.), 773-477-7330; www.piazzabella.com*
Roscoe Village people prefer the "top-notch", "homey" Italian cooking and "creative specials" at this "small and quaint" "gem" where a "really nice", "knowledgeable staff" provides "fine service"; it's no use to "hope this one stays hidden", though – "word is out" and it's "gaining in popularity", which means it now "gets crowded" and "noisy on weekends", so "make reservations."

### Piece     20 | 15 | 16 | $19

*1927 W. North Ave. (bet. Damen & Wolcott Aves.), 773-772-4422; www.piecechicago.com*
"If you need a break from traditional Chicago pizza", try the "extremely flavorful", "unique" "New Haven–style" thin-crust variety served "with all the trimmings" and a selection of "beers from around the world" ("they [also] make their own") at this "reasonably priced" Bucktown eatery; its "good energy" and "funky" staff also haul "hipsters" into its "loftlike dining room and spacious bar."

### Pierrot Gourmet     20 | 18 | 18 | $24

*Peninsula Hotel, 108 E. Superior St. (Rush St.), 312-573-6749; www.peninsula.com*
"Terrific French sandwiches and salads", "good pastries" and "great wines by the glass" combine to "deliver a simple, delicious meal in a warm and sunny space" at this "cute bistro", a River North "oasis" in the Peninsula Hotel, where "the communal table almost always has a seat"; P.S. it's also "a great place for quiet alfresco" dining.

### Pine Yard Restaurant     19 | 12 | 15 | $22

*1033 Davis St. (Oak St.), Evanston, 847-475-4940; www.pineyardrestaurant.com*
Longtime loyalists of this North Suburban Chinese "favorite" stand up for its "great", "fresh-tasting" fare (ranging "from Mandarin to Szechuan" to Cantonese) that's "better than the run-of-the-mill" competition's; still, changelings chide that "the food hasn't been the same" "since it moved" in

2000, say the "dinerlike surroundings" "need work" and throw in some service "complaints" for good measure.

### Ping Pong ⬤     21   18   16   $19
*3322 N. Broadway St. (bet. Aldine Ave. & Buckingham Pl.), 773-281-7575; www.eatpingpong.com*

"Hip" game boys 'n' girls bounce over to this "glam", "gay" Lakeview spot, a "tiny, trendy" BYO offering a "quality" "mélange of delights" (it "has a small Asian menu but does everything well") in a "stark", "spare atmosphere"; it's "cheap", too, and "nice late at night" (with a kitchen that "stays open" every evening until midnight), plus it's "fun to sit on the sidewalk" and indulge in a little "people-watching on warm days."

### Pita Inn     –   –   –   I
*9854 N. Milwaukee Ave. (Golf Rd.), Glenview, 847-759-9990*
*3910 W. Dempster St. (Crawford St.), Skokie, 847-677-0211*
*122 S. Elmhurst Rd. (Dundee Rd.), Wheeling, 847-808-7733*
*www.pitainn.com*

Whether for "quick [table] service or takeout", the "superb" Middle Eastern–Med fare (including "fresh-made pita", "tasty falafel and baba ghanoush") would be "a bargain at twice the price" at these North Suburban "gold mines" that some surveyors say serve "the best fast food" going; they're "always busy", "no matter what time of day", "but worth a little wait."

### Pizza Capri     19   13   17   $18
*1501 E. 53rd St. (Harper Ave.), 773-324-7777*
*1733 N. Halsted St. (Willow St.), 312-280-5700*
*962 W. Belmont Ave. (Sheffield Ave.), 773-296-6000*
*www.pizzacapri.com*

"Great gourmet pizza, salads and sandwiches" get the nod at this trio of "deep-dish" and "thin"-crust creators, known for "fresh, appealing" options like the "Thai chicken pie", not to mention a "nice relaxed atmosphere" and a "friendly staff"; since we're talkin' Chicago 'za, there are contentious critics who counter it's "not that impressive"; N.B. the Decor rating may not reflect a post-*Survey* expansion of the Lincoln Park branch.

### Pizza D.O.C.     21   15   16   $23
*2251 W. Lawrence Ave. (Western Ave.), 773-784-8777; www.pizza-doc.com*

"Awesome", "authentic European-style" "thin-crust" "pizza cooked in a wood-burning oven" is "elevated to a fine art" at this "favorite" Lincoln Square pie palace that also serves some "great pasta dishes"; some see it as "trendy", others as "family-oriented", but most agree it's "crowded" ever since it "has been discovered", with the impatient pointing to "slow service" as part of the problem.

**Pizza Rustica** — — — M
*3913 N. Sheridan Ave. (Sheffield Ave.), 773-404-8955*
Veterans of the 'za wars will want to check out the Venetian-
style version (thin and flaky) at this small Wrigleyville
storefront 'pizza kitchen' and BYO, which also serves other
Italian dishes made from family recipes; you can create
your own slice using various toppings (including fresh
mozzarella) or personalize a pasta dish by choosing from a
list of noodles and sauces.

**Pizzeria Uno** ◗ 22 17 18 $19
*29 E. Ohio St. (Wabash Ave.), 312-321-1000*
**Pizzeria Due** ◗
*619 N. Wabash Ave. (bet. Ohio & Ontario Sts.), 312-943-2400*
*www.unos.com*
Holding their own near the top of the pie charts, this
venerable duo delights devotees by "deep-dish"-ing up
"pizza perfection" in the form of "one-and-only" creations
that are a surefire way to "keep the family happy", even if
they're "not cheap" and you may have to "wait under less
than pleasant conditions at key dining times."

**P.J. Clarke's** ◗ 16 14 15 $23
*Embassy Suites Hotel, 302 E. Illinois St. (Columbus Dr.),
312-670-7500*
*1204 N. State Pkwy. (Division St.), 312-664-1650*
*www.pjclarkschicago.com*
While admirers groove on this "great tavern" twosome in
the Gold Coast and Streeterville for their "plentiful and
consistently good" Traditional American "comfort" fare
like "steaming hot pot pies" and "sliders, baby" (mini-
burgers), as well as a "cozy neighborhood feel" with "lots
of action", skeptics sneer "you always have to wait for
something", though, and find the "average" "bar food"
"boring" (but at least you can get it till 2 AM).

**Platiyo** 22 20 18 $31
*3313 N. Clark St. (bet. Aldine Ave. & Buckingham Pl.),
773-477-6700; www.platiyo.com*
"The owners of Mia Francesca show that they can do"
"top-shelf" "Mexican as well" at this "exciting", "thriving"
Lakeview "gem", where a "nice mix" of "flavorful" food
(including "must-try desserts") is paired with "heavenly
drinks" and "good vibes"; still, "don't expect to be seated"
promptly, even "with reservations", as the "people standing"
"at the bar" will attest.

**Poag Mahone's Carvery &** — — — M
**Ale House** ⊠
*175 W. Jackson St. (bet. S. La Salle & S. Wells Sts.), 312-566-9100;
www.poagmahone.com*
Its name means 'kiss my ass' in Gaelic, but that's the only
attitude you'll encounter at this handsome, business-casual

spot in the Loop (near the Board of Trade); it specializes in burgers, carved-meat sandwiches and other Traditional American fare, and has an Old Chicago ambiance that includes vintage stockyard photography and a 'Wall of Fame' with Chicago characters known for 'doing it their way.'

**Pompei Bakery**  19 ⟩ 13 ⟩ 15 ⟩ $13 ⟩

*2955 N. Sheffield Ave. (Wellington St.), 773-325-1900*
*1531 W. Taylor St. (Ashland Ave.), 312-421-5179*
*17 W. 744 22nd St. (S. Summit Ave.), Oakbrook Terrace, 630-620-0600*
*1261 E. Higgins Rd. (bet. National Pkwy. & N. Meacham Rd.), Schaumburg, 847-619-5001*
*www.pompeipizza.com*
Eaters erupt with enthusiasm over this small chain's "tasty" Italian edibles (including "a wide variety of pizza") that "hit the spot" for a "quick lunch", "cheap-eats dinner" or "fab carryout" "when you don't feel like cooking"; convenience and "reasonable prices" combat any criticism of the "crowded" conditions and "cafeteria-style service."

**Porter's Steakhouse** ⊠  – ⟩ – ⟩ – ⟩ E ⟩

*Hotel 71, 71 E. Wacker Dr. (bet. Michigan & Wabash Aves.), 312-462-7071*
It took a while after Fuse fizzled for another restaurant to check into Hotel 71, but this newcomer – the third outpost of a small chain – is now offering Loop meat-seekers classic cuts of prime beef and other steakhouse fare, with seafood and sandwiches rounding out the menu; N.B. breakfast and lunch are also served.

**Potbelly Sandwich Works**  20 ⟩ 14 ⟩ 17 ⟩ $9 ⟩

*One Illinois Ctr., 111 E. Wacker Dr. (Michigan Ave.), 312-861-0013* ⊠
*508 N. Clark St. (bet. Grand & Illinois Aves.), 312-644-9131*
*2264 N. Lincoln Ave. (bet. Belden & Webster Aves.), 773-528-1405*
*The Shops at North Bridge, 520 N. Michigan Ave. (Grand Ave.), 312-644-1008*
*3424 N. Southport Ave. (Roscoe St.), 773-289-1807*
*190 N. State St. (Lake St.), 312-683-1234*
*175 W. Jackson Blvd. (bet. Financial Pl. & Wells St.), 312-588-1150* ⊠
*303 W. Madison St. (Franklin St.), 312-346-1234* ⊠
*55 W. Monroe St. (Dearborn St.), 312-577-0070* ⊠
*1422 W. Webster Ave. (Clybourn Ave.), 773-755-1234*
*www.potbelly.com*
*Additional locations throughout the Chicago area*
Devoted Dagwoods have decided this "proliferating chain" of "holy-grail" sandwich specialists "far outshines the others" for its "terrific", "cheap" "hot subs" and other "wonderfully messy" "oven-toasted" bounty-between-bread, all washed down with "great shakes"; "don't let the long lines scare you" – they "move at a quick pace" thanks

to "the insane speed of the superhuman" staffers, though some surveyors wish they would "offer more seating."

### Prairie Grass Cafe                    – – – M

*601 Skokie Blvd. (bet. Dundee & Lake Cook Rds.), Northbrook, 847-205-4433; www.prairiegrasscafe.com*
Chefs Sarah Stegner and George Bumbaris (both ex Ritz-Carlton Dining Room) blend their love of quality seasonal ingredients and classic technique in their monthly changing, down-to-earth New American menus at this North Shore newcomer; the eclectic wine list was compiled by former Seasons manager Rohit Nambiar (Stegner's husband), and the casually sophisticated space is rife with wood, stone and evocative landscapes that hint at Prairie School influences.

### Privata Café                    – – – I

*935 N. Damen Ave. (Walton St.), 773-342-6681*
Now in its fourth incarnation, this Eclectic Wicker Park BYO keeps the faith with its bargain-priced Mexican-Italian fare, cooked in a central open kitchen amid a funky space with plank floors, hip artwork, high-top tables and two long settees serving as banquettes; an upright piano anchors the back wall (patrons are welcome to tickle the ivories) and a side door opens into an adjacent art gallery; N.B. don't miss the house sauces to go.

### P.S. Bangkok                    22  13  17  $20

*3345 N. Clark St. (bet. Addison St. & Belmont Ave.), 773-871-7777; www.psbangkok.com*
*2521 N. Halsted St. (bet. Fullerton Pkwy. & Wrightwood Ave.), 773-348-0072*
Thai-aholics tout the "top-notch", "authentic" food at these Lincoln Park and Wrigleyville siblings (separately owned by a brother and sister), saying it's not only "fresh" but a "super value" – and it makes for good "takeout", too; N.B. the Clark Street location serves beer and wine, as well as a "great Sunday brunch" buffet with "a mind-boggling selection", while the Halsted Street branch is BYO.

### Public Landing                    ∇ 21  23  21  $35

*200 W. Eighth St. (bet. Canal & State Sts.), Lockport, 815-838-6500; www.publiclandingrestaurant.com*
"One of the best-kept secrets" in the Southwest Suburbs, this "old"-school Traditional American deserves a look, according to fans of its "excellent dining" and "beautiful", "historic" (1844) setting "on the I&M canal"; N.B. the Decor rating may not reflect a post-*Survey* renovation.

### Puck's at the MCA                    17  18  12  $24

*Museum of Contemporary Art, 220 E. Chicago Ave.*
*(Mies van der Rohe Way), 312-397-4034; www.mcachicago.org*
Wolfgang-watchers get their "Spago fix" at this "beautiful" Streeterville "lunch spot" with "a fabulous view" and "great outdoor dining"; "as far as decor, well, it's in an art gallery,

isn't it?" – though some say it "outpaces" the "limited menu" of "good" but "pricey" New American eats; N.B. jazz fans "love the terrace" on Tuesdays "in the summertime", when live music is offered.

**Pump Room, The** ◗           22  25  23  $65
*Omni Ambassador East Hotel, 1301 N. State Pkwy. (Goethe St.), 312-266-0360; www.pumproom.com*
"Nostalgic dining" with an "old-money feel" skews New American at this Gold Coast "landmark" known for "oak panels", "deep booths" and "movie-star" "memorabilia on the walls"; proponents praise the "grand food and service" and "fancy" "Sunday champagne brunch", but antis are less pumped about the frequently "changing chefs" whose food "costs a kidney"; P.S. the "great dance floor" swings into action on weekends.

**Rainforest Cafe**                 12  22  14  $23
*605 N. Clark St. (bet. Ohio & Ontario Sts.), 312-787-1501*
*Gurnee Mills Mall, 6170 W. Grand Ave. (bet. I-94 & Hunt Club Rd.), Gurnee, 847-855-7800*
*Woodfield Mall, 121 Woodfield Mall (bet. Golf & Higgins Rds.), Schaumburg, 847-619-1900*
*www.rainforestcafe.com*
Concrete "jungle" natives and "tourists" tell us that the "simulated rainstorms", "colorful aquariums" and "all the animatronic" critters (from "elephants and gorillas" to "howling monkeys") constitute a "unique environment" that in itself is "worth a trip" to these chain outposts; discriminating diners "indifferent" to the "overpriced" American eats, though, exclaim that "entertaining" "antsy kids" is the "only reason to go."

**Raj Darbar**                      –  –  –  M
*2660 N. Halsted St. (Wrightwood Ave.), 773-348-1010; www.rajdarbar.com*
For Lincoln Parkers in search of Indian fare, this comfortably upscale spot is a popular alternative to the long trip to Devon Avenue; big portions of fresh, traditional dishes, along with some unusual offerings, are served with civility in a more tasteful setting than the average neighborhood joint – albeit with commensurate prices; N.B. the big all-you-can-eat weekend brunch is a bargain.

**Ranalli's**                       16  11  15  $18
*2301 N. Clark St. (Belden Ave.), 773-244-2300; www.ranallisonclark.com ◗*
*1925 N. Lincoln Ave. (bet. Armitage Ave. & Clark St.), 312-642-4700*
*1522 W. Montrose Ave. (bet. Ashland & Greenview Aves.), 773-506-8800; www.ranallisupnorth.com ◗*
"Reliable" "Chicago staples" for "decent pizza", these "loud, busy" "sports bars" are "great" for "happy hour" and

"people-watching" (especially the patio at the Lincoln
Avenue locale); meanwhile, though, the "mediocre decor"
and "average" edibles have some surveyors saying "you
go here to drink, not eat"; N.B. the Decor rating may not
reflect a post-*Survey* expansion of the Uptown branch.

## RA Sushi Bar Restaurant ◖     – | – | – | M

*1139 N. State St. (E. Elm St.), 312-274-0011; www.rasushi.com*
This hip Gold Coast chain link spins clubby music, slices
an extensive raw-fish selection and serves up a menu of
traditional Japanese fare; the sleek decor is all black, red
and blond wood, with hanging paper lanterns and a long
semicircular sushi bar with a waterfall-wall backdrop; best
beverage bets include the long beer list and a few sake
and creative martini selections; N.B. happy-hour bargains
run Monday–Friday, 4–7 PM.

## Raw Bar & Grill ◖     ▽ 19 | 15 | 18 | $29

*3720 N. Clark St. (bet. Grace St. & Waveland Ave.), 773-348-7291;*
*www.rawbarandgrill.com*
"The name does not really do it justice" since it's "not
[just] a raw bar" – rather, "you can find some rare treats"
from a "creative" Eclectic menu with a seafood emphasis,
partnered with a "huge selection of delicious martinis", at
this "unassuming", "romantic" Wrigleyville eatery that's a
"nice place to spend an evening with friends" or "go after
a Cubs game."

## Redfish     16 | 15 | 15 | $28

*400 N. State St. (Kinzie St.), 312-467-1600;*
*www.redfishamerica.com*
For fans of Cajun and Creole seafood, this "informal" River
North "hangout" slings "huge portions" at "reasonable
prices" in a "tavern atmosphere" (or "stay in the lounge and
watch the blues" and jazz bands on weekends); purists
propose you "don't go with high expectations", saying the
"tepid" cooking is "inconsistent" and "not authentic."

## Red Light     23 | 24 | 21 | $41

*820 W. Randolph St. (Green St.), 312-733-8880;*
*www.redlight-chicago.com*
"Amiable chef" Jackie Shen has "raised the bar several
notches" with her "imaginative", "fantabulous Asian fusion"
fare at this "kinky", "clublike" "haunt" in the Market District;
the sometimes "spicy" offerings come with "sassy service"
and "knockout drinks", but some rueful raters are red in the
face from "shouting over the loud", "pulsating music" and
aren't willing to shell out the "serious money."

## Red Lion Pub     15 | 19 | 17 | $17

*2446 N. Lincoln Ave. (Fullerton Pkwy.), 773-348-2695;*
*www.theredlionpub.com*
Royalists roar for this "nice, old-fashioned" Lincoln Park
"Brit bar" that makes you "feel like you're back in jolly old

London"; it's not just "comfortable" — it's "tacky, fusty and utterly charming", with "basic" "English pub food" (the "fish 'n' chips are a favorite, and so are the bangers and mash") and a "good selection of beers" that make it "great for an ale anytime"; P.S. "watch out for that ghost!"

### Red Star Tavern    15 | 17 | 15 | $24

*1700 Randall Rd. (Commons Dr.), Algonquin, 847-458-4500*
*1650 Premium Outlets Blvd. (Farnsworth St.), Aurora,*
*630-978-8800* ●
*1800 Tower Dr. (Aviator Rd.), Glenview, 847-486-0099* ●
*Deerfield Commons, 695 Deerfield Rd. (Waukegan Rd.),*
*Deerfield, 847-948-9700* ●
*Geneva Commons, 1602 Commons Dr. (bet. Bricher &*
*Randall Sts.), Geneva, 630-845-0845* ●
*www.redstartavern.net*

Some give these suburban satellites of a growing national group red stars for being "friendly" and offering a "large menu" of "surprisingly good" Traditional American "bar food" with "lots of beers"; still, detractors dole out demerits for what they call "average" eats and "noisy", "impersonal" settings that "look like [they were] created by consultants"; N.B. the Aurora and Algonquin sites opened post-*Survey.*

### Retro Bistro 🛇    24 | 18 | 23 | $34

*Mt. Prospect Commons, 1746 W. Golf Rd. (Busse Rd.),*
*Mt. Prospect, 847-439-2424; www.retrobistro.com*

"One of the best in the Northwest 'burbs", this "longtime favorite" is a "gift" thanks to "terrific, authentic [French] bistro food" "nicely paired" with "great wines" and served "at a reasonable cost" by an "attentive but unobtrusive" staff in an "inviting", "unstuffy" "strip-mall" setting; P.S. "the three-course prix fixe is a deal."

### Reza's    20 | 16 | 18 | $22

*5255 N. Clark St. (Berwyn Ave.), 773-561-1898*
*432 W. Ontario St. (Orleans St.), 312-664-4500*
*40 N. Tower Rd. (Butterfield Rd.), Oak Brook, 630-424-9900*
*www.rezasrestaurants.com*

This "bustling" pair of "Persian" cats comes recommended by raters who purr over the "mounds" of "well-priced", "wonderful Middle Eastern food", including a "lunch buffet that's a great deal" and "countless vegetarian" options; others get their backs up over "hit-or-miss service", though, and suggest that the "quality" is "not always consistent"; N.B. the Oak Brook branch opened post-*Survey.*

### Rhapsody    21 | 23 | 21 | $43

*Symphony Ctr., 65 E. Adams St. (bet. Michigan & Wabash Aves.),*
*312-786-9911; www.rhapsodychicago.com*

Those who applaud this Loop New American, a "pleasant dining" destination "in the Symphony Center", are wowed by the "wonderful rhapsody of flavors" in its "adventurous" fare ("like music to the ears"), which is "beautifully served" in a "sophisticated", "airy" "room" or in "a beautiful garden setting in the summer"; critics, though, cavil that the "food is great but not outstanding" and "too pricey" to boot.

### Ribs 'n' Bibs ●                     – | – | – | I
*5300 S. Dorchester Ave. (53rd St.), 773-493-0400*
"Your lips will smack" at the sight of the "melt-in-your-mouth ribs" "smoked on the spot" ("people walking by drool at the scent that billows from the chimney stack") and drenched in "tasty sauce" at this Hyde Park "BBQ pit" whose Old West–style setting is decorated with "pictures of local and national celebrities"; P.S. "it's almost strictly takeout", but there are a few "counter seats" and a sidewalk dining area.

### Rinconcito Sudamericano          ▽  22 | 11 | 20 | $22
*1954 W. Armitage Ave. (Damen Ave.), 773-489-3126*
"Huge portions" of "excellent Peruvian cuisine" combine with "helpful", "friendly service" and "affordable prices" to make this "simple" spot "one of Bucktown's best-kept secrets"; "delighted" diners recommend you "go with at least four people so you can share a variety of dishes"; N.B. a post-*Survey* move is planned.

### Ringo                            ▽  22 | 12 | 17 | $19
*2507 N. Lincoln Ave. (bet. Fullerton Pkwy. & Wrightwood Ave.), 773-248-5788*
"Now getting noticed", this "tiny neighborhood place" in Lincoln Park is "among the best" "seriously cheap" "sushi [spots] in town", and it's "BYO, so it's an even better deal" than some competitors; fence-sitters feel it's "usually good but can miss" occasionally, and per the Decor score, it's clearly "not much for ambiance."

### Rioja ⊠                           – | – | – | E
*5101 N. Clark St. (Carmen Ave.), 773-275-9191*
Once Atlantique, this tapas bar from the same owners serves up generous portions of those Spanish small plates in a whimsically decorated, earth-toned dining room; the classic and creative tastes are supplemented by moderately priced entrees and a Mediterranean-focused wine list; N.B. sidewalk seating has been added.

### Rique's                          – | – | – | I
*5004 N. Sheridan Rd. (W. Argyle St.), 773-728-6200; www.riques10.com*
Inexpensive, authentic regional Mexican eats made with fresh ingredients appeal to compadres of this casual, colorful cantina enlivening an otherwise dingy stretch of Uptown; serving from breakfast through a sensible bedtime (10 or 11 PM, depending on day of the week), it also offers *horchata* and milkshakes – or you can BYO for no charge.

### Rise
  23   22   17   $31

*3401 N. Southport Ave. (Roscoe St.), 773-525-3535;*
*www.risesushi.com*

"Follow the hip and trendy" to this "bustling" Japanese spot in Wrigleyville, where the "consistently fresh" fare is "creative", the "flavors are excellent", the "drinks are exotic" and the "modern, minimalist" environment that throbs with "clubby" music is even better "in the summer when they open the huge floor-to-ceiling windows" and "fashionable people" "crowd" the patio.

### ristorante we
  17   18   13   $42

(fka We)

*W Hotel, 172 W. Adams St. (LaSalle St.), 312-917-5608;*
*www.werestaurant.com*

The editorial 'we' wavers in its conviction concerning this "oasis of hipness in the Loop" – the 'us' crowd praises its 2004 Northern "Italian makeover" as "an improvement over the previous incarnation" thanks to "nicely done" fare and a "sharp", "low-key atmosphere", while the 'thems' think that the "mixed service" does nothing to enhance the "just-good food"; N.B. the Food rating may not reflect the post-*Survey* transition to a Tuscan steakhouse menu.

### Ritz-Carlton Café
  –   24   24   $38

*Ritz-Carlton Hotel, 160 E. Pearson St. (Michigan Ave.),*
*312-573-5160; www.fourseasons.com*

Eclectic eats from chef Kevin Hickey's new menu join signature faves like the Ritz burger and French onion soup at this "top casual dining destination" in the posh Streeterville hotel; the "well-appointed" "respite in the lobby", with a soundtrack of "running water in the fountain" and "some of the best service" around, makes a "delightful break from the hustle and bustle" of Michigan Avenue.

### RITZ-CARLTON DINING ROOM
  –   28   28   $79

*Ritz-Carlton Hotel, 160 E. Pearson St. (Michigan Ave.),*
*312-573-5223; www.fourseasons.com*

After achieving a culinary clean sweep last year (with top scores for Food, Service and Decor), this "tony" Streeterville spot saw the departure of its champion chef team, followed by the arrival of toque Kevin Hickey (ex Four Seasons Atlanta); a skew toward imaginative New American cuisine takes it in a fresh direction, though patrons still "put on the Ritz", being "treated like royalty" by a "solicitous" staff within the "luxurious", "old-world setting"; N.B. rolling dim sum and sushi have been added to the lavish brunch.

### Riva
  18   21   18   $44

*Navy Pier, 700 E. Grand Ave. (Lake Shore Dr.), 312-644-7482;*
*www.stefanirestaurants.com*

"As the sun sets and the city lights up", shore birds "show off views to visitors" at this "lakefront" Streeterville New

American serving "fresh", "simply prepared", "good-quality seafood dishes"; naysayers say it's "nice" "if you must eat on Navy Pier" but claim that "uneven", "overpriced" fare and "lukewarm" service make it best for "tourists" and the "captive Shakespeare Theatre audience."

### Rivers ⌦ 16 17 17 $33
*Mercantile Bldg., 30 S. Wacker Dr. (bet. Madison & Monroe Sts.), 312-559-1515; www.riversrestaurant.com*
A "great location" for a Loop "business lunch" or "pre-opera" dining, this "country club for traders" has a "hopping", "huge outdoor bar area during summer months" and a "view of the Chicago River" year-round; some say its "consistent" kitchen turns out "delicious" New American fare, but others snub the same as "ho-hum" and "not a good value", adding that the service is "spotty" and the scene is "frenetic" (though it's "more quiet at night").

### R.J. Grunts 18 16 18 $19
*2056 N. Lincoln Park W. (Dickens Ave.), 773-929-5363; www.leye.com*
"The '60s and '70s are alive and well" at this American "Lincoln Park institution" "where the Lettuce Entertain You food dynasty all began"; "still fun" (and "noisy") "after all these years", it's a "favorite" for "huge, juicy burgers", a "salad bar [that] rocks" and "funky" decor featuring "pictures of past waitresses" and waiters; no wonder diehards declare "don't even think about closing this place."

### RL 22 26 22 $48
*115 E. Chicago Ave. (Michigan Ave.), 312-475-1100; www.rlrestaurant.com*
Shoppers and Gold Coast diners who "want to feel like" they're "part of a Ralph Lauren ad" "dine with the landed gentry" in their "jewels and suits" amid the "unreal world" of this "clubby" American, where the "expensive", "well-presented" "rich-people comfort food" includes some "tableside prep" and a "fabulous brunch"; P.S. "sit outside for great people-watching."

### Robinson's No. 1 Ribs 19 6 13 $20
*225 S. Canal St. (bet. Adams St. & Jackson Blvd.), 312-258-8477*
*655 W. Armitage Ave. (Orchard St.), 312-337-1399*
*940 W. Madison St. (Clinton St.), Oak Park, 708-383-8452*
*www.rib1.com*
Touters of the "tender and meaty" "taste treats" at this trio of barbecue brothers are "amazed that such great ribs come from such holes in the wall"; still, those who find the overall "experience disappointing" declare them "good" but "not the best", and say the "nondescript" atmosphere means you're "better" off "taking it out" or "getting it delivered" (though the separately owned West Loop food emporium location is eat-in only).

## Rock Bottom Brewery ● 14 | 15 | 15 | $20
*1 W. Grand Ave. (State St.), 312-755-9339*
*28256 Diehl Rd. (Winfield Rd.), Warrenville, 630-836-1380*
*www.rockbottom.com*
Hoisters herald this group as being "good places" for "guys or gals" "to hang out" and "eat, talk and laugh" over "great microbrew beers" and "all-American" "bar food"; conversely, critical contributors call the "typical" "chain" profferings "predictable" and the service "haphazard", adding that the corporate moniker "is appropriate."

## Rockit Bar & Grill − | − | − | M
*22 W. Hubbard St. (bet. Dearborn & State Sts.), 312-645-6000;*
*www.rockitbarandgrill.com*
Putting a spin on comfort food, this funky, casual American hangout in River North also slings plenty of signature 'rocktails' within its raw, urban environment of exposed brick, metal, industrial light fixtures and lots of black (plus a cool display of curios and architectural artifacts); other assets include DJ entertainment on weekends, outdoor dining in season, a late-night menu and a huge second bar with pool tables upstairs.

## Roditys ● 19 | 14 | 18 | $24
*222 S. Halsted St. (bet. Adams St. & Jackson Blvd.), 312-454-0800;*
*www.roditys.com*
A "longtime", "reliable" destination for "authentic Greek food" including "any form of lamb", this Greektown "favorite" also gets points for "good service" and its status as a "great late-night spot."

## Ron of Japan 20 | 15 | 18 | $34
*230 E. Ontario St. (bet. Fairbanks Ct. & St. Clair St.), 312-644-6500*
*633 Skokie Blvd. (Dundee Rd.), Northbrook, 847-564-5900*
*www.ronofjapan.com*
Kudos for these city-and-suburban Japanese steakhouse siblings cover the "flavorful food" and "fun show" afforded by the "traditional tableside" prep ("kids love" it and even adults say it's "so campy it's a blast"); still, something is lost in translation for those who call them "dated", "cookie-cutter hibachi" havens, where you may "have to share a table" and the experience "depends on if your chef is having a good day" – plus "you'll smell like cooking oil" "for days."

## Room 22 Restaurant and Lounge − | − | − | E
*22 E. Hubbard St. (bet. State St. & Wabash Ave.), 312-527-4900;*
*www.22restaurant.com*
There's been a plethora of changes (including variations on its name) during this River North newcomer's short history, with the latest incarnation offering a creative but accessible New American menu served in a tony, modern interior with a spacious lounge and more intimate dining room; N.B. oenophiles should consider ordering a 'mixed

bottle' – three choices from the boutique list, served in chemist's beakers.

**RoSal's Italian Kitchen** ☒    ▽ 21 | 17 | 21 | $30

*1154 W. Taylor St. (Racine Ave.), 312-243-2357; www.rosals.com*
Joyous journal-ists jot that they "just love this cute, cozy" and "romantic" Southern Italian spot "with a lot of heart" in Little Italy, where the "homemade, old-country" Sicilian "feast" ferried by "friendly" folks is fit for "big appetites" and "reasonably priced", to boot; P.S. "great wines, too!"

**Rose Angelis**     22 | 19 | 20 | $28

*1314 W. Wrightwood Ave. (bet. Racine & Southport Aves.), 773-296-0081; www.roseangelis.com*
Pasta-loving Lincoln Parkers pine for the "large portions" of "decadent" Italian eats at this "homey", "unpretentious" charmer and "great date place", where it "feels like Aunt Rose herself is back in the kitchen" ("the price is also nice"); weary wags warn "they do not take reservations" for parties of fewer than eight, though, so "be prepared to wait and wait", while others wonder "what all the fuss is about."

**Rosebud, The**     20 | 17 | 18 | $33

*1500 W. Taylor St. (bet. Laflin St. and Ashland), 312-942-1117*
**Rosebud of Highland Park**
*1850 Second St. (Central Ave.), Highland Park, 847-926-4800*
**Rosebud of Naperville**
*48 W. Chicago Ave. (Washington St.), Naperville, 630-548-9800*
**Rosebud on Rush**
*720 N. Rush St. (Superior St.), 312-266-6444*
**Rosebud Theater District** ☒
*3 First National Plaza, 70 W. Madison St. (bet. Clark & Dearborn Sts.), 312-332-9500*
*www.rosebudrestaurants.com*
Offering a "truly Chicago Italian eating experience", this family of *ristoranti* includes the "favorite Little Italy" "original on Taylor" known for "huge" servings of "staples" and "professional, old-world" service in a "chaotic, jam-packed dining" room hung with "pictures of famous" patrons past; objectors oppose the "attitude", "noise" and "overpriced", "not-exceptional" eats, though, and some joke that they're "still waiting for a table", "even with reservations."

**Rosebud Steakhouse**     21 | 18 | 20 | $48

*192 E. Walton St. (Mies van der Rohe Way), 312-397-1000; www.rosebudrestaurants.com*
The Rosebud group's "interesting take on the steakhouse theme" gets the nod for "big food" that's "just plain good" and served in a "refined, clubby" space "best suited to the power lunch or dinner", especially since the staffers "make you feel like part of the club"; detractors who deem its fare "middle of the road", though, say it "could and should be better."

### Roy's
24 | 21 | 22 | $47

*720 N. State St. (Superior St.), 312-787-7599;*
*www.roysrestaurant.com*

Sated surveyors say aloha to "inspired" Hawaii Regional
cuisine, including "creative seafood" dishes, at this "fish-
lover's paradise" in River North, where "the food explodes
with tantalizing flavors" and the "nice wine selection"
includes "tasty" "house" bottles; completing this "real
surprise" are "artistry in the appearance of the dishes",
a "casual but polished" setting and "top-notch service."

### Ruby of Siam
22 | 13 | 17 | $19

*1125 Emerson St. (Ridge Ave.), Evanston, 847-492-1008*
*Skokie Fashion Sq., 9420 Skokie Blvd. (Foster Ave.), Skokie,*
*847-675-7008*
*www.rubyofsiam.com*

These North Suburban Thai twins are touted for a "large
choice" of "well-prepared and delicious" dishes that
many call "the finest" of their kind "in the area"; they're
"moderately priced", too (especially the "great-value
lunch buffet"), and the kitchens "will accommodate to
taste" on the level of spiciness – no surprise then that
some surveyors "could eat there every week."

### Rumba ⊠
14 | 19 | 13 | $38

*351 W. Hubbard St. (Orleans St.), 312-222-1226;*
*www.rumba351.com*

The "idea is on target" at this River North "theme place" –
dinner in a "sexy private banquette that's perfect for a
rendezvous" followed by "a great band and good dancing"
to "salsa the calories off"; still, diners mumble that a "major
improvement is needed" vis-à-vis the "uneven menu" of
Nuevo Latino fare, which is "unauthentic", "secondary to
the fun" and served in "small portions for the cost."

### Rushmore ⊠
23 | 20 | 19 | $45

*1023 W. Lake St. (Carpenter St.), 312-421-8845;*
*www.rushmore-chicago.com*

"Excellent quality" and "inventive", seasonal New American
"twists on comfort classics" like "to-die-for mac 'n' cheese"
appeal to eaters who "embrace" this "comfy, urban" Market
District "gem" set in a "cool minimalist room" "under the
El tracks"; a few vocal voters voice that "it would be great
if they took it down a notch and lowered the prices",
especially considering the "sterile, industrial" space with
trains "rolling overhead."

### Russell's Barbecue
18 | 10 | 12 | $14

*1621 N. Thatcher Ave. (North Ave.), Elmwood Park, 708-453-7065*
*2885 Algonquin Rd. (Rte. 53), Rolling Meadows, 847-259-5710*
*www.russellsbarbecue.com*

A "landmark" in the Western Suburbs, this "great old-
fashioned neighborhood" "throwback" with a "1930s

roadhouse atmosphere" continues to rack up plenty of
takers for its "classic" BBQ served in an "informal" setting
that's "like being on a picnic in a restaurant, wooden
benches and all"; "unimpressed" finger-lickers who
"don't get it", though, deem it "mysteriously popular",
having "expected more from a legend"; N.B. the Rolling
Meadows offshoot is unrated.

**Russian Tea Time**                    21   19   21   $34
*77 E. Adams St. (bet. Michigan & Wabash Aves.), 312-360-0000;*
*www.russianteatime.com*
"A meal fit for a commissar" awaits at this "great option"
in the Loop, where the "extensive, authentic menu" of
"delightfully different" "classic Russian cuisine" includes
"a number of vegetarian dishes" and is accompanied by
"a global selection of vodkas" "as well as caviar"; the
"opulent" setting and "warm hospitality" make you "feel
like you are getting away", plus it's "near the Symphony and
Art Institute", but nag-niks negate the "rich and heavy" food
as "overpriced" and say "service varies widely."

**RUTH'S CHRIS STEAK HOUSE**            25   20   24   $50
*431 N. Dearborn St. (Hubbard St.), 312-321-2725*
*Renaissance, 933 Skokie Blvd. (Dundee Rd.), Northbrook,*
*847-498-6889*
*www.ruthschris.com*
"The steak knives are only for show" since the "butter-
dripping prime" "aged" "beef can be cut with a fork" at
these "sizzling" city-and-suburban steakhouse chainsters,
"a sure choice when quality and service are required";
nevertheless, cranky carnivores complain that "costs add up
quickly" because "everything is à la carte", and "wish" the
"parlor-car atmosphere" "could be a bit less predictable."

**Sabatino's** ◗                        24   17   20   $29
*4441 W. Irving Park Rd. (bet. Cicero & Pulaski Aves.), 773-283-8331*
"Comfortable and consistent", this "old-time" Northern
Italian on the Northwest Side specializes in "outstanding"
"red-sauce" dishes that give "great value for the money",
and its "old-time '50s atmosphere" complete with a "piano
bar" is peopled with a "cast of characters" "right out of
the Rat Pack days"; keep in mind, though, that "you might
miss" it in its "out-of-the-way" location, so look "for the
neon sign out front."

**Sabor**                            ∇  25   22   23   $33
*Schaumburg's Town Square Ctr., 160E S. Roselle Rd.*
*(Schaumburg Rd.), Schaumburg, 847-301-1470*
Chef-owner "Christina Hernandez creates fabulous" and
"authentic" Nuevo Latino food that's paired with "wonderful"
wines" and drinks and served by staffers who "know their
stuff" within the "trendy" setting ("like in Chicago") of this
"small joint" in Schaumburg; with so much going for it, it's

a "definite favorite" and a "fresh change" for foodies in
the Northwest Suburbs.

**Sai Café**　　　　　　　　22　13　18　$29
*2010 N. Sheffield Ave. (Armitage Ave.), 773-472-8080;*
*www.saicafe.com*
"Undiminished despite all the competition", the reputation
of this Lincoln Park Japanese for "quality" fare continues
according to cohorts who covet its "melt-on-your-tongue
sushi" (served in "nice big cuts for the money"), "inventive
rolls" and "excellent cooked" items; detractors dismiss
the "lame room" as "needing a makeover", but most maki-
meisters say the food "makes up in spades" for "what
the ambiance lacks."

**Sal & Carvão Churrascaria**　　　　23　20　24　$49
*739 N. Clark St. (W. Superior St.), 312-932-1100*
*801 E. Algonquin Rd. (Roselle Rd.), Schaumburg, 847-925-0061*
*3008 Finley Rd. (Butterfield Rd.), Downers Grove, 630-512-0900*
*www.salecarvao.com*
"Bring your appetite and loose pants" to this Northwest
Suburban "meat-lover's heaven" and "low-carber's dream",
a Brazilian "churrascaria" steakhouse where 14 "different
meats nightly" are "served by roving" "gauchos" who
are "well trained and polished"; eaters who eschew it as
"expensive" might "go for lunch", which "costs less", or
consider it "more of a party/occasion place"; N.B. the
Downers Grove and River North branches are unrated.

**Salbute**　☒　　　　　　　24　15　17　$36
*20 E. First St. (bet. Garfield & Washington Sts.), Hinsdale,*
*630-920-8077; www.salbute.com*
A daily changing menu of "excellent, authentic" and yet
"creative modern Mexican food" offered up with "awesome
margaritas" weaves its spell over West Suburbanites at
this "funky little bistro-style" spot; its "festive" vibe makes
for an "entertaining night out", but "limited seating" means it
gets "crowded and noisy" ("bring a shoehorn").

**Saloon Steakhouse, The**　　　　23　20　22　$44
*Seneca Hotel, 200 E. Chestnut St. (bet. Lake Shore Dr. &*
*Michigan Ave.), 312-280-5454; www.saloonsteakhouse.com*
"Some of the best cuts of meat" and "nice fish, too", sing
a siren song to surveyors who say "try it (you'll like it)"
about this "dark and cozy" "neighborhood" steakhouse
"tucked away" from but "near the action" in Streeterville;
while it can be mercifully "quiet", "it gets a bit noisy on
weekends, so beware"; P.S. they make "a terrific martini."

**SALPICÓN**　　　　　　　25　20　23　$40
*1252 N. Wells St. (bet. Goethe & Scott Sts.), 312-988-7811;*
*www.salpicon.com*
Owners "Vince and Priscila [Satkoff] rock" at this Old Town
"gem", and the latter "gets it right" with her "high-end",

"gourmet" fare, "a whole different level" of Mexican cuisine with "sauces you want to lick off the plate"; the "tequila menu is as extensive as" the "impressive wine list", and the "festive", "intimate" setting includes the option to "sit outside under the canopy" in warm weather.

### Salvatore's Ristorante ▽ 18 18 18 $29
*525 W. Arlington Pl. (Clark St.), 773-528-1200;*
*www.salvatores-chicago.com*
Since 1977, this "hard-to-find" Lincoln Park "treasure" and "great date place" has served up traditional Northern Italian cooking that's "not so creative but consistently good" in an "upscale interior" with "generally" efficient service.

### Samah ▬ ▬ ▬ M
*3330A N. Clark St. (Buckingham Pl.), 773-248-4606;*
*www.samahlounge.com*
A dreamlike ambiance awaits visitors to this late-night Wrigleyville Middle Eastern lounge whose interior includes multiple seating areas draped and cushioned with luxurious fabrics; classic fare such as falafel and shish kebab is complemented by a range of coffee and tea drinks, belly dancing (Thursdays and Fridays) and optional hookah-puffing, but don't expect a tipple with your toke – no alcohol is served, or allowed in.

### Samba Room 21 20 18 $35
*22 E. Chicago Ave. (Washington St.), Naperville, 630-753-0985;*
*www.sambaroom.net*
Cuban and Brazilian "soul food with a bit of flair" comes to the table amid a "great atmosphere" that includes "a cigar room in the back" at this West Suburban way station; still, some Napervillians are "not impressed", and sensitive sorts say the "noise" level makes it an "auditory hell."

### San Gabriel Mexican Cafe ▬ ▬ ▬ M
*Bannockburn Green Shopping Ctr., 2535 Waukegan Rd.*
*(Half Day Rd.), Bannockburn, 847-940-0200*
North Shore noshers needn't head Downtown for upscale regional Mexican cuisine thanks to this Bannockburn bastion whose seasonal menu (by consulting chef Dudley Nieto) inventively blends modern and rustic influences; both the pumpkin-hued dining room and a selection from the deep tequila list add warmth to the dining experience; N.B. frequent tastings and dinners are offered, plus live mariachi on Thursdays.

### Sangria Restaurant and Tapas Bar ▬ ▬ ▬ M
*901 W. Weed St. (Fremont St.), 312-266-1200;*
*www.sangriachicago.com*
A small-plate sharing concept covering dishes from a whopping 24 Latin countries is the formula at this Lincoln Parker in the former Bub City space; hot and cold tapas creations – from spicy to subtle, meaty to vegetarian – are

offered up with a variety of creative sangria preparations in a relaxed, colorful setting with a big central bar, raised banquettes and a private curtained chef's table.

### San Soo Gab San ◗  – | – | – | M |
*5247 N. Western Ave. (Foster Ave.), 773-334-1589*
"Great" *kalbi* with "abundant *panch'an*", "the small dishes that are a staple of Korean food", make for a "spicy, delicious, messy experience that'll leave you stuffed and craving more" at this "always-packed" Northwest Side spot, where "cubicles provide privacy"; more particular patrons predict that "the overwhelming smell will envelop you" and "your clothes"; N.B. night-owls can 'cue till 6 AM.

### Santorini ◗  21 | 20 | 20 | $31 |
*800 W. Adams St. (Halsted St.), 312-829-8820;*
*www.santorinichicago.com*
The "friendly" folks at this "superb Greekster" ("the best fish place in Greektown") are "true to their roots", with a "great array of" "consistently" "fresh" and "good-quality" fare, "efficient service" and rustic, white-washed "decor that will make you think you are actually on Santorini"; it's a "true joy in winter" thanks to the "wood-burning fireplace", and there's sidewalk seating in summer, too, so if it's "a little more expensive than the others", fans aren't fazed.

### Sapori Trattoria  – | – | – | M |
*2701 N. Halsted St. (W. Schubert Ave.), 773-832-9999;*
*www.saporitrattoria.com*
"Consistently" "great Italian food" such as "spectacular pastas", "excellent appetizers" and "heavenly desserts" draws diners to this "intimate" Lincoln Parker, as do its "excellent wine list" and "tree-lined outdoor [space] in the summer"; P.S. "it's always crowded, so make a reservation."

### Satay  ▽ 18 | 14 | 17 | $18 |
*936 W. Diversey Pkwy. (bet. Halsted St. & Racine Ave.),*
*773-477-0100; www.satayresturant.com*
Those who "love" this Lakeviewer laud its "innovative takes" that put "a tasty spin on Asian cuisine", saying "most work well"; still, confounded contributors claim that "too many menu items" make the concept "confusing" and don't like it when the "dishes don't match the menu descriptions"; N.B. prix fixe lunch is a bargain.

### Sausalito Restaurant & Martini Bar  – | – | – | M |
*543 W. Diversey Pkwy. (Hampden Ct.), 773-248-7263;*
*www.sausalitorestaurant.com*
Tucked away in a Lakeview storefront, this Italian features moderately priced pastas and entrees, as well as designer martinis (and an all-you-can-eat weekend brunch); the cozy space comprises three dining rooms painted different shades of yellow and filled with abstract art, and there's a roomy bar where many patrons choose to dine.

## Sayat Nova
▽ 21  16  17  $24

*157 E. Ohio St. (bet. Michigan Ave. & St. Clair St.), 312-644-9159*
"If you like *Casablanca* you will enjoy" the "romantic casbah" ambiance and "scrumptious" Middle Eastern food (including "unusual Armenian" and Lebanese items and "more vegetarian dishes than most restaurants") at this "moderately priced" Streeterville "hole-in-the-wall" that's "still going strong after 30 years"; N.B. extras include DJ entertainment on the weekends and exotic hookahs.

## Scoozi!
19  19  19  $31

*410 W. Huron St. (bet. Kingsbury & Orleans Sts.), 312-943-5900;*
*www.leye.com*
"After all these years", fans of this River North pioneer Italian still "never get tired of going" for its "large, varied menu" ("love the thin-crust pizza" and "delicious pastas") served in a "cavernous", "open" space that's "festive" and "boisterous" when busy; still, some say it "once was an 'in' place" but is now a trifle "out of date", with "fairly standard" food and service that's "lacking" – in short, "not the shining star of the Lettuce group."

## Scylla
–  –  –  M

*1952 N. Damen Ave. (Armitage Ave.), 773-227-2995;*
*www.scyllarestaurant.com*
Now that Glory has faded, Scylla chef-owner Stephanie Izard (ex Spring, La Tache) has turned its former space into this relaxed Bucktown newcomer, where her emphasis on Mediterranean preparations and classical French technique puts a fresh spin on familiar seafood dishes; the bi-level space (dining room and cushy upstairs lounge) is aptly accented with art inspired by the restaurant's namesake, the mythological nymph–turned–sea monster.

## SEASONS
28  27  27  $77

*Four Seasons Hotel, 120 E. Delaware Pl., 7th fl.*
*(bet. Michigan Ave. & Rush St.), 312-649-2349;*
*www.fourseason.com*
"Excellent chef" Robert Sulatycky's "top-flight" seasonal New American cuisine "is always refined but has an edge" at this "formal-dining" "power scene" in the Gold Coast's Four Seasons Hotel, a "haven of culinary delights" where the "expense is worth it" thanks to "outstanding food", "exceptional atmosphere" (the decor "defines elegance") and the "unobtrusive", "sensitive" staff's "superb timing"; P.S. don't forget the "incredible brunch" on Sundays.

## Seasons Café ◖
23  24  26  $39

*Four Seasons Hotel, 120 E. Delaware Pl., 7th fl. (bet.*
*Michigan Ave. & Rush St.), 312-649-2349;*
*www.fourseason.com*
Within the "hushed" "luxury" of its "classy", "formal-tearoom" environment, this sister cafe to Seasons serves

"American comfort food at its best", including a "prix fixe lunch" and "wonderful" "high tea" – plus the bar is "the best martini setting" "for the fortysomething" set; a few seasoned surveyors suggest that you "spend a little extra for the main dining room", but more maintain that it's "a real match for its sibling."

**Settimana Café**   20 | 16 | 18 | $31
*2056 W. Divison St. (Hoyne Ave.), 773-394-1629;*
*www.settimanacafe.com*
"A good menu" with an extensive "selection of solid entrees" scores with "enthusiasts" of this "relatively inexpensive", "great corner Italian" spot in Wicker Park, where diners enjoy a "fun" "neighborhood cafe" feel (and a "highly recommended patio" "in summer"); still, detractors who detect "unexciting" food and some "harried" servers "have yet to be impressed"; N.B. ratings may not reflect a post-*Survey* renovation and management change.

**1776** ☒   ▽ 22 | 15 | 21 | $38
*397 Virginia St./Rte. 14 (bet. Dole & McHenry Aves.),*
*Crystal Lake, 815-356-1776; www.1776andy.com*
Colonists of the Northwest Suburbs coo about the "inspired" 650-bottle list ("the owner knows his wines"), as well as the "excellent game" dishes and "interesting food events" at this "great little" seasonal New American; in fact, fans feel it's "the best in the area", even if some traitorous town criers deem the decor "unimpressive"; N.B. the exterior was redecorated post-*Survey*.

**Shallots Bistro**   – | – | – | E
*4741 W. Main St. (Skokie Blvd.), Skokie, 847-677-3463;*
*www.shallotsbistro.com*
Chef-owner Laura Frankel has reopened her erstwhile Lincoln Park kosher kitchen in North Suburban Skokie, giving the menu a more French bistro–oriented focus while retaining former faves like stuffed veal chop and lamb tagine; the casual-chic decor is all blond wood with black-and-neon-colored walls, mirror panels and a semi-circular bar; N.B. closed Friday nights, and seasonally on Saturdays depending on when the sun sets.

**SHANGHAI TERRACE** ☒   26 | 26 | 26 | $54
*Peninsula Hotel, 108 E. Superior St., 4th fl. (bet. Michigan Ave. & Rush St.), 312-573-6744; www.chicago.peninsula.com*
Survey says this "very special", "sophisticated" "jewel within the magnificent Peninsula" in River North serves "the highest available caliber of inventive Pan-Asian cuisine" going, with "clean, fresh, delicate" flavors featured in its "pricey but perfect" provender, "impeccably" "presented" with "flawless service" in a "posh" "little lacquered jewel-box of a room"(or "outdoors on the rooftop in summer"); N.B. the Decor rating may not reflect a post-*Survey* redo.

## SHAW'S CRAB HOUSE  | 23 | 19 | 20 | $41 |
*21 E. Hubbard St. (bet. State St. & Wabash Ave.), 312-527-2722*
*1900 E. Higgins Rd. (Rte. 53), Schaumburg, 847-517-2722*
*www.shawscrabhouse.com*
This "standby" pescatory pair purveys "fresh", "simple and
expertly prepared" seafood "you can trust" in "comfy"
settings; a few fin-food fanciers feel the Schaumburg
branch "lacks the atmosphere of the [River North] location",
others that the latter is "showing its age", while some are
troubled by the "inconsistent service" and the "expensive"
eats (though each location has a "more casual" lounge
that's "a better value").

### She She  | 20 | 19 | 16 | $38 |
*4539 N. Lincoln Ave. (bet. Sunnyside & Wilson Aves.),*
*773-293-3690*
"Great for the up-and-coming" Lincoln Square area, this
"trendy" Eclectic–New American is the setting for chef-
partner Nicole Parthemore's "innovative" cooking that
"tends toward experimental"; claustrophobics care that the
"cozy" space can be "cramped" and "congested" (though
there's "fun summer dining on the huge patio"), and other
critics complain of "inconsistent food" and service.

### Shine & Morida  | 20 | 20 | 18 | $28 |
*901 W. Armitage Ave. (Fremont St.), 773-296-0101;*
*www.shinemorida.com*
The "interesting marriage of Chinese and Japanese"
cuisines at these conjoined Lincoln Park twins is "popular"
with "picky groups of eaters" who appreciate having "lots
of choices" – from "great sushi" and "unique rolls" to an
"imaginative" Mandarin menu (or even "some of each");
still, some say "service is not the priority" it could be;
N.B. the Decor rating may not reflect a post-*Survey* redo.

### Shiroi Hana  | 20 | 10 | 19 | $21 |
*3242 N. Clark St. (Belmont Ave.), 773-477-1652*
"An excellent value" satisfies surveyors who "crowd" this
"consistent" Lakeview sushi spot; even if there are "not a
whole lot of creative choices", "the basics are good" and
"fresh", "the bento boxes are a bargain" and the prices
are paltry "pocket change", even to those "on a budget."

### Shula's Steakhouse  | 22 | 19 | 21 | $50 |
*Sheraton Chicago, 301 E. North Water St. (Columbus Dr.),*
*312-670-0788*
*Wyndham Northwest Chicago, 400 Park Blvd. (Thorndale Ave.),*
*Itasca, 630-775-1499*
*www.donshula.com*
In keeping with their "elegant" "sports-bar" theme, these
members of a national steakhouse herd – virtual shrines to
"the perfect coach of the perfect team with the perfect
season" (the 1972 Miami Dolphins) – list their "good steaks"

upon a "menu written on a football"; hecklers are sidelined by the "pretty straightforward and uninspired" fare, though, especially considering the "high prices."

## Signature Room
19 | 25 | 19 | $52

*John Hancock Center, 875 N. Michigan Ave., 95th fl. (bet. Chestnut St. & Delaware Ave.), 312-787-9596; www.signatureroom.com*

"It's all about" the "magnificent views of the entire city" at this "deservedly pretentious" Streeterville "surprise at the top" of the John Hancock Building that's best "for tourists or romance"-seekers; still, some cite "sticker shock" and New American food that "needs improvement" as reasons to "just enjoy the bar" and the panorama; N.B. the West Suburban spin-off closed post-*Survey*.

## Silver Cloud Bar & Grill
17 | 12 | 17 | $19

*1700 N. Damen Ave. (Wabansia Ave.), 773-489-6212; www.silvercloudchicago.com*

"Great retro food (s'mores, mac 'n' cheese, meatloaf)" "comforts" visitors to this Bucktown American whose "cool, hip" atmosphere makes boosters "feel like [they] belong"; it does get "smoky" (the bar's cigar-friendly after 10 PM), but those who shun such clouds counter that it's "not hard to get outdoor seating."

## Silver Seafood ●
∇ 24 | 11 | 16 | $21

*4829 N. Broadway St. (Lawrence Ave.), 773-784-0668*

"If you love seafood and [Mandarin] Chinese, this is the place" prate pleased patrons of this "inexpensive, quality" spot in Uptown who recommend that you "come with an open mind" and "ask for the non-American menu" so you can sample the "real specialties"; be warned, though, that service can suffer due to the "language problem."

## Silver Spoon
– | – | – | I

*710 N. Rush St. (bet. Huron & Superior Sts.), 312-944-7100*

A spin-off of Spoon Thai, this Siamese-Japanese hybrid in a vintage Gold Coast townhouse offers a medley of classics from its primary cuisines, both cooked and cold (all of which can be adapted to vegetarian diets), plus a separate sushi menu; the space, all hushed elegance, is decorated with a mix of modern and traditional artwork from the land of the rising sun.

## Slice of Life/Hy Life Bistro ⊭
∇ 13 | 10 | 14 | $25

*4120 W. Dempster St. (bet. Crawford Ave. & Keeler St.), Skokie, 847-674-2021*

"There's no better choice on the North Shore if you or your guests keep kosher" say supporters of this "good ethnic restaurant" where two separate kitchens handle "meat and dairy"; less impressed diners declare that they "don't like the quality"; P.S. "no credit cards" accepted.

## Smith & Wollensky  | 21 | 19 | 21 | $51 |

*318 N. State St. (Wacker Dr.), 312-670-9900;*
*www.smithandwollensky.com*
Red-meat mavens who respect this "classy", "traditional"
River North "contender in the steak Olympics" say it "carries
on the tradition" of the "New York City original" with its "dry-
aged" prime beef and "sinful crackling pork shank", while
others "prefer" the "more casual" (and "cheaper") "grill
downstairs"; grumps grouse that it's "too expense account–
focused" and "not up to the quality of the flagship" in
Manhattan, but all agree "you can't beat the terrace."

## Smoke Daddy ⬤  | 20 | 14 | 17 | $20 |

*1804 W. Division St. (bet. Ashland & Damen Aves.),*
*773-772-6656; www.thesmokedaddy.com*
You can "put a little South in your mouth" at this "great
BBQ joint" and "Wicker Park institution" where the "smokin'
ribs", "live music every night" and "awful decor" are all
part of the "adventure"; still, a few feed-baggers find it
"fair to middlin'"; N.B. the Food rating may not reflect the
post-*Survey* arrival of new owners, who plan to revamp the
menu – but not the original 'cue recipe.

## socca  | – | – | – | M |

*3301 N. Clark St. (Aldine Ave.), 773-248-1155*
'European country' cuisine comes all the way to Lakeview
courtesy of toque Roger Herring (CIA grad and former
private chef to the band Phish) who whips up the likes of
classic steak frites and the namesake chickpea-flour crêpes
at this charming French-Italian bistro whose red walls are
adorned with menus and wine labels; N.B. the affordable
wine list is limited but well rounded.

## Solstice ⬤  | ▽ 22 | 22 | 20 | $32 |

*2666 N. Halsted St. (bet. Diversey & Wrightwood Sts.),*
*773-296-0304; www.solsticechicago.com*
"Gourmet food in comfort-food portions" gets the nod of
some American pub-grubbers at this "welcome" spot that
brings "the whole SoHo vibe" to Lincoln Park; decorated
with festive paintings, its welcoming interior sports several
blue-velvet banquettes, and there's also warm-weather
patio seating for summer-solstice savorers.

## Souk  | ▽ 19 | 20 | 16 | $32 |

*1552 N. Milwaukee Ave. (bet. Division St. & North Ave.),*
*773-227-1818; www.soukrestaurant.com*
"You're transported to Morocco, hookah pipes and all",
at this "hip Middle Eastern" in Wicker Park, which serves
"creative" "eats" that go "beyond the traditional" (along
with a side of "exotic [belly] dancing" on Wednesday,
Friday and Saturday evenings) to "crowds of black-wearing
hipsters"; even so, alleged "inconsistency" gives some
pen pals pause.

## South   – – – M
(fka The Room)
*5900 N. Broadway (Rosedale Ave.), 773-989-7666;*
*www.southinchicago.com*
The owners of what was once The Room have morphed their
Edgewater hipster hangout into this Southern-Southwestern
BYO, where chef Linda Raydl rustles up blackened scallops
and tempura-fried catfish with cactus; the dining area still
features exposed ductwork, brick walls and concrete floors
but is now warmed by funky furnishings such as distressed
wood shutters, copper accents and kraft paper on the tables.

## South Gate Cafe   19  19  17  $31
*655 Forest Ave. (Deerpath Ave.), Lake Forest, 847-234-8800*
"This Lake Forest standard" serves up a "blue-blood diner"
menu of American fare that provokes varying levels of
surveyor satisfaction; similarly, some say its service can
also be "great or awful", but everyone agrees the "nice
patio" "facing historic Market Square" and its ancient elms
are big draws.

## South Water Kitchen   16  18  17  $31
*Hotel Monaco, 225 N. Wabash Ave. (Upper Wacker Dr.),*
*312-236-9300; www.southwaterkitchen.com*
If you're in the Loop and looking for "your mom's food, but
better", you may like this "welcoming" American eatery that
a contingent of contributors calls "surprisingly good for a
hotel restaurant" and a "solid" "choice" for "pre-theater" or
"a reasonable business lunch"; the compass points north,
however, for those who say "service is a problem" and
there's "nothing special" about the "uninspiring" fare.

## Speakeasy Supperclub   21  20  17  $33
*1401 W. Devon Ave. (Glenwood Ave.), 773-338-0600;*
*www.speakeasysupperclub.com*
"Finally, someone realized that people in Edgewater eat
too" effuse epistolers about this "funky" Eclectic entry and
"BYO find" where "unusual, tasty" fare "with a hint of the
exotic" is treated to a "trendy" setting "with light boxes
featuring [pictures of] musicians and stars" and a "cabaret-
style" "music room" featuring occasional "live jazz"; still,
some speakers submit that "poor service is a minus."

## SPIAGGIA   26  26  25  $72
*One Magnificent Mile Bldg., 980 N. Michigan Ave., 2nd fl.*
*(Oak St.), 312-280-2750; www.spiaggiarestaurant.com*
Patrons say "pinch me" about this Gold Coast "epitome of
sophisticated dining" and "special place for special times"
that "serves its fair share of glitterati"; chef Tony Mantuano's
"heavenly, luxurious" Italian cuisine deserves its "stunning
setting" with a "view of the lake", and a "knowledgeable"
staff "anticipates any need" ("sommelier [Henry Bishop] is
first rate"); N.B. jackets are required.

### Spoon Thai        – – – M

*4608 N. Western Ave. (Wilson Ave.), 773-769-1173;*
*www.spoonthai.com*

"Exquisite and adventurous Thai food" (such as the
signature butternut blossom salad) "without the pretense"
appeals to the palates of pleased patrons, who also praise
the "authentic decor" that "adds to the overall quaint
ambiance" at this Lincoln Square neighborhood BYO;
N.B. delivery is also available.

### SPRING        26  24  24  $55

*2039 W. North Ave. (Damen Ave.), 773-395-7100;*
*www.springrestaurant.net*

A "multi-sensory experience" that's "everything a gourmet
restaurant should be", this Wicker Park New American
seafood "standout" has surveyors swooning over chef-
partner Shawn McClain's "subtle, savory" and "sublime"
dishes offered with "high-class service" in an "über-cool",
"Zen" "converted bathhouse"; a few rain on this parade,
though, calling the "austere" setting "cold" and "noisy" and
the experience "a bit overpriced."

### Square Kitchen        – – – M

*4600 N. Lincoln Ave. (W. Wilson Ave.), 773-751-1500;*
*www.squarekitchen.com*

Gracing burgeoning Lincoln Square's restaurant roster
is this casual hipster cafe serving updates on American
comfort food for brunch (Saturday and Sunday) and dinner,
including a choose-your-own-sauce option for fish and
meat entrees; neutral hues and light wood create a clean,
modern feel, and there's a spacious bar and open kitchen.

### Stained Glass Wine Bar Bistro        22  18  20  $41

*1735 Benson Ave. (bet. Church & Clark Sts.), Evanston,*
*847-864-8600; www.thestainedglass.com*

Won-over writers enjoy "a true bacchanal" starring this
"charming" North Suburbanite's "excellent" Eclectic–New
American "seasonal menu" and "good variety of [wine]
tasting options", including "plenty of by-the-glass" and
"flight" choices; they also feel "unhurried" in the "exposed-
brick" setting, though others sniff that the grape offerings
are "better than the food" and service.

### Stanley's Kitchen & Tap        19  15  17  $18

*1970 N. Lincoln Ave. (Armitage Ave.), 312-642-0007;*
*www.stanleysrestaurant.com*

The "soul-soothing" Traditional American "comfort food"
such as "excellent fried chicken" and "heavenly mac 'n'
cheese" is a "dirt-cheap" "diet-buster" at this "comfy",
"kid-friendly" Lincoln Parker where "locals" "line up"
on weekends for the "scrumptious brunch buffet" with
"Bloody Mary bar"; still, some with pickier palates pan the
offerings as "average."

### Starfish

22 | 19 | 18 | $42

*804 W. Randolph St. (Halsted St.), 312-997-2433;*
*www.starfishsushi.com*

"A definite star" and "real contender" in the eat-it-raw
rally, this "ultrahip" Market District maki-meister rolls a
"unique and different selection" of "fresh, fresh, fresh"
fish and other Japanese food ("if you're a tuna fan", check
out the flight of "different types") in "swanky sushi digs";
still, naysayers note it's "not the best in town."

### Star of Siam

17 | 12 | 16 | $19

*11 E. Illinois St. (State St.), 312-670-0100;*
*www.starofsiamchicago.com*

"Huge portions" of "no-frills", "authentic" "Thai food" fill
up fans of this River North "favorite" known for its "quick,
professional service", "reasonable prices" and "spare
space"; some feel the fare is "pretty standard", though, and
say the "staff seems tired of waiting on people."

### Stetson's Chop House

20 | 19 | 21 | $43

*Hyatt Regency, 151 E. Wacker Dr. (bet. Michigan & Stetson Aves.),*
*312-565-1234; www.hyatt.com*

Pardners pick this classic Loop steakhouse in the Hyatt
Regency for it's "prime, dry-aged beef", an example of its
"surprisingly good food (for a hotel restaurant)"; rustlers
reckon the built-in "business keeps the place" going,
though, since there are "much better steaks in Chicago."

### Stir Crazy

19 | 16 | 18 | $20

*1186 N. Northbrook Court Mall (bet. Skokie Blvd. &*
*Waukegan Rd.), Northbrook, 847-562-4800*
*Oakbrook Center Mall, 105 Oakbrook Ctr. (Rte. 83), Oak Brook,*
*630-575-0155*
*Woodfield Mall, 5 Woodfield Mall (Perimeter Dr.), Schaumburg,*
*847-330-1200*
*28252 Diehl Rd. (Windfield Rd.), Warrenville, 630-393-4700*
*www.stircrazy.com*

"A first choice for shopping-mall dining", this Asian trio
offers a choice of "arranging your own stir-fry" from "fresh
ingredients" or selecting from "very good menu items" (you
"can eat vegetarian easily", plus it's "great for children"
and "picky eaters"); "crowded, noisy" conditions make
some customers crazy, though, and others point out that
the "one-plate maximum" makes it less of a deal than its
"rivals"; N.B. the Warrenville branch opened post-*Survey*.

### Strega Nona

17 | 17 | 18 | $28

*3747 N. Southport Ave. (bet. Grace St. & Waveland Ave.),*
*773-244-0990; www.carluccirestaurant.com*

"Handy" for "a casual night out with friends" or "dinner
and a show" (the "Mercury Theater and Music Box movie
[house] are nearby"), this "affordable" Wrigleyville Italian
serves "hearty" fare "made all the more tasty by inexpensive

drinks"; though it's "popular", skeptics say the food "just isn't that good"; P.S. "sit outside to watch passersby."

**Sugar: A Dessert Bar** ◗　　19　21　13　$28

*108 W. Kinzie St. (bet. Clark St. & La Salle Blvd.), 312-822-9999*

Christine McCabe's "orgiastic desserts" ("especially the sampler") and "creative martinis" lure sugar supporters to this "decadent" River North "hot spot", with a "clubby atmosphere" variously described as "wild", "romantic and hip"; some sourpusses suggest it's "not so sweet", though, saying "everything is expensive", service from the "aloof" staff ranges from "insulting" to "nonexistent" and the confections "don't live up to the menu descriptions"; N.B. a dance floor was added post-*Survey.*

**Sullivan's Steakhouse**　　22　21　21　$48

*415 N. Dearborn St. (Hubbard St.), 312-527-3510*
*244 S. Main St. (bet. Jackson & Jefferson Aves.), Naperville, 630-305-0230*
*www.sullivansteakhouse.com*

The "buttery steaks", "terrific martinis" and "made-to-order soufflés" are "worth the wait" at these "classic" River North and West Suburban "chain steakhouses" boasting "old-style cool", "hustle-bustle", "great leather booths" and "live jazz" nightly – plus "they know how to treat you"; nevertheless, critics complain about spending "top dollar" here, claiming "nothing sets this steakhouse apart from any others."

**Suparossa**　　　　　　　∇　25　22　22　$25
(aka Cucina Biago)

*4256 N. Central Ave. (Cullom Ave.), 773-736-5828*
*7319 W. Lawrence Ave. (bet. Harlem & Oketo Aves.), Harwood Heights, 708-867-4641*
*6301 Purchase Dr. (Rte. 53), Woodridge, 630-852-1000*
*www.suparossa.com*

"Great Italian food", including "thin-crust [pizza that's] equally as good as" the "deep dish", tempts travelers to this trio of "dependable", "friendly" suburban spots, where you can expect "no surprises" – unless you count the confusing name game (the Harwood Heights branch is alternately called Cucina Biagio, and the Northwest Side location is attached to a Biagio's banquet facility).

**Superdawg Drive-In**　　23　19　20　$9

*Midway Airport, 5700 Cicero St., Concourse B (55th St.), 773-948-6300*
*6363 N. Milwaukee Ave. (Devon Ave.), 773-763-0660* ◗ ⇄
*www.superdawg.com*

Pup-lovers pack this Northwest Side "apotheosis of dawg-dom" (purveyor of the town's "top dog", and Best

Bang for the Buck in our *Survey*), panting "it should be a protected Chicago landmark" for its "flashback" "drive-in perfection" – "carhops" cater to you "in your car" while anthropomorphic "boy and girl" "wieners on the roof" ("costumed" as a strongman and a ballerina) "swoon" over each other; P.S. "the [unrated] stand at Midway Airport makes it worth wading through security lines!"

### Sushi Naniwa    21  13  19  $31
*607 N. Wells St. (bet. Ohio & Ontario Sts.), 312-255-8555; www.sushinaniwa.com*
Raters revere the "high-end sushi" at this River North "favorite" with a "friendly staff" that "flies under the radar" of many Windy City raw-fishionados; true, the "outstanding" morsels certainly "outshine" the "no-frills", "unpretentious setting", but fans feel the experience reminds them of "being in Japan" and is just "the way it should be"; P.S. "the outdoor cafe is wonderful in the summer."

### SUSHISAMBA rio    20  25  17  $47
*504 N. Wells St. (bet. Grand & Illinois Sts.), 312-595-2300; www.sushisamba.com*
The "hot", "sexy" "Chicago branch of a Miami/NYC favorite", this River North "hybrid" haven boasts a "great fusion concept", "blending Japanese and Brazilian" cuisines in its "swanky", "high-energy" (and "noisy") environment where "the people-watching can't be beat"; snubbers, though, cite "disappointing execution", "high prices" and an "inattentive staff" as evidence that it has "more buzz than substance."

### SUSHI WABI    25  19  19  $37
*842 W. Randolph St. (bet. Green & Peoria Sts.), 312-563-1224; www.sushiwabi.com*
"Urban chic" meets "stellar", "succulent sushi" as well as "a new take on traditional Japanese" cooking at this "hip" Market District "hangout" with a "*Blade Runner*–esque" vibe and "a little attitude thrown in"; though the raw treats have fans wondering "does it get any fresher?", detractors nevertheless decry the "too-small" "bar area" where folks "wait for tables" before being "squeezed in like sardines", and say the "techno" ambiance can be "too loud."

### Swordfish    –  –  –  M
*207 N. Randall Rd. (McKee St.), Batavia, 630-406-6463; www.swordfishsushi.com*
Diners desiring cutting-edge contemporary maki and other raw (and cooked) creations needn't venture Downtown thanks to this urban-chic Japanese outpost in the Western Suburbs – another successful sushi spot from the owners of Starfish and Wildfish; its tuna flights and signature martinis or boxes of sake are offered within a sleek, modern environment accented with upbeat lounge music.

## TALLGRASS
28 | 22 | 25 | $62

*1006 S. State St. (10th St.), Lockport, 815-838-5566;*
*www.tallgrassrestaurant.com*
Grateful gastronomes "thank goodness there's a real
restaurant" gracing the Southwest Suburbs – especially
considering that it's this "intimate" example of the genre
where "creative chef" and partner Robert Burcenski's
"memorable" New French fare is simply "out of this
world", the "fantastic wine list" is "extensive" and the
"staff is very knowledgeable"; N.B. both jackets and
reservations are de rigueur.

## Tango
– | – | – | M

*5 W. Jackson St. (S. Washington St.), Naperville, 630-848-1818;*
*www.tangousa.com*
An outpost of Argentina in West Suburban Naperville, this
casual steakhouse serves hot and cold tapas, steaks,
seafood and pasta, all paired with flights of wine and
sangria made tableside; the bi-level space (a bright and
noisy main floor and a quieter upstairs) is accented with
bright colors and painted motifs of suns, swirls, flowers –
and of course tango dancers.

## Tango Sur
19 | 14 | 17 | $27

*3763 N. Southport Ave. (Grace St.), 773-477-5466;*
*www.tangosur.com*
"You're here for the meat" when you visit this "authentic"
Wrigleyville "Argentinean beef joint" and "BYO", where
the "affordable yet delicious steak" and weekend "no-
reservations" policy make for "crazy waits"; note that the
"dimly lit interior" can get "crowded and noisy" ("you can
say anything there because no one will hear you"), but there
is patio and sidewalk seating in summer.

## Tank Sushi
– | – | – | M

*4514 N. Lincoln Ave. (W. Sunnyside Ave.), 773-769-2600;*
*www.tanksushi.com*
This imaginative Lincoln Square spot offers raw fish, in
addition to various small plates of cooked Asian dishes,
amid minimalist contemporary decor consisting of blond
wood and casually hip furnishings complemented by
pulsing music; N.B. those seeking privacy may opt for one
of the two tables in the tatami room, which is minus the
traditional floor seating.

## Tapas Barcelona
20 | 18 | 17 | $27

*1615 Chicago Ave. (bet. Church & Davis Sts.), Evanston,*
*847-866-9900; www.tapasbarcelona.com*
"A great place to go with a group", this North Suburban
Spanish small-plate specialist allows folks to sample "little
tastes of everything" from its "big menu of well-prepared"
and "tasty" tapas, and its "exotic dining experience" is
offered within a "colorful", "bustling" atmosphere; still, a

few faultfinders feel the fare is "unspectacular"; P.S. the
patio "is a lovely place to eat in the summer."

**Tarantino's**    21 | 18 | 19 | $34
*1112 W. Armitage Ave. (Seminary St.), 773-871-2929*
Supporters of this often "overlooked" "neighborhood"
"spot in the heart of Lincoln Park" laud its "choices
galore" of "fresh, contemporary Italian [cooking] served
up" in a "cool" and "quiet" "exposed-brick" room; most
maintain it's "great for a night out with friends or a date",
even if "service can be leisurely" sometimes; N.B. patio
dining is available.

**Tasting Room, The** ❶ 🗷    17 | 23 | 20 | $29
*1415 W. Randolph St. (Ogden Ave.), 312-942-1313;
www.tlcwine.com*
A Market District "treasure", this "intimate" New American
that reminds folks of a "living room with leather couches,
candles" and "fabulous views of the city" "is the place if you
want to try out" a "flight of wine and cheese" or some "great
appetizers" ("the desserts aren't so bad either!"); the
"tremendous selection" and "knowledgeable" staff also
help make it a "wonderful" stop "after work" or dinner.

**Tavern** 🗷    ▽ 24 | 26 | 23 | $42
*519 N. Milwaukee Ave. (bet. Cook Ave. & Lake St.),
Libertyville, 847-367-5755*
"The prize of historic downtown Libertyville", this
"hidden" haven is known for "out-of-this-world steaks"
and "excellent" New American fare, as well as "a wine
list that can't be beat for quality and affordability" (plus
a "reserve list with interesting options"); "relaxed yet
elegant" decor and an "informed", "helpful" staff are
other reasons it's a "local favorite."

**Tavern on Rush** ❶    20 | 20 | 18 | $42
*1031 N. Rush St. (Bellevue Pl.), 312-664-9600;
www.tavernonrush.com*
A Gold (Coast) rush is on for surveyors who savor the
"steak, seafood and pasta finds" found at this "flashy"
steakhouse with an "electric environment" full of "eye
candy", a "hopping bar scene" with a "great happy hour"
and a "nice outdoor dining option"; critics "cross the
street", though, to avoid what they see as "unremarkable
food" and a "cheesy" demographic ("only those with fast
cars and silicone need attend").

**Tecalitlan** ❶    ▽ 17 | 9 | 14 | $17
*1814 W. Chicago Ave. (Wood St.), 773-384-4285*
It's a Mexican standoff at this West Town old-timer, with
some championing its "tasty and cheap" "traditional" eats
(including "first-rate burritos" and "super-fresh salsa with
the chips") but others nay-saying it's "not the best"; still,
they do serve until 3 AM on weekends.

### Tempo ◑⊅
19 | 11 | 18 | $15

*6 E. Chestnut St. (State St.), 312-943-4373*

Those in search of "amazing breakfast" foods "at any hour" "shouldn't want for anything" at this "classic diner", a Greek-owned Gold Coast "godsend" "known for its waffles", "fluffy omelets" "big enough to split" and "skillets that are rumored to cure hangovers"; it's "the place for late-night Downtown dining", so "you won't be alone" (there's "always a line"), even if you "go at 2 AM"; N.B. no alcohol, no credit cards.

### 10 West ⊠
▽ 24 | 16 | 19 | $41

*10 W. Jackson Ave. (Chicago Ave.), Naperville, 630-548-3100; www.10west.net*

Enthusiasts effervesce about the Eclectic eats at this West Suburban entry in the former Elaine space, saying the "imaginative" seasonal menu – "nicely presented" by "helpful servers" in intimate rooms of a "neat" remodeled building that's one of the town's oldest former homes – "could succeed Downtown"; N.B. game is a specialty, and the boutique wine list emphasizes champagne.

### Thai Classic
23 | 14 | 20 | $18

*3332 N. Clark St. (bet. Belmont Ave. & Roscoe St.), 773-404-2000; www.thaiclassicrestaurant.com*

An "extremely varied menu" offers a "cornucopia" of "cheap", "authentic Thai food", winning friends for this Lakeview "BYO" with a "solicitous and helpful" staff, a "weekend brunch that's pure heaven" and "a few low tables" where "you can sit on the floor on pillows" for "amusing" "traditional dining"; still, some say the fare is "neither the best nor the worst" and complain that there's "no ambiance to speak of."

### Thai Pastry
22 | 10 | 17 | $16

*4925 N. Broadway St. (bet. Argyle St. & Lawrence Ave.), 773-784-5399; www.thaipastry.com*

The "amazing, affordable Thai" fare "can't be beat for the price" at this Uptown upstart in a "clean", "small storefront" space that stands up well to the competition "in the so-called better neighborhoods"; not only is the "food prepared with an unusually high [level of] care", but the "service is fast and friendly"; N.B. the "BYO" policy is also a financial bonus.

### Think Café
– | – | – | M

*2235 N. Western Ave. (Lyndale St.), 773-394-0537; www.think-cafe.com*

Take "large portions" of "well-seasoned and carefully prepared" Italian-accented Eclectic cuisine, stir in "caring, personalized service" and a dash of "incredible value", and you'll see why thoughtful respondents refer to this "casual storefront" BYO "on the fringe of Bucktown" as "a repeater."

### Three Happiness ⬤
　　　　　　　　　　　　　　　　　－　－　－　M
*209 W. Cermak Rd. (20th St.), 312-842-1964*
Still confusing folks (no wonder, as the larger spot on the corner, though older, was sold and renamed New Three Happiness), this "small and cozy" Chinatown "favorite" serves "great dim sum" and Mandarin cooking "anytime" (well, almost – till 3 AM weeknights, 24 hours on weekends); so what's the big deal if "the decor is tacky"?

### 302 WEST ⊠
　　　　　　　　　　　　　　　27　26　26　$49
*302 W. State St. (3rd St.), Geneva, 630-232-9302;*
*www.302west.net*
Superlatives abound for this "romantic" New American "dining treasure" where "terrific, modern city fare" from a "creative" daily changing menu belies the "far-outpost" setting of its "unique", "elegant-yet-casual" "old bank building" within a "postcard-perfect" West Suburban town; there's also a "great wine list", and the "yummy", "homemade desserts" alone "are well worth the trip"; N.B. after the untimely passing of chef-owner Joel Findlay in 2004, his protégé, Jeremy Lycan, continues his tradition.

### 312 Chicago
　　　　　　　　　　　　　　　19　19　19　$37
*Hotel Allegro, 136 N. La Salle St. (Randolph St.), 312-696-2420;*
*www.312chicago.com*
Surveyors who regularly speed-dial this area code–inspired Italian-American credit its "fine seasonal menu", "excellent martinis" and "irresistible neighborhood-bistro feel" for making it "a great place to forget about the chaos of the Loop" while enjoying a "power breakfast or lunch", "gourmet brunch" or a "pre- or post-theater" meal; still, crank callers are hung up on the "not overly exciting" though "perfectly passable" profferings and caution that the staff "can sometimes become overwhelmed."

### Thyme
　　　　　　　　　　　　　　　22　21　20　$43
*464 N. Halsted St. (Grand Ave.), 312-226-4300;*
*www.thymechicago.com*
"Beautiful presentation and outstanding flavor combos" distinguish chef-owner John Bubala's "well-thought-out" menu of New American–New French dishes say supporters of this "oh-so-chic", "off-the-beaten-path" Near Wester with "magical alfresco dining in the summer"; opponents opine that, while "worthy", it's "one of many comparable places" and "maybe not worth the money."

### Thyme Café
　　　　　　　　　　　　　　　－　－　－　M
*1540 N. Milwaukee Ave. (North Ave.), 773-227-1400;*
*www.thymechicago.com*
Chef-owner John Bubala's boisterous follow-up to his long-standing Thyme, this midpriced, rustic New French–New American bistro in Wicker Park features a weekly changing menu and an all-you-can-eat jazz brunch on

Sunday; set in the former Sinibar space, it has a casual, cozy feel with wood floors and bare-wood tables, mother-of-pearl inlay mirrors and a wall of artwork.

**Tien Giang**    –   –   –   I

*1104-6 W. Argyle St. (N. Winthrop Ave.), 773-275-8691*
Located on the Argyle Street restaurant strip, this double-storefront BYO also doubles up on cuisine, offering up Vietnamese and Chinese fare from morning until night (with breakfast on weekends, including Friday) in a bright, open dining room.

**Tiffin**    23   18   20   $24

*2536 W. Devon Ave. (Maplewood Ave.), 773-338-2143*
With "the best Indian food on Devon" and, per our *Survey*, in Chicago, this "favorite" Northwest Side "haunt" curries favor with its "interesting menu" of "clean, fresh and delicious" fare full of "sparkling flavor", not to mention its "energetic staff" and "nice decor" with a "soothing blue-sky scene above"; P.S. those who prefer to keep their eyes on the prize "can watch the tandoor ovens in action."

**Tilli's**    16   18   15   $23

*1952 N. Halsted St. (bet. Armitage Ave. & Willow St.), 773-325-0044; www.tillischicago.com*
"A good bite" in a "fun atmosphere" is what draws Lincoln Parkers to "mix and match different ethnic foods" at this Eclectic eatery, where you can dine "at the bar [while] watching TV", "in the dining room next to the fireplace" or "alfresco on the patio"; all that, but antis still aren't amused by what they perceive as "average" offerings.

**Tin Fish**    20   17   18   $35

*Cornerstone Ctr., 18201 S. Harlem Ave. (183rd St.), Tinley Park, 708-532-0200*
*17 W. 512 22nd St. (Midwest Rd.), Oakbrook Terrace, 630-279-0808*
*www.tf-tinfish.com*
"Fun, fresh fish" fare finds a fan base at this "consistently good" Southwest Suburban seafooder that aficionados feel is a real "find" "in a "strip mall"; conversely, critics carp about a "noisy room" and "limited offerings" that "soon [become] tiresome", as well as saying that the staff – unlike the cuisine – "is inconsistent"; N.B. the Oakbrook Terrace branch opened post-*Survey*.

**TIZI MELLOUL**    22   27   21   $39

*531 N. Wells St. (Grand Ave.), 312-670-4338; www.tizimelloul.com*
"The food is as interesting as the name" (the latter "for a mountain in Morocco") at this "posh" River North "magic carpet ride" where the "exotic", "den-of-sin" "ambiance evokes the romance of Arabian nights" and the Middle Eastern–Med menu includes both "basic" and "adventurous items" (plus "fun drinks"); for added drama, there are

hookahs, "belly dancers Sunday evenings" and a communal "round room that reminds [raters] of Jeannie's bottle."

### Toast
21 | 15 | 16 | $16

*2046 N. Damen Ave. (Dickens Ave.), 773-772-5600*
*746 W. Webster Ave. (Halsted St.), 773-935-5600*
"Interesting twists on classic" American breakfast, brunch and lunch favorites "keep the crowds coming" to this "cute", "family-friendly" Bucktown and Lincoln Park twosome; exasperated eaters, though, say to expect "spotty service", "a tight squeeze and a long wait" that can be "sometimes unbearable" "on weekends."

### Tokyo Marina
17 | 7 | 16 | $19

*5058 N. Clark St. (Carmen Ave.), 773-878-2900*
Mariners who set sail for this "funky", "dependable" Andersonville spot for "solid", "well-priced sushi" ("good carryout, too") feel it justifies "enduring the depressing decor"; for mutineers, though, a "lacking environment" and merely "decent" fare make it "not worth traveling" for.

### Tombo Kitchen ⏱
▽ 22 | 20 | 16 | $27

*3244 N. Lincoln Ave. (Melrose St.), 773-244-9885*
Complimentary correspondents call this "undiscovered" Lakeview location "better than your average sushi spot", with "a chic, downtown feel" and a "karaoke bar tucked away in the back"; on the other hand, critics cavil that it's "bested by more hip restaurants Downtown"; N.B. the Decor rating may not reflect a post-*Survey* renovation.

### Tomboy ✂
22 | 18 | 20 | $34

*5402 N. Clark St. (bet. Balmoral Ave. & Clark St.), 773-907-0636;*
*www.tomboyrestaurant.com*
"Creative, delicious" seasonal New American cooking "with interesting twists" pleases panelists who say this "quaint" yet "upscale" "old faithful" in Andersonville "continues to evolve", though some "favorites remain on the menu"; on the other hand, a few tough customers find the fare "uneven"; N.B. there's live jazz on Thursday nights.

### Tommy Nevin's Pub ⏱
15 | 16 | 16 | $21

*1450 Sherman Ave. (Lake St.), Evanston, 847-869-0450;*
*www.tommynevins.com*
"Put on your brogue" at this "almost authentic Irish" "snug" in Evanston; the "comfortable, not overly kitsched-up setting" befits the "decent, basic" American and Gaelic "grub" ("love that shepherd's pie"), and "darts" and "free live music" on weekends are additional draws; N.B. the Decor rating may not reflect a post-*Survey* renovation.

### Topo Gigio Ristorante
20 | 17 | 18 | $33

*1516 N. Wells St. (bet. Division St. & North Ave.), 312-266-9355*
"Totally untrendy", this "wonderful neighborhood Italian" offers a "varied menu" of "tasty food" that's "reliable, if not

inventive", along with some of "the best eye candy" around; most maintain it's "a fun scene in Old Town, especially in the summer" when there's "beautiful garden dining", but malcontents malign the "crowded" conditions and say certain staffers are "sometimes rude."

### TOPOLOBAMPO ⊠ | 27 | 23 | 25 | $53
*445 N. Clark St. (bet. Hubbard & Illinois Sts.), 312-661-1434; www.fronterakitchens.com*
"Master chef" Rick Bayless' "upscale" "regional Mexican" in River North ("Frontera's higher-end partner") is nothing short of a "national treasure" that "expands eaters' horizons" with "a parade of tastes" exhibiting "creativity and respect for ingredients" ("do they do it this well in Mexico?"); plus, "they've achieved margarita perfection", the "savvy sommelier" picks "wonderful wine pairings", the staff is "informative and unassuming" and the ambiance is "festive" yet "elegant."

### Toucan | – | – | – | M
*4603 N. Lincoln Ave. (Wilson Ave.), 773-989-9000*
Highlighting the multicultural influences of Caribbean cuisine, this Lincoln Square spot offers a break from the mundane; its casual storefront space has a modern cafe atmosphere, abetted by a blue mosaic bar, tropical-colored walls adorned with a toucan and a few sidewalk tables that are ideal for a weekend brunch on island time.

### Tournesol ⊠ | 22 | 20 | 22 | $37
*4343 N. Lincoln Ave. (bet. Cullom & Montrose Aves.), 773-477-8820*
The "unintimidating" and "deftly prepared bistro cuisine" at this French "storefront" in Lincoln Square is offered by "staffers who know their menu and wines" (the latter's "list has something good for every pocketbook") in a "tasteful, relaxed atmosphere" that reminds some respondents of "eating in the French countryside"; N.B. the Food rating may not reflect a post-*Survey* chef change.

### Trader Vic's ●⊠ | 16 | 21 | 18 | $36
*Palmer House Hilton, 17 E. Monroe St. (bet. State St. & Wabash Ave.), 312-917-7317; www.tradervics.com*
"Still a trip" of the "tiki" variety, this "campy" Loop Continental-"Polynesian survivor" has most agreeing that its "average" eats "taste like food of the gods" after a few of those "fancy cocktails"; restless natives nevertheless note that the drinks also "soften the blow when the check comes", and opine that this "throwback to the stone age of dining" is "cool no more."

### Trattoria Gianni | ▽ 19 | 16 | 24 | $32
*1711 N. Halsted St. (bet. North Ave. & Willow St.), 312-266-1976; www.trattoriagianni.com*
Fans of this "friendly", "classic neighborhood favorite" in Lincoln Park are fond of its "tasty" Italian food, which is

accompanied by a "good wine list"; located "across from the Steppenwolf", it's "perfect before the theater" since the "lovely service" from the "attentive" staff is "especially fast" when you have a curtain to catch.

### TRATTORIA NO. 10 🖾  24 | 20 | 21 | $37
*10 N. Dearborn St. (bet. Madison St. & Washington Blvd.), 312-984-1718; www.trattoriaten.com*
"Hidden in a [Loop] office building", this "subterranean" "fave" is a "respite from Downtown bustle", with a "well-rounded menu" of "expressive, flavorful" Italian fare, including "traditional as well as new takes on" "great handmade pastas"; some say the "grottolike dining room" is a bit "claustrophobic", "but the food and service are so good it doesn't matter!"; P.S. "check out their buffet in the bar" during the "terrific happy hour."

### Trattoria Roma  21 | 14 | 19 | $33
*1535 N. Wells St. (bet. North Ave. & Schiller St.), 312-664-7907; www.trattoriaroma.com*
To participants who praise this "perennial favorite", there's "always a great meal" of "really good [Southern] Italian food" "with a smile" at this "small but cozy" trattoria, a "great date place" "in Old Town" with a "wonderful neighborhood feel"; still, skeptics score it as "sometimes great, sometimes just ok"; P.S. there's "outdoor dining."

### Trattoria Trullo  ∇ 22 | 16 | 19 | $32
*1700 Central St. (Eastwood Ave.), Evanston, 847-570-0093; www.trattoriatrullo.com*
Delighted diarists describe this North "Suburban secret" as an "excellent neighborhood [Southern] Italian" with a "great variety" of food filled with "fresh tastes" and delivered in a "homey atmosphere"; pragmatic penmen place the decor in the "ho-hum" column, though, suggesting it "needs to expand" (even if the seasonal sidewalk seating affords a little more breathing room).

### Tre Kronor  23 | 18 | 21 | $19
*3258 W. Foster Ave. (bet. Kedzie & Kimball Aves.), 773-267-9888*
Three cheers for the "delectable" and "comforting" "Scandinavian fare" ("fantastic Swedish pancakes with lingonberries" and "amazing danishes and quiches" are among the jewels in their crown) at this "delightful", "casual" Northwest Side BYO; the "pleasant staff" and "rock-bottom prices" also contribute to the appeal, while the "cavorting gnome mural adds a sense of fun."

### Tre Via  – | – | – | M
*1575 N. Milwaukee Ave (North Ave.), 773-227-7990; www.treviachicago.com*
Named for its location at Wicker Park's prime three-way intersection, this stylish, loungey venue in the Flatiron Building offers Italian fare at neighborhood prices; settle

into an intimate booth for traditional multicourse dining or perch at the popular bar beneath the cool color-changing light fixture and graze from interesting starters, thin-crust pizzas, salads or pasta dishes – all paired with a nice little wine list, including 22 by-the-glass selections.

### Triad     – – – M

*1933 S. Indiana Ave. (Cullerton St.), 312-225-8833;*
*www.triadsushi.com*
Sushi hounds and aspiring rock stars alike favor this trendy South Loop Japanese, where an extensive menu of the raw and the cooked harmonizes with an array of sake selections, and the karaoke bar features a roster of 1,000 pop, hip-hop and classic songs; N.B. high rollers can rent a private room with an elaborate A/V system.

### Trio Atelier     – – – M

*The Homestead, 1625 Hinman Ave. (bet. Church & Davis Sts.),*
*Evanston, 847-733-8746; www.trio-restaurant.com*
Set in Evanston's quaint Homestead hotel, the former culinary laboratory Trio has been relaunched as this less expensive New French food 'workshop' under chef Dale Levitski (ex La Tache), whose simpler seasonal cuisine is served in an avant-garde dining room or in a lounge/dining area with two communal tables; though bottles from its predecessor's abundant wine cellar are still available, the focus is now on some 40 wines offered in two pour sizes.

### TRU ⌧     28   27   27   $107

*676 N. St. Clair St. (bet. Erie & Huron Sts.), 312-202-0001;*
*www.trurestaurant.com*
"Talented [toque Rick] Tramonto and [pastry chef Gale] Gand's one-two punch" has grateful gastronomes gushing about this "extraordinary" New French "event-dining" "extravaganza", the Most Popular restaurant in our *Survey*; from the "serene, minimalist decor" and "choreographed service" to the "help of knowledgeable sommelier" Scott Tyree, it's a "seamless" Streeterville "food-as-theater" "spectacle", and if a few "nitpickers" find it "over the top" ("you can easily spend four hours for dinner") and beyond "expensive", the majority nevertheless advises you to just "spend the money and do it."

### Tsuki     – – – M

*1441-45 W. Fullerton Ave. (bet. Clifton St. & Racine Ave.),*
*773-883-8722; www.tsuki.us*
The owners of Ringo bring their sexy sushi to Lincoln Park via this Japanese venue where small plates for sharing join traditional and radical raw-fish options on an extensive menu; high-style design elements include a stone water wall behind the bar, wavy blue banquettes for lounging upon, a steel 'stream' in the floor and a spectacular, crescent-shaped glass sushi bar lit from within.

## Tsunami
20 | 20 | 17 | $37

*1160 N. Dearborn St. (Division St.), 312-642-9911;*
*www.tsunamichicago.com*

"One of the original high-end sushi places", this "hip" Gold
Coast "charmer" for the "beautiful people" offers a "great
selection" of raw fish and "excellent Japanese entree
choices" "downstairs [and a] hot lounge upstairs" (or "sit
outside and people-watch"); still, some say that the food is
"not so memorable" and cite "slow service" and "high
prices" as concerns.

## Tucci Benucch
17 | 16 | 17 | $26

*900 N. Michigan Ave., 5th fl. (Walton St.), 312-266-2500;*
*www.leye.com*

"Good while shopping", this "comfortable, inviting" Lettuce
Entertain You Italian is "not your typical mall restaurant" to
proponents who praise its "good old-fashioned food" and
"moderate" pricing; weary wordsmiths, though, dog it as
"disappointing" due to "hit-or-miss" meals.

## Tufano's Vernon Park Tap ⬠
21 | 13 | 19 | $23

*1073 W. Vernon Park Pl. (bet. Harrison & Racine Sts.),*
*312-733-3393*

"They treat you like family" at this "authentic old [Southern]
Italian", a Near South Side institution that's "quite the
Chicago experience" for hearty eaters who enjoy "huge
dishes" of "dependable" (and "cheap") "traditional" fare –
plus it's a "good place to spot pols"; just the same, jaded
jurists say "don't expect great service and atmosphere";
N.B. no reservations for parties of fewer than eight.

## Turquoise
– | – | – | M

*2147 W. Roscoe St. (bet. Damon & Western Aves.), 773-549-3523;*
*www.turquoisedining.com*

Traditional and modern Turkish cuisine, along with some
Med items, make up the bill of fare at this handsome Roscoe
Villager whose tasteful, warm-wood dining room is accented
with bright pendant light fixtures and framed artwork; in
warm weather, the sidewalk cafe is a nice spot for a
designer martini, *raki* (Turkish ouzo), native wine or *ayran* (a
non-alcoholic drink of yogurt, salt and soda).

## Tuscany
21 | 17 | 19 | $32

*3700 N. Clark St. (Waveland Ave.), 773-404-7700*
*1014 W. Taylor St. (Morgan St.), 312-829-1990*
*1415 W. 22nd St. (Rte. 83), Oak Brook, 630-990-1993*
*550 S. Milwaukee Ave. (bet. Dundee & Hintz Rds.),*
*Wheeling, 847-465-9988*
*www.stefanirestaurants.com*

"Well-done basics" and "a few inventive options" win
friends for this "popular", "cheerful" "Northern Italian Little
Italy favorite" and its sibs; "crowded and noisy" conditions,
"long waits" and "spotty service" at certain branches put

off some prospective diners, though, and others suggest that "the suburban locations don't measure up."

**Tweet**  ⊘  — | — | — | M

*5020 N. Sheridan Rd. (Foster St.), 773-728-5576;*
*www.tweet.biz*

This small Uptown venue serves up creative Eclectic fare at bargain prices upon naked tables in a funky, earth-toned dining room accented with a wall of mirrors, colorful throw pillows along long banquettes and work by area artists; N.B. there's a full bar, but credit cards are still not accepted.

**Twin Anchors**  23 | 13 | 17 | $26

*1655 N. Sedgwick St. (bet. Eugenie St. & North Ave.),*
*312-266-1616; www.twinanchorsribs.com*

"Ridiculously tasty ribs" inspire a "citywide reputation" (and "extraordinary waits") for this "old-school" BBQ "blast", "Old Town's best bet for charm and satisfaction" with a "historic bar" ("no brass and glass") and "friendly service"; spoilers who say the slabs are "somewhat disappointing" given "the hype" and rate the decor as "ramshackle" "don't see what all the fuss is about."

**Twist**  22 | 19 | 18 | $26

*3412 N. Sheffield Ave. (Clark St.), 773-388-2727*

A Spanish-Eclectic "twist on the usual tapas" that "combines foods and flavors you would never imagine" "at reasonable prices" turns some surveyors into small-plate savorers at this "welcome" Lakeview option; still, "jostled" judges jab at "tables" that "are way too tight" in this "claustrophobic" "closet-cum-restaurant" – though the "sidewalk tables are a little better."

**Twisted Lizard, The**  16 | 15 | 15 | $20

*1964 N. Sheffield Ave. (Armitage Ave.), 773-929-1414;*
*www.thetwistedlizard.com*

"Simple Mexican" meals meet "fantastic margaritas" to the satisfaction of a segment of surveyors at this "reliable, low-cost choice" in Lincoln Park, where the "low-ceilinged" "subterranean" setting has a "college feel" (appropriate since it's "steps away from DePaul"); dropouts, though, dis the food as "mediocre."

**Twisted Spoke**  ◐  19 | 15 | 14 | $18

*3369 N. Clark St. (Roscoe St.), 773-525-5300*
*501 N. Ogden Ave. (Grand Ave.), 312-666-1500*
*www.twistedspoke.com*

"Real bikers and wannabes" who "dine side by side" at this "funky" Near West Traditional American and its Wrigleyville spin-off favor the "great bar food", "fun brunch" (they make a "mean Bloody Mary"), "kitschy atmosphere" and "wonderful rooftop" dining (at the original) – and devoted diehards declare "don't be put off by the too-cool-for-school staff."

## Udupi Palace  ▽ 22 11 18 $16
*2543 W. Devon Ave. (bet. Maplewood Ave. & Rockwell St.),
773-338-2152*
*Market Square, 730 E. Schaumburg Rd. (N. Plum Grove Rd.),
Schaumburg, 847-884-9510*
*www.udupipalace.com*
Cohorts of this Northwest Side BYO "storefront" "return"
for the "memorably" "superb and surprisingly creative"
South Indian "veggie food" and say it's "good for novices",
too (the Schaumburg branch also serves meat dishes and
has a liquor license); N.B. the Decor score may not reflect
a post-*Survey* remodeling of the original location.

## Uncle Julio's Hacienda  17 15 15 $25
*855 W. North Ave. (Clybourn Ave.), 312-266-4222*
*2360 Fountain Square Dr. (Butterfield Rd.), Lombard,
630-705-9260* ⬕
Enthusiastic eaters who esteem this Old Town option and its
South Suburban sequel for their "right-on Tex-Mex taste"
tell us they also love the "yummy swirls" "concocted of
frozen margarita and sangria", as well as their "convenient
locations" (and parents purport they're "the ultimate kids'
places"); still, laggards lament what they see as "assembly-
line", "chain-store" offerings and "crowded" confines.

## Uncommon Ground  19 19 16 $16
*3800 N. Clark St. (Grace St.), 773-929-3680;
www.uncommonground.com*
"One of the best coffeehouses in the city", this "adorable"
Wrigleyville Eclectic combines "a nice, varied menu" of
"good, comforting food" (including vegetarian options)
with a "laid-back" setting including a "cozy fireplace";
there's also nightly entertainment "featuring poetry
readings", "live music" and "open-mike" events – now if
only the "friendly staff" wasn't so "inconsistent"; N.B. the
Decor rating may not reflect a post-*Survey* expansion.

## Uno Di Martino  – – – M
*2122 W. Lawrence Ave. (Hamilton Ave.), 773-878-1326*
Brothers Martino and Geronimo Ontiveros, both Mia
Francesca alumni, cook up hearty Italian eats at this
casual Lincoln Square trattoria with medieval castle decor
that's a holdover from the previous tenant – an incongruity
that's easily overlooked given the affordable prices and
equally wallet-friendly BYO policy.

## Usagi Ya  – – – M
*1178 N. Milwaukee Ave. (Division St.), 773-292-5885*
This funky storefront with pop art on the walls and Pan-
Asian food on the plates melds nicely with its Ukrainian
Village neighborhood; expect an extensive sushi list with
scads of specialty maki, plus an even longer menu of
Japanese, Vietnamese and other Eastern offerings, both

cold and cooked; tip: the long raw-fish bar and two horseshoe booths by the front windows are the hot seats.

**Va Pensiero**  25 | 22 | 24 | $50
*Margarita Inn, 1566 Oak Ave. (Davis St.), Evanston, 847-475-7779; www.va-p.com*
The cooking is "imaginative and traditional at the same time" at this "lush", "romantic" North Suburban Italian "favorite", where the "attentive" staff is "coddling", the Boot-centric "wine cellar is a joy" and the "lovely old-hotel" setting is "civilized" (you can also "dine under the stars" on the terrace); still, some free spirits find it "stiff", "staid" and "overpriced"; N.B. the Food rating may not reflect a post-*Survey* chef change.

**Venus Mezedopolion**  – | – | – | M
*820 W. Jackson Blvd. (bet. Green & Halsted Sts.), 312-714-1001; www.venuschicago.com*
Savory Cyprian meze such as swordfish kebabs, octopus in wine and slow-baked lamb are the specialty of this Greektown Greek-Med, whose open kitchen offers them as à la carte dishes or part of combination platters; the large, sunny space, including a bar shaped like an ancient boat, conjures up the Aegean, especially on weekends when there's traditional live *rembetika* music.

**Veranda**  – | – | – | M
*28 Orland Square Dr. (LaGrange Rd.), Orland Park, 708-226-9100*
The Southwest Suburbs are home to this upscale-casual New American with a Mediterranean accent whose entrees include cedar-plank salmon and brick-oven flatbread pizzas from a central stone-hearth oven; design highlights run to oversized wood columns, a gold color scheme and vintage artwork, plus – naturally – an outdoor veranda; N.B. a separate lounge offers an extensive martini list and live entertainment.

**Vermilion**  ▽ 22 | 23 | 16 | $40
*10 W. Hubbard St. (bet. Dearborn & State Sts.), 312-527-4060*
Adventurous palates perceiving "magical flavors" in the "fusion of Indian and Latin cuisines" (with "more [of the former] than [the latter]") praise the "unique", "tasty" fare at this "awesome", "funky" River Norther, where diners "can order tapas or entrees" in a fashionably "elegant" setting; paradoxically, pensive penmen postulate that management still has "a few kinks to work out", mostly in terms of service; N.B. outdoor seating is available.

**Via Carducci**  22 | 16 | 19 | $29
*1419 W. Fullerton Ave. (Southport Ave.), 773-665-1981; www.viacarducci.com*
"Hot and hearty" "authentic Southern Italian", including "fantastic pasta" and "thin-crust pizza", pairs with a "terrific wine list" at this "great neighborhood find" in Lincoln Park;

fans' "hopes" that it remain "relatively undiscovered" seem to be fading, with regulars reporting that it "can be crowded", though a post-*Survey* "expansion" − including the addition of an adjacent wine bar − "promises to make it even better."

### Viand Bar & Kitchen                ▽ 20 | 21 | 17 | $31
*155 E. Ontario St. (St. Clair St.), 312-255-8505;*
*www.viandchicago.com*
Voters vaunt the "different twist to typical tapas" at this "great addition to" Streeterville, saying they "love the concept" of seasonal New American "small plates" "to share with friends" amid a "hip decor" so deceptive you'd "never think you are in a restaurant attached to a Courtyard by Marriott" hotel; P.S. there are also "plenty of wines by the glass to choose from, at all price points."

### Via Veneto                18 | 14 | 17 | $26
*6340 N. Lincoln Ave. (Drake St.), 773-267-0888;*
*www.viavenetochicago.com*
*Amici* of this "popular" Northwest Sider opt for the "old-fashioned Italian cooking without pretense", including "homemade pasta" at "fair prices", and insinuate that "if you don't feel like family here, you never had one"; still, some who "remember the Peterson Avenue" original wonder whether the current "digs are an improvement" and suggest that "service has gone south" since the 2002 move.

### Viceroy of India                ▽ 19 | 12 | 14 | $20
*2520 W. Devon Ave. (bet. Campbell & Maplewood Aves.),*
*773-743-4100*
*19W 555 Roosevelt Rd. (Highland Ave.), Lombard, 630-627-4411*
*www.viceroyofindia.com*
"Authentic Indian" dining on Devon and in the Western Suburbs comes in the form of "generous portions" of "fresh food" at these subcontinental siblings that are also "wonderful for large parties"; "it isn't mandatory" that you "spend quite a bit of money" (the "buffet lunch" is a bargain).

### Vic's Classic Italian Steakhouse ▽ 20 | 17 | 16 | $33
(fka Giannotti Steak House)
*17 W. 400 22nd St. (bet. Midwest Rd. & Rte. 83), Oakbrook Terrace,*
*630-833-2700; www.vicsonline.com*
Serving "straight-ahead Italian for big appetites", this West Suburban steakhouse satisfies supporters of its signature beef, "eight-finger cavatelli with marinara sauce", "great chicken Vesuvio" and "excellent specials"; still, the "unimpressed" opine that it's only "ok for the price."

### Victory's Banner                ▽ 21 | 12 | 17 | $13
*2100 W. Roscoe St. (Hoyne Ave.), 773-665-0227;*
*www.victorysbanner.com*
The "tasty breakfasts" and "fresh" "vegetarian food" at this Roscoe Villager are not just a "health-conscious"

option – enlightened eaters say the Eclectic fare is so "creative you won't miss the meat"; though "service is kind and responsive", some surveyors are unnerved by the "bizarro atmosphere", and others say that the "austere" lunch fare is "disappointing"; still, there's "always a line out the door on weekends."

## Vie ☒ 　　　　　　　　– | – | – | M |
*4471 Lawn Ave. (Burlington Ave.), Western Springs, 708-246-2082; www.vierestaurant.com*
Paul Virant (ex Blackbird) goes out on his own in the Western Suburbs with this casually upscale New American entry focusing on seasonal, artisanal, global ingredients – and boasting the town's first post-Prohibition liquor license; housed in a two-story red brick building near the commuter train station, its sleek decor features a wood-burning fireplace that warms the space in cold weather.

## Vien Dong ☒ 　　　　　　– | – | – | I |
*3227 N. Clark St. (W. Belmont Ave.), 773-348-6879; www.viendongrestaurant.com*
An exhaustive menu of bargain-priced Vietnamese vittles – some familiar, some not, but all with helpful translations – along with some Chinese chow keep the faithful packing the simple setting of this busy BYO, a taste of Argyle Street in an unassuming Lakeview storefront.

## Village, The 　　　　　　18 | 19 | 20 | $29 |
*The Italian Village Restaurant Complex, 71 W. Monroe St., 2nd fl. (bet. Clark & Dearborn Sts.), 312-332-7005; www.italianvillage-chicago.com*
"Picture the *Lady and the Tramp* Italian restaurant setting and you have" this longtime Loop "standby" (the top floor of its namesake three-restaurant complex), where "old-time waiters make" the "well-prepared" "classic chow" "a little more special"; grumps grouse it's "getting stale" and hopefuls who "expected more exciting food" find it "boring", but most maintain it's a "great pre-theater option."

## Vinci 　　　　　　　　22 | 20 | 20 | $35 |
*1732 N. Halsted St. (Willow St.), 312-266-1199; www.vincichicago.com*
Chef-owner "Paul LoDuca makes you feel like part of his family" and cooks up "consistently good" "refined-but-rustic" Italian with "outstanding seasonal variations" at this "lovely" Lincoln Park "favorite" with "enough elbow room", a "warm atmosphere" and a "reasonably priced wine list"; P.S. it's "good for Steppenwolf or Royal George patrons."

## Vintage Wine Bar 　　　　– | – | – | M |
*1942 W. Division St. (bet. Damen & Winchester Aves.), 773-772-3400; www.vintage-chicago.com*
Wicker Park has warmed up to this unpretentious wine bar with a New American small-plates menu, a handful of

desserts and a wide-ranging 100-label vino list (30 by the glass); design highlights include an imposing brick archway that anchors the bar, a 22-ft. illuminated bottle storage display, a lounge area with fireplace and outdoor dining.

### Vive La Crepe       ▽  16  14  17  $17

*1565 Sherman Ave. (bet. Davis & Grove Sts.), Evanston, 847-570-0600; www.vivelacrepe.com*

"For Sunday brunch or a light" repast, this "charming" Evanston New French crêperie finds a following for its "tasty" combos in both "meal and dessert" varieties ranging from chicken Marsala to bananas Foster; still, naysayers nag that the noshes are "not authentic" and "uninspired."

### Vivere ⊠       22  23  22  $43

*The Italian Village Restaurant Complex, 71 W. Monroe St. (bet. Clark & Dearborn Sts.), 312-332-4040; www.italianvillage-chicago.com*

A "hip, romantic" "place to impress" that's "convenient to all of the Downtown attractions", this "magically theatrical", "over-the-top" "Italian experience" offers "more modern", "sophisticated" "choices than The Village", its "upstairs" sibling, but shares the "unbelievable wine list" of its downstairs triplet, La Cantina Enoteca; "obliging" service from an "efficient" staff also makes it a living "treat."

### Vivo       22  21  21  $38

*838 W. Randolph St. (bet. Green & Peoria Sts.), 312-733-3379; www.vivo-chicago.com*

Made from "fresh ingredients", the "excellent" Italian cuisine is "full of flavor" at this "delicious" "date place" overseen by an "energetic, friendly and informative staff" in a "hip" "architectural warehouse" setting (which was the "first outpost on the Market District's" now-"great Randolph strip"); qualifiers quibble, though, that the "quite-loud" ambiance makes it "tough to talk."

### Volare       22  16  21  $35

*201 E. Grand Ave. (St. Clair St.), 312-410-9900; www.volarerestaurant.com*

"A real find", this "down-home Italian" Streeterville "treat" is a "dependable" "good value", plus "they know how to provide the extras" (in case the "large portions" of "tasty" fare aren't big enough for ya); critics complain that it's "crowded and noisy" and "there's no place to wait", but diehards deem it "well worth it"; N.B. the Decor rating may not reflect a post-*Survey* remodeling.

### Volo Restaurant & Wine Bar       –  –  –  M

*2008 W. Roscoe St. (Damen Ave.), 773-348-4600; www.volorestaurant.com*

From the originator of Kitsch'n on Roscoe comes this New American small-plates-and-flights way station in Roscoe Village, an upscale loftlike space with two outdoor dining

environments and an evolving seasonal menu from chef
Stephen Dunne (ex Spago, mk) that pairs organic and
housemade foodstuffs with a juicy global wine list.

**Vong's Thai Kitchen**                    21 | 21 | 20 | $34
*6 W. Hubbard St. (State St.), 312-644-8664; www.leye.com*
Those who feel they've "finally got it right" at this River
North redo of the former Vong say it's "better now that they
downscaled", while still serving "impressively diverse",
"tasty Thai food with a twist" that's "a perfect sensory
experience" when "enjoyed" along with its "cool look" and
"attentive service"; still, sophisticates say "something's
missing" now that it's "less esoteric and more populist",
and wallet-watchers think it's "expensive" for the genre.

**Walker Bros.**                            23 | 17 | 19 | $14
**Original Pancake House**
*825 W. Dundee Rd. (bet. Arlington Hts. Rd. & Rte. 53),
Arlington Heights, 847-392-6600*
*1615 Waukegan Rd. (bet. Chestnut & Lake Aves.), Glenview,
847-724-0220*
*620 Central Ave. (bet. Green Bay Rd. & 2nd St.), Highland Park,
847-432-0660*
*Lake Zurich Theatre Development, 767 S. Rand Rd. (Rte. 22),
Lake Zurich, 847-550-0006*
*200 Marriott Dr. (Milwaukee Ave.), Lincolnshire, 847-634-2220*
*153 Green Bay Rd. (bet. Central & Lake Aves.), Wilmette,
847-251-6000*
Flapjack fans love this chain of "consistent, efficient, fun"
American "breakfast icons" for their "heavenly", "carbo-
craver" eats that amount to "glorious morning excess" (and
"don't forget pancakes are good for lunch and dinner", too);
"snappy service" and "wood-and-stained-glass decor"
with "old-time charm" also make them well "worth" the
inevitable "long waits", especially "on weekends."

**Wave** ◗                                 17 | 21 | 18 | $42
*W Chicago Lakeshore, 644 N. Lake Shore Dr. (Ontario St.),
312-255-4460; www.waverestaurant.com*
"Funky" decor sets a "great standard" at this Streeterville
Eclectic "scene" spot in the W Chicago Lakeshore, where
the seafood is "artfully prepared" and there's a "fun"
"happy hour"; still, some testifiers tell us the tide has gone
out on this "trendy spot", claiming it's "all flash and no
substance" and saying the "setting is better than the food."

**Weber Grill**                             19 | 17 | 17 | $32
*Hilton Garden Inn, 539 N. State St. (Grand Ave.), 312-467-9696*
*2331 Fountain Sq. Dr. (Meyers Rd.), Lombard, 630-953-8880*
*220 N. Milwaukee Ave. (Lake Cook Rd.), Wheeling, 847-215-0996*
*www.webergrillrestaurant.com*
"You can't beat the taste" boom boosters of these city-
and-suburbans "based on a backyard BBQ" concept,

complete with "gigantic" Webers ("grill envy starts here")
sizzling with "basic preparations" of "very American"
vittles in somewhat "fancy" but "family-ish" confines; still,
"do-it-at-home" sorts sear the food as "standard", saying
it unduly "lightens the pocketbook", and suggest there's
"something wrong with the service."

### Webster's Wine Bar ◑          17   21   20   $23
*1480 W. Webster Ave. (bet. Ashland Ave. & Clybourn St.),
773-868-0608; www.websterwinebar.com*
There's a "terrific vibe" at this "cool" Eclectic Lincoln Park
"vino bar" and "date place" with "comfortable sofas"; the
"helpful staff" "is good with suggestions" on pairing the
"many by-the-glass selections" or "great flights" from the
"fantastic wine list" "with a cheese plate" or other light
fare, though picky eaters peg the "passable" provender as
"pricey" and "merely an accoutrement."

### West Town Tavern ⊠          25   22   24   $36
*1329 W. Chicago Ave. (Throop St.), 312-666-6175;
www.westtowntavern.com*
"Go west and strike gold" at this West Town tastemaker
where "Drew and Susan [Goss] keep it simple and
incredibly delicious", dishing up "upscale" yet "down-
home" New American "comfort" cooking supported by a
"well-honed wine list"; the "professional and friendly
service" also contributes to the "casual, inviting" vibe of
its "quaint", "cozy" "neighborhood" setting.

### White Fence Farm          22   18   21   $19
*Joliet Rd. (2 mi. south of I-55), Lemont, 630-739-1720;
www.whitefencefarm.com*
"A nostalgia trip" to the Southwest Suburbs is on the
itinerary for fans of this "tried-and-true" "family place"
where Traditional American fodder like "famous fried
chicken and fritters" is laid out in a "huge" "down-on-the-
farm" setting; still, feuders feel it's "a bit corny" and "tired";
P.S. there are "lots of fun things" for you and the "kids" "to
look at while you're waiting."

### Wiener's Circle, The ◑≠          21   6   14   $7
*2622 N. Clark St. (Wrightwood Ave.), 773-477-7444*
"When you must [have] a Chicago dog", "the Circle is
the stop to make" for some of the "best" ones around,
including "perfect chardogs" and "kick-ass red hots" (not
to mention "great burgers"); "late-night, après-partying"
people should "be prepared" to get their "cheese fries
with attitude" from "the potty-mouthed counter women",
whose "comedy" "sideshow" of "verbal assaults" and "R-
rated obscenities" makes for a "hilarious experience."

### WILDFIRE          23   21   20   $37
*159 W. Erie St. (bet. La Salle & Wells Sts.), 312-787-9000
235 Parkway Dr. (Milwaukee Ave.), Lincolnshire, 847-279-7900*

(continued)
**WILDFIRE**
*Oakbrook Center Mall, 232 Oakbrook Ctr. (Rte. 83), Oak Brook,*
*630-586-9000*
*1300 Patriot Blvd. (E. Lake Ave.), Glenview, 847-657-6363*
*1250 E. Higgins Rd. (National Pkwy.), Schaumburg, 847-995-0100*
*www.wildfirerestaurant.com*
Pyromaniacs prefer the "done-to-perfection steaks", "fine
seafood" and other "succulent, hearty" American fare from
the "wood-burning" oven and rotisserie (try the "great
crusted filets") at "this Lettuce Entertain You" trio in the
city and suburbs, where the "always-packed" "supperclub atmosphere" can get "wild", especially after a few of
those "great martinis"; N.B. the Schaumburg and Glenview
branches are unrated.

**Wildfish**                          ▽ 24 | 22 | 18 | $33 |
*Arlington Town Square, 60 S. Arlington Heights Rd.*
*(Northwest Hwy.), Arlington Heights, 847-870-8260;*
*www.wildfishcontemporary.com*
Relieved raw-fish fanatics are "surprised to find" such
"excellent", "wonderfully fresh" "Downtown-style" sushi
(including "innovatively presented" and "interesting maki
rolls") in a Northwest "Suburban location"; the "unique"
Japanese menu also features "smokin'" cooked items,
which are served in a "hot and hip" setting that makes for
a "most enjoyable experience."

**Wishbone**                          20 | 15 | 17 | $19 |
*3300 N. Lincoln Ave. (School St.), 773-549-2663*
*1001 W. Washington Blvd. (Morgan St.), 312-850-2663*
*www.wishbonechicago.com*
"Southern classics", "brunch favorites" and "excellent
vegetarian choices" merge on the menu at this "kitschy"
chicken-themed duo where a "crowd" "of all ages and
races" "lines" up for "reliable" "down-home cookin'"
served in a "crowded", "colorful", "kid-friendly" context
with "wild murals"; P.S. it's "modestly priced", too.

**Wolfgang Puck's Grand Café**        17 | 18 | 18 | $27 |
*Century Theatre Complex, 1701 Maple Ave. (Church St.),*
*Evanston, 847-869-9653; www.wolfgangpuck.com*
Visitors who value its "well-prepared" New American
cuisine (including "crave-worthy salads" and "exotic
pizza") call this "informal", "upscale" North Suburban
cafe a "crowd-pleaser"; grouches who gripe it's not all
that "grand" say "it's a brand name" only, with "overpriced",
"lackluster" noshes that are "not as good as expected."

**Woo Lae Oak**                       – | – | – | M |
*3201 Algonquin Rd. (Newport Dr.), Rolling Meadows, 847-870-9910*
An upscale temple of Korean comestibles, this Suburban
Northwest member of an international chain boasts a vast

space and a menu to match: beneath the main dining room's grand domed ceiling, staffers barbecue for you at your table or serve you an intriguing tasting menu of unusual items at a relative bargain; N.B. there's a separate bar for soju-sipping and socializing.

**X/O Chicago** ◑      _ | _ | _ | M
3441 N. Halsted St. (W. Newport Ave.), 773-348-9696;
www.xochicago.com
Named for the premium cognac designation, this hot boîte in Lakeview offers tasting flights of boutique brandies plus wines from around the globe with its ever-changing plethora of Eclectic small plates; the chic dining rooms incorporate organic materials along with floor-to-ceiling booths perfect for privacy lovers; N.B. late-night loungers can convene until 2 AM (3 AM on Saturdays).

**Yard House**      _ | _ | _ | M
1880 Tower Dr. (Patriot Blvd.), Glenview, 847-729-9273;
www.yardhouse.com
A North Suburban installation of a southern Californian chain, this 10,000-sq.-ft. newcomer combines a 100-plus item menu of New American 'fusion' fare with a whopping 130 beers in pints, half-yards and yards – plus specialty martinis and beer blends with unusual flavors; the upscale-casual space is heavy on wood and stainless steel, with an oval bar where patrons can watch sports on monitors.

**Yoshi's Café**      25 | 16 | 22 | $39
3257 N. Halsted St. (Belmont Ave.), 773-248-6160;
www.yoshiscafe.com
Loyalists love this "Lakeview institution" for its very "distinctive", "ingenious" New American cuisine with "French-Asian fusion" overtones but "without pretension or trendiness" from the namesake chef-owner, "who just keeps trucking along" after more than 20 years; he and "his wife are incredibly hospitable" and make you feel "like they are serving you in their home"; N.B. the Decor rating may not reflect a post-*Survey* renovation.

**Zealous**      22 | 24 | 22 | $66
419 W. Superior St. (Sedgewick St.), 312-475-9112;
www.zealousrestaurant.com
Devotees are "dazzled" by "this fine-dining" venue "hidden" in River North, a "special-occasion" "expense-account" spot with a "spectacular", "spare space" in which "imaginative" chef Michael Taus' "marvelous menu" of "delicious gourmet" New American cuisine is "well prepared" "and beautifully presented" along with an "exceptional wine list"; not "all palates" report "such a pleasant surprise", though, with some finding the fare "too complicated" and "not up to the price level"; P.S. "if you have a group, book the bamboo grove."

**Zest**                         21   20   21   $37
*Hotel InterContinental, 525 N. Michigan Ave. (Illinois Ave.),*
*312-321-8766; www.chicago.interconti.com*
A "great spot for 21st-century grazers", this Streeterville
New American offers "nice, light, modern food" in a "cool",
"beautiful space" that's "rarely crowded" and affords a view
of the "Mag Mile"; plus, "who would expect to find such a
reasonably priced restaurant at the Hotel InterContinental?"

**Zia's Trattoria**              23   18   20   $29
*6699 N. Northwest Hwy. (bet. Harlem & Touhy Aves.),*
*773-775-0808; www.ziaschicago.com*
Won-over wordsmiths warble about the "classy",
"consistent" Italian menu (augmented by "ambitious
specials") that's "equal to more expensive places" at
this "homey" Edison Park "family-owned trattoria" with
a "cozy", "brick-walled dining room"; still, the "noise"
and "crowded" conditions are ancillary annoyances.

# Chicago Indexes

**CUISINES**
**LOCATIONS**
**SPECIAL FEATURES**

# CUISINES

**Afghan**
Kabul House

**American (New)**
Adelle's
Alinea
Allen's – New Amer.
Amber Cafe
Aria
Atwater's
Bank Lane Bistro
Bijan's Bistro
Bin 36
Bistro Marbuzet
Blackbird
Black Duck Tavern
Blue Line Club Car
Blue Water Grill
Blu 47
BOKA
Brett's Café Amer.
Butter
Cab's Wine Bar
Café Absinthe
Cafe Selmarie
Canoe Club
Charlie's on Leav.
Charlie Trotter's
Chef's Station
Chestnut Grill
Cielo
Cité
Courtright's
Crofton on Wells
David's Bistro
Dunlays
erwin american
Feast
Fio
Flo
Frankie J's
Grand Lux Cafe
Green Dolphin St.
Green Zebra
Improv Kitchen
Jack's on Halsted
Jacky's Bistro

Jane's
Jilly's Cafe
JP Chicago
Kevin
La Fette
L8
Leo's Lunchroom
Lovell's/Lake Forest
Magnolia Cafe
Maison
Masck
Menagerie
Meritage/Wine
M. Henry
Milk & Honey
mk
Naha
Next Door Bistro
North Pond
Oceanique
One North
one sixtyblue
120 Ocean Place
Park Grill
Pepper Lounge
Philander's Oak Park
Prairie Grass Cafe
Puck's at MCA
Pump Room
Rhapsody
Ritz-Carlton Café
Riva
Rivers
Room 22
Rushmore
Seasons
1776
She She
Signature Room
Solstice
South
South Gate Cafe
Spring
Square Kitchen
Stained Glass Bistro
Tasting Room

Tavern
302 West
Thyme
Thyme Café
Tomboy
Veranda
Viand Kitchen
Vie
Vintage Wine Bar
Volo
West Town Tavern
Wolfgang Puck Café
Yard House
Yoshi's Café
Zealous
Zest

## American (Traditional)
American Girl
Ann Sather
Atwood Cafe
Avenue Ale Hse.
Bandera
Bar Louie
Barn of Barrington
Berghoff
Billy Goat Tavern
Black Duck Tavern
Bluegrass
Bongo Room
Boston Blackie's
Breakfast Club
Bubba Gump Shrimp
Burgundy Inn
Cal. Pizza Kitchen
Charlie's Ale Hse.
Cheesecake Factory
Chicago Firehouse
Clubhouse
Cornelia's
Corner Grille
Cullen's B&G
Dell Rhea's Chicken
Drake Bros.' Steak
18 Esperienza
Fadó Irish Pub
Flatlander's
Flo
Fluky's

Four Farthings
Gale Street Inn
Genesee Depot
Goose Is. Brewing
Grace O'Malley's
Gracie's on Webster
Green Door Tavern
Grill on the Alley
Gulliver's Pizzeria
Hackney's
Hard Rock Cafe
Heartland Cafe
Hemmingway's
Hot Chocolate
Hugo's Frog/Fish
Ina's
Irish Oak
Jake Melnick's
J. Alexander's
Joey's Brickhouse
John Barleycorn
Lawry's Prime Rib
Lou Mitchell's
L. Woods Lodge
Mac's
Marché
Margie's Candies
Medici on 57th
Mike Ditka's
Miller's Pub
Mill Race Inn
Millrose
Misto
Mity Nice Grill
Moody's Pub
Motel
Mrs. Park's Tavern
Nookies
Northside B&G
Oak Tree
O'Neil's
Original Pancake Hse.
Petterino's
Phil & Lou's
Pizzeria Uno/Due
P.J. Clarke's
Poag Mahone's
Porter's Steak

Public Landing
Rainforest Cafe
Red Star Tavern
Ritz-Carlton Café
R.J. Grunts
RL
Rock Bottom Brew.
Rockit B&G
Seasons Café
Silver Cloud B&G
South Gate Cafe
South Water Kitchen
Stanley's Kitchen
312 Chicago
Toast
Tommy Nevin's Pub
Twisted Spoke
Walker Bros. Pancake
Weber Grill
White Fence Farm
Wildfire

### Argentinean
Costumbres Argentinas
Tango
Tango Sur

### Armenian
Sayat Nova

### Asian
Alice & Friends Veg.
Big Bowl
Catch 35
China Grill
Chinoiserie
Flat Top Grill
Green Ginger
Karma
L'anne
Moto
Penang
Ping Pong
Red Light
Satay
Shanghai Terrace
Stir Crazy

### Austrian
Edelweiss
Glunz Bavarian

### Barbecue
Aloha Grill
BD's Mongolian
Carson's Ribs
Dick's Last Resort
Famous Dave's
Fat Willy's
Fireplace Inn
Hecky's
Joe's Be-Bop Cafe
Lem's BBQ
Merle's Smokehouse
Ribs 'n' Bibs
Robinson's Ribs
Russell's BBQ
Smoke Daddy
Twin Anchors
Weber Grill

### Brazilian
Fogo de Chão
Sal & Carvão
Samba Room
Sushisamba rio

### Cajun
Blue Bayou
Davis St. Fishmkt.
Dixie Kitchen
Heaven on Seven
House of Blues
Maple Tree Inn
Pappadeaux Seafood
Redfish

### Californian
Acqualina
Caliterra B&G

### Caribbean
Calypso Cafe
Julio's Cocina
Marina Cafe
Toucan

### Chinese
(* dim sum specialist)
Ben Pao
Best Hunan
Chen's
Dee's

Dragon Court
Dragonfly Mandarin
Emperor's Choice
Evergreen
Fornetto Mei
Furama*
Golden Budha
Hai Yen
Happy Chef Dim Sum*
Jewel of India
Koi
Lao Sze Chuan
LuLu's Dim Sum*
Moon Palace
New Three Happiness*
Opera
P.F. Chang's
Phoenix*
Pine Yard
Shine & Morida
Silver Seafood
Three Happiness*
Tien Giang

## Coffee Shops/Diners
Chicago Diner
Ed Debevic's
Lou Mitchell's
Manny's
Milk & Honey
Nookies
Tempo

## Colombian
La Fonda Latino
Las Tablas

## Continental
Café La Cave
Dover Straits
Grille on Laurel
Le P'tit Paris
Lobby, The
Lutnia
Lutz Continental
Narcisse
Trader Vic's

## Costa Rican
Irazu

## Creole
Blue Bayou
Heaven on Seven
House of Blues
Marina Cafe
Pappadeaux Seafood
Redfish

## Cuban
Cafe Bolero
Cafe 28
Miramar
Samba Room

## Delis
Bagel
Cold Comfort Cafe
Manny's
Mrs. Levy's Deli
Potbelly Sandwich

## Eclectic
Aria
Avenues
Bite
Blind Faith Café
CHIC Cafe
Chinoiserie
Cru Cafe/Wine
Deleece
Eclectic
Ember Grille
Feast
Flight
foodlife
Gracie's on Webster
Hilary's Urban
Iggy's
Jane's
John's Place
Kit Kat Lounge
Kitsch'n
Lula
Mj2 Bistro
Moto
Narcisse
Orange
Park Grill
Privata Café
Raw Bar & Grill

She She
Speakeasy Supperclub
Stained Glass Bistro
Sugar Dessert Bar
10 West
Think Café
Tilli's
Toast
Tweet
Twist
Uncommon Ground
Victory's Banner
Wave
Webster's Wine
X/O Chicago
Zest

## English
Red Lion Pub

## Ethiopian
Ethiopian Diamond
Mama Desta's

## Filipino
Coobah

## Fondue
Fondue Stube
Geja's Cafe
Melting Pot

## French (Bistro)
Albert's Café
Bank Lane Bistro
Barrington Bistro
Bêtise Bistro
Bistro Banlieue
Bistro Campagne
Bistro Kirkou
Bistro Marbuzet
Bistro 110
Bistrot Margot
Bistrot Zinc
Brasserie Jo
Café Bernard
Cafe Central
Café le Coq
Cafe Matou
Cafe Pyrenees

Café 36
Cerise
Chez François
Chez Joel
Cyrano's
D & J Bistro
Firefly
Froggy's French
Hemmingway's
Jacky's Bistro
KiKi's Bistro
La Crêperie
La Sardine
La Tache
Le Bouchon
Miramar
Mon Ami Gabi
Pierrot Gourmet
Retro Bistro
Shallots Bistro
socca
Tournesol

## French (Classic)
Froggy's French
la petite folie
Le Vichyssois

## French (New)
Ambria
Atwater's
Brasserie Jo
Café des Architectes
Carlos'
CHIC Cafe
Cité
Dining Rm. at Kendall
Everest
Gabriel's
Jilly's Cafe
Kevin
L'anne
Le Colonial
Le Français
Le Lan
Les Deux Autres
Les Nomades
Le Titi de Paris
Maison

Marché
Mimosa
NoMI
Oceanique
Olives
Pasha
Pasteur
Ritz-Carlton Din. Rm.
Tallgrass
Thyme
Thyme Café
Trio Atelier
Tru
Vive La Crepe

## German
Berghoff
Edelweiss
Glunz Bavarian
Lutz Continental
Mirabell

## Greek
Artopolis Bakery
Athena
Costa's
Greek Islands
Noyes St. Café
OPA Estiatorio
Papagus Taverna
Parthenon
Pegasus
Roditys
Santorini
Venus Mezedopolion

## Hamburgers
Billy Goat Tavern
Boston Blackie's
Ed Debevic's
Goose Is. Brewing
Green Door Tavern
Hackney's
Pete Miller's
P.J. Clarke's
R.J. Grunts
Superdawg Drive-In
Twisted Spoke
Wiener's Circle

## Hawaii Regional
Roy's

## Hawaiian
Aloha Grill

## Hot Dogs
Al's #1 Beef
Fluky's
Gold Coast Dogs
Hot Doug's
Superdawg Drive-In
Wiener's Circle

## Indian
Essence of India
Gaylord Indian
Hema's Kitchen
India House
Indian Garden
Jewel of India
Klay Oven
Monsoon
Mt. Everest
Mysore Woodland
Raj Darbar
Tiffin
Udupi Palace
Vermilion
Viceroy of India

## Irish
Abbey Pub
Chief O'Neill's Pub
Cullen's B&G
Fadó Irish Pub
Grace O'Malley's
Irish Oak
Tommy Nevin's Pub

## Israeli
Hashalom

## Italian
(N=Northern; S=Southern)
Al Dente Café
A Milano
Amore (N)
Angelina (S)
Anna Maria Pasteria

Antico Posto
a tavola (N)
Aurelio's Pizza
Bacchanalia (N)
Bacino's
Balagio
Ballo
BaPi (N)
Basil Leaf Cafe (N)
bella! Bacino's
Bella Notte (S)
Bice Grill (N)
Bice Ristorante (N)
Blandino's Sorriso (N)
Bruna's
Buca di Beppo (S)
Buona Terra (N)
Butera Ristorante
Cafe Borgia
Café Luciano
Café Spiaggia
Caliterra B&G (N)
Campagnola
Cannella's
Carlucci (N)
Carmine's
Cielo (N)
Club Lago (N)
Club Lucky
Coco Pazzo (N)
Coco Pazzo Cafe (N)
Convito Italiano
Cornelia's
Cucina Bella
Dave's Italian (S)
Del Rio (N)
Dinotto (N)
Dolce
18 Esperienza
EJ's Place (N)
Enoteca Piattini (S)
Erie Cafe
Figo Ristorante (N)
Filippo's (S)
Flourchild's
Follia (N)
Fornetto Mei
Francesca's (N)

Francesco's Hole (S)
Gabriel's
Gilardi's
Gio (N)
Gioco (N)
Graziano's Pizza
Grotto
Harry Caray's
La Bocca/Verità
La Cantina Enoteca
La Cucina/ Donatella
La Donna
La Fontanella
La Gondola
La Piazza
La Scarola
La Strada
La Vita (N)
L8
Leonardo's (N)
Lucca's
Lucia
Maggiano's (S)
Mario's Gold Coast
Merlo (N)
Mia Cucina
Mia Francesca
Mimosa
Misto
Next Door Bistro
Nick & Tony's
Noyes St. Café
O'Famé
O'Neil's
Osteria Via Stato
Pane Caldo (N)
Papa Milano (S)
Pasha
Pasta Palazzo
Phil Stefani's
Piazza Bella
Pizza Capri (N)
Pizza Rustica
Pompei Bakery
Privata Café
ristorante we (N)
RoSal's (S)
Rose Angelis

Rosebud
Sabatino's (N)
Salvatore's (N)
Sapori Trattoria
Sausalito
Scoozi!
Settimana Café
socca
Spiaggia
Strega Nona
Suparossa (S)
Tarantino's
312 Chicago
Topo Gigio
Trattoria Gianni
Trattoria No. 10
Trattoria Roma (S)
Trattoria Trullo (S)
Tre Via
Tucci Benucch
Tufano's Vernon Pk. (S)
Tuscany (N)
Uno Di Martino
Va Pensiero
Via Carducci (S)
Via Veneto
Vic's Classic Steak
Village (N)
Vinci
Vivere
Vivo
Volare
Zia's Trattoria

## Japanese
(* sushi specialist)
Akai Hana*
Amy Thai*
Benihana*
Bluefin*
Bob San*
Chen's*
Coast Sushi*
Dee's*
Hama Matsu*
Heat*
Indie Cafe*
Itto Sushi*
Izumi Sushi*

Japonais*
Kamehachi*
Kaminari*
Katsu Japanese*
Kaze Sushi*
Kizoku Sushi*
Koi*
Kuni's*
Kyoto*
Matsuya*
Matsu Yama*
Meiji*
Mirai Sushi*
New Japan*
Oysy*
RA Sushi*
Ringo*
Rise*
Ron of Japan
Sai Café*
Shine & Morida*
Shiroi Hana*
Silver Spoon*
Starfish*
Sushi Naniwa*
Sushisamba rio*
Sushi Wabi*
Swordfish*
Tank Sushi*
Tokyo Marina*
Tombo Kitchen*
Triad*
Tsuki*
Tsunami*
Usagi Ya*
Wildfish*

## Jewish
Bagel
Mrs. Levy's Deli

## Korean
Amitabul
Chicago Kalbi
Hama Matsu
Jin Ju
Koryo
San Soo Gab San
Woo Lae Oak

## Kosher
Shallots Bistro
Slice of Life

## Lebanese
Aladdin's Eatery
Fattoush
Kan Zaman
Sayat Nova

## Mediterranean
Acqualina
Aladdin's Eatery
Andies
Artopolis Bakery
Avec
Café des Architectes
Costa's
Isabella Estiatorio
Lucca's
Naha
Pita Inn
Scylla
Souk
Tizi Melloul
Turquoise
Venus Mezedopolion
Veranda

## Mexican
Adobo Grill
Blue Cactus
Cafe 28
Caliente
Chilpancingo
De Cero
Don Juan
Dorado
El Jardin
El Presidente
Frontera Grill
Hacienda Tecatitlan
Hot Tamales
Irazu
Ixcapuzalco
La Cazuela Mariscos
Lalo's
Las Bellas Artes
La Taberna Tapatia

Lindo Mexico
Lupita's
Nuevo Leon
Platiyo
Privata Café
Rique's
Salbute
Salpicón
San Gabriel Mexican
Tecalitlan
Topolobampo
Twisted Lizard

## Middle Eastern
Andies
Babylon Kitchen
Maza
Old Jerusalem
Pita Inn
Samah
Souk
Tizi Melloul

## Moroccan
Hashalom

## Nepalese
Mt. Everest

## Noodle Shops
Joy Yee's Noodle
Lincoln Noodle Hse.
Penny's Noodle

## Norwegian
Tre Kronor

## Nuevo Latino
Coobah
Mambo Grill
Mas
Nacional 27
Rumba
Sabor
Sangria
Vermilion

## Pacific Northwest
Meritage/Wine

## Pakistani
Hema's Kitchen

### Persian/Iranian
Noon-O-Kabab
Reza's

### Pizza
Art of Pizza
Aurelio's Pizza
Bacino's
bella! Bacino's
Bricks
Cal. Pizza Kitchen
Chicago Pizza/Grinder
Dave's Italian
Edwardo's Pizza
Flourchild's
Gioco
Giordano's
Graziano's Pizza
Gulliver's Pizzeria
La Gondola
Lou Malnati Pizza
My Pie Pizza
Nancy's Stuffed Pizza
Original Gino's
Piece
Pizza Capri
Pizza D.O.C.
Pizza Rustica
Pizzeria Uno/Due
Pompei Bakery
Ranalli's
Trattoria Roma
Wolfgang Puck Café

### Polynesian
Trader Vic's

### Puerto Rican
Coco

### Russian
Russian Tea Time

### Sandwiches
Al's #1 Beef
Bagel
Chicago Sammies
Cold Comfort Cafe
Corner Bakery
Mr. Beef

Mrs. Levy's Deli
Potbelly Sandwich

### Scottish
Duke of Perth

### Seafood
Bluepoint Oyster
Bob Chinn Crab Hse.
Bubba Gump Shrimp
Canoe Club
Cape Cod Room
Catch 35
Chinn's Fishery
Davis St. Fishmkt.
Dick's Last Resort
Don Roth's
Don's Fishmarket
Dover Straits
Drake Bros.' Steak
Emperor's Choice
Erie Cafe
Froggy's French
Grillroom
Half Shell
Hugo's Frog/Fish
Joe's Sea/Steak
Keefer's
La Cazuela Mariscos
Lobby, The
McCormick & Schmick
Nick & Tony's
Nick's Fishmarket
Nine
Oceanique
120 Ocean Place
Pacific Blue
Pappadeaux Seafood
Parkers' Ocean Grill
Pete Miller's
Raw Bar & Grill
Redfish
Riva
Santorini
Scylla
Shaw's Crab Hse.
Shula's Steak
Silver Seafood
Spring

Sullivan's Steak
Tin Fish
Topo Gigio
Wave
Wildfire

## Small Plates
Andalucia
Arco de Cuchilleros
Avec
BOKA
Cafe Ba-Ba-Reeba!
Café Iberico
Dolce
Emilio's Tapas
Enoteca Piattini
Flight
1492 Tapas
La Tasca
Maza
Menagerie
Mesón Sabika
Sangria
Tango
Tapas Barcelona
Twist
Vermilion
Viand Kitchen
Vintage Wine Bar
Volo
X/O Chicago

## Soul Food
Army & Lou's
BJ's Market
House of Blues
Negro League Café

## South American
El Nandu
Julio's Cocina
La Peña
Mas
Nacional 27
Rinconcito Sudamer.

## Southern
Army & Lou's
BJ's Market
Bluegrass

Dixie Kitchen
Fat Willy's
House of Blues
Joe's Be-Bop Cafe
LuLu's Dim Sum
South
Wishbone

## Southwestern
Bandera
South

## Spanish
(* tapas specialist)
Andalucia
Arco de Cuchilleros
Cafe Ba-Ba-Reeba!
Café Iberico
Emilio's Tapas
La Tasca
Mesón Sabika
Rioja*
Tapas Barcelona
Twist

## Steakhouses
Benihana
Bogart's Charhouse
Butera Ristorante
Capital Grille
Carmichael's Steak
Catch 35
Chicago Chop Hse.
Chicago Prime Steak
Club Lago
Don Roth's
Drake Bros.' Steak
EJ's Place
El Nandu
Erie Cafe
Fogo de Chão
Gene & Georgetti
Gibsons Steak
Golden Budha
Grille on Laurel
Grill on the Alley
Grillroom
Grotto
Harry Caray's

Hugo's Frog/Fish
Keefer's
Kinzie Chophouse
Las Tablas
Magnum's Steak
Mike Ditka's
Morton's Steak
Myron & Phil's Steak
Nick & Tony's
Nine
Palm
Pete Miller's
Phil Stefani's
Porter's Steak
Red Star Tavern
Ron of Japan
Rosebud Steak
Ruth's Chris Steak
Sal & Carvão
Saloon Steak
Shaw's Crab Hse.
Shula's Steak
Smith & Wollensky
Stetson's Chop Hse.
Sullivan's Steak
Tango Sur
Tavern
Tavern on Rush
Vic's Classic Steak
Wildfire

## Swedish
Ann Sather
Tre Kronor

## Tex-Mex
Uncle Julio's

## Thai
Amarind's
Amy Thai
Aroma
Arun's
Indie Cafe
Mama Thai
P.S. Bangkok
Ruby of Siam

Silver Spoon
Spoon Thai
Star of Siam
Thai Classic
Thai Pastry
Vong's

## Turkish
A La Turka
Cousin's
Turquoise

## Vegetarian
(* vegan)
Alice & Friends Veg.*
Amitabul*
Andies
Blind Faith Café
Chicago Diner
Ethiopian Diamond
Green Zebra*
Handlebar*
Heartland Cafe
Hema's Kitchen
Kabul House
Karyn's Cooked*
Karyn's Fresh Corner*
Lula
Mama Desta's
Maza
Mysore Woodland
Narcisse
Reza's
Sayat Nova
Slice of Life
Udupi Palace
Victory's Banner
Wishbone

## Vietnamese
Hai Yen
Le Colonial
Le Lan
Pasteur
Tien Giang
Usagi Ya
Vien Dong

# LOCATIONS

## DOWNTOWN

### Loop
Aria
Atwood Cafe
bella! Bacino's
Berghoff
Billy Goat Tavern
Boston Blackie's
Catch 35
China Grill
Corner Bakery
Everest
Giordano's
Gold Coast Dogs
Golden Budha
Grillroom
Heaven on Seven
La Cantina Enoteca
La Strada
Miller's Pub
Morton's Steak
Mrs. Levy's Deli
Nick & Tony's
Nick's Fishmarket
One North
Palm
Park Grill
Petterino's
Poag Mahone's
Porter's Steak
Potbelly Sandwich
Rhapsody
ristorante we
Rivers
Rosebud
Russian Tea Time
South Water Kitchen
Stetson's Chop Hse.
312 Chicago
Trader Vic's
Trattoria No. 10
Village
Vivere

### River North
Allen's – New Amer.
Al's #1 Beef
Avenues
Ballo
Bar Louie
Ben Pao
Big Bowl
Bijan's Bistro
Billy Goat Tavern
Bin 36
Blandino's Sorriso
Blue Water Grill
Brasserie Jo
Buca di Beppo
Café Iberico
Cal. Pizza Kitchen
Carson's Ribs
Cerise
Chicago Chop Hse.
CHIC Cafe
Chilpancingo
Club Lago
Coco Pazzo
Corner Bakery
Crofton on Wells
Cyrano's
Ed Debevic's
Ember Grille
Erie Cafe
Fadó Irish Pub
Fluky's
Fogo de Chão
1492 Tapas
Frontera Grill
Gaylord Indian
Gene & Georgetti
Giordano's
Grand Lux Cafe
Green Door Tavern
Hard Rock Cafe
Harry Caray's
Heaven on Seven

House of Blues
India House
Joe's Sea/Steak
Kamehachi
Kan Zaman
Karyn's Cooked
Keefer's
Kevin
KiKi's Bistro
Kinzie Chophouse
Kitsch'n
Kizoku Sushi
Klay Oven
Lalo's
Lawry's Prime Rib
L8
Le Lan
Lobby, The
Lou Malnati Pizza
Maggiano's
Mambo Grill
Masck
Melting Pot
mk
Motel
Mr. Beef
Nacional 27
Naha
Narcisse
Original Gino's
Osteria Via Stato
Oysy
Pasha
P.F. Chang's
Phil Stefani's
Pierrot Gourmet
Pizzeria Uno/Due
Potbelly Sandwich
Rainforest Cafe
Redfish
Reza's
Rock Bottom Brew.
Rockit B&G
Room 22
Rosebud
Roy's
Rumba
Ruth's Chris Steak

Sal & Carvão
Scoozi!
Shanghai Terrace
Shaw's Crab Hse.
Smith & Wollensky
Star of Siam
Sugar Dessert Bar
Sullivan's Steak
Sushi Naniwa
Sushisamba rio
Tizi Melloul
Topolobampo
Vermilion
Vong's
Weber Grill
Wildfire
Zealous

## Streeterville

Bandera
Benihana
Bice Grill
Bice Ristorante
Billy Goat Tavern
Boston Blackie's
Bubba Gump Shrimp
Cal. Pizza Kitchen
Caliterra B&G
Cape Cod Room
Capital Grille
Charlie's Ale Hse.
Cheesecake Factory
Chestnut Grill
Cité
Coco Pazzo Cafe
Corner Bakery
Dick's Last Resort
Drake Bros.' Steak
Emilio's Tapas
foodlife
Grill on the Alley
Indian Garden
Joe's Be-Bop Cafe
Kamehachi
Le P'tit Paris
Les Nomades
Mity Nice Grill
Mrs. Park's Tavern

Original Pancake Hse.
P.J. Clarke's
Puck's at MCA
Ritz-Carlton Café
Ritz-Carlton Din. Rm.
Riva
Ron of Japan
Saloon Steak

Sayat Nova
Shula's Steak
Signature Room
Tru
Viand Kitchen
Volare
Wave
Zest

## CITY NORTH

### Andersonville/Edgewater
Andies
Ann Sather
Charlie's Ale Hse.
Corner Grille
Ethiopian Diamond
Francesca's
Hama Matsu
Indie Cafe
Jin Ju
La Donna
La Fonda Latino
La Tache
Leonardo's
M. Henry
Moody's Pub
Pasteur
Reza's
Rioja
South
Speakeasy Supperclub
Tokyo Marina
Tomboy

### Gold Coast
Albert's Café
American Girl
Big Bowl
Bistro 110
Bistrot Zinc
Café des Architectes
Café Luciano
Café Spiaggia
Carmine's
Chicago Sammies
Cielo
Corner Bakery
Cru Cafe/Wine

Edwardo's Pizza
Fornetto Mei
Gibsons Steak
Grotto
Hugo's Frog/Fish
Jake Melnick's
Le Colonial
Mario's Gold Coast
McCormick & Schmick
Merlo
Mike Ditka's
Morton's Steak
NoMI
Oak Tree
Pane Caldo
Papa Milano
P.J. Clarke's
Pump Room
RA Sushi
RL
Rosebud Steak
Seasons
Seasons Café
Silver Spoon
Spiaggia
Tavern on Rush
Tempo
Tsunami
Tucci Benucch

### Lakeview/Wrigleyville
A La Turka
Amy Thai
Angelina
Ann Sather
Arco de Cuchilleros
Art of Pizza
Bagel

Bar Louie
Blue Bayou
Buca di Beppo
Burgundy Inn
Cafe 28
Caliente
Chen's
Chicago Diner
Coobah
Cornelia's
Cousin's
Cullen's B&G
Deleece
Duke of Perth
El Jardin
erwin american
Firefly
Flat Top Grill
Genesee Depot
Giordano's
Goose Is. Brewing
Half Shell
Heaven on Seven
Improv Kitchen
Irish Oak
Jack's on Halsted
Joey's Brickhouse
John Barleycorn
Kit Kat Lounge
Koryo
La Crêperie
Lucca's
Mama Desta's
Matsuya
Matsu Yama
Menagerie
Mia Francesca
Monsoon
Nancy's Stuffed Pizza
Nookies
Orange
Penny's Noodle
Pepper Lounge
Ping Pong
Pizza Capri
Pizza Rustica
Platiyo
Potbelly Sandwich

P.S. Bangkok
Raw Bar & Grill
Rise
Samah
Satay
Sausalito
Shiroi Hana
socca
Strega Nona
Tango Sur
Thai Classic
Tombo Kitchen
Tuscany
Twist
Twisted Spoke
Uncommon Ground
Vien Dong
X/O Chicago
Yoshi's Café

### Lincoln Park/DePaul/Sheffield
Aladdin's Eatery
Al Dente Café
Alinea
Aloha Grill
Ambria
Bacino's
Basil Leaf Cafe
Black Duck Tavern
BOKA
Bricks
Butera Ristorante
Cafe Ba-Ba-Reeba!
Café Bernard
Charlie's Ale Hse.
Charlie Trotter's
Chicago Pizza/Grinder
Dee's
Dunlays
Edwardo's Pizza
El Presidente
Emilio's Tapas
Enoteca Piattini
Fattoush
Filippo's
Four Farthings
Geja's Cafe
Gold Coast Dogs

Goose Is. Brewing
Gracie's on Webster
Green Dolphin St.
Hema's Kitchen
Itto Sushi
J. Alexander's
John Barleycorn
John's Place
JP Chicago
Kabul House
Karyn's Fresh Corner
Kyoto
La Gondola
Lalo's
Las Tablas
Lindo Mexico
Bar Louie
Lou Malnati Pizza
Maza
Merlo
Mon Ami Gabi
My Pie Pizza
Nookies
North Pond
O'Famé
Original Gino's
Original Pancake Hse.
Pasta Palazzo
Penny's Noodle
Pizza Capri
Pompei Bakery
Potbelly Sandwich
P.S. Bangkok
Raj Darbar
Ranalli's
Red Lion Pub
Ringo
R.J. Grunts
Robinson's Ribs
Rose Angelis
Sai Café
Salvatore's
Sangria
Sapori Trattoria
Shine & Morida
Solstice
Stanley's Kitchen
Tarantino's

Tilli's
Toast
Trattoria Gianni
Tsuki
Twisted Lizard
Via Carducci
Vinci
Webster's Wine
Wiener's Circle

## Old Town
Adobo Grill
Bistrot Margot
Cal. Pizza Kitchen
Cucina Bella
Dinotto
Fireplace Inn
Flat Top Grill
Heat
Kamehachi
La Fette
Nookies
Old Jerusalem
Salpicón
Topo Gigio
Trattoria Roma
Twin Anchors
Uncle Julio's

## Rogers Park/West Rogers Park
Carson's Ribs
Fluky's
Fondue Stube
Gulliver's Pizzeria
Heartland Cafe
La Cazuela Mariscos
La Cucina/ Donatella

## Uptown/Lincoln Square
Acqualina
Alice & Friends Veg.
Andalucia
Andies
Anna Maria Pasteria
Bistro Campagne
Cafe Selmarie
Charlie's on Leav.
Dorado
Essence of India

Frankie J's
Furama
Glunz Bavarian
Gold Coast Dogs
Hai Yen
La Bocca/Verità
Lincoln Noodle Hse.
Magnolia Cafe
Pizza D.O.C.
Ranalli's
Rique's

She She
Silver Seafood
Spoon Thai
Square Kitchen
Tank Sushi
Thai Pastry
Tien Giang
Toucan
Tournesol
Tweet
Uno Di Martino

## CITY NORTHWEST

### Bucktown
Ann Sather
Babylon Kitchen
Bar Louie
Bluefin
Café Absinthe
Cafe Bolero
Cafe Matou
Club Lucky
Coast Sushi
Cold Comfort Cafe
Costumbres Argentinas
Feast
Hot Chocolate
Irazu
Ixcapuzalco
Jane's
Le Bouchon
Margie's Candies
Meritage/Wine
My Pie Pizza
Northside B&G
Piece
Rinconcito Sudamer.
Scylla
Silver Cloud B&G
Think Café
Toast

### Humboldt Park
Coco

### Logan Square
Buona Terra
Dunlays

El Nandu
Fat Willy's
Lula

### Northwest Side/ Ravenswood
Abbey Pub
Amitabul
Arun's
Chicago Kalbi
Chief O'Neill's Pub
Gale Street Inn
Giordano's
Hashalom
Hema's Kitchen
Hot Doug's
Indian Garden
Jewel of India
Katsu Japanese
La Peña
Las Tablas
Lutnia
Lutz Continental
Mirabell
Mysore Woodland
Nancy's Stuffed Pizza
Noon-O-Kabab
Sabatino's
San Soo Gab San
Suparossa
Superdawg Drive-In
Tiffin
Tre Kronor
Udupi Palace

Via Veneto
Viceroy of India

## O'Hare Area/Edison Park
Berghoff
Big Bowl
Billy Goat Tavern
Bin 36
Café La Cave
Carlucci
David's Bistro
Don Juan
Flatlander's
Flourchild's
Gibsons Steak
Giordano's
Gold Coast Dogs
Harry Caray's
Kamehachi
Lou Mitchell's
Morton's Steak
Nick's Fishmarket
Original Gino's
Walker Bros. Pancake
Wildfire
Zia's Trattoria

## Roscoe Village
Brett's Café Amer.
Kaze Sushi
Kitsch'n

La Taberna Tapatia
Piazza Bella
Turquoise
Victory's Banner
Volo
Wishbone

## Wicker Park
Adobo Grill
Blue Line Club Car
Bob San
Bongo Room
Green Ginger
Green Zebra
Handlebar
Hilary's Urban
Leo's Lunchroom
Lucia
Mas
Milk & Honey
Mirai Sushi
Penny's Noodle
Privata Café
Settimana Café
Smoke Daddy
Souk
Spring
Thyme Café
Tre Via
Vintage Wine Bar

# CITY SOUTH

## Chinatown
Dragon Court
Emperor's Choice
Evergreen
Happy Chef Dim Sum
Joy Yee's Noodle
Lao Sze Chuan
Moon Palace
New Three Happiness
Penang
Phoenix
Three Happiness

## Far South Side
Army & Lou's
BJ's Market

Flo
Gold Coast Dogs
Lem's BBQ
Marina Cafe
Negro League Café
Original Pancake Hse.

## Hyde Park/Kenwood
Bar Louie
Calypso Cafe
Dixie Kitchen
Edwardo's Pizza
la petite folie
Medici on 57th
Original Pancake Hse.

Pizza Capri
Ribs 'n' Bibs

**Near South Side**
Lalo's
Nuevo Leon
Tufano's Vernon Pk.

**Printer's Row**
Edwardo's Pizza
Hackney's

**South Loop**
Bar Louie
Billy Goat Tavern
Chicago Firehouse
Corner Bakery
Gioco
Grace O'Malley's
Manny's

**East Village**
Hacienda Tecalitlan

**Far West**
Amarind's

**Greektown**
Artopolis Bakery
Athena
Butter
Costa's
Giordano's
Greek Islands
Parthenon
Pegasus
Roditys
Santorini
Venus Mezedopolion

**Little Italy/University Village**
Al's #1 Beef
Bar Louie
Chez Joel
Francesca's
Lao Sze Chuan
La Vita
Pompei Bakery

Opera
Orange
Oysy
Triad

**Southwest Side**
Bacchanalia
Blu 47
Bruna's
Giordano's
Gold Coast Dogs
Harry Caray's
La Fontanella
Lalo's
Lou Malnati Pizza
Manny's
Pegasus
Superdawg Drive-In

## CITY WEST

RoSal's
Rosebud
Tuscany

**Market District**
Aroma
Bar Louie
Bluepoint Oyster
De Cero
Dragonfly Mandarin
Flat Top Grill
Follia
Ina's
Izumi Sushi
La Sardine
Marché
Moto
one sixtyblue
Red Light
Rushmore
Starfish
Sushi Wabi
Tasting Room
Vivo

**Near West**
Bella Notte

Breakfast Club
Cannella's
Dining Rm. at Kendall
Hecky's
Iggy's
Japonais
La Scarola
Misto
Thyme
Twisted Spoke

## Ukrainian Village
a tavola
Bite
Blue Cactus
Mac's
Usagi Ya

## West Loop
Amore
Avec
Bacino's
Billy Goat Tavern
Blackbird
Carmichael's Steak
Gold Coast Dogs
Lou Mitchell's
Meiji
Nine
Phil & Lou's
Robinson's Ribs
Wishbone

## West Town
Tecalitlan
West Town Tavern

## SUBURBS

## Suburban North
Akai Hana
Aladdin's Eatery
Al's #1 Beef
A Milano
Bagel
Bank Lane Bistro
Bar Louie
BD's Mongolian
Benihana
Best Hunan
Bêtise Bistro
Blind Faith Café
Bluegrass
Bob Chinn Crab Hse.
Boston Blackie's
Buca di Beppo
Cafe Central
Café Luciano
Cafe Pyrenees
Cal. Pizza Kitchen
Campagnola
Carlos'
Carson's Ribs
Cheesecake Factory
Chef's Station
Chinoiserie
Convito Italiano

Dave's Italian
Davis St. Fishmkt.
Del Rio
Dixie Kitchen
Don Roth's
Don's Fishmarket
Dover Straits
Edwardo's Pizza
EJ's Place
Famous Dave's
Filippo's
Fio
Flat Top Grill
Flight
Fluky's
Francesca's
Francesco's Hole
Froggy's French
Gabriel's
Gale Street Inn
Gilardi's
Gio
Gold Coast Dogs
Grille on Laurel
Hackney's
Hecky's
Hot Tamales
Jacky's Bistro

# Chicago – Locations

J. Alexander's
Jilly's Cafe
Joy Yee's Noodle
Kabul House
Kamehachi
Karma
Koi
Kuni's
Kyoto
Lalo's
Le Français
Lou Malnati Pizza
Lovell's/Lake Forest
LuLu's Dim Sum
Lupita's
L. Woods Lodge
Maggiano's
Merle's Smokehouse
Mesón Sabika
Mimosa
Miramar
Mt. Everest
Myron & Phil's Steak
New Japan
Next Door Bistro
Noyes St. Café
Oceanique
Olives
O'Neil's
OPA Estiatorio
Original Gino's
Oysy
Palm
Pete Miller's
P.F. Chang's
Pine Yard
Pita Inn
Prairie Grass Cafe
Rainforest Cafe
Red Star Tavern
Ron of Japan
Rosebud
Ruby of Siam
Ruth's Chris Steak
San Gabriel Mexican
Shallots Bistro
Slice of Life
South Gate Cafe

Stained Glass Bistro
Stir Crazy
Tapas Barcelona
Tommy Nevin's Pub
Trattoria Trullo
Trio Atelier
Tuscany
Va Pensiero
Vive La Crepe
Walker Bros. Pancake
Weber Grill
Wildfire
Wolfgang Puck Café
Yard House

## Suburban NW
Al's #1 Beef
Aurelio's Pizza
BaPi
Barn of Barrington
Barrington Bistro
Benihana
Big Bowl
Bistro Kirkou
Boston Blackie's
Cal. Pizza Kitchen
Carson's Ribs
Cheesecake Factory
Chicago Prime Steak
D & J Bistro
Dover Straits
Eclectic
Edelweiss
Famous Dave's
Francesca's
Gaylord Indian
Graziano's Pizza
Hackney's
India House
Indian Garden
Julio's Cocina
Kaminari
Lalo's
La Tasca
Le Titi de Paris
Le Vichyssois
Lou Malnati Pizza
Maggiano's

Magnum's Steak
Melting Pot
Mia Cucina
Millrose
Mj2 Bistro
Morton's Steak
Nancy's Stuffed Pizza
Original Gino's
Original Pancake Hse.
Pappadeaux Seafood
Pompei Bakery
Rainforest Cafe
Red Star Tavern
Retro Bistro
Russell's Barbecue
Sabor
Sal & Carvão
1776
Shaw's Crab Hse.
Shula's Steak
Stir Crazy
Suparossa
Lao Sze Chuan
Tavern
Udupi Palace
Walker Bros. Pancake
Wildfire
Wildfish
Woo Lae Oak

## Suburban South
Al's #1 Beef
Aurelio's Pizza
Balagio
Bogart's Charhouse
Cafe Borgia
Dixie Kitchen
Maple Tree Inn
Original Pancake Hse.

## Suburban SW
Al's #1 Beef
Aurelio's Pizza
Balagio
Bogart's Charhouse
Buca di Beppo
Canoe Club
Courtright's
Dell Rhea's Chicken

Famous Dave's
Francesca's
Gold Coast Dogs
Hackney's
Original Gino's
Public Landing
Suparossa
Tallgrass
Tin Fish
Veranda
White Fence Farm

## Suburban West
Adelle's
Amber Cafe
Antico Posto
Atwater's
Aurelio's Pizza
Avenue Ale Hse.
Balagio
Bar Louie
BD's Mongolian
bella! Bacino's
Benihana
Bistro Banlieue
Bistro Marbuzet
Buca di Beppo
Cab's Wine Bar
Café le Coq
Café 36
Cal. Pizza Kitchen
Carlucci
Catch 35
Cheesecake Factory
Chez François
Chinn's Fishery
Clubhouse
Costa's
Dolce
Ed Debevic's
Edwardo's Pizza
18 Esperienza
Emilio's Tapas
Famous Dave's
Figo Ristorante
Flat Top Grill
Francesca's
Greek Islands

Heaven on Seven
Hemmingway's
Hugo's Frog/Fish
Indian Garden
Isabella Estiatorio
J. Alexander's
Joy Yee's Noodle
Kyoto
Lalo's
L'anne
Lao Sze Chuan
La Piazza
Las Bellas Artes
Les Deux Autres
Lou Malnati Pizza
Maggiano's
Magnum's Steak
Maison
Mama Thai
Melting Pot
Mesón Sabika
Mill Race Inn
Mon Ami Gabi
Morton's Steak
Mysore Woodland
Nancy's Stuffed Pizza
Nick & Tony's
120 Ocean Place
Original Gino's
Original Pancake Hse.
Pacific Blue

Papagus Taverna
Pappadeaux Seafood
Parkers' Ocean Grill
Penny's Noodle
P.F. Chang's
Philander's Oak Park
Pompei Bakery
Red Star Tavern
Reza's
Robinson's Ribs
Rock Bottom Brew.
Rosebud
Russell's BBQ
Sal & Carvão
Salbute
Samba Room
Stir Crazy
Sullivan's Steak
Swordfish
Tango
10 West
302 West
Tin Fish
Tuscany
Uncle Julio's
Viceroy of India
Vic's Classic Steak
Vie
Weber Grill
Wildfire

# SPECIAL FEATURES

(Indexes list the best in each category. Multi-location restaurants' features may vary by branch.)

## Additions
(Properties added since the last edition of the book)

Acqualina
Al Dente Café
Alinea
Aloha Grill
Amber Cafe
A Milano
Amore
Amy Thai
Aroma
Babylon Kitchen
Ballo
BaPi
Bluegrass
Blue Water Grill
Blu 47
Butter
Campagnola
Canoe Club
Charlie's on Leav.
Chestnut Grill
China Grill
Coco
Costumbres Argentinas
De Cero
Dining Rm. at Kendall
Dolce
Dorado
Dragon Court
Dragonfly Mandarin
Drake Bros.' Steak
18 Esperienza
Ember Grille
Essence of India
Fattoush
Figo Ristorante
Flatlander's
Flourchild's
Fornetto Mei
Golden Budha
Grace O'Malley's
Grille on Laurel
Hacienda Tecalitlan
Hecky's
Hot Chocolate
Hot Doug's
Improv Kitchen
Indie Cafe
Jewel of India
Joey's Brickhouse
JP Chicago
Kaminari
Kan Zaman
Karyn's Cooked
Karyn's Fresh Corner
Kaze Sushi
Kizoku Sushi
Koi
La Cucina/ Donatella
La Fette
La Fontanella
La Vita
L8
Le Lan
Leonardo's
Marina Cafe
Matsu Yama
Meiji
Melting Pot
Miramar
Mj2 Bistro
Moon Palace
Motel
Negro League Café
OPA Estiatorio
Osteria Via Stato
Pacific Blue
Pizza Rustica
Porter's Steak
Prairie Grass Cafe
Raj Darbar
Rioja
Rique's
Rockit B&G

Room 22
Samah
San Gabriel Mexican
Sausalito
Scylla
Shallots Bistro
Silver Spoon
socca
South
Thyme Café
Tien Giang
Toucan
Triad
Trio Atelier
Tsuki
Turquoise
Uno Di Martino
Usagi Ya
Venus Mezedopolion
Veranda
Vie
Vien Dong
Vintage Wine Bar
Volo
Woo Lae Oak
X/O Chicago
Yard House

## Breakfast

(See also Hotel Dining)
Abbey Pub
Albert's Café
Ann Sather
Army & Lou's
Bagel
Bar Louie
bella! Bacino's
Berghoff
Billy Goat Tavern
Bin 36
Bite
Blind Faith Café
Bongo Room
Breakfast Club
Cafe Selmarie
Cheesecake Factory
Chicago Diner
Cold Comfort Cafe

Corner Bakery
Corner Grille
David's Bistro
Davis St. Fishmkt.
Dixie Kitchen
Ed Debevic's
Flo
foodlife
Furama
Hackney's
Harry Caray's
Heartland Cafe
Heaven on Seven
Hemmingway's
Hilary's Urban
Ina's
Irazu
John's Place
Kitsch'n
Leo's Lunchroom
Lou Mitchell's
Lula
Manny's
M. Henry
Milk & Honey
Mill Race Inn
Millrose
Mrs. Levy's Deli
Nick & Tony's
Nookies
Nuevo Leon
Oak Tree
Orange
Original Pancake Hse.
Pegasus
Phoenix
Ranalli's
San Soo Gab San
Slice of Life
Superdawg Drive-In
Tecalitlan
Tempo
Three Happiness
Tilli's
Toast
Tommy Nevin's Pub
Tre Kronor
Uncommon Ground

Viand Kitchen
Victory's Banner
Walker Bros. Pancake
Wishbone

## Brunch
Adobo Grill
American Girl
Andies
Angelina
Ann Sather
Atwater's
Atwood Cafe
Avenues
Bar Louie
Barn of Barrington
Bêtise Bistro
Bistro Campagne
Bistro Marbuzet
Bistro 110
Bistrot Margot
Bistrot Zinc
Bite
BJ's Market
Blue Cactus
Bongo Room
Brett's Café Amer.
Buona Terra
Café des Architectes
Cafe Selmarie
Café Spiaggia
Cafe 28
Caliterra B&G
Calypso Cafe
Cerise
Charlie's Ale Hse.
Cheesecake Factory
Chicago Diner
CHIC Cafe
Chilpancingo
Clubhouse
Coobah
Corner Grille
Cullen's B&G
Davis St. Fishmkt.
Deleece
Dick's Last Resort
Dixie Kitchen

Dunlays
erwin american
Fio
Flo
Follia
Four Farthings
Frankie J's
Frontera Grill
Grand Lux Cafe
Green Ginger
Hackney's
Heaven on Seven
Hemmingway's
Hilary's Urban
House of Blues
Jack's on Halsted
Jane's
Jilly's Cafe
John's Place
Kitsch'n
La Crêperie
La Donna
Las Bellas Artes
La Tache
Leo's Lunchroom
Lobby, The
Mac's
Magnolia Cafe
Meritage/Wine
Mesón Sabika
M. Henry
Mike Ditka's
Milk & Honey
Millrose
Nick & Tony's
North Pond
Northside B&G
Noyes St. Café
Orange
Pizza Capri
P.J. Clarke's
Platiyo
Privata Café
P.S. Bangkok
Pump Room
ristorante we
Ritz-Carlton Café
Ritz-Carlton Din. Rm.

RL
Salpicón
Sangria
Seasons
She She
Signature Room
Silver Cloud B&G
Smith & Wollensky
South Water Kitchen
Square Kitchen
Stanley's Kitchen
Sushisamba rio
Tavern on Rush
Thai Classic
312 Chicago
Tilli's
Toast
Tre Kronor
Tweet
Twisted Spoke
Uncommon Ground
Vermilion
Viceroy of India
Vinci
Walker Bros. Pancake
Wishbone
Yoshi's Café

### Buffet Served
(Check availability)
Avenues
Barn of Barrington
Clubhouse
Dell Rhea's Chicken
Dick's Last Resort
Drake Bros.' Steak
Edwardo's Pizza
Ember Grille
Essence of India
Flatlander's
Flat Top Grill
Furama
Gaylord Indian
Grace O'Malley's
Hemmingway's
Hilary's Urban
India House
Indian Garden

Jewel of India
Karyn's Fresh Corner
Klay Oven
La Fonda Latino
Lao Sze Chuan
Lobby, The
Mt. Everest
Negro League Café
Porter's Steak
P.S. Bangkok
Puck's at MCA
Raj Darbar
Reza's
Ritz-Carlton Din. Rm.
Robinson's Ribs
RoSal's
Ruby of Siam
Seasons
Signature Room
Stanley's Kitchen
Thai Classic
Tiffin
Udupi Palace
Viceroy of India
Vic's Classic Steak

### Business Dining
Alinea
Aria
Atwood Cafe
Avenues
Balagio
Ben Pao
Bice Ristorante
Bistro Kirkou
Blackbird
Bluepoint Oyster
Blue Water Grill
Brasserie Jo
Café des Architectes
Caliterra B&G
Capital Grille
Carlucci
Carmichael's Steak
Catch 35
Charlie Trotter's
Chez François
Chicago Chop Hse.

Chicago Prime Steak
Coco Pazzo
Crofton on Wells
David's Bistro
Drake Bros.' Steak
Erie Cafe
Everest
Fogo de Chão
Gene & Georgetti
Gibsons Steak
Golden Budha
Grill on the Alley
Grillroom
Grotto
Harry Caray's
Japonais
Joe's Sea/Steak
Karma
Keefer's
Kevin
Kinzie Chophouse
Lawry's Prime Rib
Le Colonial
Le Français
Les Nomades
Le Titi de Paris
Magnum's Steak
McCormick & Schmick
Mike Ditka's
mk
Morton's Steak
Mrs. Park's Tavern
Naha
Nick & Tony's
Nick's Fishmarket
Nine
NoMI
One North
one sixtyblue
120 Ocean Place
Palm
Park Grill
Petterino's
Phil Stefani's
Porter's Steak
Rhapsody
ristorante we
Ritz-Carlton Din. Rm.

Rivers
RL
Roy's
Ruth's Chris Steak
Sal & Carvão
Saloon Steak
Seasons
Shaw's Crab Hse.
Slice of Life
Smith & Wollensky
South Water Kitchen
Spiaggia
Sullivan's Steak
312 Chicago
Topolobampo
Tuscany
Vivere
Vivo
Vong's
Weber Grill

## BYO

Aladdin's Eatery
Amitabul
Amy Thai
Andalucia
Ann Sather
Babylon Kitchen
Bite
Blue Cactus
Butera Ristorante
Café le Coq
CHIC Cafe
Chinoiserie
Coast Sushi
Cold Comfort Cafe
Convito Italiano
Courtright's
Don Roth's
Dorado
Dragon Court
El Presidente
Essence of India
Fattoush
Follia
Frankie J's
Genesee Depot
Gibsons Steak

Giordano's
Hama Matsu
Happy Chef Dim Sum
Hashalom
Hecky's
Hema's Kitchen
Hilary's Urban
Indie Cafe
Irazu
Jewel of India
Joy Yee's Noodle
Kabul House
Kan Zaman
Karyn's Fresh Corner
La Cazuela Mariscos
La Cucina/ Donatella
Lao Sze Chuan
Las Tablas
Leonardo's
Leo's Lunchroom
Lincoln Noodle Hse.
Lucia
Masck
Matsu Yama
Medici on 57th
Melting Pot
M. Henry
Morton's Steak
My Pie Pizza
Mysore Woodland
Nancy's Stuffed Pizza
Nookies
Nuevo Leon
Old Jerusalem
Orange
Original Gino's
Penny's Noodle
Ping Pong
Pizza Rustica
Privata Café
P.S. Bangkok
Ranalli's
Ringo
Rique's
Robinson's Ribs
Ruby of Siam
Satay
South

Speakeasy Supperclub
Spoon Thai
Tango Sur
Thai Classic
Thai Pastry
Think Café
Tien Giang
Tombo Kitchen
Tournesol
Tre Kronor
Tweet
Udupi Palace
Uno Di Martino
Vien Dong

## Celebrity Chefs
(Listed under their primary restaurants)
Alinea, *Grant Achatz*
Ambria, *Gabino Sotelino*
Arun's, *Arun Sampanthavivat*
Avec, *Koren Grieveson*
Avenues, *Graham Elliot Bowles*
Bistro 110, *Dominique Tougne*
Blackbird, *Paul Kahan*
Café le Coq, *Stephen Chiappetti*
Campagnola, *M. Altenberg*
Charlie's/Leav., *C. Socher*
Charlie Trotter's, *Charlie Trotter*
Chilpancingo, *Geno Bahena*
Crofton on Wells, *Suzy Crofton*
erwin, *Erwin Drechsler*
Everest, *Jean Joho*
Frontera Grill, *Rick Bayless*
Gioco, *Corcoran O'Connor*
Hot Chocolate, *Mindy Segal*
Jack's on Halsted, *Jack Jones*
Keefer's, *John Hogan*
Kevin, *Kevin Shikami*
Le Bouchon, *J-C Poilevey*
Le Français, *Roland Liccioni*
Le Titi de Paris, *M. Maddox*
Le Vichyssois, *Bernard Cretier*
Mas, *John Manion*
mk, *Michael Kornick*
Nacional 27, *Randy Zweiban*
Naha, *Carrie Nahabedian*
North Pond, *Bruce Sherman*

one sixtyblue, *Martial Noguier*
Opera, *Paul Wildermuth*
Prairie Grass, *Stegner/ Bumbaris*
Red Light, *Jackie Shen*
Salpicón, *Priscila Satkoff*
Spiaggia, *Tony Mantuano*
Spring, *Shawn McClain*
Tallgrass, *Robert Burcenski*
Thyme, *John Bubala*
Topolobampo, *Rick Bayless*
Tru, *Rick Tramonto, Gale Gand*
West Town Tavern, *Susan Goss*
Zealous, *Michael Taus*

## Child-Friendly

(Alternatives to the usual
fast-food places; * children's
menu available)
Aloha Grill
American Girl*
Ann Sather
Antico Posto*
Artopolis Bakery
Bandera*
BD's Mongolian
Benihana*
Berghoff*
Big Bowl
Bob Chinn Crab Hse.*
Bongo Room
Breakfast Club
Bubba Gump Shrimp*
Cafe Selmarie
Cal. Pizza Kitchen*
Carson's Ribs*
Cheesecake Factory*
Chicago Sammies
Chicago Pizza/Grinder
Corner Bakery
Dave's Italian
Davis St. Fishmkt.*
Dell Rhea's Chicken*
Dick's Last Resort*
Ed Debevic's*
Edwardo's Pizza*
Famous Dave's*
Flatlander's*
Flat Top Grill*

Flourchild's*
Fluky's*
foodlife*
Gold Coast Dogs
Grand Lux Cafe*
Graziano's Pizza*
Gulliver's Pizzeria*
Hackney's*
Hard Rock Cafe*
Harry Caray's*
Heaven on Seven*
Hecky's
Hilary's Urban
Hot Doug's*
House of Blues*
Ina's*
Jake Melnick's*
John's Place*
Joy Yee's Noodle
Kitsch'n*
Lawry's Prime Rib*
Lincoln Noodle Hse.
Lou Malnati Pizza*
Lou Mitchell's*
LuLu's Dim Sum
Lutz Continental
Maggiano's*
Manny's*
Margie's Candies*
Marina Cafe
Mill Race Inn*
Mity Nice Grill*
Oak Tree
OPA Estiatorio
Orange*
Original Gino's*
Original Pancake Hse.*
Papagus Taverna*
Pegasus
P.F. Chang's
Pizza Capri*
Pizza D.O.C.
Pizzeria Uno/Due*
Potbelly Sandwich
Rainforest Cafe*
R.J. Grunts*
Robinson's Ribs*
Rock Bottom Brew.*

# Chicago – Special Features

Ron of Japan*
Russell's BBQ*
Scoozi!*
Stanley's Kitchen*
Stir Crazy*
Tempo
Toast*
Tucci Benucch*
Tufano's Vernon Pk.
Twin Anchors*
Uncle Julio's*
Uncommon Ground*
Walker Bros. Pancake*
White Fence Farm*
Wishbone*

## Cigars Welcome

Al Dente Café
Avenue Ale Hse.
Ballo
Bistro 110
Blandino's Sorriso
Bluepoint Oyster
Café Luciano
Capital Grille
Carlucci
Carmichael's Steak
Carmine's
Carson's Ribs
Chestnut Grill
Chicago Chop Hse.
Chicago Prime Steak
Cité
Clubhouse
Club Lago
Coco Pazzo
Courtright's
Cru Cafe/Wine
D & J Bistro
Dell Rhea's Chicken
Dick's Last Resort
18 Esperienza
El Nandu
Erie Cafe
Famous Dave's
Fornetto Mei
Four Farthings
Froggy's French

Gale Street Inn
Gene & Georgetti
Gibsons Steak
Gilardi's
Goose Is. Brewing
Greek Islands
Green Dolphin St.
Green Door Tavern
Grill on the Alley
Grillroom
Grotto
Hacienda Tecalitlan
Hackney's
Harry Caray's
Hugo's Frog/Fish
Kamehachi
Karma
Keefer's
Kinzie Chophouse
La Cantina Enoteca
Las Tablas
La Strada
Le Vichyssois
Lovell's/Lake Forest
Magnum's Steak
McCormick & Schmick
Mike Ditka's
Mill Race Inn
Morton's Steak
Narcisse
Nick's Fishmarket
Nine
NoMI
120 Ocean Place
Palm
Parkers' Ocean Grill
Pasha
Pete Miller's
Philander's Oak Park
Phil Stefani's
P.J. Clarke's
Pump Room
Red Star Tavern
Retro Bistro
Riva
Rock Bottom Brew.
Rosebud
Rumba

Russell's BBQ
Ruth's Chris Steak
Sabatino's
Sabor
Saloon Steak
Salvatore's
Samba Room
Santorini
Seasons
Shaw's Crab Hse.
Shula's Steak
Signature Room
Silver Cloud B&G
Silver Seafood
Smith & Wollensky
Smoke Daddy
Souk
Spiaggia
Sugar Dessert Bar
Sullivan's Steak
Suparossa
Superdawg Drive-In
Tavern
Tavern on Rush
Tecalitlan
Tilli's
Tin Fish
Tommy Nevin's Pub
Topo Gigio
Topolobampo
Tuscany
Twisted Spoke
Veranda
Vermilion
Viand Kitchen
Volare
Weber Grill
White Fence Farm
Zia's Trattoria

## Critic-Proof

(Gets lots of business
despite so-so food)
Bar Louie
Billy Goat Tavern
Ed Debevic's
Rainforest Cafe
Rock Bottom Brew.

## Dancing

Ballo
Barn of Barrington
Coco
Dover Straits
Drake Bros.' Steak
Gale Street Inn
Hacienda Tecalitlan
La Peña
Lutnia
Nacional 27
Narcisse
Nine
Pump Room
Rumba
Sayat Nova
Souk
Tango
Vermilion
Vic's Classic Steak

## Delivery/Takeout

(D=delivery, T=takeout)
Adobo Grill (T)
Akai Hana (D,T)
Aladdin's Eatery (D,T)
A La Turka (T)
Andies (D,T)
Athena (T)
Bella Notte (D,T)
Benihana (T)
Berghoff (T)
Bijan's Bistro (D,T)
Bluepoint Oyster (D,T)
Bob Chinn Crab Hse. (D,T)
Buca di Beppo (T)
Cafe Ba-Ba-Reeba! (T)
Café Spiaggia (T)
Chilpancingo (T)
Coco Pazzo Cafe (T)
Crofton on Wells (T)
D & J Bistro (T)
Davis St. Fishmkt. (T)
Don Juan (T)
Emilio's Tapas (T)
erwin american (T)
Famous Dave's (D,T)
Filippo's (D,T)

foodlife (D,T)
Francesca's (D,T)
Gale Street Inn (D,T)
Gene & Georgetti (T)
Gibsons Steak (T)
Gioco (T)
Heaven on Seven (D,T)
Hema's Kitchen (D,T)
Jack's on Halsted (T)
Japonais (D,T)
Joe's Sea/Steak (D,T)
Keefer's (T)
La Sardine (T)
Las Bellas Artes (T)
La Scarola (T)
La Tasca (T)
Lawry's Prime Rib (T)
Le Colonial (D,T)
Lula (T)
L. Woods Lodge (D,T)
Maggiano's (T)
Meritage/Wine (T)
Mesón Sabika (T)
Mia Francesca (T)
Mirai Sushi (T)
Mon Ami Gabi (T)
Nick & Tony's (T)
Old Jerusalem (D,T)
Opera (T)
Orange (T)
Papagus Taverna (D,T)
Parthenon (D,T)
Penang (D,T)
Pierrot Gourmet (T)
Platiyo (T)
Poag Mahone's (D,T)
Potbelly Sandwich (D,T)
Privata Café (D,T)
Red Light (T)
R.J. Grunts (T)
Rock Bottom Brew. (T)
RoSal's (T)
Rosebud (D,T)
Salbute (D,T)
Saloon Steak (D,T)
San Soo Gab San (D,T)
Scoozi! (T)
Shaw's Crab Hse. (D,T)

Smith & Wollensky (T)
Souk (T)
Sullivan's Steak (T)
Sushi Naniwa (D,T)
Sushi Wabi (D,T)
Swordfish (T)
Tarantino's (D,T)
Tizi Melloul (T)
Trattoria Roma (D,T)
Tre Via (D,T)
Twin Anchors (T)
Village (D,T)
Volare (D,T)
Yoshi's Café (T)

## Dining Alone
(Other than hotels and places
with counter service)
Amitabul
Ann Sather
Bar Louie
Bite
Blind Faith Café
Breakfast Club
Chicago Diner
Corner Bakery
Flat Top Grill
Fluky's
foodlife
Gold Coast Dogs
Heartland Cafe
Hilary's Urban
Hot Doug's
Indie Cafe
Kaze Sushi
Kinzie Chophouse
Kizoku Sushi
Koi
Leo's Lunchroom
Lula
Manny's
Meiji
Moody's Pub
Nookies
Noyes St. Café
Oak Tree
Penny's Noodle
Puck's at MCA

Reza's
Toast
Triad
Tsuki
Tweet
Usagi Ya
Viand Kitchen
Wiener's Circle

## Entertainment

(Call for days and times of performances)
Abbey Pub (Irish/rock)
A La Turka (belly dancing)
American Girl (musical)
Avenue Ale Hse. (jazz)
Barn of Barrington (DJ/band)
Blue Bayou (blues/jazz)
Cafe Bolero (Latin jazz)
Cafe 28 (Latin)
Catch 35 (piano)
Chicago Chop Hse. (piano)
Chicago Prime Steak (jazz)
Chief O'Neill's Pub (Irish)
Costa's (piano)
Cousin's (tango)
Cyrano's (cabaret)
Dover Straits (bands)
Edelweiss (German)
El Nandu (guitar)
Emilio's Tapas (flamenco)
Enoteca Piattini (jazz)
Filippo's (jazz)
Fio (jazz)
Flight (jazz)
Frankie J's (comedy)
Geja's Cafe (flamenco guitar)
Gilardi's (piano)
Green Dolphin St. (jazz)
Hackney's (varies)
Hard Rock Cafe (varies)
House of Blues (blues)
Irish Oak (Irish/rock)
Julio's Cocina (Brazilian/jazz)
Kit Kat (female impersonators)
Lalo's (DJ/mariachi)
La Strada (piano)
La Taberna Tapatia (DJ)

Lobby, The (jazz)
Lutnia (piano)
Mesón Sabika (flamenco guitar)
Mia Cucina (piano)
Mill Race Inn (bands)
Millrose (piano)
Myron & Phil's Steak (piano)
Nacional 27 (DJ/jazz)
Nick's Fishmarket (jazz)
Parkers' Ocean Grill (jazz/piano)
Pasha (flamenco/Latin)
Philander's Oak Park (jazz)
Pump Room (jazz/swing)
Redfish (blues/jazz)
Ritz-Carlton Din. Rm. (piano)
Rock Bottom Brew. (karaoke)
Rumba (DJ/salsa lessons)
Sabatino's (guitar/piano)
Sabor (varies)
Salvatore's (piano)
Sayat Nova (DJ)
Shaw's Crab Hse. (blues/jazz)
Signature Room (jazz)
Smoke Daddy (blues/jazz)
Souk (belly dancing)
Speakeasy (cabaret/jazz)
Sugar Dessert Bar (DJ)
Sullivan's Steak (jazz)
Sushi Wabi (DJ)
302 West (jazz )
Tizi Melloul (belly dancing)
Tombo Kitchen (karaoke)
Uncommon Ground (open mike)
Webster's Wine (band)

## Fireplaces

Andies
Atwater's
Barn of Barrington
Bêtise Bistro
Bistrot Margot
Blue Line Club Car
Boston Blackie's
Café La Cave
Carlucci
Chen's
Chestnut Grill
Clubhouse

Costa's
Courtright's
Cru Cafe/Wine
Dee's
Dell Rhea's Chicken
Don Roth's
Don's Fishmarket
Dover Straits
Dunlays
Edelweiss
Enoteca Piattini
Erie Cafe
Famous Dave's
Fireplace Inn
Flatlander's
Flourchild's
Francesca's
Gale Street Inn
Gene & Georgetti
Gibsons Steak
Greek Islands
Grille on Laurel
Hacienda Tecalitlan
Half Shell
Hecky's
Japonais
Jewel of India
John's Place
Koi
Les Nomades
Lovell's/Lake Forest
Magnum's Steak
Maison
McCormick & Schmick
Melting Pot
Mill Race Inn
Millrose
Misto
Moody's Pub
My Pie Pizza
Narcisse
Nick & Tony's
Northside B&G
Prairie Grass Cafe
Red Star Tavern
Reza's
RL
Sai Café

Santorini
Smith & Wollensky
South Gate Cafe
Tallgrass
Tilli's
Tommy Nevin's Pub
Tsunami
Uncommon Ground
Va Pensiero
Via Carducci
Vic's Classic Steak
Vie
Vintage Wine Bar
Walker Bros. Pancake
Webster's Wine
White Fence Farm

## Game in Season
Allen's – New Amer.
Ambria
Atwater's
Avenues
Bank Lane Bistro
Barrington Bistro
Bêtise Bistro
Bice Ristorante
Bin 36
Bistro Banlieue
Bistro Campagne
Bistro Kirkou
Bistro 110
Bistrot Margot
Bistrot Zinc
Blue Water Grill
BOKA
Brasserie Jo
Brett's Café Amer.
Buona Terra
Cab's Wine Bar
Café Absinthe
Café Bernard
Café des Architectes
Café La Cave
Café le Coq
Cafe Matou
Cafe Pyrenees
Café 36
Carlos'

Charlie Trotter's
Chestnut Grill
Chez François
Courtright's
Crofton on Wells
Cyrano's
D & J Bistro
De Cero
erwin american
Froggy's French
Gabriel's
Hemmingway's
Hot Doug's
Katsu Japanese
Kaze Sushi
Keefer's
Kevin
La Fette
la petite folie
La Tache
Le Bouchon
Le Français
L8
Les Nomades
Le Titi de Paris
Le Vichyssois
Lovell's/Lake Forest
Merlo
Mimosa
Misto
mk
Monsoon
Naha
Narcisse
North Pond
Oceanique
O'Neil's
120 Ocean Place
Opera
Park Grill
Philander's Oak Park
Puck's at MCA
Pump Room
Raw Bar & Grill
Ritz-Carlton Din. Rm.
RL
Room 22
Rushmore

Russian Tea Time
Salbute
Salpicón
Sapori Trattoria
Seasons
1776
Speakeasy Supperclub
Stained Glass Bistro
Stetson's Chop Hse.
Sushisamba rio
Tallgrass
Tarantino's
10 West
Think Café
302 West
Thyme
Tomboy
Tre Kronor
Va Pensiero
Vie
Vivere

## Historic Places

(Year opened; * building)
1844 Public Landing*
1847 Mesón Sabika*
1858 Don Roth's*
1865 Crofton on Wells*
1866 Barn of Barrington*
1880 West Town Tavern*
1881 Twin Anchors*
1883 Eclectic*
1884 Thyme Café*
1886 Cold Comfort Cafe*
1890 John Barleycorn
1890 Pizzeria Uno/Due*
1890 Webster's Wine*
1893 Tavern*
1895 Club Lago*
1897 Tallgrass*
1900 Vivo*
1901 South Gate Cafe*
1909 Pompei Bakery
1918 Drake Bros.' Steak
1920 Chef's Station*
1921 Green Door Tavern
1921 Margie's Candies
1923 Lou Mitchell's
1927 Village*

1927 Vivere*
1929 Fluky's
1930 Del Rio*
1930 Russell's BBQ
1930 Tufano's Vernon Pk.*
1933 Bruna's
1933 Cape Cod Room
1933 Mill Race Inn
1934 Billy Goat Tavern
1935 Miller's Pub
1937 Café le Coq*
1938 Al's #1 Beef
1938 Pump Room
1939 Hackney's
1941 Gene & Georgetti
1942 Manny's
1945 Ann Sather
1945 Army & Lou's
1946 Dell Rhea's Chicken
1948 Superdawg Drive-In
1951 Papa Milano
1954 White Fence Farm
1955 La Cantina Enoteca
1955 Pizzeria Uno/Due

## Hotel Dining

Belden-Stratford Hotel
  Ambria
  Mon Ami Gabi
Carleton Hotel
  Philander's Oak Park
Crowne Plaza Hotel
  Karma
Doubletree Guest Suites Hotel
  Mrs. Park's Tavern
Doubletree Hotel
  Gibsons Steak
Drake Hotel
  Cape Cod Room
  Drake Bros.' Steak
Embassy Suites Hotel
  P.J. Clarke's
Fairmont Chicago Hotel
  Aria
Fitzpatrick Hotel
  Benihana
Four Seasons Hotel
  Seasons
  Seasons Café

Hard Rock Hotel
  China Grill
Herrington Inn
  Atwater's
Hilton Garden Inn
  Weber Grill
Holiday Inn
  Harry Caray's
Homestead Hotel
  Trio Atelier
Hotel 71
  Porter's Steak
Hotel Allegro
  312 Chicago
Hotel Burnham
  Atwood Cafe
Hotel InterContinental
  Zest
Hotel Monaco
  South Water Kitchen
Hyatt Regency
  Stetson's Chop Hse.
Le Méridien Hotel
  Cerise
Margarita Inn
  Va Pensiero
Omni Ambassador East
  Pump Room
Omni Chicago Hotel
  Cielo
Palmer House Hilton
  Trader Vic's
Park Hyatt Chicago
  NoMI
Peninsula Hotel
  Avenues
  Lobby, The
  Pierrot Gourmet
  Shanghai Terrace
Red Roof Inn
  Coco Pazzo Cafe
Renaissance
  Ruth's Chris Steak
Ritz-Carlton Hotel
  Ritz-Carlton Café
  Ritz-Carlton Din. Rm.
Seneca Hotel
  Saloon Steak

Sheraton Chicago
  Shula's Steak
Sofitel Chicago Water Tower
  Café des Architectes
Swissôtel
  Palm
Tremont Hotel
  Mike Ditka's
W Chicago Lakeshore
  Wave
Westin Hotel
  Ember Grille
  Grill on the Alley
Westin River North
  Kamehachi
W Hotel
  ristorante we
Wyndham Chicago
  Caliterra B&G
Wyndham Northwest Chicago
  Shula's Steak

## Jacket Required
Ambria
Carlos'
Charlie Trotter's
Le Français
Les Nomades
Spiaggia
Tallgrass
Tru

## Late Dining
(Weekday closing hour)
Al Dente Café (3 AM)
Al's #1 Beef (varies)
Andies (12 AM)
Athena (12 AM)
Avec (12 AM)
Ballo (12 AM)
Bar Louie (varies)
Bijan's Bistro (3:30 AM)
Billy Goat Tavern (2 AM)
Blue Line Club Car (12 AM)
Bob San (12 AM)
Caliterra B&G (12 AM)
Chestnut Grill (1 AM)
Coast Sushi (12 AM)
Coobah (1 AM)

Costumbres Argentinas (12 AM)
Cru Cafe/Wine (12:30 AM)
Dick's Last Resort (12:45 AM)
Dragon Court (12 AM)
Dunlays (varies)
El Presidente (24 hrs.)
Ember Grille (2 AM)
Emperor's Choice (12:30 AM)
Evergreen (12 AM)
Fireplace Inn (12 AM)
Flight (1 AM)
Gibsons Steak (varies)
Giordano's (12 AM)
Gold Coast Dogs (varies)
Gracie's on Webster (2 AM)
Greek Islands (12 AM)
Gulliver's Pizzeria (1 AM)
Handlebar (12 AM)
Happy Chef Dim Sum (2 AM)
Hugo's Frog/Fish (12 AM)
Iggy's (3:15 AM)
Improv Kitchen (2 AM)
Itto Sushi (12 AM)
Izumi Sushi (2 AM)
Jake Melnick's (1 AM)
John Barleycorn (12 AM)
Kamehachi (1:30 AM)
Kit Kat Lounge (12 AM)
Lao Sze Chuan (varies)
La Taberna Tapatia (2 AM)
L8 (12 AM)
Lem's BBQ (2 AM)
Lou Mitchell's (varies)
Mac's (12 AM)
Margie's Candies (12 AM)
Melting Pot (varies)
Miller's Pub (2 AM)
Moody's Pub (1 AM)
Motel (2 AM)
Nancy's Stuffed Pizza (2 AM)
Narcisse (1 AM)
NoMI (12 AM)
Nookies (varies)
Northside B&G (2 AM)
Nuevo Leon (12 AM)
Parthenon (12 AM)
Pasha (3 AM)
Pegasus (varies)

Penang (1 AM)
Pepper Lounge (12 AM)
Pete Miller's (12:30 AM)
Phil & Lou's (12 AM)
Ping Pong (12 AM)
Pizzeria Uno/Due (varies)
P.J. Clarke's (2 AM)
Pump Room (12 AM)
Ranalli's (varies)
RA Sushi (1 AM)
Raw Bar & Grill (1 AM)
Red Star Tavern (varies)
Reza's (varies)
Ribs 'n' Bibs (12 AM)
Rock Bottom Brew. (varies)
Roditys (12 AM)
Samah (12:30 AM)
Sangria (12 AM)
San Soo Gab San (12 AM)
Santorini (12 AM)
Silver Seafood (1 AM)
Smoke Daddy (1 AM)
Solstice (2 AM)
Sugar Dessert Bar (12 AM)
Superdawg Drive-In (1 AM)
Sushi Wabi (12 AM)
Tasting Room (12 AM)
Tavern on Rush (12 AM)
Tecalitlan (12 AM)
Tempo (24 hrs.)
Three Happiness (varies)
Tombo Kitchen (12 AM)
Tommy Nevin's Pub (12:30 AM)
Tre Via (1 AM)
Twisted Spoke (varies)
Vintage Wine Bar (2 AM)
Webster's Wine (2 AM)
Wiener's Circle (4 AM)

## Meet for a Drink
(Most top hotels and the
following standouts)
Abbey Pub
Allen's – New Amer.
A Milano
Avenue Ale Hse.
Ballo
Bandera

Bar Louie
Bijan's Bistro
Billy Goat Tavern
Bin 36
Bistro 110
Blue Bayou
Blue Line Club Car
Bluepoint Oyster
Blue Water Grill
BOKA
Brasserie Jo
Butter
Cab's Wine Bar
Café des Architectes
Canoe Club
Catch 35
Charlie's Ale Hse.
Chicago Prime Steak
Chief O'Neill's Pub
China Grill
Coobah
Cru Cafe/Wine
Dolce
Enoteca Piattini
Firefly
Flight
Four Farthings
Frontera Grill
Gibsons Steak
Goose Is. Brewing
Green Door Tavern
Grotto
Harry Caray's
Iggy's
Jake Melnick's
Japonais
Joe's Sea/Steak
John Barleycorn
Keefer's
L8
Mambo Grill
Marché
McCormick & Schmick
Meritage/Wine
Mike Ditka's
Millrose
Miramar
mk

Moody's Pub
Motel
Nacional 27
Nine
NoMI
Northside B&G
One North
one sixtyblue
Osteria Via Stato
P.J. Clarke's
Platiyo
Prairie Grass Cafe
Red Light
Red Star Tavern
Rhapsody
RL
Rock Bottom Brew.
Rockit B&G
Rosebud Steak
Rumba
Scoozi!
Shaw's Crab Hse.
Signature Room
Smith & Wollensky
South Water Kitchen
Stained Glass Bistro
Sugar Dessert Bar
Sullivan's Steak
Sushisamba rio
Tasting Room
Tavern on Rush
10 West
312 Chicago
Tizi Melloul
Trader Vic's
Trattoria No. 10
Twisted Spoke
Volo
Wave
Webster's Wine
X/O Chicago

**Microbreweries**
Flatlander's
Goose Is. Brewing
Millrose
Piece
Rock Bottom Brew.

**Old City Feel**
Abbey Pub
Army & Lou's
Bacchanalia
Bagel
Berghoff
Billy Goat Tavern
Bruna's
Cape Cod Room
Carson's Ribs
Charlie's Ale Hse.
Chicago Chop Hse.
Club Lago
Geja's Cafe
Gene & Georgetti
Green Door Tavern
John Barleycorn
Lawry's Prime Rib
Le P'tit Paris
Lou Mitchell's
Lutz Continental
Manny's
Margie's Candies
Miller's Pub
Moody's Pub
Papa Milano
Pizzeria Uno/Due
P.J. Clarke's
Pump Room
Rosebud
Trader Vic's
Tufano's Vernon Pk.

**Outdoor Dining**
(G=garden; P=patio;
S=sidewalk; T=terrace;
W=waterside)
Albert's Café (S)
Allen's – New Amer. (P)
Andalucia (P)
Arco de Cuchilleros (P)
a tavola (G)
Athena (G)
Atwater's (P)
Avec (S)
Bice Ristorante (S)
Bijan's Bistro (S)
Bistro Campagne (G)

Bistro 110 (S)
Bistrot Margot (S)
Blackbird (S)
Blandino's Sorriso (P,W)
Brasserie Jo (S)
Cafe Ba-Ba-Reeba! (P)
Carmichael's Steak (G)
Carmine's (P)
Charlie's Ale Hse. (G,P,S,W)
Chez Joel (P)
Coco Pazzo (P)
Coco Pazzo Cafe (P)
Cucina Bella (P,S)
Cyrano's (S)
Edwardo's Pizza (P)
El Jardin (G)
Feast (G)
Flight (P)
Four Farthings (P,S)
Frontera Grill (P)
Greek Islands (P,S)
Green Dolphin St. (P,W)
Iggy's (P)
Isabella Estiatorio (P)
Japonais (P)
John Barleycorn (P,S)
John's Place (S)
Kamehachi (P,S)
Kitsch'n (G,P,S)
Le Colonial (S,T)
Lucca's (G)
Lutz Continental (G)
Maggiano's (P)
Mas (S)
Meritage/Wine (G)
Mesón Sabika (G,P)
Mill Race Inn (P,W)
Moody's Pub (G)
NoMI (G)
North Pond (P)
Northside B&G (G)
Papagus Taverna (S)
Park Grill (P)
Pegasus (T)
P.F. Chang's (P)
Phil Stefani's (S)
Potbelly Sandwich (P)
Public Landing (T,W)

Puck's at MCA (P,W)
RL (P)
Rock Bottom Brew. (G)
Rosebud (P,S,W)
Salvatore's (G,P)
Shanghai Terrace (T)
Smith & Wollensky (G,P,T,W)
South Gate Cafe (P,S)
Sushisamba rio (S)
Tapas Barcelona (G,P)
Tavern on Rush (P,S)
Thyme (G,P,T)
Tommy Nevin's Pub (G)
Tuscany (G,P)
Twisted Lizard (P,S)
Twisted Spoke (P)
Va Pensiero (T)

## People-Watching
Adobo Grill
American Girl
A Milano
Avec
Ballo
Berghoff
Bice Ristorante
Bin 36
Bistro 110
Blackbird
Blue Water Grill
BOKA
Bongo Room
Brasserie Jo
Butter
Carmine's
Chicago Chop Hse.
Coco Pazzo
Coobah
Follia
Gibsons Steak
Green Zebra
Grill on the Alley
Harry Caray's
Japonais
Keefer's
Le Colonial
Manny's
Marché

Mirai Sushi
Miramar
mk
Motel
Naha
Narcisse
Nine
NoMI
one sixtyblue
Opera
Rosebud
Rosebud Steak
Scoozi!
Spring
Sushisamba rio
Tavern on Rush
Vermilion
Wave

## Power Scenes

Alinea
Ambria
Avenues
Bice Ristorante
Capital Grille
Catch 35
Charlie Trotter's
Chicago Chop Hse.
Coco Pazzo
Everest
Gene & Georgetti
Gibsons Steak
Grill on the Alley
Hugo's Frog/Fish
Keefer's
Le Français
Les Nomades
mk
Morton's Steak
Naha
NoMI
Ritz-Carlton Café
Ritz-Carlton Din. Rm.
RL
Ruth's Chris Steak
Seasons
Smith & Wollensky
Spiaggia

Spring
Tru
Zealous

## Private Rooms
(Restaurants charge less at off times; call for capacity)
Ambria
Athena
Ben Pao
Berghoff
Bin 36
Brasserie Jo
Buca di Beppo
Caliterra B&G
Capital Grille
Catch 35
Charlie Trotter's
Chicago Chop Hse.
Club Lucky
Costa's
Edwardo's Pizza
Emilio's Tapas
Everest
Famous Dave's
Francesca's
Frontera Grill
Gabriel's
Gene & Georgetti
Gibsons Steak
Gioco
Goose Is. Brewing
Greek Islands
Joe's Sea/Steak
Kamehachi
Keefer's
Mesón Sabika
Mia Francesca
Misto
mk
Naha
Nick & Tony's
Nine
NoMI
Northside B&G
one sixtyblue
Park Grill
Pasteur

Pete Miller's
Red Light
Rock Bottom Brew.
Rosebud
Russian Tea Time
Ruth's Chris Steak
Scoozi!
Shaw's Crab Hse.
Smith & Wollensky
Spiaggia
Sushisamba rio
Tallgrass
10 West
312 Chicago
Tizi Melloul
Topolobampo
Trattoria Roma
Trio Atelier
Tru
Va Pensiero
Vivo
Wildfire

**Prix Fixe Menus**
(Call for prices and times)
Ambria
Arun's
Avenues
Bank Lane Bistro
Bin 36
Bistro 110
Caliterra B&G
Carlos'
Charlie Trotter's
Chez François
Courtright's
Cyrano's
D & J Bistro
Everest
Fogo de Chão
Froggy's French
Gabriel's
La Sardine
Le Français
Les Nomades
mk
Moto
NoMI

North Pond
Oceanique
one sixtyblue
Pump Room
Red Light
Retro Bistro
Roy's
Sal & Carvão
Salpicón
Seasons
Shanghai Terrace
Signature Room
Spiaggia
Spring
Stained Glass Bistro
Tallgrass
Topolobampo
Tournesol
Tru
Zealous

**Quick Bites**
Aladdin's Eatery
Albert's Café
Aloha Grill
Art of Pizza
Artopolis Bakery
Babylon Kitchen
Bagel
Bar Louie
BD's Mongolian
Berghoff
Bice Grill
Big Bowl
Bijan's Bistro
Billy Goat Tavern
Bin 36
Cafe Selmarie
Chicago Sammies
Chicago Pizza/Grinder
Cold Comfort Cafe
Corner Bakery
Cru Cafe/Wine
El Presidente
Flat Top Grill
Fluky's
foodlife
Gold Coast Dogs

Hot Chocolate
Hot Doug's
Lem's BBQ
Lincoln Noodle Hse.
Manny's
Mrs. Levy's Deli
Noon-O-Kabab
Oak Tree
Old Jerusalem
Pegasus
Penny's Noodle
Pierrot Gourmet
Pompei Bakery
Potbelly Sandwich
Puck's at MCA
Russell's BBQ
Stained Glass Bistro
Stir Crazy
Superdawg Drive-In
Tasting Room
Tempo
Uncommon Ground
Viand Kitchen
Webster's Wine
Wiener's Circle

## Quiet Conversation

Akai Hana
Albert's Café
Amitabul
Aria
Arun's
Bank Lane Bistro
Barn of Barrington
Barrington Bistro
Best Hunan
Bêtise Bistro
Bistro Banlieue
Café Bernard
Café des Architectes
Café La Cave
Cafe Matou
Cafe Pyrenees
Cafe Selmarie
Café Spiaggia
Caliterra B&G
Cape Cod Room
Carlos'

Charlie Trotter's
Chicago Prime Steak
Chinoiserie
Cité
Convito Italiano
D & J Bistro
Don Roth's
Dover Straits
erwin american
Everest
Fondue Stube
Gale Street Inn
Gaylord Indian
Geja's Cafe
Genesee Depot
Hashalom
Itto Sushi
Jilly's Cafe
Kevin
Klay Oven
Kyoto
La Crêperie
La Gondola
Las Bellas Artes
Lawry's Prime Rib
Le Français
Le P'tit Paris
Les Nomades
Le Titi de Paris
Le Vichyssois
Lovell's/Lake Forest
Lucca's
Mill Race Inn
Mimosa
New Japan
North Pond
Oceanique
One North
120 Ocean Place
Pierrot Gourmet
Pump Room
Rhapsody
Ritz-Carlton Café
Ritz-Carlton Din. Rm.
Rivers
RL
Ron of Japan
Russian Tea Time

Salvatore's
Seasons
Seasons Café
1776
Shanghai Terrace
Shiroi Hana
Signature Room
Slice of Life
South Gate Cafe
South Water Kitchen
Tallgrass
Tasting Room
Tavern
302 West
Trattoria No. 10
Tre Kronor
Tru
Va Pensiero
Via Veneto
Village
Vinci
Vivere
Vong's
Zealous

## Raw Bars
Bluepoint Oyster
Blue Water Grill
Bob Chinn Crab Hse.
Brasserie Jo
Butter
Cape Cod Room
Catch 35
Davis St. Fishmkt.
Half Shell
Hama Matsu
JP Chicago
120 Ocean Place
Pappadeaux Seafood
RA Sushi
Raw Bar & Grill
Riva
Shaw's Crab Hse.
Shine & Morida
Sushisamba rio
Swordfish
Tin Fish
Wave

## Romantic Places
Ambria
Avenues
Barrington Bistro
Bistro Banlieue
Bistro Campagne
Bistro Kirkou
Bistrot Margot
Bistrot Zinc
BOKA
Butter
Café Absinthe
Café Bernard
Café La Cave
Cafe Pyrenees
Cape Cod Room
Carlos'
Charlie Trotter's
Chez François
Chez Joel
Chinoiserie
Cité
Coco Pazzo
Courtright's
Crofton on Wells
Cyrano's
D & J Bistro
Dolce
Eclectic
Enoteca Piattini
erwin american
Everest
Fio
Fondue Stube
1492 Tapas
Froggy's French
Geja's Cafe
Gioco
Green Dolphin St.
Grotto
Jacky's Bistro
Japonais
Jilly's Cafe
KiKi's Bistro
La Crêperie
La Sardine
La Tache
Le Bouchon

Le Colonial
Le Français
L8
Le P'tit Paris
Les Nomades
Le Titi de Paris
Le Vichyssois
Meritage/Wine
Mill Race Inn
mk
Mon Ami Gabi
Monsoon
Nacional 27
Naha
Narcisse
NoMI
Oceanique
Pane Caldo
Pasteur
Pump Room
Rhapsody
Rioja
Ritz-Carlton Din. Rm.
RL
RoSal's
Rushmore
Seasons
1776
Shanghai Terrace
Signature Room
Solstice
Souk
South Gate Cafe
Spring
Stained Glass Bistro
Tallgrass
Tango Sur
Tasting Room
Tavern
302 West
Tizi Melloul
Topo Gigio
Tru
Va Pensiero
Vermilion
Vinci
Vivo
Vong's

Wave
Webster's Wine
Wildfish

**Senior Appeal**
Albert's Café
Andies
Ann Sather
Army & Lou's
Bacchanalia
Bagel
Barn of Barrington
Berghoff
Bogart's Charhouse
Bruna's
Buca di Beppo
Café Luciano
Cannella's
Cape Cod Room
Carson's Ribs
Dave's Italian
Davis St. Fishmkt.
Dell Rhea's Chicken
Del Rio
Don Roth's
Don's Fishmarket
Dover Straits
Edelweiss
Fireplace Inn
Fondue Stube
Francesco's Hole
Gale Street Inn
Hackney's
La Cantina Enoteca
La Gondola
La Strada
Lawry's Prime Rib
Le P'tit Paris
Le Vichyssois
Lou Mitchell's
Lutnia
Lutz Continental
Margie's Candies
Miller's Pub
Mill Race Inn
Mirabell
Myron & Phil's Steak
Next Door Bistro
Nick's Fishmarket

Oak Tree
Original Pancake Hse.
Papa Milano
Pump Room
Rosebud
Russell's BBQ
Russian Tea Time
Sabatino's
South Gate Cafe
Tre Kronor
Tufano's Vernon Pk.
Via Veneto
Vic's Classic Steak
Village
Walker Bros. Pancake
White Fence Farm

## Singles Scenes

Adobo Grill
Bar Louie
BOKA
Café Iberico
Charlie's Ale Hse.
Clubhouse
Cullen's B&G
Dick's Last Resort
Fadó Irish Pub
Four Farthings
Genesee Depot
House of Blues
Joe's Be-Bop Cafe
L8
Mike Ditka's
Moody's Pub
Narcisse
Nine
Northside B&G
Pasha
P.J. Clarke's
Ranalli's
Red Light
Rock Bottom Brew.
Rockit B&G
Scoozi!
Stanley's Kitchen
Sushisamba rio
Tavern on Rush
Tilli's
Wave

## Sleepers

(Good to excellent food, but
little known)
Army & Lou's
Atwater's
Bacchanalia
Bistro Kirkou
Bite
Brett's Café Amer.
Bruna's
Buona Terra
Cab's Wine Bar
Cafe Bolero
Cafe Borgia
Café le Coq
Cannella's
Cold Comfort Cafe
Eclectic
Edelweiss
Ethiopian Diamond
Fio
Hai Yen
Hemmingway's
Irazu
Izumi Sushi
Julio's Cocina
Kyoto
La Cantina Enoteca
La Fonda Latino
La Gondola
L'anne
Las Bellas Artes
Mama Thai
Maple Tree Inn
Misto
Noon-O-Kabab
Phil & Lou's
Public Landing
Rinconcito Sudamer.
Ringo
RoSal's
Sabor
Sayat Nova
1776
Shiroi Hana
Silver Seafood
Solstice
Stetson's Chop Hse.

Suparossa
Tavern
10 West
Tombo Kitchen
Trattoria Trullo
Udupi Palace
Vermilion
Viand Kitchen
Vic's Classic Steak
Victory's Banner
Wildfish

## Teen Appeal
Ann Sather
Arco de Cuchilleros
Aurelio's Pizza
Bacino's
Bandera
BD's Mongolian
bella! Bacino's
Big Bowl
Buca di Beppo
Cal. Pizza Kitchen
Cheesecake Factory
Chicago Pizza/Grinder
Dick's Last Resort
Edwardo's Pizza
EJ's Place
El Jardin
Famous Dave's
Flat Top Grill
Fluky's
Giordano's
Gold Coast Dogs
Grand Lux Cafe
Hackney's
Hard Rock Cafe
Harry Caray's
Heaven on Seven
Hot Doug's
Hot Tamales
Ina's
Jake Melnick's
Joy Yee's Noodle
Lincoln Noodle Hse.
Lindo Mexico
Lou Malnati Pizza
Lou Mitchell's

LuLu's Dim Sum
L. Woods Lodge
Margie's Candies
Mity Nice Grill
My Pie Pizza
Nancy's Stuffed Pizza
Nookies
Original Gino's
Original Pancake Hse.
Penny's Noodle
Pizzeria Uno/Due
Pompei Bakery
Potbelly Sandwich
Rainforest Cafe
Ranalli's
R.J. Grunts
Robinson's Ribs
Russell's BBQ
Stanley's Kitchen
Stir Crazy
Suparossa
Superdawg Drive-In
Tempo
Toast
Uncle Julio's
Walker Bros. Pancake
Wiener's Circle
Wishbone

## Theme Restaurants
Fogo de Chão
Fondue Stube
Geja's Cafe
Hard Rock Cafe
Hecky's
House of Blues
Rainforest Cafe

## Trendy
Acqualina
Adobo Grill
Alinea
A Milano
Avec
Ballo
Bin 36
Bistro Campagne
Blackbird
Blue Water Grill

BOKA
Bongo Room
Butter
Café Iberico
Charlie's on Leav.
China Grill
Coobah
De Cero
Fogo de Chão
Follia
Frontera Grill
Gibsons Steak
Gioco
Green Zebra
Hot Chocolate
Hot Doug's
Indie Cafe
Japonais
JP Chicago
La Tache
Le Bouchon
L8
Marché
Mas
Meiji
Mia Francesca
Mirai Sushi
Miramar
mk
Motel
Naha
Narcisse
Nine
NoMI
one sixtyblue
Opera
Osteria Via Stato
Platiyo
Prairie Grass Cafe
Red Light
Scylla
Spring
Starfish
Sushisamba rio
Sushi Wabi
Tournesol
Vermilion
Volo

Wave
West Town Tavern
X/O Chicago

## Views
Atwater's
Avenues
Blandino's Sorriso
Cielo
Cité
Courtright's
Drake Bros.' Steak
Ember Grille
Everest
Flight
Lobby, The
Marina Cafe
Mill Race Inn
NoMI
North Pond
OPA Estiatorio
Park Grill
Puck's at MCA
Riva
Rivers
Seasons
Signature Room
Smith & Wollensky
South Gate Cafe
Spiaggia
Tasting Room

## Visitors on Expense Account
Alinea
Ambria
Arun's
Avenues
Bice Ristorante
Blackbird
Bob Chinn Crab Hse.
Caliterra B&G
Cape Cod Room
Capital Grille
Carlos'
Catch 35
Charlie Trotter's
Chicago Chop Hse.
Coco Pazzo

Courtright's
Crofton on Wells
Everest
Gene & Georgetti
Gibsons Steak
Heat
Joe's Sea/Steak
Keefer's
Kevin
Lawry's Prime Rib
Le Colonial
Le Français
Les Nomades
Le Titi de Paris
Lobby, The
mk
Morton's Steak
Naha
Nine
NoMI
North Pond
Oceanique
one sixtyblue
Palm
Pump Room
Ritz-Carlton Din. Rm.
RL
Rosebud Steak
Roy's
Ruth's Chris Steak
Saloon Steak
Seasons
Shanghai Terrace
Shaw's Crab Hse.
Signature Room
Smith & Wollensky
Spiaggia
Spring
Tallgrass
Topolobampo
Tru
Vivere
Wave
Zealous

## Wine Bars
Avec
Cab's Wine Bar

Café Bernard
Chestnut Grill
Cru Cafe/Wine
Cucina Bella
Cyrano's
Flight
Meritage/Wine
Stained Glass Bistro
Tasting Room
Vintage Wine Bar
Volo
Webster's Wine

## Winning Wine Lists
Alinea
Allen's – New Amer.
Ambria
Arun's
Avec
Avenues
Bin 36
Bistrot Margot
Blackbird
BOKA
Cab's Wine Bar
Café 36
Campagnola
Capital Grille
Carlos'
Charlie Trotter's
Coobah
Courtright's
Cru Cafe/Wine
Cyrano's
Del Rio
Everest
Flight
Fogo de Chão
Gabriel's
Geja's Cafe
Green Zebra
Heat
Isabella Estiatorio
Japonais
La Sardine
Le Français
Le P'tit Paris
Les Nomades

Le Titi de Paris
Meritage/Wine
Miramar
mk
Moto
Naha
NoMI
North Pond
Oceanique
one sixtyblue
Pane Caldo
Rhapsody
Ritz-Carlton Din. Rm.
Salpicón
Seasons
1776
Signature Room
Smith & Wollensky
Spiaggia
Spring
Stained Glass Bistro
Sugar Dessert Bar
Tallgrass
Tasting Room
302 West
Thyme
Topolobampo
Trattoria No. 10
Tru
Va Pensiero
Vivere
Webster's Wine
West Town Tavern
Zealous
Zest

**Worth a Trip**
Arlington Heights
   Le Titi de Paris
Evanston
   Campagnola
   Jacky's Bistro
   Va Pensiero
Geneva
   302 West
Highland Park
   Carlos'
Highwood
   Miramar
Hinsdale
   Salbute
Lakemoor
   Le Vichyssois
Lake Zurich
   Bistro Kirkou
   D & J Bistro
Lockport
   Tallgrass
Mt. Prospect
   Retro Bistro
Northbrook
   Prairie Grass Cafe
Tinley Park
   Tin Fish
Western Springs
   Vie
Wheeling
   Le Français
Willow Springs
   Courtright's

# Milwaukee

# Milwaukee's Most Popular

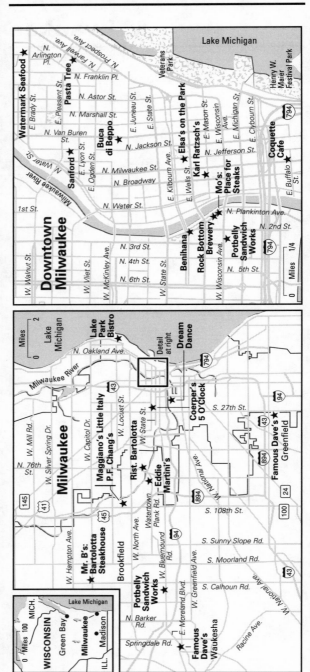

Lake Michigan

Watermark Seafood

N. Arlington Pl.

N. Farwell Ave.

N. Prospect Ave.

Veterans Park

Henry W. Maier Festival Park

Pasta Tree

E. Brady St.

N. Franklin Pl.

E. Pleasant St.

N. Astor St.

N. Marshall St.

E. Juneau St.

E. State St.

Elsa's on the Park

Karl Ratzsch's

N. Wisconsin Ave.

E. Mason St.

E. Michigan St.

E. Clybourn St.

794

Coquette Cafe

N. Van Buren St.

Buca di Beppo

N. Lyon St.

E. Ogden St.

N. Jackson St.

Sanford

N. Water St.

N. Milwaukee St.

Mo's: Place for Steaks

N. Jefferson St.

E. Buffalo St.

N. Broadway

N. Water St.

1st St.

N. Plankinton Ave.

N. 2nd St.

Downtown Milwaukee

Benihana

Rock Bottom Brewery

Potbelly Sandwich Works

794

W. Walnut St.

N. 3rd St.

W. Vliet St.

W. McKinley Ave.

N. 4th St.

N. State St.

N. 6th St.

W. State St.

W. Wisconsin Ave.

N. 5th St.

Miles

1/4

0

Miles

2

Lake Michigan

Lake Park Bistro

0

N. Oakland Ave.

Detail at right

Dream Dance

794

Milwaukee River

43

Coerper's 5 O'Clock

S. 27th St.

94

W. Mill Rd.

Maggiano's Little Italy

P.F. Chang's

W. Locust St.

W. State St.

43

Famous Dave's Greenfield

N. 76th St.

W. Capitol Dr.

W. Silver Spring Dr.

Rist. Bartolotta

Eddie Martini's

W. National Ave.

894

145

41

45

Watertown Plank Rd.

894

24

100

Milwaukee

S. 108th St.

Mr. B's: Bartolotta Steakhouse

W. North Ave.

94

S. Sunny Slope Rd.

W. Hampton Ave.

Brookfield

Potbelly Sandwich Works

W. Bluemound Rd.

W. Greenfield Ave.

S. Moorland Rd.

43

N. Barker Rd.

E. Moreland Blvd.

S. Calhoun Rd.

S. National Ave.

Famous Dave's Waukesha

Springdale Rd.

Racine Ave.

Lake Michigan

MICH.

Miles 100

Green Bay

WISCONSIN

Milwaukee

Madison

ILL.

236

# Top Ratings

## Most Popular

1. Maggiano's
2. Sanford
3. P.F. Chang's
4. Lake Park Bistro
5. Potbelly Sandwich
6. Eddie Martini's
7. Buca di Beppo
8. Coquette Cafe
9. Elsa's on the Park
10. Dream Dance
11. Mr. B's
12. Rist. Bartolotta
13. Mo's
14. Coerper's
15. Watermark Seafood
16. Famous Dave's
17. Karl Ratzsch's
18. Pasta Tree
19. Rock Bottom Brew.
20. Benihana

## Top 10 Food

**29** Sanford
Watermark Seafood
**27** Dream Dance
Rist. Bartolotta
**26** Immigrant Rm./Wine

Heaven City
Three Bros.
Eddie Martini's
Riversite
**25** Coquette Cafe

## By Cuisine

**American (New)**
**29** Sanford
**27** Dream Dance
**26** Heaven City

**American (Traditional)**
**26** Riversite
**22** Elsa's on the Park
**21** Jake's

**Eclectic**
**26** Immigrant Rm./Wine
**24** Tess
**23** Eagan's

**Italian**
**27** Rist. Bartolotta
**25** Mangia
Osteria del Mondo

**Japanese**
**24** Nanakusa
**20** Hama
**18** Benihana

**Mexican**
**23** Rey Sol
**22** Taqueria Azteca
**21** Cempazuchi

**Seafood**
**29** Watermark Seafood
**26** Eddie Martini's
**24** River Lane Inn

**Steakhouses**
**26** Eddie Martini's
**25** Mr. B's
**24** Coerper's

# Top Food

## By Location

**Downtown**
27 Dream Dance
25 Osteria del Mondo
24 Milwaukee Chop

**East Side**
29 Sanford
   Watermark Seafood
25 Lake Park Bistro

**Outlying Areas**
26 Immigrant Rm./Wine
   Heaven City
   Riversite

**South Side**
26 Three Brothers
24 Il Mito
23 Rey Sol

**Third Ward**
25 Coquette Cafe
24 Nanakusa
22 Third Ward Caffe

**West Side**
27 Rist. Bartolotta
26 Eddie Martini's
25 Singha Thai

# Top 10 Decor

27 Bjonda
26 Lake Park Bistro
   Immigrant Rm./Wine
   Nanakusa
   Sanford

25 Riversite
   Heaven City
24 Coast
   Eddie Martini's
   Karl Ratzsch's

# Top 10 Service

29 Sanford
27 Immigrant Rm./Wine
26 Dream Dance
   Eddie Martini's
24 Watermark Seafood

   Riversite
   Lake Park Bistro
23 Rist. Bartolotta
   Heaven City
   Celia

# Best Buys

1. Potbelly Sandwich
2. Singha Thai
3. Rey Sol
4. Taqueria Azteca
5. Elsa's on the Park

6. Famous Dave's
7. Edwardo's
8. King & I
9. Cempazuchi
10. Three Brothers

subscribe to zagat.com

# Milwaukee
# Restaurant Directory

**Au Bon Appétit** ⌧    ▽ 20 | 11 | 20 | $23 |
*1016 E. Brady St. (Astor St.), 414-278-1233;*
*www.aubonappetit.com*
A "wonderful" pair of "on-site owners" really "puts [their] hearts into" this "charming" Mediterranean-Lebanese on fashionable Brady Street – host Costi Helou "always tries to make you comfortable" within the "tightly packed" dining room, and red-toqued chef Rihab Aris "loves to discuss" her French-influenced "ethnic fare", which includes lots of vegetarian items and a "great chocolate mousse."

**Bacchus**    – | – | – | E |
*Cudahy Towers, 925 E. Wells St. (Prospect Ave.), 414-765-1166;*
*www.bacchusmke.com*
Joe Bartolotta (Lake Park Bistro, Ristorante Bartolotta) breathes new life into the Downtown space that once housed the Boulevard Inn, transforming it into a big-city New American with mirrors, square lampshades and brown-leather banquettes; chef Brandon Wolff (ex Dream Dance) mans the high-profile kitchen, turning out trademarks such as braised beef short ribs, day-boat scallops with parsnip puree and Australian rack of lamb, all confidently served by a knowledgeable staff.

**Barossa**    – | – | – | M |
*235 S. Second St. (W. Oregon St.), 414-272-8466;*
*www.barossawinebar.com*
This two-year-old Eclectic offers an innovative, organic-leaning, vegetarian-friendly menu – Indian lamb chops, chicken EOS, tempeh Marbella, vegan ratatouille tart – within an exposed-brick-and-hardwood dining room well suited to its Fifth Ward converted-warehouse neighborhood; N.B. a Friday-nights-only nightclub called B Side recently opened on the second floor.

**Benihana**    18 | 16 | 19 | $31 |
*850 N. Plankinton Ave. (2nd St.), 414-270-0890;*
*www.benihana.com*
See review in the Chicago Directory.

**Bjonda** ⌧    23 | 27 | 21 | $46 |
*7754 Harwood Ave. (Watertown Plank Rd.), Wauwatosa,*
*414-431-1444; www.bjonda.com*
The two sisters who own this "urbane" Wauwatosa "Eclectic" in a "slightly hidden location", "Marija and Vesna Madunic, have done an excellent job" creating an "upscale yet relaxing" "eye-candy" space with "stark but appealing Decor" that's No. 1 in our *Survey*; their "creative" menu, "a fusion of European and Asian cuisines", yields "well-prepared", "outstanding results", "and small touches" such as "tuffets for women's purses" "make the dinner even better", though some suggest they're "still working out" "service kinks."

**Buca di Beppo**                    16 │ 18 │ 17 │ $25 │
*1233 North Van Buren St. (Juneau Ave.), 414-224-8672;*
*www.bucadibeppo.com*
See review in the Chicago Directory.

**Caterina's**                ▽ 24 │ 19 │ 25 │ $31 │
*9104 W. Oklahoma Ave. (S. 92nd St.), 414-541-4200*
"Lots of regulars" rave about the "authentic dishes and
flavors" at this "excellent Italian" on the Southwest Side
that has "wonderful service" and a "great family" behind
it; "there's a reason it's been around for years" – namely,
the "wholesome, good" (if a bit "heavy") food – and "the
complimentary antipasto tray is worth the trip!"

**Celia** ⊠                    24 │ 23 │ 23 │ $48 │
*Pfister Hotel, 424 E. Wisconsin Ave. (Milwaukee St.),*
*414-390-3832; www.pfister-hotel.com*
"Located in the historic Pfister Hotel", "the grande dame of
Milwaukee" inns, this "white-tablecloth" Continental strikes
many as "a cut above" thanks to a "sophisticated menu",
"outstanding wine list" and "respectful", "knowledgeable"
staff; not everyone reports "a great experience", though,
with "disappointed" detractors downgrading it for "being
in a basement (albeit a well-decorated one)"; N.B. the Food
rating may not reflect a post-*Survey* chef change.

**Cempazuchi**                    21 │ 20 │ 20 │ $25 │
*1205 E. Brady St. (Franklin Pl.), 414-291-5233;*
*www.cempazuchi.com*
With a "unique" mix of "authentic traditional entrees" and
"more inventive" dishes (as well as "multiple choices of
tequila" yielding "perfectly prepared margaritas"), this
"relaxed, casual" yet "upscale" spot is definitely "not your
typical Mexican", and its "inviting Brady Street location",
overseen by a "friendly staff", offers an "enjoyable scene
for people-watching", too; P.S. don't miss the "to-die-for
moles" or "creative" "perch tacos, a funky Wisconsin twist."

**Coast**                    21 │ 24 │ 19 │ $33 │
*O'Donnell Park Complex, 931 E. Wisconsin Ave. (Astor St.),*
*414-727-5555; www.coastrestaurant.com*
A "must-try", this "outstanding hot spot" "on the lakefront"
features "fantastic decor with a matching" "marvelous
view" "of the Milwaukee Art Museum's brilliant [Santiago]
Calatrava addition", as well as a "creative", "primarily
seafood-based menu" that "tempts" with a "variety" of
"delicious" New American dishes "from all over the map";
still, some suggest service is "a little rough."

**Coerper's 5 O'Clock Club** ⊠        24 │ 13 │ 20 │ $41 │
*2416 W. State St. (24th St.), 414-342-3553*
"Mammoth", "mountain-high, "melt-in-your-mouth" cuts
have made this "classic" "old-fashioned steakhouse" a

"Milwaukee tradition" for more than half a century, so "don't let" the "tough" Central City neighborhood, "legendary reservations process" ("you must call at 4 PM on Tuesday afternoon for the next" Saturday), "unique system" of "ordering at the bar" or "no-ambiance" decor "deter you" – this "throwback" is "worth the trials."

### Coquette Cafe ⊗          25 | 22 | 23 | $33 |
*316 N. Milwaukee St. (St. Paul Ave.), 414-291-2655;*
*www.coquettecafe.com*
"Tucked away" in the "trendy" Third Ward, this "charming bistro" (the "more casual" and "affordable" French "little sister" of award-winning chef Sandy D'Amato's "renowned Sanford") features "homey" yet "nuanced" selections (folks "love" the "excellent hanger steak") "served with a Midwestern lack of pretension" "in a warm setting"; P.S. proximity to a plethora of play purveyors makes it a "great" "place for pre- or post-theater dining."

### Crawdaddy's ⊗          24 | 19 | 20 | $28 |
*6414 W. Greenfield Ave. (National Ave.), 414-778-2228;*
*www.foodspot.com/crawdaddys*
"Noise", "long waits" and a "no-reservations" policy (for parties of fewer than eight) can't stop locals from "crowding" this "always-hoppin'" "New Orleans–style" eatery on the West Side; "arrive early" for the "extensive and ever-changing menu" of "very good Cajun"-Creole fare – including, as the name suggests, "great seafood" selections – all served in "large portions" that Big Easy lovers "guarantee" will leave you more than "satisfied."

### Dancing Ganesha          22 | 20 | 20 | $27 |
*1692-94 N. Van Buren St. (Brady St.), 414-220-0202;*
*www.dancingganesha.com*
When you "want something a little different", drop in to this "inventive" East Side Indian that "puts a unique twist on" subcontinental fare via a "creative menu" marked by "deep, rich flavors"; perhaps it's "not the most authentic", but most say it's "a sure bet", especially if you "venture to order the edgier" offerings – "they'll make you dance!"

### DREAM DANCE ⊗          27 | 23 | 26 | $53 |
*Potawatomi Bingo Casino, 1721 W. Canal St. (16th St.),*
*414-847-7883; www.paysbig.com*
"Hidden away" in Downtown's Potawatomi Bingo Casino is this "classy" "special-occasion" venue, a "little pot of dining gold" featuring a "fantastic", "innovative [New] American" menu that "showcases local specialties" and is "superbly served" by "outstanding" staffers who go "above and beyond"; still, it's "not a dream for" those who "can't get past" its "incongruous setting" "upstairs" from a "smoke-filled" "gambling hall"; N.B. the Food rating may not reflect a post-*Survey* chef change.

### Eagan's                     23 | 21 | 20 | $30
*1030 N. Water St. (State St.), 414-271-6900*
"Pre- and post-theater" crowds direct their hunger for
"fresh seafood" ("the lobster BLT is a must", as is the
"outstanding sushi") toward this "consistently" "excellent"
Eclectic "just across the street" from Downtown's Marcus
Center for the Performing Arts; "large-scale Impressionist-
style" murals frame the "crowded" (on show nights) and
"noisy" bar/dining room, drawing in "everyone from visiting
NBA players to ladies who lunch."

### Eddie Martini's              26 | 24 | 26 | $51
*8612 Watertown Plank Rd. (84th St.), 414-771-6680*
Diners "step back in time" at this "crowded", "clubby"
steakhouse, a West Side "favorite" for "mouthwatering"
meat and "delicious seafood"; "personable" "team"
"servers in white coats" "make you feel like a favorite",
though some say service "can get overdone" – and you'd
better "plan on spending a boatload of money"; N.B. the
Food rating may not reflect a post-*Survey* chef change.

### Edwardo's Natural Pizza       18 | 10 | 14 | $17
*10845 Bluemound Rd. (Hwy. 100), 414-771-7770*
*700 E. Kilbourn Ave. (Van Buren St.), 414-277-8080*
*www.edwardos.com*
See review in the Chicago Directory.

### Elliot's Bistro               17 | 19 | 18 | $33
*2321 N. Murray Ave. (North Ave.), 414-273-1488;*
*www.elliotsbistro.com*
This "fun" and "charming" East Side French with a mural
(painted by chef-owner Pierre Briere) and a whimsical hat
collection is "refreshing" to diners who fall for its "good,
basic" bistro cuisine (to wit: "great boeuf bourguignon",
bouillabaisse, chocolate mousse, crêpes suzette); still,
contrarians aren't swept away, calling it merely "ok."

### Elm Grove Inn, The 🗷         20 | 18 | 20 | $44
*13275 Watertown Plank Rd. (Elm Grove Rd.), Elm Grove,
262-782-7090; www.elmgroveinn.com*
Admirers assert that the "very good" New American–
Eclectic "cuisine won't disappoint" at this "dependable"
Elm Grove "roadhouse" with "elegant", "calm Colonial
decor", calling it a "secret in the suburbs" to which
"Milwaukeeans forget to go"; still, others claim "its better
days are long gone", reporting that it's "pricey" and "uneven
ever since the ownership changed a few years ago" with
the departure of locally noted chef Nico Derni.

### Elsa's on the Park ●          22 | 23 | 18 | $23
*833 N. Jefferson St. (E. Wells St.), 414-765-0615; www.elsas.com*
A "late-night crowd" of "stylish" "be-seens" takes to this
"hip, happening" Downtown American bar overlooking

Cathedral Square, a "loud", "trendy", "big-city" space where "killer hamburgers big enough to share" and "good sandwiches" are washed down with all manner of cocktails, including "great martinis"; still, whistleblowers wail that "spotty service" from certain "indifferent servers" "is a bummer"; N.B. the Decor rating may not reflect a post-*Survey* face-lift.

### Famous Dave's
18 | 15 | 16 | $19

*5077 S. 27th St. (Edgerton Ave.), Greenfield, 414-727-1940*
*2137 E. Moreland Blvd. (Springdale St.), Waukesha, 262-522-3210*
*www.famousdaves.com*
See review in the Chicago Directory.

### Gilbert's
▽ 26 | 27 | 23 | $46

*327 Wrigley Drive (Center St.), Lake Geneva, 262-248-6680;*
*www.gilbertsrestaurant.com*
A "quiet place for an intimate dinner", this "top-flight" "classic dining delight" set in a "beautifully restored" 30-room, 1885 Queen Anne mansion seduces diners with its "superb views" of Lake Geneva, "outstanding" (mostly organic, Pacific Rim–influenced) New American cuisine enhanced with greens and herbs from an on-site garden and "excellent service" from a staff that "anticipates your every need"; N.B. jackets are suggested.

### Giovanni's
22 | 17 | 22 | $35

*1683 N. Van Buren St. (Brady St.), 414-291-5600;*
*www.giovannismilwaukee.com*
Aficionados of "excellent homemade Italian dishes" "walk away happy" after a visit to this family-run Downtown "classic" known for "knowing its veal so well" (the owner and namesake, Giovanni Safina, cuts it himself); the "old-fashioned" atmosphere "transports" lovers of the "old country" back to a time "when good service and leisurely dining were in vogue."

### Golden Mast Inn
21 | 23 | 21 | $34

*W349 N5293 Lacy Ln. (Lake Dr.), Okauchee, 262-567-7047;*
*www.weissgerbers.com/goldenmast*
A "lovely setting" and "great Friday fish" fry lure "throngs" to this "dependable" flagship of the Weissgerber family's Waukesha County "dining empire"; fans "trust" in its menu, saying it "blends the best of German cuisine" with an American menu, but pooh-poohers purport that the "prime viewing" of Lake Okauchee – and not the "nothing-special" fare – "is the draw here."

### Hama
20 | 13 | 16 | $32

*333 W. Brown Deer Rd. (Port Washington Rd.), 414-352-5051*
California (sushi) dreamers "in the Heartland" find a "fresh", "original" Asian-fusion "twist" on the classic raw-fish fare at this "imaginative" North Shore strip-mall spot; defenders dub it an "all-time favorite" and declare that their "out-of-

town friends go ga-ga" for it, though detractors dis it as "overpriced" and say the space "could use an update."

### HEAVEN CITY 26 25 23 $40
*S91 W27850 National Ave./Hwy. ES (Edgewood Ave.),*
*Mukwonago, 262-363-5191; www.heavencity.com*
"Knowing the history of this" "worth-a-drive" New American set "in an old house" "hidden" in Mukwonago "is half the fun"; reportedly a "former" "gangster hideout", "religious retreat and house of ill repute" (at different times), it's now a "fun, funky place" with "many theme nights" (folks "love May Mushroom Madness") and "a maze of small, romantic rooms"; N.B. the ratings may not reflect a post-*Survey* change of ownership.

### Il Mito ◙ 24 23 22 $30
*605 W. Virginia St. (6th St.), 414-276-1414; www.ilmito.com*
Diners land on "an island of wonderful food" when they enter the "fun, hip atmosphere" of this "upbeat" South Side "oasis" located at "the foot of the striking Sixth Street Viaduct"; "knowledgeable chef-owner" "Michael Feker has staked a claim to serious cuisine" with his "different take on Italian", dishing up "fusion that works", including "innovative specials"; P.S. it's "a great lunch spot."

### IMMIGRANT ROOM & 26 26 27 $60
### WINERY, THE ◙
*American Club, 419 Highland Dr. (School St.), Kohler,*
*920-457-8888; www.destinationkohler.com*
"Top-notch service", "superb food" and "an incredible setting" inside Kohler's American Club Resort have diners immigrating to this "ultimate" Eclectic, a "wonderful" (if "pricey") place that leaves "every sense satisfied"; its "lovely", "old European-style" dining room is "a treat for a special occasion" or to signal "a spectacular end to a day on the golf course or at the spa"; P.S. the separate Winery Bar offers "unique appetizers" and "outstanding wines", plus "their cheese selection is the best" around.

### Jackson Grill ◙ ▽ 28 18 23 $35
*3736 W. Mitchell St. (38th St.), 414-384-7384;*
*www.milwaukeefood.com*
"The word is out" on this "tiny" South Side steakhouse "retreat" that's "reminiscent of a supper club from the past"; owner Jimmy Jackson, son of noted late Milwaukee restaurateur Ray, serves a "small but incredible menu" ("excellent steaks", "to-die-for" specials), but be sure to "come early", as this place can get quite "busy."

### Jake's Fine Dining ◙ 21 17 20 $33
*21445 W. Capitol Dr. (Barker Rd.), Brookfield, 262-781-7995;*
*www.foodspot.com/jakes*
Carnivores in touch with their "old supper club" side note the "high quality" and "expert knowledge" of this

"reliable", "cozy" Brookfield steakhouse that's been offering "wonderful prime rib", "high-quality steaks" and "great" "haystack onion" rings before its "grand stone fireplace" for more than four decades; still, critics contend that "time has passed [it] by", claiming it's been "surpassed by several other places" in town.

### Karl Ratzsch's    23 | 24 | 22 | $36

*320 E. Mason St. (bet. Broadway & Milwaukee St.), 414-276-2720; www.karlratzsch.com*
"Often overlooked" "by locals", this "über-Teutonic" Downtown has nonetheless "passed the test of time and changing dining habits", making it to the ripe old age of 101 on the strength of "old-world charm", "warm service" and some of the most "authentic" "traditional dishes" (sauerbraten, schnitzel, roast goose) "this side of the Rhine River"; but while many laud this "longtime gem" as the "epitome of Milwaukee's German heritage", others opine that "the grande dame" is showing her age.

### King & I, The    22 | 17 | 19 | $24

*823 N. Second St. (bet. Kilbourn Ave. & Wells St.), 414-276-4181; www.kingandirestaurant.com*
"The king brings the heat" say those "never disappointed" by this Downtown Thai with its "large selection" of "high-quality" dishes, which feature "unmatched flavors" and are made "as spicy as you want"; the "nice Midwest service" also ranks with loyal subjects, but unimpressed populists purport that the place is "less than authentic"; N.B. the West Side branch closed post-*Survey*.

### Knick, The ◑    21 | 21 | 19 | $26

*Knickerbocker Hotel, 1030 E. Juneau Ave. (N. Astor St.), 414-272-0011; www.theknickrestaurant.com*
"Be sure to wear your black" to fit in "with the 'in' crowd" lounging at the bar or on the "great" front patio ("a favorite during the summer") of this "trendy", "happening" Eclectic, whose "proximity to Downtown attractions is perfect"; ardent Knicksters praise the "creatively prepared and presented" fare, although an "inconsistent" kitchen and "outrageously expensive" drinks are complaints of grousers.

### Lake Park Bistro    25 | 26 | 24 | $45

*Lake Park Pavilion, 3133 E. Newberry Blvd. (Lake Park Rd.), 414-962-6300; www.lakeparkbistro.com*
With this East Side "French jewel", restaurateur Joe Bartolotta "has created a masterpiece" inside a "perfect setting" – Frederick Law Olmsted–designed Lake Park ("romantics" recommend that you "ask for a table by the window with a view of Lake Michigan"); fans exclaim "Seine-sational!" about the "top-shelf", "consistently wonderful" "classic and modern bistro fare", but even devotees deride the "unacceptable noise level."

### MAGGIANO'S LITTLE ITALY
| 20 | 18 | 19 | $28 |

*Mayfair Mall, 2500 N. Mayfair Rd. (W. North Ave.), Wauwatosa, 414-978-1000; www.maggianos.com*
See review in the Chicago Directory.

### Mangia
| 25 | 20 | 21 | $33 |

*5717 Sheridan Rd. (bet. 57th & 58th Sts.), Kenosha, 262-652-4285*
Respondents who rave about this "wonderful" Kenosha Italian "halfway between Milwaukee and Chicago" "almost don't want to tell anyone about it so [they] can keep it [their] own little secret"; "imaginative entrees" served in "huge portions" and "warm surroundings" make it a "diamond in the rough" that's "always a delight" and "worth the drive from" the Windy City.

### Milwaukee Chop House ☒
| 24 | 20 | 21 | $47 |

*Hilton Hotel City Center, 633 N. Fifth St. (bet. Michigan St. & Wisconsin Ave.), 414-226-2467; www.milwaukeechophouse.com*
Expecting "big red-meat portions"? – you'll find them, as well as an "upbeat" atmosphere, at this Hilton Hotel City Center spot that friends find to be "one of the best chophouses in" town; still, those who feel they've been "clipped and chopped at this place" caution that service can be "sketchy" and insist that the "expensive" food "doesn't live up to its pretensions."

### Mimma's Cafe
| 21 | 21 | 20 | $36 |

*1307 E. Brady St. (Arlington Pl.), 414-271-7337; www.mimmas.com*
A place where regulars "savor every bite", this Italian "anchor of Brady Street" is an East Side "destination" for pasta (and "people-watching") thanks to chef/co-owner Mimma Megna's "personal touch"; despite its "reputation", though, some let-down" surveyors find fault with "overpriced" selections and "tired" dishes, declaring that the "haunt" is "not what it used to be."

### Mo's: A Place for Steaks ☒
| 23 | 20 | 22 | $53 |

*720 N. Plankinton Ave. (Wisconsin Ave.), 414-272-0720; www.mosaplaceforsteaks.com*
"Eat your heart out, Lawry's!" gush groupies of this "clubby", "classy", "always-busy" Downtown steakhouse "frequented by celebrities" and "dignitaries" who groove on its "top-notch" meat "cooked to perfection"; friends say owner "Johnny V [Vassallo] knows his steaks" and "has a winner" here, but foes feel the "overhyped" experience suffers from an "overpriced" menu and the "attitude" of some "overbearing" staffers.

### Mr. B's: A Bartolotta Steakhouse
| 25 | 21 | 23 | $45 |

*17700 W. Capitol Dr. (Calhoun Rd.), Brookfield, 262-790-7005; www.mrbssteakhouse.com*
The "flavor of real fire" from "a wood-burning oven" infuses the "tender, melt-in-your-mouth" filets ("including Kobe

beef") served with "great sides and desserts" at this "high-end" (read: "expensive") Brookfield steakhouse, part of the Joe Bartolotta empire; the "warm colors" and "cozy" feel of its "charming" "rustic" setting are also favored, but the kitchen takes licks from some who say it yields "uneven experiences."

### Nanakusa                    24   26   20   $37
*408 E. Chicago St. (Milwaukee St.), 414-223-3200*
"Fresh", "spectacular sushi" and a "beautiful" "minimalist interior" make this Third Ward Japanese a "surprise find" in a "beer and bratwurst town" cries the "hipper-than-average crowd" that frequents the "trendy" venue (home of a 16-seat tatami room); diners are divided, though, on whether the staff is "knowledgeable and helpful" or "less than stellar", while "high prices" have grumblers griping "don't forget to take out a home-equity loan before dining."

### North Shore Bistro              20   19   18   $31
*River Point Village, 8649 N. Port Washington Rd. (Brown Deer Rd.), 414-351-6100; www.northshorebistro.com*
Boosters believe this "comfortable" "neighborhood staple" (sister restaurant of Downtown's The Knick) "has a lot to offer" the North Shore – "imaginative" New American fare, a "casual" yet "upscale feel" and a "friendly" staff; critics concede it's a "solid choice for locals" but cite sometimes "spotty service" and a somewhat "pretentious menu" that "tries a little too hard" as evidence that it's "not worth a special trip."

### Osteria del Mondo               25   23   23   $43
*1028 E. Juneau Ave. (N. Astor St.), 414-291-3770; www.osteria.com*
"Take someone you want to impress" to chef-owner Marc Bianchini's "elegant", "special date" place, a "nice surprise for Downtown Milwaukee" that satisfied supporters say shines like a "supernova" (though, unlike that short-lived celestial phenomenon, it has lasted for more than a decade); with its "authentic" Northern Italian cuisine, "good wine selection" and "charming", "comfortable" front patio, it "stacks up against any other for quality", even if the "crowds and critics tend to overlook" it.

### Pacific Rim                    20   20   19   $39
*830 N. Old World Third St. (Kilbourn Ave.), 414-277-8100; www.pacificrim-restaurant.com*
"There's nothing else like" this Downtown "Asian fusion" spot (around the corner from its older Thai sibling, The King & I) that's "making its presence felt" with an "ambitious" "concept new to Milwaukee"; some report experiences that were "not as good as anticipated", but enthusiasts insist that it "succeeds more often than not" and predict that, "like a fine wine, it will only get better with time."

**Palms**   20  21  19  $29
*221 N. Broadway (bet. Buffalo & Chicago Sts.), 414-298-3000*
Monkey lovers "go on a taste safari" at this "simian-inspired", Asian-influenced New American, a "lively" "jewel of the Third Ward" that supporters call a "convenient spot for a just-right bite before a show" Downtown thanks to "lots of variety"; still, the "creative decor" with paintings of "chimps everywhere" "can be off-putting for some", and others insist that "nothing" on the "strange menu" "really sticks out as excellent."

**Pasta Tree, The**   24  18  20  $28
*1503 N. Farwell Ave. (Curtis Pl.), 414-276-8867*
This "old favorite" on the East Side serves "top-notch" Northern Italian fare along with "innovative specials" in a "small, narrow" space that supporters say makes you feel "like you're in Europe"; what's an "intimate and romantic" "date" place to some, however, strikes "claustrophobics" as "cramped" ("we call it the Pasta Closet"), but still a majority maintains that "the food is worth the tight surroundings."

**P.F. CHANG'S CHINA BISTRO**   20  19  18  $26
*Mayfair Mall, 2500 N. Mayfair Rd. (W. North Ave.), Wauwatosa, 414-607-1029; www.pfchangs.com*
See review in the Chicago Directory.

**Pleasant Valley Inn**   ∇ 22  21  23  $31
*9801 W. Dakota St. (Dakota & 99th Sts.), 414-321-4321; www.foodspot.com/pleasantvalleyinn*
"Tucked away in a residential neighborhood", this "hidden secret" of the Southwest Side is a pleasant place to get your fill of "consistently good" "roadhouse-style" American fare, including "standard" options such as filet mignon, fresh salmon and New York–style cheesecake; a family operation, it's a "locals' joint" that "gives you the feeling you're in a fine supper club in the north woods."

**Polonez**   ∇ 26  19  24  $22
*4016 S. Packard Ave. (bet. Lunham Ave. & Rte. 32), 414-482-0080; www.foodspot.com/polonez*
"You feel like part of the [Burzynski] family", "sampling authentic Polish food" such as "wonderful" pierogi, sausages, potato pancakes and Hunter's stew along with "a selection of vodkas" at this "homey", family-owned South Side spot; the "staff is great", too, but '-ski' wannabes go for the "old-country" cuisine, not the unpretentious decor.

**Potbelly Sandwich Works**   20  14  17  $9
*135 W. Wisconsin Ave. (Plankinton Ave.), 414-226-0014*
*17800 W. Bluemound Rd. (bet. Brookfield & Calhoun Rds.), Brookfield, 262-796-9845*
*www.potbelly.com*
See review in the Chicago Directory.

### Red Circle Inn ⊠　　　▽ 24 | 18 | 23 | $41
*N44 W33013 Watertown Plank Rd. (Hwy. C), Nashotah,*
*262-367-4883; www.foodspot.com/redcircleinn*
Dating to 1848, this "neat" Nashotah place (reputedly the state's oldest restaurant) conjures up "good memories" for longtime admirers, who say it's "worth" the drive for its "outstanding" Continental cuisine; some style watchers call the dining room "über-kitschy", but there's "great atmosphere in the bar" – plus "old-fashioned drinks."

### Rey Sol　　　23 | 15 | 22 | $21
*2338 W. Forest Home Ave. (Lincoln Ave.), 414-389-1760;*
*www.foodspot.com/reysol*
"You feel like you're at a home in Mexico" when visiting this "authentic South Side Mexican" where the "exceptionally tasty", "not-your-run-of-the-mill" "feasts" feature such specialties as red snapper and Yucatán-style shredded pork; its "excellent quality" lures fans to the questionable area, which some call the restaurant's "biggest detraction."

### RISTORANTE BARTOLOTTA　　　27 | 23 | 23 | $41
*7616 W. State St. (Harwood Ave.), Wauwatosa, 414-771-7910;*
*www.bartolottaristorante.com*
"Anything Bartolotta touches is great", so it's no surprise followers brave a "high noise level" and "on-top-of-each-other" tables to get a piece of his longest-running endeavor, this West Side "favorite" where "dreamy" Northern Italian fare and "gracious service" find a "rustic", "comfortable" yet "classy" home; remember, though, that "reservations are a must", since "crowds" of "smiling people" mean it's "still hard to get into after all these years."

### River Lane Inn ⊠　　　24 | 17 | 21 | $35
*4313 W. River Ln. (Brown Deer Rd.), 414-354-1995*
"Wonderful opportunities to try" "great seafood" (including some Cajun-Creole specialties such as the "best blackened fish around") abound at this "off-the-beaten-path" North Shore spot, the casual counterpart to Jim Marks' The Riversite; "popular with locals", it's a "fantastic place" that fans feel is "like an old friend or a favorite sweater", though a few naysayers negate the menus as "a little tired."

### Riversite, The ⊠　　　26 | 25 | 24 | $43
*11120 N. Cedarburg Rd. (Mequon Rd.), Mequon,*
*262-242-6050*
"A beautiful view of the Milwaukee River", "exceptional wines" and the skills of "creative" chef Tom Peschong keep this "reliable", "upscale" North Shore American on its audience's A-list; "superbly hospitable" owner Jim Marks is often "present and will guide you through the myriad choices", which include "extraordinary appetizers" and "excellent seafood" selections; P.S. the "nice setting" is "especially lovely when the snow flies."

# Milwaukee

F D S C

**Rock Bottom Brewery**    14 | 15 | 15 | $20
*740 N. Plankinton Ave. (bet. Wells St. & Wisconsin Ave.),*
*414-276-3030; www.rockbottom.com*
See review in the Chicago Directory.

**Roots Restaurant and Cellar**    – | – | – | E
*1818 N. Hubbard St. (Vine St.), 414-374-8480;*
*www.rootsmilwaukee.com*
Putting down roots in the up-and-coming Brewers Hill
area, this dramatic venue with beautiful city views features
two spaces – an upscale upper level serving seasonally
changing Cal–Asian fusion fare and a more casual cellar
with a sandwich-and-salad focus; N.B. both menus use
ingredients grown on the restaurant's proprietary farm.

**Saffron Indian Bistro**    – | – | – | I
*17395D-1 Blue Mound Rd. (bet. Brookfield & Calhoun Rds.),*
*Brookfield, 262-784-1332*
Droves of weekday suit-wearers queue up for the popular
lunch buffet at this Indian yearling set in a Brookfield strip
mall; in the evenings, diners crowd its sparsely decorated
space to enjoy selections such as butter chicken, lobster
masala, tandoori rabbit and saffron-mango cheesecake.

**SANFORD** ⌘    29 | 26 | 29 | $66
*1547 N. Jackson St. (Pleasant St.), 414-276-9608;*
*www.sanfordrestaurant.com*
"If I only had one meal left, I would have it here" attest
acolytes "astounded" by this "intimate", "elegant" East Side
New American mecca that "defines gourmet in Milwaukee",
setting "the standard" by scoring this *Survey*'s top honors
for both Food and Service; "genius" co-owner and "chef
Sanford D'Amato amazes with his spectacular cooking" and
"adventurous menu", while the "fantastic" staff provides
"outstanding service", ensuring that this "true culinary
experience" is "worth the splurge."

**Savoy Room, The** ⌘    22 | 20 | 19 | $37
*ShoreCrest Hotel, 1962 N. Prospect Ave. (North Ave.),*
*414-270-9933*
Though local legend Sally Papia was tragically killed
in a car accident in early 2005, her final venture – this
ShoreCrest Hotel Italian steakhouse she opened in 2002 –
continues to uphold "her standards", with "excellent-value"
food that's "as good as ever" (including "great steaks"
"hidden in a delectable mound of onion rings"); still, some
find it "a little bit pricey for the overall quality."

**Sebastian's** ⌘    ▽ 28 | 24 | 27 | $34
*6025 Douglas Ave. (5 Mile Rd.), Caledonia, 262-681-5465;*
*www.sebastiansfinefood.com*
"Tell your friends" about this Caledonia New American
whose "outstanding" menu selections are "unique enough

**vote at zagat.com**    251

for the most discriminating palate but won't disappoint jaded steak eaters"; add in "warm, comfortable decor" and "great service" and you'll see why addicts aver that "if you can find" this "off-the-beaten-track" restaurant, "you'll be back the next night."

### Singha Thai
25　16　19　$19

*2237 S. 108th St. (Lincoln Ave.), 414-541-1234;*
*www.singhathai.com*
Though "any of the curries are great", regulars of this "awesome" West Side Thai know to "go to the back page" of its "expansive menu" "for house specialties", including Singha beef, charcoal chicken, crispy shrimp and spicy noodles; "don't expect to be wowed" by "its typical strip-mall" location, "but at least you aren't paying for frills."

### Sticks N Stones ☒
22　22　22　$43

*2300 N. Pilgrim Square Dr. (North Ave.), Brookfield, 262-786-5700;*
*www.sticksandstonesrestaurant.com*
The "only elegant choice in the area", this Brookfield New American segments surveyors – supporters say its staff is "attentive" and its "creative seafood" is "excellent" and "a decent value" (the "meat dishes, as well"), while bone-breakers bellow that the "food is never a wow" and "service is sometimes off"; "horrible acoustics" are another reason name-callers would much rather "go to [its sibling spot] Eddie Martini's instead."

### Tandoor
▽　24　10　21　$20

*1117 S. 108th St. (Washington St.), 414-777-1600*
"Authentic" curries, tandoori and vegetarian dishes that are not only "fantastic" but also a "great bargain" ("the lunch buffet is not to be missed") have supporters of this West Side spot saying they "wouldn't eat anywhere else for Indian", so "don't be afraid" of the unremarkable decor – "the food will make you feel comfortable."

### Taqueria Azteca
22　17　17　$20

*119 E. Oklahoma Ave. (Chase Ave.), 414-486-9447*
If you're "not looking for standard taco fare", you've come to the right place according to advocates of this "inventive" South Side Mexican who advise you to "order off the specials board" (known for "unique", "fresh" choices including twists on standard quesadillas) then "cool your palate" with "chunky guacamole" and "super margaritas" – you "will be rewarded with a delicious meal."

### Tess
24　18　20　$35

*2499 N. Bartlett Ave. (Bradford Ave.), 414-964-8377*
"A funky old corner tavern"-cum-bistro, this East Sider is just the ticket for a "diverse menu" of "ambitious" Eclectic eats that locals say "succeeds almost all the time" (the "seafood and pastas are very good", but "save room for dessert"); some "criticize" its "cramped" dining room for

"lacking atmosphere", but all agree the "fabulous" "walled-in patio" is "exceptional."

### Third Ward Caffe ⊠                22 | 22 | 20 | $30

*225 E. St. Paul Ave. (bet. Broadway & Water St.), 414-224-0895;*
*www.foodspot.com/thirdwardcaffe*

"It's not hip, it's not happening", but this "established" Northern Italian joint that "put down roots when the Third Ward wasn't cool" could "easily become a habit"; caffe-crashers go crazy for its "warm, intimate atmosphere" and "reliable" fare, including "seasonal offerings" of "fabulous pastas" such as "excellent pumpkin ravioli."

### THREE BROTHERS ⊅            26 | 17 | 22 | $27

*2414 S. St. Clair (Russell Ave.), 414-481-7530*

Owners Branko and Patricia Radicevic "treat you like family the minute you walk in the door" of their "one-of-a-kind" Serbian set in an old South Side Schlitz tavern that oozes "simple", "old-world charm"; ranging from "well-dressed businessmen to everyday anarchists", the "crowd" "spends hours" at this "authentic" "fixture" sampling the likes of burek, chicken paprikash and goulash – all foods that "warm your heart."

### WATERMARK SEAFOOD            29 | 24 | 24 | $42

*1716 N. Arlington Pl. (Brady St.), 414-278-8464;*
*www.watermarkseafood.net*

"Chic" yet "comfortable", this East Side "underwater treasure" has "instant-classic" potential thanks to chef-owner and "seafood magician" Mark Weber (Lake Park Bistro's former top toque), whose daily changing menu of "simple, subtle, perfect" dishes showcases "fresh" fin fare; even if certain staffers seem "a bit challenged", it's still "a fantastic addition to the Milwaukee scene."

### Zarletti ⊠                    – | – | – | M

*741 N. Milwaukee St. (E. Mason St.), 414-225-0000*

Co-owner and self-taught chef Brian Zarletti's Italian grandma–inspired meals (pan-seared salmon, pasta al pomodoro, veal with lemon sauce, tiramisu) lend homey appeal to this Downtown newcomer set in an intimate corner storefront on nightlife-mecca Milwaukee Street; so, too, does the modern, chocolate-walled interior accented with fresh blooms from the proprietors' own flower shop.

# Milwaukee Indexes

## CUISINES
## LOCATIONS
## SPECIAL FEATURES

# CUISINES

## American (New)
Bacchus
Coast
Dream Dance
Elm Grove Inn
Gilbert's
Heaven City
North Shore Bistro
Palms
Sanford
Sebastian's
Sticks N Stones

## American (Traditional)
Eddie Martini's
Elsa's on Park
Golden Mast Inn
Jackson Grill
Jake's Fine Dining
Pleasant Valley Inn
Riversite
Rock Bottom Brew.

## Asian Fusion
Hama
Pacific Rim
Roots

## Barbecue
Famous Dave's

## Cajun
Crawdaddy's

## Californian
Roots

## Chinese
P.F. Chang's

## Continental
Celia
North Shore Bistro
Red Circle Inn

## Creole
Crawdaddy's

## Delis
Potbelly Sandwich

## Eclectic
Barossa
Bjonda
Eagan's
Elm Grove Inn
Immigrant Room
Knick
Tess

## French
Elliot's Bistro

## French (Bistro)
Coquette Cafe
Lake Park Bistro

## German
Golden Mast Inn
Karl Ratzsch's

## Hamburgers
Elsa's on Park

## Indian
Dancing Ganesha
Saffron Indian Bistro
Tandoor

## Italian
(N=Northern; S=Southern)
Buca di Beppo
Caterina's
Giovanni's
Il Mito (S)
Maggiano's (S)
Mangia
Mimma's Cafe
Osteria del Mondo (N)
Pasta Tree (N)
Rist. Bartolotta (N)
Third Ward Caffe (N)
Zarletti

## Japanese
(* sushi specialist)
Benihana*
Hama*
Nanakusa

## Lebanese
Au Bon Appétit

## Mediterranean
Au Bon Appétit

## Mexican
Cempazuchi
Rey Sol
Taqueria Azteca

## Pizza
Edwardo's Pizza

## Polish
Polonez

## Sandwiches
Potbelly Sandwich

## Seafood
Eagan's
Eddie Martini's

River Lane Inn
Sticks N Stones
Watermark Seafood

## Serbian
Three Brothers

## Steakhouses
Benihana
Coerper's 5 O'Clock
Eddie Martini's
Jackson Grill
Jake's Fine Dining
Milwaukee Chop Hse.
Mo's: Steak
Mr. B's: Steak
Savoy Room

## Thai
King & I
Singha Thai

# LOCATIONS

## MILWAUKEE

**Brewers Hill**
Roots

**Central City**
Coerper's 5 O'Clock

**Downtown**
Bacchus
Benihana
Buca di Beppo
Celia
Coast
Dream Dance
Eagan's
Edwardo's Pizza
Elsa's on Park
Karl Ratzsch's
King & I
Knick
Milwaukee Chop Hse.
Mo's: Steak
Osteria del Mondo
Pacific Rim
Potbelly Sandwich
Rock Bottom Brew.
Zarletti

**East Side**
Au Bon Appétit
Cempazuchi
Dancing Ganesha
Elliot's Bistro
Giovanni's
Lake Park Bistro
Mimma's Cafe
Pasta Tree

Sanford
Savoy Room
Tess
Watermark Seafood

**Fifth Ward**
Barossa

**North Shore**
Hama
North Shore Bistro
River Lane Inn

**South Side**
Il Mito
Jackson Grill
Polonez
Rey Sol
Taqueria Azteca
Three Brothers

**Southwest Side**
Caterina's
Pleasant Valley Inn

**Third Ward**
Coquette Cafe
Nanakusa
Palms
Third Ward Caffe

**West Side**
Crawdaddy's
Eddie Martini's
Edwardo's Pizza
Singha Thai
Tandoor

## OUTLYING AREAS

**Brookfield**
Jake's Fine Dining
Mr. B's: Steak
Potbelly Sandwich
Saffron Indian Bistro
Sticks N Stones

**Caledonia**
Sebastian's

**Elm Grove**
Elm Grove Inn

**Greenfield**
Famous Dave's

## Kenosha
Mangia

## Kohler
Immigrant Room

## Lake Geneva
Gilbert's

## Mequon
Riverside

## Mukwonago
Heaven City

## Nashotah
Red Circle Inn

## Okauchee
Golden Mast Inn

## Waukesha
Famous Dave's

## Wauwatosa
Bjonda
Maggiano's
P.F. Chang's
Rist. Bartolotta

# SPECIAL FEATURES

(Indexes list the best in each category. Multi-location restaurants' features may vary by branch.)

## Additions
(Properties added since the last edition of the book)
Bacchus
Barossa
Saffron Indian Bistro
Zarletti

## Brunch
Eagan's
Elliot's Bistro
Golden Mast Inn
Knick
Lake Park Bistro
Palms
Polonez
Tess

## Buffet Served
(Check availability)
King & I
Polonez
Saffron Indian Bistro
Tandoor

## Business Dining
Bacchus
Bjonda
Celia
Coast
Coquette Cafe
Eagan's
Eddie Martini's
Elm Grove Inn
Giovanni's
Il Mito
Jake's Fine Dining
Karl Ratzsch's
Knick
Lake Park Bistro
Milwaukee Chop Hse.
Mo's: Steak
Mr. B's: Steak
North Shore Bistro
Pacific Rim

Rist. Bartolotta
River Lane Inn
Riversite
Saffron Indian Bistro
Sticks N Stones
Watermark Seafood

## Catering
Au Bon Appétit
Bjonda
Buca di Beppo
Crawdaddy's
Dancing Ganesha
Elm Grove Inn
Famous Dave's
Gilbert's
Giovanni's
King & I
Knick
Mangia
North Shore Bistro
Pacific Rim
Red Circle Inn
Rey Sol
Sticks N Stones

## Celebrity Chefs
(Listed under their primary restaurants)
Au Bon Appétit, *Rihab Aris*
Bacchus, *Brandon Wolff*
Jackson Grill, *Jimmy Jackson*
Mimma's Cafe, *Mimma Megna*
Osteria/Mondo, *Marc Bianchini*
Riversite, *Tom Peschong*
Sanford, *Sandy D'Amato*
Watermark Sea., *Mark Weber*

## Child-Friendly
(Alternatives to the usual fast-food places; * children's menu available)
Benihana*
Bjonda*

Caterina's
Cempazuchi
Coast*
Edwardo's Pizza*
Famous Dave's*
Gilbert's*
Giovanni's
Golden Mast Inn*
Hama
Il Mito
Immigrant Room
Karl Ratzsch's*
Knick
Lake Park Bistro*
Maggiano's*
Mangia*
Mimma's Cafe
Osteria del Mondo
Pacific Rim
Palms
Pasta Tree
P.F. Chang's
Pleasant Valley Inn
Potbelly Sandwich*
Rey Sol
Rist. Bartolotta
River Lane Inn
Riversite
Rock Bottom Brew.*
Singha Thai*
Sticks N Stones
Taqueria Azteca
Tess
Third Ward Caffe
Watermark Seafood

### Cigars Welcome
Bjonda
Elm Grove Inn
Famous Dave's
Gilbert's
Giovanni's
Golden Mast Inn
Heaven City
Osteria del Mondo

### Cool Loos
Bjonda
Buca di Beppo

Eddie Martini's
Lake Park Bistro
Savoy Room

### Critic-Proof
(Gets lots of business despite
so-so food)
Rock Bottom Brew.

### Delivery/Takeout
(D=delivery, T=takeout)
Benihana (T)
Bjonda (T)
Buca di Beppo (T)
Cempazuchi (T)
Crawdaddy's (T)
Dancing Ganesha (T)
Elsa's on Park (T)
Famous Dave's (D,T)
Giovanni's (T)
Hama (T)
Il Mito (T)
King & I (T)
Knick (T)
Maggiano's (T)
Mimma's Cafe (T)
Nanakusa (T)
North Shore Bistro (T)
Palms (T)
Pasta Tree (T)
Polonez (T)
Potbelly Sandwich (D,T)
Rey Sol (D,T)
River Lane Inn (T)
Rock Bottom Brew. (T)
Roots (T)
Singha Thai (T)
Tandoor (T)
Taqueria Azteca (T)
Third Ward Caffe (T)

### Dessert
Bjonda
Celia
Dancing Ganesha
Dream Dance
Eddie Martini's
Elm Grove Inn
Hama

Lake Park Bistro
Mimma's Cafe
Palms
Sanford
Watermark Seafood

## Dining Alone
(Other than hotels and places with counter service)
Benihana
Bjonda
Cempazuchi
Coquette Cafe
Hama
Lake Park Bistro
Nanakusa
North Shore Bistro
Potbelly Sandwich
Rock Bottom Brew.
Singha Thai
Tandoor
Watermark Seafood

## Dramatic Interiors
Bjonda
Dancing Ganesha
Elsa's on Park
Karl Ratzsch's
Lake Park Bistro
Sanford

## Entertainment
(Call for days and times of performances)
Coast (jazz/reggae)
Elm Grove Inn (classical guitar)
Gilbert's (jazz)
Golden Mast Inn (piano)
Immigrant Room (piano)
Karl Ratzsch's (piano)
North Shore Bistro (jazz)
Rey Sol (piano)
Rock Bottom Brew. (karaoke)
Sticks N Stones (piano)

## Fireplaces
Bjonda
Coast
Elm Grove Inn

Gilbert's
Golden Mast Inn
Heaven City

## Game in Season
Bjonda
Celia
Coast
Coquette Cafe
Dream Dance
Eddie Martini's
Elliot's Bistro
Gilbert's
Golden Mast Inn
Heaven City
Immigrant Room
Zarletti

## Historic Places
(Year opened; * building)
1847  Red Circle Inn
1875  Gilbert's*
1890  Elsa's on Park*
1904  Karl Ratzsch's
1918  Immigrant Room*
1935  Elm Grove Inn
1940  Golden Mast Inn*
1951  Three Brothers
1952  Coerper's 5 O'Clock

## Holiday Meals
(Special prix fixe meals offered at major holidays)
Celia
Golden Mast Inn
Immigrant Room

## Hotel Dining
Hilton Hotel City Center
    Milwaukee Chop Hse.
Knickerbocker Hotel
    Knick
Pfister Hotel
    Celia
ShoreCrest Hotel
    Savoy Room

## Jacket Required
Immigrant Room

### Late Dining
(Weekday closing hour)
Elsa's on Park (1AM)
Knick (12AM)

### Local Favorites
Caterina's
Cempazuchi
Coerper's 5 O'Clock
Crawdaddy's
Elsa's on Park
King & I
Knick
Lake Park Bistro
Mimma's Cafe
Mr. B's: Steak
North Shore Bistro
Pasta Tree
Pleasant Valley Inn
Rist. Bartolotta
River Lane Inn
Riversite
Sanford
Singha Thai
Taqueria Azteca
Third Ward Caffe
Three Brothers

### Meet for a Drink
(Most top hotels and the
following standouts)
Bacchus
Barossa
Bjonda
Cempazuchi
Coast
Coquette Cafe
Crawdaddy's
Dancing Ganesha
Eagan's
Eddie Martini's
Elsa's on Park
Giovanni's
Il Mito
Jackson Grill
Knick
Lake Park Bistro
Mo's: Steak
Nanakusa

North Shore Bistro
Osteria del Mondo
Palms
Rock Bottom Brew.
Savoy Room
Sticks N Stones
Taqueria Azteca
Tess
Watermark Seafood
Zarletti

### Old City Feel
Karl Ratzsch's
Three Brothers

### Outdoor Dining
(G=garden; P=patio;
S=sidewalk; T=terrace;
W=waterside)
Coast (P)
Eagan's (S)
Edwardo's Pizza (P)
Gilbert's (W)
Giovanni's (P)
Golden Mast Inn (P,W)
Il Mito (P)
Knick (P)
Lake Park Bistro (P,W)
Maggiano's (P)
Mangia (P)
North Shore Bistro (P)
Osteria del Mondo (P)
Palms (S)
Pasta Tree (P)
P.F. Chang's (P)
Potbelly Sandwich (P,S)
Rist. Bartolotta (S)
River Lane Inn (P)
Riversite (P,W)
Rock Bottom Brew. (P)
Roots (P)
Savoy Room (S)
Taqueria Azteca (P)
Tess (P)
Third Ward Caffe (S)
Watermark Seafood (P)

### People-Watching
Bacchus
Bjonda

Coast
Coquette Cafe
Eagan's
Eddie Martini's
Elsa's on Park
Il Mito
Knick
Maggiano's
Mimma's Cafe
Mo's: Steak
Nanakusa
North Shore Bistro
Palms
Pasta Tree
P.F. Chang's
Rist. Bartolotta
River Lane Inn
Rock Bottom Brew.
Sanford
Savoy Room
Sticks N Stones
Three Brothers
Watermark Seafood

## Power Scenes
Bacchus
Eddie Martini's
Lake Park Bistro
Mo's: Steak
Mr. B's: Steak
Savoy Room

## Private Rooms
(Restaurants charge less at off times; call for capacity)
Bjonda
Buca di Beppo
Celia
Coast
Coquette Cafe
Eddie Martini's
Edwardo's Pizza
Elm Grove Inn
Famous Dave's
Gilbert's
Golden Mast Inn
Hama
Heaven City
Immigrant Room

King & I
Maggiano's
Mangia
Mimma's Cafe
Mr. B's: Steak
Nanakusa
Osteria del Mondo
Pacific Rim
Polonez
Red Circle Inn
River Lane Inn
Riversite
Rock Bottom Brew.
Sebastian's
Sticks N Stones

## Prix Fixe Menus
(Call for prices and times)
Bjonda
Elliot's Bistro
Gilbert's
Immigrant Room
Lake Park Bistro
Red Circle Inn
Rey Sol

## Quick Bites
Edwardo's Pizza
Elsa's on Park
Famous Dave's
Hama
Knick
Tandoor

## Quiet Conversation
Au Bon Appétit
Barossa
Bjonda
Celia
Dream Dance
Eddie Martini's
Elliot's Bistro
Elm Grove Inn
Golden Mast Inn
Il Mito
Jake's Fine Dining
Karl Ratzsch's
Milwaukee Chop Hse.
Osteria del Mondo

Pacific Rim
Pasta Tree
Polonez
Red Circle Inn
Riversite
Sanford
Third Ward Caffe
Watermark Seafood

## Raw Bars
Benihana
Eagan's
Hama
Nanakusa

## Reserve Ahead
Bjonda
Buca di Beppo
Coast
Coerper's 5 O'Clock
Eddie Martini's
Elliot's Bistro
Gilbert's
Heaven City
Il Mito
Lake Park Bistro
Mo's: Steak
Osteria del Mondo
Riversite
Sanford
Tess
Watermark Seafood

## Romantic Places
Dancing Ganesha
Golden Mast Inn
Heaven City
Il Mito
Immigrant Room
Lake Park Bistro
Mimma's Cafe
Osteria del Mondo
Pasta Tree
Red Circle Inn
Riversite
Third Ward Caffe
Three Brothers
Watermark Seafood
Zarletti

## Senior Appeal
Elm Grove Inn
Giovanni's
Golden Mast Inn
Immigrant Room
Jake's Fine Dining
Karl Ratzsch's
Pleasant Valley Inn
Polonez
Red Circle Inn
Riversite
Three Brothers

## Singles Scenes
Barossa
Bjonda
Crawdaddy's
Eagan's
Elsa's on Park
Knick
Mo's: Steak
Nanakusa
Palms
Rock Bottom Brew.

## Sleepers
(Good to excellent food, but little known)
Au Bon Appétit
Caterina's
Gilbert's
Jackson Grill
Pleasant Valley Inn
Polonez
Red Circle Inn
Sebastian's
Tandoor

## Special Occasions
Bacchus
Benihana
Bjonda
Celia
Coerper's 5 O'Clock
Dream Dance
Eddie Martini's
Elm Grove Inn
Gilbert's
Golden Mast Inn

Heaven City
Il Mito
Immigrant Room
Jake's Fine Dining
Karl Ratzsch's
Lake Park Bistro
Mangia
Milwaukee Chop Hse.
Mimma's Cafe
Mo's: Steak
Mr. B's: Steak
Osteria del Mondo
Pacific Rim
Pasta Tree
Pleasant Valley Inn
Red Circle Inn
Rist. Bartolotta
Riversite
Sanford
Sebastian's
Third Ward Caffe
Three Brothers
Watermark Seafood

## Tasting Menus
Bjonda
Elliot's Bistro
Gilbert's

## Teen Appeal
Buca di Beppo
Edwardo's Pizza
Maggiano's
P.F. Chang's
Potbelly Sandwich
Rock Bottom Brew.

## Theme Restaurants
Buca di Beppo
Famous Dave's
Maggiano's
P.F. Chang's

## Trendy
Bacchus
Barossa
Bjonda
Cempazuchi
Coast
Dancing Ganesha

Eddie Martini's
Elsa's on Park
Il Mito
Knick
Lake Park Bistro
Maggiano's
Mo's: Steak
Palms
P.F. Chang's
Rist. Bartolotta
Sanford
Zarletti

## Valet Parking
Bjonda
Celia
Coast
Gilbert's
Giovanni's
Immigrant Room
Karl Ratzsch's
Knick
Mo's: Steak
Osteria del Mondo
P.F. Chang's
Rist. Bartolotta
Zarletti

## Views
Bacchus
Coast
Gilbert's
Golden Mast Inn
Knick
Lake Park Bistro

## Visitors on Expense Account
Barossa
Coquette Cafe
Eagan's
Edwardo's Pizza
Il Mito
King & I
Knick
Maggiano's
North Shore Bistro
Polonez
Rey Sol
Rock Bottom Brew.

Saffron Indian Bistro
Singha Thai
Tandoor
Taqueria Azteca

## Winning Wine Lists

Bacchus
Barossa
Coquette Cafe
Dream Dance
Lake Park Bistro
Mangia
Milwaukee Chop Hse.
Osteria del Mondo
Rist. Bartolotta
Sanford
Watermark Seafood

## Worth a Trip

Caledonia
    Sebastian's
Kenosha
    Mangia
Kohler
    Immigrant Room
Lake Geneva
    Gilbert's
Mukwonago
    Heaven City
Nashotah
    Red Circle Inn
Okauchee
    Golden Mast Inn

# Wine Vintage Chart

This chart is designed to help you select wine to go with your meal. It is based on the same 0 to 30 scale used throughout this *Survey*. The ratings (prepared by our friend **Howard Stravitz,** a law professor at the University of South Carolina) reflect both the quality of the vintage and the wine's readiness for present consumption. Thus, if a wine is not fully mature or is over the hill, its rating has been reduced. We do not include 1987, 1991–1993 vintages because they are not especially recommended for most areas. A dash indicates that a wine is either past its peak or too young to rate.

| | '85 | '86 | '88 | '89 | '90 | '94 | '95 | '96 | '97 | '98 | '99 | '00 | '01 | '02 | '03 |
|---|---|---|---|---|---|---|---|---|---|---|---|---|---|---|---|
| **WHITES** | | | | | | | | | | | | | | | |
| **French:** | | | | | | | | | | | | | | | |
| Alsace | 24 | – | 22 | 28 | 28 | 27 | 26 | 25 | 25 | 26 | 25 | 26 | 27 | 25 | – |
| Burgundy | 26 | 25 | – | 24 | 22 | – | 28 | 29 | 24 | 23 | 26 | 25 | 23 | 27 | 24 |
| Loire Valley | – | – | – | – | 24 | – | 20 | 23 | 22 | – | 24 | 25 | 23 | 27 | 26 |
| Champagne | 28 | 25 | 24 | 26 | 29 | – | 26 | 27 | 24 | 24 | 25 | 25 | 26 | – | – |
| Sauternes | 21 | 28 | 29 | 25 | 27 | – | 21 | 23 | 26 | 24 | 24 | 24 | 28 | 25 | 26 |
| **Germany** | 25 | – | 25 | 26 | 27 | 25 | 24 | 27 | 24 | 23 | 25 | 24 | 29 | 27 | – |
| **California (Napa, Sonoma, Mendocino):** | | | | | | | | | | | | | | | |
| Chardonnay | – | – | – | – | – | – | – | 24 | 26 | 25 | 25 | 24 | 27 | 29 | – |
| Sauvignon Blanc/Semillon | – | – | – | – | – | – | – | – | – | 25 | 25 | 23 | 27 | 28 | 26 |
| **REDS** | | | | | | | | | | | | | | | |
| **French:** | | | | | | | | | | | | | | | |
| Bordeaux | 24 | 25 | 24 | 26 | 29 | 22 | 26 | 25 | 23 | 25 | 24 | 28 | 26 | 23 | 24 |
| Burgundy | 23 | – | 21 | 24 | 26 | – | 26 | 28 | 25 | 22 | 28 | 22 | 24 | 27 | – |
| Rhône | 25 | 19 | 27 | 29 | 29 | 24 | 25 | 23 | 24 | 28 | 27 | 27 | 26 | – | 25 |
| Beaujolais | – | – | – | – | – | – | – | – | – | – | 23 | 24 | – | 25 | 28 |
| **California (Napa, Sonoma, Mendocino):** | | | | | | | | | | | | | | | |
| Cab./Merlot | 27 | 26 | – | 21 | 28 | 29 | 27 | 25 | 28 | 23 | 26 | 23 | 27 | 25 | – |
| Pinot Noir | – | – | – | – | – | – | – | – | 24 | 24 | 25 | 24 | 26 | 29 | – |
| Zinfandel | – | – | – | – | – | – | – | – | – | – | – | 26 | 26 | – | – |
| **Italian:** | | | | | | | | | | | | | | | |
| Tuscany | – | – | – | – | 25 | 22 | 25 | 20 | 29 | 24 | 28 | 26 | 25 | – | – |
| Piedmont | – | – | – | 27 | 28 | – | 23 | 27 | 27 | 25 | 25 | 28 | 23 | – | – |

subscribe to zagat.com